Mau Mau
Memoirs

Mau Mau Memoirs

History, Memory, and Politics

Marshall S. Clough

LYNNE
RIENNER
PUBLISHERS

BOULDER
LONDON

Published in the United States of America in 1998 by
Lynne Rienner Publishers, Inc.
1800 30th Street, Boulder, Colorado 80301

and in the United Kingdom by
Lynne Rienner Publishers, Inc.
3 Henrietta Street, Covent Garden, London WC2E 8LU

Library of Congress Cataloging-in-Publication Data
Clough, Marshall S.
    Mau Mau memoirs : history, memory, and politics / by Marshall S.
Clough.
        p. cm.
    Includes bibliographical references and index.
    ISBN 1-55587-537-8 (hc   :   alk. paper)
    1. Mau Mau—Biography—History and criticism.   2. Mau Mau—
Historiography.   3. Kenya—Politics and government—To 1963—
Historiography.   4. Autobiography.   I. Title.
DT433.577.C58   1997
967.62'03—dc21   97-36869
                                                                                                       CIP

British Cataloguing in Publication Data
A Cataloguing in Publication record for this book
is available from the British Library.

Printed and bound in the United States of America

The paper used in this publication meets the requirements
of the American National Standard for Permanence of
Paper for Printed Library Materials Z39.48-1984.

5 4 3 2 1

To my parents,
Awana Styles Clough and Ralph Nelson Clough

Contents

Acknowledgments

From the day in 1974 when I bought a plate in a Nairobi shop imprinted with the image of the captive Dedan Kimathi on a stretcher until the present, I have been fascinated by the history and memory of Mau Mau. Mau Mau memory has gone through many changes in Kenya, and these developments are a principal concern of this book. Meanwhile, I am struck how in Britain and in the United States, when Mau Mau is remembered, it continues to be exoticized, as in the expression "mau mauing" that appears occasionally in the U.S. media as a description of the harassment of white authority figures by radical African-American activists. In Western popular culture, Mau Mau resurfaces from time to time, most bizarrely as the label "mau mau" for a line of trendy men's clothes in Britain. In Kenya, the memory of Mau Mau remains too serious to be made light of in such a way.

This book has grown from the kernel of a paper presented at the Annual Meeting of the African Studies Association in Boston in November 1993, thanks to the encouragement of Lynne Rienner. I would like to express my appreciation to the Kenya National Archives, the Public Record Office in London, and the Rhodes House Library in Oxford for allowing me access to their archival sources. I would like to thank the Faculty Research and Publications Board and the Life of the Mind/Honors Program at the University of Northern Colorado for providing financial support for research, and the Board of Trustees of the University of Northern Colorado for granting me sabbatic leave in the autumn semester of 1995–1996. Thanks also to my colleagues of the History Department Seminar for their valuable comments on drafts of Chapters 1 and 6.

I would like to express my great appreciation to Kennell A. Jackson, Jr., as my mentor at Stanford and my coeditor of *A Bibliography on Mau Mau* (Stanford, 1975). I would like to thank Cora Presley, Wunyabari Maloba, Anthony Clayton, John Spencer, John Lonsdale, James Olney, and Greet Kershaw, either for advice and comments on this project or for exchanging views and ideas about Mau Mau with me over the years. And special thanks to Jim and Nurit Wolf, for their generous granting of a "Pinecliff Residential Fellowship" for my sabbatic leave; the Wolfs' secluded cabin in the Colorado mountains provided me with solitude for reflection and quiet for writing. I would also like to thank Wambui Waiyaki Otieno, for allowing me access to her autobiographical manuscript (forthcoming from Lynne Rienner Publishers); Sally Glover and Jean Hay, at Lynne Rienner Publishers, for their assistance; and Keith Rakoske, the cartographer. And I must mention the invaluable encouragement of my wife, Tony Clough, and my friends Tim and Christine Jensen-Fox, Susan Nelson, and Pam De Vore.

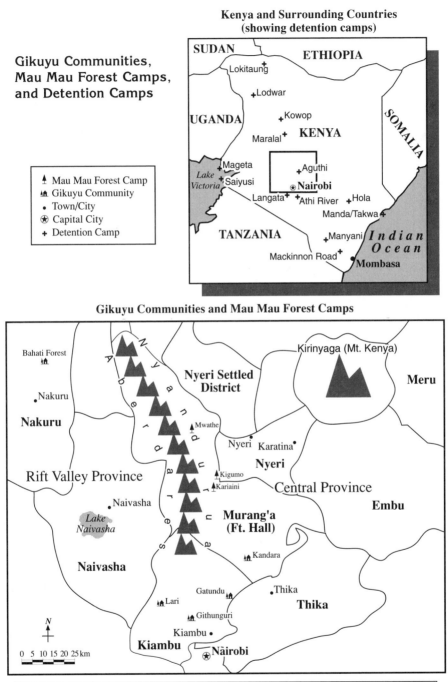

Gikuyu Communities, Mau Mau Forest Camps, and Detention Camps

Kenya and Surrounding Countries
(showing detention camps)

SUDAN ETHIOPIA

Lokitaung

Lodwar

UGANDA

Kowop

Maralal KENYA

SOMALIA

Mageta
Lake Aguthi
Victoria Saiyusi
Nairobi
Langata Athi River Hola
Manda/Takwa

TANZANIA Manyani *Indian Ocean*

Mackinnon Road Mombasa

🔺 Mau Mau Forest Camp
🏠 Gikuyu Community
• Town/City
✪ Capital City
✚ Detention Camp

Gikuyu Communities and Mau Mau Forest Camps

Bahati Forest

Nakuru

Nakuru

Nyeri Settled District

Kirinyaga (Mt. Kenya)

Meru

Mwathe

Nyeri Karatina

Nyeri

Rift Valley Province

Kigumo
Kariaini

Central Province

Embu

Naivasha

Lake Naivasha

Murang'a (Ft. Hall)

Kandara

Naivasha

Gatundu Thika

Lari

Thika

N

Githunguri

0 5 10 15 20 25 km

Kiambu

Kiambu Nairobi

Map Design and Production: Keith Rokoske Map Sources: *Fighting Two Sides*, Clough, 1990; *"Mau Mau" Detainee*, Kariuki, 1963; *MapArt* Digital Base Map of East Africa; *National Atlas of Kenya*, Third Edition, 1970; *Mau Mau From Within*, Njama and Barnett, 1966

Introduction

The future historian of these times may find it difficult to get our side of the story. . . . But in my narrative of the camps and our strange life together inside them he may perhaps see some glimpses of the truth and justice of the movements of unity, and he may begin to understand why we do not regard the soldiers of the forest as "hardcore," "terrorists," or murderers, but as the noblest of our fighters for freedom.

—*Josiah Mwangi Kariuki*[1]

I have written about the Mau Mau movement and revolt of 1952–57— why it started and how it was conducted. I have told the story A–Z omitting nothing, for I was one of those in the forest. . . . What I did and saw with my own hands and eyes I have put in this book.

—*H. Kahinga Wachanga*[2]

I continue to gaze into the valley bottom of the memory. And my fear now is that as soon as a memory forms it immediately takes on the wrong light, mannered, sentimental as war and youth always are, becomes a piece of narrative written in the style of the time, which can't tell us how things really were but only how we thought we saw them. I don't know if I am destroying the past or saving it, the past hidden in that besieged village.

—*Italo Calvino*[3]

The Presentation of Mau Mau

In 1963 Oxford University Press published a slim autobiographical volume that would change the way the world looked at the revolt in Kenya the British had called "Mau Mau." As a *London Times* reviewer commented, "Now for the first time we get the other side of the picture, in the words of one who, as a Mau Mau hardcore detainee, saw himself not as a sufferer from some deep spiritual sickness but as a loyal patriot struggling for his country's freedom from alien rule."[4] While *"Mau Mau" Detainee,* by a young Kenyan named J. M. Kariuki, carried the imprimatur of an

1

introduction by Margery Perham, one of the most distinguished British scholars on Africa, it was the story itself that impressed some readers and angered others. Ngugi wa Thiong'o, then a reporter for the *Nation* in Nairobi, remembers that the book "was immediately the center of a critical rage and storm."[5] The pages seemed to echo British memoirs of Japanese prison camps along the Burma Railway, but in this case the British themselves were the brutal camp officers and their African detainees were those who suffered, died, or endured to gain their freedom. Kariuki's memoir had elements of heroism. But it was difficult for the British (and for some Kenyans) to accept that an account of Mau Mau could be an heroic story.

Before 1963 the story of Mau Mau had been controlled by its enemies. The British government line—that the revolt was an atavistic eruption of "African savagery" rather than a legitimate response to real grievances—had dominated discussions of Kenya in the 1950s. Western journalists and writers of fiction had generally accepted this official version and translated it into sensationalistic images of terror; lurid descriptions of "oath rituals" and massacres in the press and in popular books like Robert Ruark's best-selling novel *Something of Value* had overshadowed petitions of protest from Mau Mau activists in the detention camps that appeared occasionally in left-wing newspapers in Britain or in debates in the House of Commons. The deaths of eleven detainees in Hola Camp in 1958 did lead to an uproar about the government's policies of repression, but not to questioning of the official version of the basic nature of Mau Mau itself. The official British report, *Historical Survey of the Origins and Growth of Mau Mau* (1960), seemed to represent the last word on Mau Mau as a political and social pathology.

Even dissenting voices during the Emergency had often included denunciations of Mau Mau actions in their attacks on British policies and practices in Kenya. In *African Journeys* (1955), for example, a book very critical of British policy, Fenner Brockway commented on how disturbing he found the "nature" of Mau Mau. "I am thinking now not only of the Lari massacres, where infants at the breast were slashed to death with their mothers (and the victims here were fellow Africans), but of the cold-blooded oath-taking ceremonies with their filthy obscenities, reflecting the power which crude witchcraft still has over some Kikuyu minds."[6] Kenyan critics could also feel compelled to attack both sides. Muga Gicaru, in his bitter attack on British Kenya and the settlers, *Land of Sunshine* (1958), wrote that government policies have given "the Mau Mau, both black and white, fertile ground to flourish."[7] Jomo Kenyatta, imprisoned and detained since 1952 as the "manager" of Mau Mau, was careful in his statements at Maralal in 1961 to emphasize his distaste for all violence and his commitment to constitutional progress toward majority rule and independence.

The persistence of the British version made Mau Mau something of an embarrassment in the early 1960s. For the British, for why were they willing to allow a transition to majority rule under Jomo Kenyatta's leadership when they had earlier maintained his responsibility for directing Mau Mau? For many new African politicians, because they were constitutional and modernist, and had done little for the African freedom struggle before 1952 when the revolt began. Even potentially for Kenyatta himself, for some advisers believed that if he wanted to shed the onus of responsibility for Mau Mau violence, emerge as a credible moderate leader in the eyes of both the British and Kenyans of all ethnic groups, and reassure the settlers (to prevent a flight of whites and their capital), he would have to repudiate any "debt" to the hard men of Mau Mau that might affect his ability to rule the country after independence.

"Mau Mau" Detainee complicated the interpretation of the 1950s for politicians and scholars alike. To begin with, Kariuki questioned the use of "Mau Mau" at all, arguing that rebels never called it by that name, that the term was imposed by the British, and that he was only using it (within quotation marks) because it had unfortunately gained worldwide recognition.[8] His characterization of the movement itself as a rational response to both government restrictions on constitutional politics and settler exploitation of the African peasantry undercut the standard British interpretation of Mau Mau as a reactionary and obscurantist secret society manipulated by unscrupulous politicians. Kariuki's descriptive language was different: the "gangsters," "thugs," or "terrorists" were now the "freedom fighters." Moreover, as Kenya moved toward independence in 1963, Kariuki warned African leaders in Kenya not to forget those who had fought the British. Though Kariuki regarded Kenyatta as a hero, he distinguished that father figure of Kenyan nationalism from the politicians who had emerged since 1954.

Less than a decade after the end of the revolt, therefore, Mau Mau was already being reinterpreted, and this process of historical revision was beginning with a personal account, a memoir of revolt and detention. Over the next two decades, numerous autobiographical writings on Mau Mau would be published, forming, as Luise White has pointed out, a unique body of writing on revolt in the continent, for there is as yet "no comparable literature anywhere else in Africa."[9] These personal narratives would assume a role in ongoing debates—public and academic—about the place of the revolt in the forging of the Kenyan nation. Controversy over Mau Mau was just beginning with the coming of independence to Kenya and the role of memory in molding history, the role of history in shaping the present, and the responsibility of the present to the past all would be issues of debate in the years to come.

It is the premise of this book that Mau Mau has been difficult to assimilate into the usable historical memory of Kenya because of its own perceived nature—its violence, its apparent radicalism, and the ethnic and regional character of its support—and because of the disparity between the explicit and implicit goals of the movement and the sociopolitical system, carried over from colonial times, which has dominated the independent nation. In 1988, the historian Frederick Cooper made an observation as relevant to the first twenty-five years of independence as it is to the present. "In Kenya, Mau Mau has become a politically charged topic, and discussing it has become a way—in some cases a risky way—of saying something about the present. The voices of the past and the present mix with each other, but perhaps this angry disharmony, this clash of voices, itself reveals the most."[10]

Within Kenya, the ongoing controversy about Mau Mau has involved academic historians, Mau Mau veterans, creative writers, politicians, and members of the general public. It has pitted a radical Gikuyu historian, Maina wa Kinyatti, whose two books have made bold claims for Mau Mau as a radical nationalist challenge to both colonialism and neocolonialism, against three historians from western Kenya, William R. Ochieng', E. S. Atieno Odhiambo, and especially B. A. Ogot. Ogot's 1972 article argued the need for a historiography of Mau Mau that would include the anti–Mau Mau loyalists; his 1977 essay stigmatized the Mau Mau songs (*nyimbo*) as exclusivist rather than national.[11] The controversy has involved creative writers like Ngugi wa Thiong'o and Micere Githae Mugo, who have used literature to preserve the memory of Mau Mau "heroes" like Dedan Kimathi and to popularize Mau Mau political values. It has engaged politicians as well, from Jomo Kenyatta, who attempted first to suppress and then manipulate the history of Mau Mau; to Bildad Kaggia, who tried to build a career on pro–Mau Mau populism; to Daniel arap Moi, who has allied with certain ex–Mau Mau leaders like Kariuki Chotara while suppressing other Mau Mau sympathizers (jailing both Maina wa Kinyatti and Mau Mau memoirist Gakaara wa Wanjau). Mau Mau veterans have either directly engaged in these controversies (Bildad Kaggia, J. M. Kariuki) or have been drawn into them by the publication of their own memoirs and those of others (Mohamed Mathu, Kahinga Wachanga, Gakaara wa Wanjau).

Mau Mau has received considerable scholarly attention ever since the 1966 publication of Carl Rosberg and John Nottingham's pathbreaking book, *The Myth of "Mau Mau": Nationalism in Kenya,* which established scholarly grounding for its interpretation as a rational, predictable outgrowth of nationalist opposition to British rule and settler domination. The Dutch scholar Rob Buijtenhuijs has written three books in which he charges Rosberg and Nottingham with oversimplification, stresses the complexity of the movement, and engages the issue of Mau Mau and historical memory. The last decade has seen an outpouring of writings about Mau Mau, both within Kenya and without, some conservative like David Throup's *Social and Political Origins of Mau Mau* (1988), concerned mainly with elucidating the background to Mau Mau in official British policy decisions, others populist like Tabitha Kanogo's *Squatters and the Roots of Mau Mau* (1987) and Frank Furedi's *The Mau Mau War in Perspective* (1989), both of which investigate the social background of the movement and the war among the squatters of the Rift Valley; still others are concerned with describing previously neglected groups involved in Mau Mau, like Cora Presley's *Kikuyu Women, the Mau Mau Rebellion, and Social Change in Kenya* (1992). Throughout the period Bruce Berman and John Lonsdale have written searching essays on explaining Mau Mau (both in its own time and in historiography), collected in the two-volume work *Unhappy Valley* in 1992.[12]

The national representativeness of Mau Mau has been a matter of recent debate. The last decade has seen the publication of two comprehensive studies of Mau Mau, one by the North American anthropologist Robert B. Edgerton, *Mau Mau: An African Crucible* (1989) and the other by the Kenyan historian Wunyabari Maloba, *Mau Mau and Kenya: An Analysis of a Peasant Revolt* (1993), both of which question the national character of the revolt.[13] In a significant article published in 1991, E. S. Atieno Odhiambo observes that "For four decades, Mau Mau has been the conjuncture around which Kenya's pasts and Kenya's possible futures have been debated, contested and fought over."[14] He goes on to charge that Gikuyu, whether historians or members of the political elite, want to control Mau Mau, both to determine what is to be remembered and to use the role of their group in the revolt to make present political claims.[15] John Lonsdale, aware that Atieno Odhiambo's impression is common outside Central Kenya, argues that struggles over the meaning of Mau Mau represent a debate, in history and active present memory, over "civic virtue" that is not peculiarly Gikuyu but which represents a "moral ethnicity" (as opposed to the discredited "political tribalism") shared by other indigenous traditions.[16]

From the publication of Kariuki's *"Mau Mau" Detainee,* the personal accounts of Mau Mau have been drawn into the debate. In 1972 B. A. Ogot complained that "the interpretation of the Mau Mau uprising which is gaining currency is largely based on the accounts of radicals" and called on those who were loyalist during the Emergency to write their personal stories.[17] Generally speaking, personal narratives of Mau Mau have been received in Kenya not as disinterested efforts to preserve history but as the expressions of active participants in the ongoing struggle about historical memory and present politics. Outside Kenya, historians have sometimes criticized these accounts by questioning their accuracy or representativeness but have also used them extensively to support their own interpretations of the movement and the revolt. This book takes the position that these personal narratives are important as sources for understanding Mau Mau history and as documents in the ongoing "Mau Mau debate." *Mau Mau Memoirs* considers the importance of these books as part of a Mau

Mau discourse on the revolt (in contrast to other discourses), uses them to reconstruct the history of the movement, studies them as commentaries on independent Kenya and its relation to its past, and weighs the role they have played in the national historical memory of Mau Mau.

This book is a close study of thirteen of these "Mau Mau memoirs," defined as personal accounts by Africans that focus primarily on the experience of the authors during the Kenya Emergency as guerrilla fighters, detainees, members of the "passive wing," or civilians whose lives were directly affected by the revolt and the counterinsurgency. The accounts are J. M. Kariuki's *"Mau Mau" Detainee* (1963), Karari Njama's and Donald Barnett's *Mau Mau from Within* (1966), Waruhiu Itote's *"Mau Mau" General* (1967), Charity Waciuma's *Daughter of Mumbi* (1969), Kiboi Muriithi's *War in the Forest* (1971), Joram Wamweya's *Freedom Fighter* (1971), Karigo Muchai's *The Hardcore* (1973), Ngugi Kabiro's *Man in the Middle* (1973), Mohamed Mathu's *The Urban Guerrilla* (1974), Bildad Kaggia's *Roots of Freedom* (1975), H. Kahinga Wachanga's *The Swords of Kirinyaga* (1975), Gucu G. Gikoyo's *We Fought for Freedom* (1979), and Gakaara wa Wanjau's *Mau Mau Author in Detention* (1988). I am using the term "memoirs" to describe them as a group, though some are more truly autobiographies (full life stories) while others are "life histories." (These terms are discussed more fully later in this chapter.)

This study makes use of but does not attempt to deal intensively with other first-person accounts that touch on Mau Mau but are either primarily about other matters, do not reflect a personal experience of the period, do not deal mainly with the time of the Emergency, are unpublished and/or incomplete, are presented as fiction, or are included in scholars' works written for other purposes. Harry Thuku's *An Autobiography* (1970), for example, includes a chapter dealing with the Emergency period, but is much more concerned with his political activities in the 1920s and 1930s. Muga Gicaru's *Land of Sunshine* (1958) and R. Mugo Gatheru's *Child of Two Worlds* (1964) are used only sparingly because the authors were outside Kenya during the Emergency. Henry Muoria's interesting but confusing memoir, *I, the Gikuyu and the White Fury* (1994) is valuable to historians mostly for its appendices of Muoria's writings from the late 1940s and early 1950s; as editor of the important periodical *Mumenyereri*, Muoria would seem to have a lot to say about Mau Mau, but his memoir is limited to the 1946–1952 period. Eliud Mutonyi's *Mau Mau Chairman* is unpublished and incomplete. Muthoni Likimani's book of stories, *Passbook Number F.47927* (1985), while autobiographical in some places and valuable in reflecting womens' experiences of Mau Mau, is described by its author as fiction and therefore is used but not intensively studied here. The stories of Gikuyu women recorded by Jean Davison in *Voices from Mutira* (1989) are referred to but not included for close study because they are too fragmentary, deal only partially with Mau Mau, and were recorded for scholarly purposes unconnected to the study of the revolt as such. Other personal accounts have not been used intensively for similar reasons.

Mau Mau Memoirs relies primarily on personal accounts for its description and analysis of the movement, but draws as well on other materials. Archival records, unpublished personal papers, and the wealth of fine scholarly writings on Mau Mau are used to strengthen the narrative and the analysis and are employed for comparison and contrast with the autobiographical materials.

Autobiography, Memoir, and Colonial Africa

Though autobiographies and memoirs have much in common, there are some differences between them. Autobiographies are above all personal reflections of individual experience, especially of "the growth of the personality," as Monika Schipper puts it.[18] Memoirs on the other hand deal more with exterior events. Moreover, autobiographies tend to deal with a whole life up to the time of writing, while memoirs, though they may include earlier events, tend to focus on a particular period, a time of significance to the community or nation as much as to the individual.

Although autobiographies and memoirs are usually studied as forms of literature, they are also accounts of the past, and most personal narratives have been written as historical records. Like all works of history, memoirs must be considered both as accounts of the past and reflections of or even commentaries on the time in which they were written. As personal accounts, however, memoirs are a special sort of history and a particular kind of commentary, describing a set of unique experiences and reflecting a distinct perspective. For the most part, writers of memoirs are neither professional writers nor historians. Sometimes they are public figures who believe that their key roles in large historical events have given them a knowledge and insight few historians can claim; in other cases, the authors of memoirs may be ordinary people with special experiences, whose personal accounts can sometimes be as valuable as the public figures because theirs is a view from below.

To illustrate the historical value of memoirs from below, let us look at twentieth-century Europe. There are political memoirs of World War I (Churchill, Lord Grey, etc.), but for the Western Front experience historians of Britain turn instead to books like Siegfried Sassoon's *Memoirs of an Infantry Officer* (1930), Robert Graves's *Goodbye to All That* (1929), and Vera Brittain's *Testament of Youth* (1933). Turning to World War II, while Charles de Gaulle's memoirs are rich with information, for the story of the Resistance in France itself, historians consult such personal accounts as Lucie Aubrac's *La Résistance* (1958) and Robert Noireau's *Le temps de partisans* (1955). Finally, in a real sense, the Nazi death camps can only be understood (if at all) by reading the memoirs of survivors, such as Elie Wiesel's *Night* (1960) and Primo Levi's *Survival in Auschwitz* (1961). Indeed, the immense upheavals of twentieth-century Europe have led to the outpouring of personal narratives testifying to their human cost, and many of the most valuable accounts to historians have not been political memoirs but the painful personal stories of survivors of the front lines and the camps.

Autobiography and memoir are of course Western genres, and twentieth-century European writers like Graves, Noireau, and Levi had an extensive tradition to refer to and build on, as the quote from Italo Calvino that opens this introduction makes clear. By contrast, the traditional cultures of Africa preserved the past by means of oral transmission through the generations, and the communal nature of African society tended to stress the historical role of the group as a whole more than the particular contributions of any one person. Personal accounts of Africa did begin to appear in the late eighteenth and early nineteenth centuries, significantly as narratives of African experiences of the slave trade. The most famous of these was *The Travels of Olaudah Equiano,* written by an Ibo from Nigeria who was captured as a slave while a child, spent many years in captivity, finally won his freedom, and joined the anti–slave trade cause.[19] Books like Equiano's *Travels* were the European equivalent of African-American slave narratives such as those of Frederick Douglass, written to expose the evils of slavery and to contribute to the campaign for abolition.[20] They helped to win some understanding for African cultures, but their effect was blunted by the decline of slave trading, the rise of social Darwinist and racist attitudes in Europe, and the popularity of personal accounts and autobiographical fiction written by European explorers and travelers in Africa. Richard Burton, David Livingstone, Henry Morton Stanley, and Joseph Conrad shaped nineteenth-century European readers' perceptions of the continent and their images of its people.

During the colonial period that followed, a number of British colonial officials, military men, missionaries, and settlers published autobiographies and memoirs of their experiences in Africa. Narratives such as Sir Harry Johnston's *The Story of My Life* (1920), F. P. Crozier's *Five Years Hard* (1932), and Lord Cranworth's *Kenya Chronicles* (1939) portrayed the role of European empire builders in Africa as a worthy struggle to bring civilization and modern progress to a backward continent, while the actions of the Africans themselves—bit players in a European drama played out against the backdrop of their own homeland—tended to provide moral lessons or comic relief. Some of the most widely read and influential European personal accounts of colonial Africa were written by Kenya settlers. Isak Dinesen's *Out of Africa* (1938), Llewelyn Powys's *Black Laughter* (1924), and Beryl Markham's *West with the Night* (1942) were three of the best known of a series of settler memoirs published between

World War I and 1950. Kenyan memoirs may have enjoyed particular popularity because of the image of the country in the British mind—open, rolling plains under an enormous sky, endless herds of wild animals, and noble savages carrying spears and shields. Kenya was the Wild West of the early twentieth century, and the settlers played the parts of pioneers. *Out of Africa* achieved classic status in Europe, and its author won a reputation as one of the foremost interpreters of Africa and Africans, a reputation later bitterly attacked by Ngugi wa Thiong'o.[21] Into Dinesen's settlers' Eden came a snake called Mau Mau, changing the tone of European accounts of the 1950s. In autobiographical settler polemics of the time, such as Ione Leigh's *In the Shadow of the Mau Mau* (1954) and J. F. Lipscomb's *White Africans* (1955), and in the memoirs of whites who fought Mau Mau in the police and the military—such as William Baldwin's *Mau Mau Manhunt* (1957) or Ian Henderson's *The Hunt for Kimathi* (1958)—the characterization of Africans changed, and the "savagery" that earlier memoirists had found appealing now seemed like menace (see Chapter 2).

In colonial Africa in the 1930s, 1940s, and 1950s, as more Africans gained Western education and confronted the challenges of European domination, more turned to personal narratives themselves. In his classic study of African autobiographies, *Tell Me Africa,* James Olney comments that African writers of personal narratives have three motivations for writing that European or American authors might not share: "to preserve a disappearing world, to describe the African milieu to outside readers, and . . . to describe a representative case of a peculiarly African experience."[22] To these I must add a fourth motivation, one especially important for understanding colonial autobiographies and memoirs in countries dominated by settler minorities: the desire to defend their people against misrepresentation and repression by the European colonialists. The prototypical South African memoirs, for example—Peter Abrahams's *Tell Freedom* (1954), Ezekiel Mphahlele's *Down Second Avenue* (1959), and Bloke Modisane's *Blame Me on History* (1963)—although they do not deal with nationalism or revolt, are political in effect, for the system turned their personal narratives into acts of resistance. It should be no surprise, considering African traditions, that all four motivations are more collective than individual. Olney believes that the main characteristic that sets an African autobiography apart from a Western autobiography is that the "African autobiography implies by its very nature and displays in its performance a communality of existence that is unknown in the Western world."[23] One of Olney's prime examples is a book usually thought of as a work of anthropology, Jomo Kenyatta's *Facing Mt. Kenya: The Tribal Life of the Gikuyu* (1938). Kenyatta's authority for his anthropological observations is primarily his own experience as a Gikuyu who grew up in the culture; in effect, Kenyatta is writing a kind of communal autobiography, or in Olney's words, "both ethnography and autobiography."[24] If *Facing Mt. Kenya* is a kind of autobiography, its purpose is in large part political—to represent the African cause (and the Gikuyu cause in particular) in opposition to the British: to defend Gikuyu land against settlers, Gikuyu customs against missionaries, and the Gikuyu right to rule themselves against government officials and their collaborators, the chiefs.

The Mau Mau memoirs are rooted in Kenyatta's version of the deep past, however some may disagree with him about recent history, the present, and the future. The beloved ancestral land, the idealized community, the honored, timeless customs are all imperiled by British conquest, land alienation, and colonial rule. Resistance, whether nonviolent or violent, is an ancestral imperative, a social expectation, and a pressing personal need. As Gakaara wa Wanjau puts it:

> This is the naked truth: before the coming of the white man, our land was a land of joy and plenty, we had plentiful food and large herds of goats and cows, and our people were people of wealth and dignity and great warriors. And the white man did not usher in an era of peace. On the contrary, he introduced an era of perpetual war, war with ourselves as we struggle with desperate and hopeless poverty and deprivation. We have to come to grips with a realisation of this bitter truth; for until we change the situation our plight will remain one of sorrow and tears.[25]

The Mau Mau Memoirs as History

This study will look first at the importance of these memoirs as sources for the history of Mau Mau and as reflections on that history—thus as both primary documents by direct participants and secondary interpretions of the movement written after the fact. Following Christiana Pugliese, I will use full names or the single name commonly used by the author himself or herself.[26] I am also using "Gikuyu" instead of "Kikuyu" to refer to both people and language, following the lead of Gakaara wa Wanjau.

J. M. Kariuki, author of *"Mau Mau" Detainee,* was born in 1926 into a Nyeri family living near Bahati Forest in the Rift Valley, graduated from secondary school in 1952, and spent the years from 1953 to 1960 in detention camps. Kariuki's memoir opposed a new account of the 1950s to the British version and began a new discourse about the revolt and about Kenya's colonial history; it was also critical of African politicians of the 1960s who took advantage of Mau Mau's sacrifices to advance their own interests. As an account of the fighting revolt, however, the memoir was limited, for Kariuki spent almost the entire Emergency in detention.[27]

The memoirs of Karari Njama and Waruhiu Itote, published in 1966 and 1967, provided a more complete picture, for both dealt in detail with the war in the forest. These two memoirs characterized the Mau Mau guerrillas as both politically self-conscious and militarily skilled, very different from their portrayal in the police and military memoirs by Baldwin, Henderson, and Kitson. Karari Njama, born in 1926 to a squatter family in the Rift Valley and who later returned to Nyeri, completed a junior secondary education. Author with North American scholar Donald Barnett of *Mau Mau from Within,* he had served during the revolt in Nyandarua (Aberdares), acting as secretary to General Dedan Kimathi and as liaison officer among various units of fighters. His story was a detailed description of Mau Mau organization and operations in the most important sector of the fighting. Waruhiu Itote, born in 1922 and educated through Standard III elementary level, came from South Tetu, Nyeri, cradle of many Mau Mau guerrillas. The author of *"Mau Mau" General,* a veteran of the fighting in Burma during World War II, was one of the most renowned Mau Mau leaders, commander of the guerrillas on Kirinyaga (Mt. Kenya) before his capture in 1954. His memoirs of his career as "General China" offered invaluable insight into the point of view of the fighting leadership, provided revealing detail on relations between the forest bands and the "passive wing," and included a self-conscious and quite detailed description of Mau Mau oaths specifically designed to counter the negative image of oathing in British texts. (Waruhiu Itote's second book, *Mau Mau in Action,* published in 1979, was not a personal narrative.)[28]

Although the memoirs of Kariuki, Njama, and Itote offered new perspective from the African side of the conflict, in each case it was a view from the top. Until the late 1960s, no memoirs had appeared that dealt with the experiences of rank-and-file fighters, or the passive wing, or women. The memoir of Charity Waciuma, *Daughter of Mumbi* (1969), was very different from the first accounts of the Emergency. Waciuma, born in 1939 and a recipient of a secondary education, was a teenager during the 1950s and spent most of the decade in a village in Kandara Division, Murang'a. Though she did not fight for or serve Mau Mau, she was a sympathizer and her brief memoir contained unforgettable descriptions of the harrowing conditions in an "Emergency village." Her female perspective on the Gikuyu experience of Mau Mau was unprecedented, though Wambui Otieno's account will add another female voice when it is published.[29]

Shortly thereafter the first stories of rank-and-file Mau Mau fighters appeared, Kiboi Muriithi's *War in the Forest* (1971), written with the assistance of Peter Ndoria, and Joram Wamweya's *Freedom Fighter* (1971). Muriithi, a man of some secondary education, had been born in Nyeri in 1930; Wamweya, whose education in missionary and independent schools ended with Standard II, was born in Kiambu in 1928. Both men had fought as guerrillas for extended periods, Muriithi on Kirinyaga and Wamweya in Kiambu and the Rift Valley, but both had remained soldiers, never rising to any high position of command. Theirs were unquestionably popular accounts, Wamweya's in particular reading like an adventure story. These memoirs offered valuable insight into the motivations, experiences, and points of view of the average Mau Mau recruit.[30]

The Muriithi and Wamweya memoirs were followed in short order by three personal histories edited from tapes by Donald Barnett, Karari Njama's editor. *The Hardcore: The Story of Karigo Muchai* (1973) recounts the experiences of a Kiambu veteran of World War II born in 1914; Muchai, a man of limited education, had been a long-term detainee and survivor of the beatings at Hola. *Man in the Middle: The Story of Ngugi Kabiro* (1973) tells the story of a well-educated member of the passive wing in Nairobi, born in Kiambu in 1929, who supplied arms and ammunition to the movement. *The Urban Guerrilla: The Story of Mohamed Mathu* (1974) is the account of a guerrilla from South Tetu, Nyeri, a man of some secondary education born in 1931, who fought for several years in and around Nairobi. These pamphlets, in addition to recounting the three men's experiences in Mau Mau, raise questions about the political system of independent Kenya.[31]

This tendency was even clearer in the autobiography of Bildad Kaggia, *Roots of Freedom,* published in 1975. Born in 1922, Kaggia was a primary school graduate who educated himself further in the British army; though from Kandara in Murang'a, he had lived for some time in both Dagoretti and Nairobi. After founding his own independent religious group, acting as a militant trade unionist, and serving as an elected member of the radical Nairobi branch of the Kenya African Union, Kaggia became a leader of the Mau Mau "Central Committee" in Nairobi. His book revealed much new information about the struggle in Nairobi before the Emergency. Arrested in October 1952, Kaggia spent eight years in detention with Kenyatta and other leaders. Upon his release, he joined the Kenya African National Union and was elected to Parliament. After a frustrating period in the ruling party during which his proposals for land redistribution (especially to Mau Mau veterans) and social justice made little progress, he and Oginga Odinga founded the Kenya People's Union. Kaggia was defeated in the election of 1966, spent some months in prison in 1969, and rejoined KANU later that year. Though he prudently made no references to the banned KPU in his autobiography, he discussed in detail his disapproval of the scramble for power in the early 1960s. *Roots of Freedom* both attacked the "lies" of the British and challenged the contention of the elite after independence that "we all fought for freedom" and now Kenyans should forget the past.[32]

In the same year Kaggia's autobiography appeared, H. Kahinga Wachanga published *The Swords of Kirinyaga,* edited by Robert Whittier. Wachanga, who obtained a secondary education up to Form II, was born in 1923 in Mukurwe-ini Division of Nyeri. One of the founding members of the "40 Group" (*Anake a 40*), an officer in the forests, and a prominent negotiator with the British, Wachanga was the most important fighting leader to publish his memoirs since Waruhiu Itote. In addition to providing valuable inside information about the guerrilla war, Wachanga challenged the accuracy of the accounts of Waruhiu Itote and Karari Njama (not surprising in the latter case, for Njama had criticized him), questioning the role of Dedan Kimathi and the "Kenya Parliament," and extolling Stanley Mathenge and the "Kenya Riigi" (see Chapter 5).[33]

Gucu G. Gikoyo's memoir *We Fought for Freedom* (1979), also published in Swahili as *Tulipigania Uhuru*, also took sides. Gikoyo was born in Ithanga, Murang'a, in 1934; his father, a strong traditionalist, made sure that he received no Western education at all, which made him unusual among the memoirists, but not among the guerrillas. Gikoyo had served the War Council as a killer of informers and later had fought in Murang'a with generals Matenjagwo and Kago. Like Wachanga, Gikoyo deplored Kimathi's influence over the fight in the forests, and portrayed a more sympathetic Mathenge; in addition, his characterization of the daring General Kago introduced a fresh hero to rival Kimathi and Mathenge.[34]

In 1983, at the urging of Ngugi wa Thiong'o and Maina wa Kinyatti, the writer and editor Gakaara wa Wanjau published a diary of his detention camp experience in Gikuyu, a book reissued in English translation five years later as *Mau Mau Author in Detention* (1988). Wanjau, born in Tumutumu, Nyeri, in 1921, had completed a year of Alliance High School before he was expelled after a student strike. He joined the army and served as a noncommissioned clerical officer during World War II. An editor, writer, and composer of nationalist songs in Gikuyu during the late 1940s, Gakaara Wanjau became notorious to the British as the author of *The Creed of Gikuyu and Mumbi* and was swept up with the first detainees. The bulk of his book was a verbatim transcription of his diaries (smuggled out of detention camp and preserved by his wife), which detailed his experiences in Kajiado, Takwa, and Manda camps, providing the memoir with a wealth of concrete detailed information, followed by a section recreated from memory on Athi River camp and on his experiences after release from detention.[35]

The Mau Mau Memoirs: History, Memory, and Politics

This study will also analyze the Mau Mau memoirs as a critique of the public memory of Mau Mau in independent Kenya. Over the past fifteen years a scholarly literature has developed on history and memory, from broad theoretical multinational studies like Benedict Anderson's *Imagined Communities* (1983), to studies of historical memory over time in one country like Michael Kammen's *Mystic Chords of Memory* (1990), to highly focused studies of memory of a specific period in a single nation like Henry Rousso's *The Vichy Syndrome: History and Memory in France*

Since 1944 (1994). Historians are increasingly interested in the phenomenon of national historical memory, which as Anderson points out can be "a
narrative of identity" that involves selective forgetting as well as a kind of
creative remembering.[36] Rousso, a scholar of the historical memory of
occupation and collaboration in France, is particularly concerned with the
link between the search for what Kammen calls "a usable past" and contemporary politics, in his case the connection between the contested memory of 1940–1944 and the efforts of contemporary French public figures to
deal with the "Vichy syndrome."[37] In Kenya control of public memory has
always been contended. The authors of Mau Mau memoirs have not only
advanced their version of the past, but their narratives often have
expressed, implicitly or explicitly, criticism of contemporary Kenya's treatment of its past and of the gap between the reality of the present day and
the promise of the violent struggle for liberation.

At the end of the acknowledgements to his memoir, Gakaara wa
Wanjau writes, "A nation which does not know its own history is a dead
nation."[38] But which version of its past should a nation know? The Mau
Mau memoirists are determined to redeem the past by destroying the negative version of the revolt first propagated by the British. In Bildad Kaggia's
words, "The *mzungu* (white) explanations are not just unconvincing, they
are lies which must be corrected. 'Mau Mau' must be represented in its true
perspective. It must be recognized and praised for the true liberation movement it was, the first of its kind on the continent."[39] Kaggia was well
aware, however, that the British discourse was not the only kind ex–Mau
Mau had to face. The independent Kenyan government had its own perspective on the past, and had developed a discourse on decolonization that
emphasized nonviolence and consensus.

Kenya had turned its back on white rule but had become independent
by constitutional means. The Kenyatta regime, which came to stress order,
stability, and economic continuity with colonial times, was soon reconciled
with the British and the white settlers, and the new government was dominated by men who had entered politics in 1957 and after, in many cases
while the Mau Mau leaders were still in detention. Kenyatta and the government—most of whose members were from Kiambu, a Gikuyu district
with a reputation for comparative quiescence during Mau Mau—felt the
need to emphasize national unity, of all Gikuyu and of all ethnic groups in
Kenya. The mood at the top was typified by Kenyatta's calls for national
reconciliation, and by his oft-repeated comment that "We all fought for
uhuru." This new Kenyan official version of the nationalist struggle was
best exemplified by *Suffering Without Bitterness* (1968), a narrative of
Kenyatta's career and collection of his speeches that contains little about
Mau Mau itself but a great deal about Kenyatta's personal suffering; its
themes are pride in the achievement of independence, unwillingness to
dwell on the past, condemnation of divisiveness, and hope for a future of

unity and prosperity.[40] Kenyatta and his government, most remaining settlers, and many Africans outside Central Kenya took the position that the
past should be set aside in the interests of the present. The Emergency was
the most traumatic experience of the colonial past, and the ethnic-based
violence and counterviolence of Mau Mau was at the center of the
Emergency. As far as these Kenyans were concerned, the violent Mau Mau
revolt was not part of the independent nation's "usable past."

Most Mau Mau authors did not find this an acceptable perspective on
the troubled history of Kenya. The attitude of some was influenced by personal bitterness, for few of the ex–forest fighters or detainees found themselves sharing in the political or economic spoils of independence. As
Mohamed Mathu put it:

> I should like to remind those African leaders who now condemn Mau Mau
> and tell us to forget our past struggles and suffering, that their present
> positions of power . . . would not have been realized except for our sacri-
> fices. I would also warn them that we did not make these sacrifices just to
> have Africans step into the shoes of our former European masters.[41]

Taken as a whole, certain grievances were particularly important to the
Mau Mau authors: the condemnation of Mau Mau and the suppression of or
distortion of its history, the lack of punishment for chiefs and home guards
for abuses committed during the Emergency, the wealth and prominence of
certain loyalists in independent Kenya, the failure of the government to
provide land for ex-fighters, the emergence of an elite who acted like the
old colonial masters, and the lack of social justice in independent Kenya.
The demand for retribution was somewhat muted in the memoirs—except
for Charity Waciuma's impassioned rage at the "TRAITORS" and her vow
that her time for revenge would come—perhaps because the Mau Mau, as
defeated rebels, were not in a strong position of power.[42] However, most
authors did feel that the continued power of collaborators within a socioeconomic system that had remained largely unchanged from colonial times
was a betrayal of Mau Mau principles. J. M. Kariuki, detainee turned populist politician, believed that only a new future would redeem the sufferings
of the past, not only for Mau Mau veterans but for all Kenyans.

> Our leaders must realize that we have put them where they are, not to sat-
> isfy their ambitions nor so that they can strut about in fine clothes and
> huge Cadillacs as ambassadors and ministers, but to create a new Kenya
> in which everyone will have an opportunity to educate himself to his
> fullest capabilities, in which no one will die or suffer through lack of
> medical facilities, and in which each person will earn enough to eat for
> himself and his family.[43]

As Kenya moved in a neocolonial direction in the 1960s and 1970s, the
Mau Mau authors contributed to the critique of independent Kenya also

expressed by commentators like Ngugi wa Thiong'o and the historian Maina wa Kinyatti, who used the memoirs in their radical interpretation of past and present. In the 1980s, after the death of Kenyatta and a brief "populist" period under his successor, dissenters mounted an increasingly harsh assault on the regime of President Moi. Mau Mau served some dissenters as a symbol and as an historical rallying point of opposition, though others—particularly intellectuals from outside Central Kenya—saw the use of Mau Mau in this way as nationally divisive. The debate over history and memory grew heated once again, and the Mau Mau memoirs assumed new relevance as accounts of the past and commentaries on the present.

Using the Mau Mau Memoirs

In assessing any sources, historians have to weigh their reliability. Personal accounts like the Mau Mau memoirs may enjoy a certain automatic credibility with the general public, but also suffer from the skepticism of scholars. It is important, however, for historians not to be too quick to reject the evidence of untutored memoirists, for, as James Goodwin has pointed out in commenting on narratives like the autobiography of Nate Shaw, recent personal accounts have served to "democratize" the genre and provide insight unavailable before.[44] All autobiographers, not just the highly educated, have to contend with the issue of truthfulness in personal narrative, as John Barbour demonstrates in his discussion of Malcolm X; Barbour argues that successful personal narratives are characterized by a constant interplay between conscience and imagination.[45] Moreover, in the case of the Mau Mau memoirs, as in the case of the African-American slave narratives they resemble in certain ways, the burden of truthfulness is heavy, for the memoirists represent others as much as themselves; as John Sekora puts it, such personal narratives are "both instrument and inscription of a powerful collective memory."[46]

As a record of the past, a memoir does have potential drawbacks from an historian's point of view. Unlike a diary, it does not date from the event but is a recollection subject to the distortions of time. Unlike most archival documents, it is an account whose reliability and credibility may be undermined by the personal interests of the author. Moreover, a memoir is an inevitably partial account whose narrative fullness may conceal the author's fragmentary grasp of the facts, possibly exacerbated by eagerness to place himself or herself at the center of events. Another potential problem lies in the author's collaboration with someone else. Political memoirs, such as Michael Blundell's *So Rough a Wind* (1963), are often ghostwritten, but so are other personal narratives.

So the historian must use personal narratives with care. On the other hand, autobiographies and memoirs have compensating advantages compared to other sources of the past. Even if available, diaries may be fragmentary and unreflective compared to a memoir written some years later. For example, Robert Kee, in his introduction to his memoir of the Second World War, notes how useless his own carefully maintained diaries came to be when he turned to writing a personal account of his experiences.[47] Archival sources, such as government reports of an event, while very useful, may themselves suffer from misunderstanding and bias, a particular problem when the government officials are foreigners ruling over a people whose ways and customs are strange to them. In such cases autobiographies, memoirs, and other personal narratives provide a necessary cross-check for the historian. Moreover, personal accounts often reflect the perspectives of those on the scene better than do sources like archival documents. Indeed, that is one of the reasons they are written in the first place. The large collection of British, French, and German memoirs of the trenches of World War I were written in part as correctives to the pervasive government propaganda that had completely distorted what had really happened on the Western Front. Memoirs are also of interest for another reason. As personal historical accounts written years after the event, they tend to reflect the time of their composition as well as shed light on the past; in studying such personal narratives, historians can learn not only about the past but also about debates over that past. When we look at continuing public controversies over the presentation of history in countries as diverse as Germany, France, Russia, the United States, and South Africa, we realize the important role personal accounts can play.

Historians of twentieth-century Africa have always used personal accounts as sources. Most of this documentation has been in the form of oral history, interviews collected (primarily by Western anthropologists and historians) from African informants. The early published life history, *Baba of Karo* (1954), transcribed and edited by Mary F. Smith, has been followed by a number of others such as Patricia Romero's recent collection, *Life Histories of African Women* (1988).[48] Susan Geiger has written extensively on life histories, including a methodological article on their collection and use.[49] In the case of Kenya, many studies of the colonial period have been based in part on oral history interviews with elders. Recorded and published life stories have also played a role, from Margery Perham's *Ten Africans* in 1936 to Jean Davison's *Voices from Mutira* in 1989, the latter of which contains short narrative fragments of Mau Mau experiences.[50]

The role of autobiographies and memoirs in understanding Kenyan history has received some scholarly attention, notably in articles by William Ochieng' and B. A. Ogot and in a dissertation and book by Christiana Pugliese, though no one has yet written a full-length study of the Mau Mau memoirs in particular.[51] Ochieng', their most severe critic, is skeptical of the historical value of autobiography in general, and of the historical credibility of the Mau Mau narratives especially, commenting that "the Mau

Mau autobiographies are a poor guide as to what the Mau Mau movement was all about."[52] Rob Buijtenhuijs is similarly critical. In *Mau Mau Twenty Years After* (1973), he accuses J. M. Kariuki and Waruhiu Itote of having "spawned a new myth, the African myth of Mau Mau" and of having crossed the line "between fact and fancy"; in his introduction to *Essays on Mau Mau* (1982), he criticizes "most of the ex freedom-fighters who published their memoirs" for focusing on "their own role and that of their associates" and downplaying the actions of others.[53] In his criticisms of the memoirs David Maughan-Brown in *Land, Freedom, and Fiction* (1985) broadly questions the historical credibility of accounts written after the fact "with benefit of hindsight," an observation that could be made of course about most twentieth-century personal narratives.[54] In his *Mau Mau and Kenya: An Analysis of a Peasant Revolt* (1983), Wunyabari Maloba's discussion reveals much about academic reservations concerning the Mau Mau personal narratives. Maloba acknowledges that the memoirs "are stories of great courage, singular determination, and perseverance" but maintains that they are "weak on analysis of the movement itself," particularly of its causes, its ideology, and the motivations of its members.[55]

Maloba's comments suggest uncertainty about whether to treat the Mau Mau memoirs as primary documents ("stories of great courage") or secondary histories ("weak on analysis") comparable but inferior to academic studies of the revolt. (Of course, *Mau Mau from Within* is both first-person narrative and academic history, but Njama and Barnett are responsible for different narratives within the same book covers.) Maloba's uncertainty is understandable; while the memoirs are the stories of Mau Mau participants and thus first-person accounts, they are also productions well after the events they describe, and therefore works of history. But the Mau Mau memoirists are different from historians: they are veterans of the experiences they describe, they are not professionally trained in the production of history, and they have produced engagé accounts not grounded in assumptions of scholarly detachment. Their narratives try to recreate the past both in detail and in feel, and in their accounts analysis may be embedded rather than prominently displayed. In my view, the scholarly skepticism toward the memoirs is understandable but exaggerated. Several of the critics in fact use the memoirs heavily to support some of their most significant arguments; Buijtenhuijs's criticisms of the memoirs in *Essays on Mau Mau,* for example, are undercut by his tendency to rely heavily on four of the personal narratives—those by Wachanga, Kaggia, Mathu, and Kariuki—to support some of his most important points. Indeed, his discussion of Mau Mau oathing in the book is persuasive mainly because he uses the memoirs so effectively.

Other scholars have not only used the memoirs but directly acknowledged their importance to the understanding of Mau Mau. In her article "One Voice Speaking for Many" (1983), Carol Neubauer argues for the importance of the Gikuyu personal narratives in the study of Mau Mau through analyses of J. M. Kariuki, R. Mugo Gatheru, and Charity Waciuma.[56] Luise White, in her provocative essay, "Separating the Men from the Boys" (1990), suggests that historians have not used the memoirs as much as they might "because of intellectuals' distrust of popular literature," and argues that the memoirs are valuable precisely because as popular literature they show "sensitivity to local concerns," and calls for an effort "to bring Mau Mau participants into the academic debate on Mau Mau." For as White observes, "The very subjectivity—and vulnerability—of the autobiographer's 'I' offers historians a political authenticity that disinterested observers do not have."[57] In his last essay in the second volume of *Unhappy Valley,* John Lonsdale uses the memoirs to enrich his discussion of Gikuyu political thought. This present book is part of the effort to give the Mau Mau memoirs the attention they deserve, not only by using them but by highlighting their importance.

Of course, the Mau Mau memoirs do need to be used with care. One matter of concern is the role of editors/collaborators. More than half the memoirs were written with the active assistance of editors or other writers, and in at least six of these cases the outside person was British or North American. While in most cases there is little reason to believe that the information in the assisted accounts is inaccurate or that these accounts differ in spirit from those that are primarily the responsibilty of the authors themselves, editing is a creative process, and the editors may have had a critical role in selection, organization, and perhaps in the tone of some passages. In her biography of Gakaara wa Wanjau, Christiana Pugliese questions what she believes to be stylistic distortions of his account by translator Ngigi Njoroge and editor Maina wa Kinyatti.[58] There is also reason to believe that the radical political convictions of Donald Barnett had some influence over the presentation of the three memoirs he edited from tapes, those of Karigo Muchai, Ngugi Kabiro, and Mohamed Mathu. However, to make a comparison, the role of white editors, often abolitionists, in the preparation and publication of the African-American slave narratives has been a matter of debate among American scholars but those personal accounts are still treated as important historical sources.[59] The important role of editors or co-writers should not invalidate the historical value of the Mau Mau memoirs, but readers need to be aware of the collaborators' potential influence.

As in European resistance memoirs, it is not surprising that in these accounts national ends, group ends, and personal ends can be conflated, and historians need to be sensitive to this. Convinced of the justice of their cause, the authors emphasize the positive within Mau Mau and condemn the movement's opponents, not only the British but the Gikuyu loyalists and other Africans hostile to Mau Mau. All the authors are Gikuyu, but most seem to believe genuinely that they were fighting for all Africans.

Detachment tends to be foreign to such engagé accounts, which means that the memoirs capture quite faithfully the spirit of the revolt itself but may at times miss some facts and distort the reality of the 1950s as experienced by others, especially loyalists of Central Kenya and those of other ethnic groups. Finally, the memoirs include only one account written by a woman and no accounts written by loyalists.

In addition to these general caveats about the memoirs taken as a group, historians need to be aware of particular problems. Several of the authors, Waruhiu Itote and Kahinga Wachanga in particular, are concerned with justifying their own actions during the revolt. Itote was the first important Mau Mau general to be captured; because he cooperated with the British in arranging surrender negotiations with groups still in the forest, he is very sensitive to attacks on his integrity, and devotes several chapters of his book to justifying his actions. Wachanga is keen to defend himself against the attacks of Karari Njama, and his memoir may be influenced by his effort to clear his reputation. Joram Wamweya tries hard to build up his personal role, possibly exaggerating his importance. With the exceptions of Waruhiu Itote, Karari Njama, and Kahinga Wachanga, none of these authors was in a position to become personally familiar with more than his own area of operations; nevertheless, some of them tend to report second-hand information about other areas that may not be reliable, a point that Kahinga Wachanga makes quite forcibly in *The Swords of Kirinyaga*. "Most leaders operated in one small area only and therefore knew what happened in other locations by hearsay only. The story of Mau Mau actions has often been distorted as a result."[60] It is clear from these accounts that Mau Mau was an enormously complex movement, with committees and army groups overlapping and occasionally conflicting with each other. It is not always clear that the authors can unravel these complexities them-selves. (Of course, the secrecy essential to Mau Mau partially explains this.) Finally, there is an important difficulty in accepting these memoirs as indicative of a general "Mau Mau perspective": eleven of thirteen authors are people of some education, which by their own admission was not typi-cal of members of the movement.

If these and other factors are taken into account, the Mau Mau memoirs can be of great value as historical sources. I am mindful of both the pos-sible fallibility of memory, as expressed so vividly by Italo Calvino in the passage from "Memories of a Battle" (a reflection on his own partisan experience) that opens this chapter, and the strength of memory in oral cul-tures like the Gikuyu; in addition, several memoirists used surviving jour-nals to help them reconstruct events.[61] Even though I am well aware that the long speeches in the memoirs could not have been reproduced verbatim, I am not troubled by this, confident that the sense is generally accurate, as Thucydides caught the sense of speeches within his oral culture and related them in his history of the Peloponnesian War. In writing *Mau Mau*

Memoirs, I have treated information from personal experience or observation as most reliable, as less reliable information reported to the author on events that had recently occurred, and information the author learned much later as least reliable. I have weighed the closeness of the individual to the matters reported, the similarity of his/her account to records in other memoirs or in archival documents, and the plausibility of the account given the general circumstances. I have treated with skepticism passages that seem to be infused with Marxist ideological fervor or other revolutionary hyperbole, and regard descriptions of unlikely military success with a grain of salt. When Karari Njama describes victory in a minor ambush with home guards, I treat this as credible; when Kiboi Muriithi reports General Tanganyika's men raising "hundreds of guns" to shoot down a spotter plane, I am very doubtful.[62] As Walter Laqueur points out, exaggeration has been a fault of guerrilla memoirists at least since the time of the Spanish insurrection against Napoleon.[63] I am careful with dates in the memoirs, as I have found dating in general to be imprecise. Information in a memoir that is negative toward the movement I usually take seriously, though not necessarily if it is directed against another leader with whom the author has a known quarrel. If used with care and double-checked against other evidence, the memoirs can be invaluable for the light they shed on a range of historical issues.

I intend to go further, however. Since 1963 the memory of Mau Mau has challenged the neocolonial direction of African-ruled Kenya and disturbed the national integration of the country. Most of the memoirists are aware of the problematic legacy of Mau Mau, and thus a study of the memoirs is a contribution to the ongoing debate about Kenya's historical memory.

The plan for *Mau Mau Memoirs* is as follows: Chapter 2 will present a brief summary of Kenya's colonial history and discuss the discourses on Mau Mau of first the British and then the independent Kenyan regime. Chapter 3 will analyze the presentation of Mau Mau in the three earliest memoirs, those of J. M. Kariuki, Karari Njama, and Waruhiu Itote. Chapter 4 will use the memoirs as a whole to discuss the Mau Mau movement and its oaths. Chapter 5 will discuss the guerrilla war, while Chapter 6 will discuss the experience of detention. Chapter 7 will use the memoirs to discuss the experience of Mau Mau veterans from 1960 to 1975. Finally, Chapter 8 will use the memoirs to discuss the historical interpretation of Mau Mau and deal with Mau Mau in Kenya's historical memory.

Notes

1. J. M. Kariuki, *"Mau Mau" Detainee: The Account by a Kenya African of his Experiences in Detention Camps 1953–1960,* foreword by Margery Perham (London: Oxford, 1963).

2. H. Kahinga Wachanga, *The Swords of Kirinyaga: The Fight for Land and Freedom,* ed. Robert Whittier (Nairobi: East African Publishing House, 1975), p. xxi.

3. Italo Calvino, "Memories of a Battle," in Italo Calvino, *The Road to San Giovanni* (New York: Doubleday, 1995), p. 85.

4. Anonymous, "Kenyan Patriot?," *Times Literary Supplement,* Aug. 9, 1963; see also Clyde Sanger, "A Kikuyu Tells His Story," *Manchester Guardian Weekly,* Aug. 8, 1963.

5. Ngugi wa Thiong'o, "J. M.—A Writer's Tribute," in Ngugi wa Thiong'o, *Writers in Politics* (London: Heinemann, 1981), p. 82.

6. Fenner Brockway, *African Journeys* (London: Gollancz, 1955), p. 169.

7. Muga Gicaru, *Land of Sunshine: Scenes of Life in Kenya before Mau Mau* (London: Lawrence and Wishart, 1958), p. 169.

8. Kariuki, *Detainee,* p. 24.

9. Luise White, "Separating the Men from the Boys: Constructions of Gender, Sexuality, and Terrorism in Central Kenya, 1939–1959," *International Journal of African Historical Studies,* vol. 23, no. 1 (1990), p. 2.

10. Frederick Cooper, "Mau Mau and the Discourses of Decolonization," *Journal of African History,* vol. 29 (1988), p. 313.

11. Maina wa Kinyatti, ed., *Thunder from the Mountains: Mau Mau Patriotic Songs* (London: Zed, 1980); Maina wa Kinyatti, ed., *Kenya's Freedom Struggle: The Dedan Kimathi Papers* (London: Zed, 1987); B. A. Ogot, "Revolt of the Elders: An Anatomy of the Loyalist Crowd in the Mau Mau Uprising 1952–1956," in B. A. Ogot, ed., *Politics and Nationalism in Colonial Kenya* (Nairobi: East African Publishing House, 1972), pp. 134–38; B. A. Ogot, "Politics, Culture, and Music in Central Kenya: A Study of Mau Mau Hymns, 1951–1956," *Kenya Historical Review,* vol. 5, no. 2 (1977), pp. 275–86.

12. Carl Rosberg and John Nottingham, *The Myth of "Mau Mau": Nationalism in Kenya* (New York: Praeger, 1966); Robert Buijtenhuijs, *Le mouvement Mau Mau: Une révolte paysanne et anti-coloniale en Afrique noire* (The Hague: Mouton, 1971), *Mau Mau Twenty Years After: The Myth and the Survivors* (The Hague: Mouton, 1973), *Essays on Mau Mau: Contributions to Mau Mau Historiography* (Leiden: African Studies Center, 1982); David Throup, *Political and Social Origins of Mau Mau, 1945–53* (London: James Currey, 1987); Tabitha Kanogo, *Squatters and the Roots of Mau Mau* (London: James Currey, 1987); Frank Furedi, *The Mau Mau War in Perspective* (London: James Currey, 1989); Cora Presley, *The Mau Mau Rebellion, Kikuyu Women, and Social Change* (Boulder: Westview, 1992); Bruce Berman and John Lonsdale, *Unhappy Valley,* 2 vols. (London: James Currey, 1992).

13. Robert B. Edgerton, *Mau Mau: An African Crucible* (New York: Macmillan, 1989); Wunyabari Maloba, *Mau Mau and Kenya: An Analysis of a Peasant Revolt* (Bloomington: Indiana, 1993).

14. E. S. Atieno Odhiambo, "The Production of History in Kenya: The Mau Mau Debate," *Canadian Journal of African Studies,* vol. 25, no. 2 (1991), p. 300.

15. Ibid., pp. 301, 306.

16. John Lonsdale, "The Moral Economy of Mau Mau: Wealth, Poverty and Civic Virtue in Kikuyu Political Thought," in Berman and Lonsdale, *Unhappy Valley,* vol. 2, pp. 466–68.

17. Ogot, "Revolt of the Elders," pp. 147–148.

18. Monika Schipper, *Beyond the Boundaries: Text and Context in African Literature* (Chicago: Ivan R. Dee, 1990), p. 125.

19. Olaudah Equiano, *The Interesting Narrative of the Life of Olaudah Equiano,* 2 vols. (London, 1789).

20. Henry Louis Gates, Jr., introduction to *The Classic Slave Narratives,* ed. Henry Louis Gates (New York: Mentor, 1987), p. xiv.

21. Ngugi wa Thiong'o, *Detained: A Writer's Prison Diary* (London: Heinemann, 1981), pp. 35–37.

22. James Olney, *Tell Me Africa: An Approach to African Literature* (Princeton: Princeton University Press, 1973), p. 27.

23. Ibid., p. 57.

24. Jomo Kenyatta, *Facing Mt. Kenya: The Tribal Life of the Gikuyu* (London: Secker and Warburg, 1938); Olney, *Tell Me Africa,* p. 81.

25. Gakaara wa Wanjau, *Mau Mau Author in Detention,* trans. Paul Ngigi Njoroge (Nairobi: Heinemann, 1988).

26. Christiana Pugliese, "Author, Publisher, and Gikuyu Nationalist: The Life and Writings of Gakaara wa Wanjau" (Ph.D. thesis, University of London, 1993), pp. 624–25.

27. Kariuki, *Detainee,* Ch. 1.

28. Karari Njama and Donald L. Barnett, *Mau Mau from Within* (New York: Monthly Review, 1966); Waruhiu Itote, *"Mau Mau" General* (Nairobi: East African Publishing House, 1967).

29. Charity Waciuma, *Daughter of Mumbi* (Nairobi: East African Publishing House, 1969). Wambui Otieno's account, tentatively titled *Mau Mau's Daughter,* will be published by Lynne Rienner Publishers.

30. Kiboi Muriithi and Peter Ndoria, *War in the Forest* (Nairobi: East African Publishing House, 1971); Joram Wamweya, *Freedom Fighter* (Nairobi: East African Publishing House, 1971).

31. Karigo Muchai, *The Hardcore,* ed. Donald Barnett (Richmond, B.C.: Liberation Support Movement, 1973); Ngugi Kabiro, *Man in the Middle,* ed. Donald Barnett (Richmond, B.C.: Liberation Support Movement, 1973); Mohamed Mathu, *The Urban Guerrilla,* ed. Donald Barnett (Richmond, B.C.: Liberation Support Movement, 1974).

32. Bildad Kaggia, *Roots of Freedom* (Nairobi: East African Publishing House, 1975).

33. Wachanga, *Swords.*

34. Gucu G. Gikoyo, *We Fought for Freedom: Tulipigania Uhuru* (Nairobi: East African Publishing House, 1979).

35. Wanjau, *Mau Mau Author.*

36. Benedict Anderson, *Imagined Communities: Reflections on the Origin and Spread of Nationalism,* 2nd ed. rev. (New York: Verso, 1993), p. 205.

37. Michael Kammen, *Mystic Chords of Memory: The Transformation of Tradition in American Culture* (New York: Knopf, 1991), p. 6; Henry Rousso, *The Vichy Syndrome: History and Memory in France Since 1944,* trans. Arthur Goldhammer (Cambridge: Harvard, 1994), Ch. 1.

38. Wanjau, *Mau Mau Author,* p. ix.

39. Kaggia, *Roots of Freedom,* p. 193.

40. Jomo Kenyatta, *Suffering Without Bitterness: The Founding of the Kenya Nation* (Nairobi: East African Publishing House, 1968).

41. Mathu, *Urban Guerrilla,* p. 87.

42. Waciuma, *Daughter of Mumbi,* p. 130.

43. Kariuki, *Detainee,* p. 181.

44. James Goodwin, *Autobiography: The Self-Made Text* (New York: Twayne, 1993), pp. 18–19.

45. John D. Barbour, *The Conscience of the Autobiographer* (New York: St. Martin's, 1992), pp. 26, 30–31.

46. John Sekora, "Is the Slave Narrative a Species of Autobiography?" in *Studies in Autobiography,* ed. James Olney (New York: Oxford, 1977), p. 111.

47. Quoted in Paul Fussell, *The Great War and Modern Memory* (London: Oxford, 1977), p. 311.

48. Mary F. Smith, *Baba of Karo* (New York: Philosophical Library 1955); Patricia Romero, ed., *Life Histories of African Women* (London: Ashfield, 1988).

49. Susan Geiger, "Women's Life Histories: Method and Content," *Signs,* 11:2 (1986), pp. 344-51; *TANU Women,* her collective biography of women political activists in Tanzania, is in press at Heinemann.

50. Margery Perham, ed., *Ten Africans* (London: Faber and Faber, 1936); Jean Davison, *Voices from Mutira* (Boulder: Lynne Rienner, 1989). A revised edition of *Voices from Mutira* was published in 1996, but my references are to the 1989 edition.

51. William R. Ochieng', "Autobiography in Kenyan History," *Ufahamu,* vol. 14, no. 2 (1985), pp. 80–101; B. A. Ogot, "Kenyan Autobiography," *Ufahamu,* vol. 14, no. 2 (1985); Pugliese, "The Life Story."

52. Ochieng', "Autobiography," p. 91.

53. Buijtenhuijs, *Mau Mau Twenty Years After,* pp. 46–48; Buijtenhuijs, *Essays,* pp. 1–2.

54. David Maughan-Brown, *Land, Freedom, and Fiction: History and Ideology in Kenya* (London: Zed, 1985), p. 56.

55. Maloba, *Mau Mau and Kenya,* p. 16.

56. Carol Neubauer, "One Voice Speaking for Many: The Mau Mau Movement and Kenya Autobiography, " *Journal of Modern African Studies,* vol. 21, no. 1 (1983), pp. 113–31.

57. White, "Separating the Men from the Boys," p. 2.

58. Pugliese, "Gakaara wa Wanjau," p. 145.

59. See John W. Blassingame, "Using the Testimony of Ex-Slaves: Approaches and Problems," in *The Slave's Narrative,* ed. Charles T. Davis and Henry Louis Gates (New York: Oxford, 1985), pp. 78–83.

60. Wachanga, *Swords,* p. 31.

61. This point is made by Robert Whittier, preface to Wachanga, *Swords,* p. viii.

62. Muriithi, *War in the Forest,* p. 51.

63. Walter Laqueur, *Guerrilla: A Historical and Critical Study* (Boston: Little, Brown, 1976), p. 33.

Mau Mau and Its Interpreters

When to this religious aspect of the movement the great power exercised by the magical and mystical acts that accompany the actual oath-taking are added, it is not difficult to see how it became possible to make so many normally peace-loving Kikuyu into the fanatical, murdering maniacs that they have become under Mau Mau.

—L. S. B. Leakey[1]

Mau Mau has three objects. The first is to bind its adherents to itself by such compelling oaths that thereafter their minds and their bodies and their morals are irrevocably in the power of the cult; the second object is to destroy Christianity and all forms of authority, and to install itself as both law and religion; and the third object is to drive the European out of Kenya and to usurp his place in the White Highlands.

—J. F. Lipscomb[2]

We are determined to have independence in peace, and we shall not allow hooligans to rule Kenya. We must have no hatred toward one another. Mau Mau was a disease which had been eradicated, and must never be remembered again.

—Jomo Kenyatta[3]

M ilitarily the British defeated Mau Mau in four years (1952–1956), but they found the political challenge it posed a more thorny problem. Though the colonial government came to accept the legitimacy of constitutional African nationalism in Kenya, they completely rejected Mau Mau itself and until 1961 treated its convicted "manager," Jomo Kenyatta, as a pariah. They constructed a discourse that explained Mau Mau as a regression to the past, condemned the guerrillas as "savages" and "maniacs," and justified counterinsurgency, detention, and "rehabilitation" as necessary antidotes to this political and spiritual sickness.

The rapid transition to African majority rule between 1960 and 1963 and the release of Jomo Kenyatta to lead the new nation seemed at first inconsistent, but the British could justify it by altering the discourse to uncouple Jomo Kenyatta from Mau Mau. The moderate, pro-capitalist, and pro-Western stance of the new government seemed to validate the alteration, and this regime itself, led by Kenyatta, shaped a new discourse about Kenya's colonial history that centered on constitutional anticolonialism, downplayed the role of Mau Mau, condemned violence, and called for reconciliation of all Kenyans in the spirit of "forgive and forget."

This chapter is divided into three parts: a brief summary of Kenya's colonial history from 1896 to 1963; a consideration of the "myth of Mau Mau" that the British constructed during and just after the revolt; and an analysis of the discourse on decolonization of the independent Kenyan regime, which drew on both the British myth and the critique of the Kenya Emergency by British and Kenyan dissenters.

Kenya, 1895–1963

Building Colonial Kenya, 1895–1940

While the takeover of Kenya was bloody (leaving memories that would be drawn on during the Mau Mau revolt), imperial conquest was the common experience of most African countries. Kenya Colony, however, began to assume its own particular character when Governor Eliot pledged to create a "white man's country" dominated by European farmers in the temperate highlands, working their estates with a labor pool of African peasants. The government alienated land from pastoralists like the Maasai and agricultural peoples like the Gikuyu to create a large reserved area for Europeans in the center and west of the country. The economic position of the settlers was soon bolstered by political power in the Legislative Council, in the Executive Council, and on government boards. Though they never reached the strength that enabled the while Rhodesians to gain internal self-rule, they dominated all others for decades, always hoping to win autonomy inside the empire.[4]

The construction of a "white man's country" had drastic effects on Kenyan Africans. Subjected to racial discrimination and restricted in their political rights, Africans faced difficult circumstances throughout the colonial period, and the Gikuyu were affected more than most other groups. Land alienation and government restrictions on further expansion weakened their traditions of pioneering and land ownership. The British imposition of chieftaincy replaced patterns of decentralized local self-rule through councils and *athamaki* (big men). Government demands for taxes and labor imposed new challenges on Gikuyu society, forcing men to work away from their homes, introducing the monetary system, and driving up the price of items in the local areas through inflation. Changes imposed by the government were exacerbated by the new settler influence over the land

and the economy and by the ideological and social challenges posed by the actions of Christian missionaries. Yet the early colonial period also opened up opportunities for Africans, especially for the Gikuyu, who lived closest to Nairobi, the radiating point of change, and to the "White Highlands," the main area of European settlement. By the beginning of World War I, many Gikuyu, especially those of the southernmost district of Kiambu, had expanded their cultivation to sell produce in the city. Others had become accustomed to travel from their homes to find work and were using the money they earned for their own purposes and not solely for paying taxes. Other families moved to settle as squatters on settler estates in the Rift Valley, where they planted farms and raised large herds of goats. Moreover, after a period of skepticism, Gikuyu began to respond to the opportunities offered by missionary schools. Among Europeans the Gikuyu gained a reputation as a "progressive" people.[5]

In 1919, tax increases, wage cuts, and new threats to Gikuyu land provoked rural Gikuyu in Kiambu to found the first African political group, the reformist Kikuyu Association (KA). Urban Africans soon founded the more militant East African Association (EAA), headed by the charismatic Harry Thuku, who was very critical of chiefs. The British government responded by arresting Thuku and banning his organization after a bloody confrontation in 1922. The split between the KA and the EAA established a pattern of division between Gikuyu moderates and militants, replicated in 1924 when Gikuyu from Murang'a formed the Kikuyu Central Association (KCA). Members of the KCA took a secret oath to defend the soil of the Gikuyu. The KA and the KCA, though they shared similar goals and though neither sought direct confrontation with the government, were natural rivals, for they represented different elites—the KA included the chiefs and conservative mission converts, while the KCA represented ambitious young men opposed to chiefly control of Gikuyu politics. Women apparently had no role at all in the KA, and were allowed to work with the KCA only as auxiliaries. The gap between the groups widened in 1929 when, against the wishes of most Gikuyu Christians, some missionaries insisted that Christians give up the tradition of female circumcision. While some Gikuyu agreed, led by KA chiefs and mission elders, others led by the KCA repudiated the missionaries and many left to form their own churches and schools. The cultural crisis of identity between noncircumcisers and circumcisers would last into the time of Mau Mau.[6]

In spite of this bitter division, Gikuyu could agree on the need to recover the alienated lands. Both the KA and the KCA had petitioned for redress for years, and the arrival of the Kenya Land Commission in 1932 to hear testimony raised high expectations. Harry Thuku, back from detention and leader of the KCA, and Chief Koinange wa Mbiyu acted as the main spokesmen for the Gikuyu, assisted by the organization of the Gikuyu lineages. The KLC report in 1934, recommending that the white highlands status be made permanent and providing only compensation to the Gikuyu, ultimately destroyed the KA. When the government implemented the KLC's recommendations in 1940 in the area of Limuru, Kiambu, a dispute erupted between those who accepted and those who refused, an argument that would have violent consequences at Lari in 1953.[7]

The mid-1930s was a volatile time for Gikuyu politics. With Jomo Kenyatta living in England, conflicts over the leadership of the KCA led to a split in 1935, when Harry Thuku left to form the pro-government Kikuyu Provincial Association (KPA). George K. Ndegwa revived the KCA in 1938, leading to several years of intense political activity. The campaign for Githunguri Teachers College led to cooperation between the KCA and the male circumcision groups and strengthened the link between the KCA and the independent schools. The KCA also established close ties to other disaffected African groups elsewhere in Kenya, recalling the united campaign of the early 1920s and also looking forward to the politics of the Kenya African Union (KAU). The government banned the revived KCA and detained its leaders at the beginning of World War II in 1940.[8]

Toward Confrontation, 1945–1952

World War II served as a catalyst for change, leading to rising international opposition to colonialism and an upsurge of African nationalism across the continent. In Kenya, a number of Africans (including Waruhiu Itote, Bildad Kaggia, Karigo Muchai, and Gakaara wa Wanjau) had enlisted in the British forces, and these veterans expected their service to be rewarded by employment opportunities and political reform. When the British instead implemented the policies of "the second colonial occupation" and largely ignored African demands for change, they created a potentially explosive situation that was exacerbated by the self-assertiveness of the settler community. European politicians began to lay plans for autonomy under minority control, heartened by the influx of new settlers and inspired by the Rhodesian-led movement toward federation in British Central Africa. At the local level in the highlands, settlers followed up their success in forcing destocking in the late 1930s by demanding new contracts to further limit the freedom of Gikuyu squatters to use the land.[9]

African discontent soon emerged, expressed through political parties, labor unions, and informal protest organizations. As the people most affected by the second colonial occupation, the Gikuyu dominated protest, not only in their homeland of Central Kenya, but in their expansion areas of the Rift Valley, Nairobi, and Mombasa. As political and economic frustrations grew, divisions widened between those with a perceived stake in the system—the older, the landed, the educated, colonial job-holders, and the adherents of mainline Christian sects—who favored moderate, constitutional reform, and others on the outside, who were often younger, landless or underemployed, less well educated, or members of independent Christian sects. Some members of this second group were willing to consider more radical means, including the use of violence, to achieve substantive change. The Kikuyu Central Association, banned but still active underground, revived with the return of its leaders, and the Kenya African Union, founded in 1946 and led by the widely popular Jomo Kenyatta, built a strong Gikuyu base as well as recruiting Kamba, Luo, and members of other ethnic groups. Labor unrest exploded in the 1940s in Mombasa and Nairobi, fueled by political discontent as well as urban circumstances, low wages, and conditions of work. In Central Kenya and the Rift Valley, local disputes over landholding, land use, wages, and working conditions contributed to the political ferment. Officials were alarmed by the breadth and depth of African discontent.[10]

Initially, African politics remained in the moderate hands of the leaders of the KCA and KAU, but within a few years control slipped from their grasp. The veterans of the KCA continued to work with the Gikuyu lineage organization called *Mbari,* and the leaders of both together devised a new oath of unity in the mid-1940s, more militant than the original KCA oath but not involving coercion or violence. KAU, with its wider membership and broader ethnic appeal, relied on mass meetings more than oathing but like the KCA called for such moderate and constitutional reforms as more African representation in the Legislative Council, a new land commission, and reforms in African education. A new generation of radicals in Nairobi—in the labor unions, the "40 Group" of young activists, and the African press—were growing restive under what they saw as the weak older leadership. Meanwhile, the Olenguruone confrontation between Gikuyu farmers and the government in the late 1940s radicalized many Gikuyu in the Rift Valley and led to the development of a more militant oath tradition. A critical turning point came in 1951, when the radicals ousted the moderate leadership of the Nairobi branch of KAU. At about the same time the close cooperation between the Kiambu KCA, led by Koinange wa Mbiyu, and the Gikuyu radicals from Nairobi, led by Fred Kubai, broke down and the oathing campaign fragmented and became more aggressive, leading to the emergence of the secret movement the British called "Mau Mau." Militant leaders like Kaggia, Kubai, Wachanga, Mutonyi, and Itote dominated the secret movement, used violence to enforce its authority (driving the minority of "loyalist" Gikuyu onto the defensive), and began collecting guns.[11]

Emergency and Revolt, 1952–1960

The administration of Governor Philip Mitchell refused to acknowledge that the steep rise of crime, African political unrest, and deteriorating race relations indicated that Kenya faced a serious crisis. When a new governor,

Evelyn Baring, arrived on September 30, 1952, he conferred with officials and settlers about the oathing and the violence in Nairobi, Nyeri, and the Rift Valley, otherwise showing little interest in African opinion. The assassination of the powerful chief Waruhiu wa Kung'u on October 9 convinced Baring to ask the Colonial Office for a declaration of emergency, to begin with the arrest of a list of leading Africans headed by Jomo Kenyatta.[12]

Though news of this "Jock Scott" operation leaked out, few of the politicians, labor leaders, and journalists targeted made any serious efforts to evade it; on October 20 the government all but beheaded the African nationalist movement in Central Kenya, moving in the coming months to ban some labor unions, close the Gikuyu independent schools, and eventually outlaw KAU itself, while preparing for a political "show trial" of Kenyatta and five other leaders. However, though the memoirs and other evidence show that Jock Scott had initially demoralized the secret movement, the government failed to fully exploit their advantage, suggesting that both Nairobi and London (still fully engaged in Malaya) believed that Mau Mau had been suppressed.[13]

Official complacency allowed the remnants of the Mau Mau central committee and the other committees to recuperate and prepare for armed struggle. Gikuyu, Embu, and Meru militants began to assemble in camps in the forests of Nyandarua and Kirinyaga, excellent terrain for hit-and-run guerrilla warfare. Meanwhile, supporters in Nairobi collected arms, ammunition, and medical supplies, recruited young fighters, and established supply lines, while others in the reserve areas passed on the supplies and recruits to the forest. More important to individual bands than the support from Nairobi was the backing they received from their home locations, often only a few miles away; small groups passed back and forth between the camps and the rural communities, bringing food, news, and information about security force operations.

In early 1953 Mau Mau went on the offensive in the reserve areas, in Nairobi, and to a lesser extent in the settled areas of the highlands, targeting especially chiefs and their families and supporters, African police, and Christians who had refused the oath or actively opposed the secret movement. Operating mostly at night, Mau Mau fighters assaulted or killed individual loyalists, set fire to homes and schools, and attacked police patrols or isolated police posts. By mid-1953, Mau Mau actions had transformed certain locations of Nairobi, much of Nyeri and Murang'a, and most of the forest fringes of Gikuyuland into no-go areas at night for loyalists and the local security forces. Attacks on the loyalist community of Lari, on the Naivasha police station, and on settler families in the highlands heightened the impression that the Mau Mau were winning.[14]

In June 1953, General George Erskine arrived to take charge of the British counterinsurgency. He set about coordinating the forces at his disposal—regular troops of the British army, battalions of the King's African

Rifles, the Kenya Regiment (a settler unit), the Kenya Police, the Kenya Police Reserve, the Kenya Police Air Wing, and local "tribal police"—with the assistance of the new "War Council" composed of officials, settlers, and military. Better intelligence, aggressive patrolling, and air reconnaissance and bombing kept the bands on the move. More important to Erskine's overall strategy were his efforts to separate the bands from their civilian supporters. Taking a leaf from General Templer's Malaya counterinsurgency book, he began an aggressive campaign of "food denial," which involved concentrating much of the rural Gikuyu population in fortified "Emergency villages" to cut them off from the guerrillas, placing them under curfew, and putting them to work digging a great ditch between their communities and the forest. But the most important element in the new British strategy was Operation Anvil in April 1954, which rounded up and screened most of the Gikuyu, Embu, and Meru residents of Nairobi, deporting some to detention camps, repatriating most of the others, and devastating the Mau Mau support system in the capital.[15]

The situation for Mau Mau in the forests and the reserves soon became critical. Despite their efforts to coordinate, the leaders became increasingly divided over different strategies, government surrender initiatives, growing suspicions between educated and illiterate forest fighters, and their own personality conflicts and struggles for power. By mid-1955 the counterinsurgency and their own internal problems had essentially halted any concerted action among forest groups. As Mau Mau went into decline, the fortunes of the loyalists rose. The Kikuyu Guard, initially poorly armed and unmotivated, became an effective fighting force, which brutalized civilians but also suffered more casualties and killed more Mau Mau and than any other counterinsurgency unit.[16]

In the Gikuyu reserve areas, British civilian authorities had begun to implement the Swynnerton Plan of land consolidation, hoping to achieve what M. P. K. Sorrenson has called a "counter-revolution in the Kikuyu country."[17] There were good agricultural arguments for land consolidation, but there were also compelling political arguments. Rights to the new consolidated farms would only be granted to loyalists; the British hoped thereby to form a core of politically conservative, property-owning Gikuyu yeomen and a smaller group of gentry, who would resist any future social revolution as against their own interests. Land consolidation was the political capstone on the edifice of counterinsurgency.

Meanwhile, the British had interned in detention camps more than 80,000 men and women, mostly Gikuyu, Embu, and Meru, but including a number of Kamba, Luo, Luhya, and other groups. Camp officers and guards were expected to extract both information and confessions from the detainees, turn them against Mau Mau, and send them home "rehabilitated." The government effectively turned aside or ignored criticisms of the actions of the security forces in the field, but it ultimately proved more difficult to keep the truth about conditions in the camps and prisons from getting out. In 1959, in an ill-advised effort to force hardcore detainees to work at the high-security camp at Hola, a group of warders beat and killed eleven men. The ensuing scandal led to the end of the camp system.[18]

Decolonization in Kenya

In 1954 the government began to reform the Legislative Council and lift restrictions on African political activity. With Kenyatta and older leaders still in detention, African politics in the late 1950s came to be dominated by union men like Tom Mboya, younger Gikuyu like J. G. Kiano who had not participated in the KCA or in Mau Mau, and politicians from other ethnic groups, like Oginga Odinga of the Luo. Political change was coming, but only with deliberate speed, and its watchword was "multiracialism," which meant the continued influence of Europeans out of all proportion to their numbers. The pace of change would soon accelerate. In 1958, Oginga Odinga's call for the release of Kenyatta (soon taken up by all African politicians) and the Africans' boycott of the Lennox-Boyd constitution undermined multiracialism and put pressure on the British government. These developments, and the Hola scandal, the costs of continued British rule, and violence in Nyasaland (Malawi) contributed to an important reconsideration of British policy by Harold Macmillan and his colonial secretary, Ian Macleod, leading to the Lancaster House conference on Kenya in 1960.[19]

MacLeod still hoped to control African "radicalism," however, relying on Michael Blundell and his New Kenya Group (NKG), which had close ties to urban businesses and multinational corporations, to work with African "moderates" of the Kenya African Democratic Union (KADU)—generally politicians from smaller ethnic groups—to maintain continuity and protect British interests against the Kenya African National Union (KANU), dominated by an alliance of Gikuyu and Luo. Ultimately this strategy failed. Kenyatta's release and triumphant return in August 1961, was a symbolic watershed—a yielding of the British government to African public opinion, a repudiation of the official association of Kenyatta with Mau Mau, and a victory for KANU.[20]

The majority party itself, however, was divided from within along fault lines of region, personality, faction, policy, and ideology. The British ban on national political parties for Africans had not been lifted until 1960, so that parochial power had become entrenched in some places. The personal conflict between Luo politicians Tom Mboya and Oginga Odinga began to assume Cold War overtones as Mboya accepted support from the USA and Odinga from the Eastern Bloc. Among Gikuyu politicians, ex–Mau Mau like Bildad Kaggia and Fred Kubai clashed with new men like J. G. Kiano and Kariuki Njiri, whose support was ex-loyalist, particularly on land and other economic issues. When independence came in December 1963, the celebrations of *uhuru* took place against a backdrop of political uneasiness and economic uncertainty.[21]

The British Version of Mau Mau

The Shaping of a Discourse

Mau Mau and the Emergency must be understood in the context of developments in Britain, the empire, and the world as a whole. Although the government wished to decolonize slowly for economic and strategic reasons, the British public's focus on internal affairs, Cold War attacks by the Soviets, and intense criticism from Third World leaders like Nehru and Nkrumah put British colonial policy under pressure. Moreover, guerrilla warfare and terrorism in Palestine and Malaya, followed by the engagement with the United Nations in Korea, severely taxed British political resolve and military resources. But a rearguard action was still possible, especially in Africa south of the Sahara, where Soviet influence was weak, where the British still held a preponderance of military power, and where British officials and settlers could yet pose as upholders of "civilized" values.

The eruption of Mau Mau shocked Europeans in Kenya by its intense violence, but also tended to confirm the underlying suspicions of many whites about Kenyan Africans. To British officials and missionaries, the revolt represented a rejection of the Western, Christian values they believed they had labored for two generations to inculcate in African society. To many settlers this outbreak of "savagery" proved the fundamentally primitive character of Africans, for it was led by the Gikuyu, once considered the most progressive of Kenyan ethnic groups; indeed, Mau Mau—while threatening the settlers physically and haunting them psychologically—made it possible for them to argue their case for the perpetuation of white control of Kenya.

The European anti–Mau Mau discourse developed in tandem with the repression of the revolt by white officials, soldiers, and settlers. Official Kenya took the lead. In October 1952, the Kenya government was faced with three challenges: to deal immediately with the disorder and violence, to justify the drastic measures taken to suppress the movement, and to explain its own failure to prevent the situation from developing. Sensitive on the one hand to the attacks of settlers and British conservatives, who complained bitterly of their failure to act sooner, and on the other hand to criticisms from the left wing in Britain and Nehru in India, who questioned whether the Emergency was not really a disguised effort to suppress the constitutional nationalism of the Kenya African Union, officials in Nairobi moved quickly to control the representation of the revolt.

The government statement issued to the press on October 29 summed up the official position on Mau Mau:

> Mau Mau is a secret Society confined almost entirely to the Kikuyu tribe. It seems clear that it is a recrudescence of a society known as the Kikuyu Central Association which was proscribed for subversive activities in 1940. It has been resuscitated by Africans desirous of achieving a form of African tyranny (with Kikuyu predominance) and personal power through the exploitation of tribal feeling and superstition. It encourages race hatred and is virulently anti-European and anti-Christian in character. It pursues its aims by forcible administration of secret oaths to men, women, and children, and by the intimidation of witnesses and law-abiding Africans. It resorts to methods of a most brutal and inhuman kind, including murder, the mutilation of bodies, arson and the maiming of domestic animals. This subversive society has attracted to it the worst criminals in the Kikuyu tribe, and is held in abhorrence by responsible members of all races.[22]

Subversive, superstitious, tribalist, racist, anti-Christian, intimidating, brutal, criminal, committed to winning personal power for a few individuals and to establishing an ethnic tyranny—clearly Mau Mau was a pariah movement with which there could be no understanding, no compromise. By implication, the government bore no responsibility through political repressiveness or economic neglect for the rise of such a movement. Oliver Lyttleton, secretary of state for the colonies, made this explicit at a press conference in Nairobi in November, stating unequivocally that Mau Mau "is not the direct child of economic conditions and is not intended or designed to improve them."[23] If Gikuyu rebels turned their backs on constitutional avenues of political advancement, rejected the hard road of gradual economic progress in their own reserves, and spurned modernity in favor of a regression to the past, the Kenya government could not be blamed.

Retrospective self-justification, however, was obviously not enough. The political effort to counter Mau Mau required effective propaganda, directed both inward toward Africans and outward. Members of the Kenya Information Services put the skills the British had learned from two world wars to the task of supporting the counterinsurgency effort through various media, including bilingual handbills and filmstrips and soundtrucks blaring through the African locations. Radio broadcasts in English, Swahili, Gikuyu, and other African languages disseminated the official message over the airwaves to Kenyan Africans. Official pamphlets, such as *The Mau Mau in Kenya* (London, 1954) and the bilingual *The Kikuyu Who Fight Mau Mau/Wakikuyu Wanaopigana na Mau Mau* (Nairobi, 1955) publicized the evils of the Mau Mau movement and the heroism of the Gikuyu who fought against it.[24] The government also held frequent press conferences for local, British, and international reporters eager for copy about the trial of Jomo Kenyatta, the "Lari massacre," and attacks on settler farms. Even though officials in Britain and Kenya sometimes complained about press sensationalism, they did largely control the story of Mau Mau that appeared in most newspapers and magazines around the world.[25] This served official purposes within Kenya and allowed London to portray Mau Mau as a parochial phenomenon, unconnected to the general movement of African nationalism or the worldwide upsurge of communism.

Official press releases and propaganda statements may have initiated the rhetorical attack on Mau Mau, but more important in the long run were certain in-depth studies of the movement, particularly J. C. Carothers's *The Psychology of Mau Mau* (1955) and two books by L. S. B. Leakey, *Mau Mau and the Kikuyu* (1953) and *Defeating Mau Mau* (1954). Both men had close links to the government. Carothers, a psychiatrist who had worked in Mathare Mental Hospital from 1938 to 1950, formulated the influential psychological interpretation of Mau Mau. Carothers held that the Gikuyu were a backward people with a "forest psychology," whose inability to adjust to the modern world had led from personal anxiety and cultural confusion to a full-blown mass sociopathology that expressed itself in violence and witchcraft.[26] In his books, Leakey—paleontologist, self-professed "white African," and Special Branch officer—drew on his knowledge of language, customs, and society both to explain some Gikuyu grievances and to interpret Mau Mau through the study of political hymns and oaths. Leakey used his positions as an adopted Gikuyu "insider," with close links to conservative elders in Kiambu District (listening to them about Mau Mau as well as talking to them), and as an anthropologist to insist on the radical "otherness" of Mau Mau, its distance from both original Gikuyu values and the values of Christianity. As Bruce Berman and John Lonsdale have pointed out, however, Leakey was hardly neutral within the Gikuyu political context, carrying strong animus against the Kikuyu Central Association and against Jomo Kenyatta personally.[27] Leakey argued that Mau Mau was so dangerous because it offered a new faith that, through the manipulation of oath-taking and magic, was able "to make so many normally peace-loving Kikuyu into the fanatical, murdering maniacs that they have become under Mau Mau."[28] Both Carothers and Leakey included in their writings liberal prescriptions for reform, but these suggestions were often ignored while their attacks on Mau Mau became grist for other writers, some hostile not only to Mau Mau but to African politics in general.

Like L. S. B. Leakey, most missionaries could be included among the white liberal community in Kenya and some also had inside knowledge from years living in Central Kenya. Canon T. F. C. Bewes, Africa secretary of the Church Missionary Society, both condemned Mau Mau as a direct threat to generations of labor in building a Gikuyu Christian community and criticized abuses on the government side that victimized Mau Mau supporters and committed Christians indiscriminately.[29] Missionaries attacked Mau Mau as a perverted alternative religion, practicing rituals and preaching a faith directly inimical to Christianity; they also criticized harsh actions by the security forces as threatening to polarize Kenya along racial lines. While missionaries helped to construct the British "myth of Mau Mau," their questioning of the counterinsurgency provided ammunition for critics of the Emergency at home (see next section).

Kenyan settlers (like Afrikaners and white southerners in the United States) had always been sensitive to criticism and had responded aggressively to apparent threats to their way of life. Mau Mau was the most serious test of all; as Anthony Clayton puts it, the settlers saw Mau Mau as a "sinister challenge of 'them or us.'"[30] Settlers had tended to show ambivalence toward the Gikuyu, sometimes lumping them with other Africans as lazy and shiftless, at other times praising or criticizing them for their industry; in Elspeth Huxley's novel of Mau Mau, *A Thing To Love*, on one page farmer Colonel Foxley reflects that young Gikuyu men "liked doing nothing better than any race he had ever known," while five pages later his daughter Pat describes the family's cook Karioki as "a real, shrewd Kikuyu with charm and alertness and an eye for profit as keen as any Jew's."[31] Because the Gikuyu more than any other Africans worked for the settlers as servants and laborers, their involvement in Mau Mau was seen as a particularly wounding betrayal. Huxley and other settler authors attempted to shape the British discourse on Mau Mau in an effort to discredit the rebels, the revolt itself, and the left-wing defenders of African nationalism in Kenya in Britain (who could be portrayed as being soft on Mau Mau).

Let us look at three of the best-known settler books. Charles Wilson's *Before the Dawn in Kenya* (which went through three printings between October 1952 and January 1953) used nineteenth-century travelers' accounts to make the case that the arrival of Europeans had saved East Africa from complete stagnation, and argued in his conclusion that Mau Mau was "nothing less than a return to the darkness, superstition, and cruelty of primitive heathenism."[32] Ione Leigh, whose family ran a coffee plantation, used her book *In the Shadow of the Mau Mau* (1954), which drew heavily on both Wilson and Leakey, to contrast the good relations between benevolent settlers and "irresponsible" but "amiable and trusting" Africans before Mau Mau with the poisonous racial atmosphere of the Emergency. Leigh blamed the outbreak of the revolt on "extremists abroad" and their local African collaborators like Kenyatta, who planted the "disease" of Mau Mau in order to exploit the "savage instincts of the African."[33] Her descriptions of those "instincts" at work, in her chapters on the Lari massacre and on the killings of upcountry settlers, were harrowing accounts of gruesome atrocities illustrated by graphic photographs. J. F. Lipscomb's settler *apologias, White Africans* (1955) and *We Built a Country* (1956), were not written with the same racist and sensationalist verve as Leigh, and he devoted most of *White Africans* to a discussion of the essential contribution of settlers to the development of Kenya. In his chapter on the contemporary crisis, however, he discussed Mau Mau as "a revolting and highly contagious disease" transmitted by irresponsible Europeans to ambitious educated Gikuyu and in turn to the "misguided and ignorant mass" and argued that Mau Mau would have to be permanently exiled and the future built by loyalists working with Asians and Europeans.[34]

Three memoirs of the counterinsurgency also contributed to the Mau Mau myth: William Baldwin's *Mau Mau Manhunt* (1957), Ian Henderson's *The Hunt for Kimathi* (1958), and Frank Kitson's *Gangs and Counter-Gangs* (1960). Baldwin was an American adventurer who arrived broke in Kenya in April 1954, joined the Kenya Police Reserve, and served in the General Service Unit. As Dane Kennedy comments, Baldwin's account is "frankly racist," yet the racism is oddly naive, as if Baldwin could not understand why anyone would criticize him or other police for killing surrendered Mau Mau.[35] Ian Henderson was both more respectable and more influential; as a scion of an established settler family, a fluent Gikuyu speaker, the Special Branch officer in charge of preparing witnesses for the trial of Kenyatta, a leader of "pseudo-gangs," and the man responsible for capturing Dedan Kimathi, Henderson's engagé personal account in the form of an adventure story was a key document expressing the myth of Mau Mau. Though Henderson repected Kimathi as a wily antagonist, he saw him as the charismatic embodiment of evil and his followers as "savage, vicious, unpredictable as a rabid dog," as "fanatics who . . . enjoyed killing children and slitting open the stomachs of pregnant women."[36] Henderson's single-minded pursuit of Kimathi through the Nyandarua forests is reminiscent of Richard Meinertzhagen hunting down a man-eating lion in early colonial days; in this account, Kimathi and his comrades lose their human characteristics and become beasts to be tracked down and exterminated, while Henderson emerges as the hero of the piece. Frank Kitson, a major in the regular army who helped to organize military intelligence for the counterinsurgency (including the running of pseudo-gangs in Kiambu District), wrote a more detached memoir that revealed sympathy for Mau Mau guerrillas as individuals and respect for them as antagonists, but condemned Mau Mau as a movement in terms similar to the other personal accounts. Kitson's description of a "sweep" of Gikuyu women he commanded through the bush of Kiambu in search of the remnants of General Waruingi's band is a memorable depiction of the dehumanization of their guerrilla opponents by the officers of the counterinsurgency.[37] Kitson's attitude might have been influenced by the military's official *A Handbook of Anti–Mau Mau Operations* (1954), which expressed respect for Mau Mau fieldcraft but not for the qualities of Africans in general, even those in the security forces. "The African is simple, and not very intelligent, but very willing if treated in the right way. Do not regard him as a slave or an equal."[38]

Of the works of fiction about Mau Mau in the 1950s, Robert Ruark's *Something of Value* (1955) was by far the most widely read. Indeed, to quote John Lonsdale, the novel "must, alas, be the best known account of Mau Mau," for it remained in print from 1955 to 1980; moreover, the film version, starring Rock Hudson and Sidney Poitier (1957) with a cameo introduction by Winston Churchill, was seen by millions of people worldwide.[39] Ruark, a successful American novelist and journalist with five books to his credit, spent three years researching his novel, drawing on the writings of Huxley, Leakey, and Kenyatta and on conversations with settler friends. Although he claimed that *Something of Value* "is not a political book," in his foreword he described *Facing Mount Kenya* as "an explicit blueprint for the terror," admonished his readers that "to understand Africa you must understand a basic impulsive savagery," and called Mau Mau "a symptomatic ulcer of the evil and unrest which currently afflicts the world."[40] *Something of Value* explained Mau Mau as the predictable result when basically primitive Africans are corrupted by Westernization and education and then exploited by cynical agitators. In spite of his research, Ruark was deplorably ignorant about Kenyan affairs—for example, he identified Jomo Kenyatta as the leader of the "Kenya Provincial Association"—but *Something of Value* was really about violence, especially mindless, orgiastic violence. Two key scenes in the novel make this clear: a description of a *batuni* oath-taking in the forest, during which the character Njogu decapitates a small boy in the arms of his father to use his blood to consecrate the oath ("The boy's blood surged, bubbling frothy like a flood, onto his father's face"), and a portrayal of a settler farmhouse after a Mau Mau attack, during which the hero, settler and white hunter Peter McKenzie, views the carnage in his sister's living room the morning after the family has been brutally chopped to death by *pangas*. "For the first time in his life Peter McKenzie was sick in the presence of blood. The room was soaked in it, swimming with it. . . . There were separate big pools of blood, sticky, coagulated, crusty now. A long slick trail of blood led from one of the easy chairs to end in a thick pool under the piano."[41] In a book with many horrific scenes these two stand out, and the visceral reaction they provoke is designed to convince readers that the British and the settlers are fighting a brutal, barbaric enemy. The settlers in *Something of Value* have their faults, but Ruark clearly believes they are the right side, the white side.

In 1957, with Mau Mau under control, the British government commissioned F. D. Corfield, an official who had served for two years with the War Council in Kenya, to research and write the report *Historical Survey of the Origins and Growth of Mau Mau*, which finally appeared in May 1960. Well aware that "the *Mau Mau* uprising caused worldwide interest," Corfield wrote his report as much for the general public as for his official audience, in order to convice the world at large what can occur "when

African nationalism runs riot."[42] His debt to other writers of the myth of Mau Mau, especially Carothers and Leakey, was evident throughout; he aimed at being definitive rather than original. The irresponsible outside agitators, the scheming and ambitious African politicians, and the backward Gikuyu masses appear again in his pages as Corfield attempted to discredit once and for all not only Mau Mau but the KCA, KAU, and Jomo Kenyatta. In his conclusion, he wrote:

> It has been suggested that had the hand of co-operation been given to Jomo Kenyatta, history would have taken a different turn, and there would have been no Mau Mau. But all the evidence points otherwise . . . without the freedom afforded them by a liberal Government, Jomo Kenyatta and his associates would have been unable to preach their calculated hymn of hate and to exploit, through the medium of perverted witchcraft and of intimidation, the almost inevitable grievances which must accompany the rapid evolution of a primitive society. Can anyone imagine what kind of African State would have arisen in Kenya on the foundation of Mau Mau, which sought to eliminate all non-African influence and which, by the unspeakable debauchery of its oaths, achieved the terrible result of breaking and debasing the dignity of thousands of human souls.[43]

Examining the British "Myth of Mau Mau"

When Carl Rosberg and John Nottingham coined the phrase "myth of 'Mau Mau,'" in the title of their revisionist study published in 1966, they knew that their use of "myth" for the British explanation of the revolt was to turn the old orthodoxy on its head, for Europeans in the 1950s had characterized Mau Mau itself as an "apotheosis of unreason." Rosberg and Nottingham, careful to place the British term "Mau Mau" in quotation marks and treating the "myth" essentially as a seamless whole, analyzed and rejected this discourse on the revolt as inaccurate and apolitical, and argued instead that the secret movement was "an integral part of an ongoing, rationally conceived nationalist movement."[44]

Since 1966 every scholar of Mau Mau has had to take this study into account, and some have chosen to revisit the British myth as well. In *Mau Mau: Twenty Years After* (1973) Rob Buijtenhuijs goes beyond Rosberg and Nottingham's general description to analyze various expressions of the myth by officials, settlers, missionaries, scholars, and popular writers, stressing the advantages the British government derived from disseminating this version, and the long-term effects their virtual monopoly of discourse on Mau Mau in the 1950s had on worldwide perceptions of the revolt.[45] David Maughan-Brown analyzes British writings on Mau Mau in greater depth and argues that an essentially uniform discourse affected the depiction of the revolt in novels written by both European and by African authors.[46] Other scholars have questioned his approach, exploring the complexities and even contradictions in different British descriptions of Mau Mau. John Lonsdale, for example, in "Mau Maus of the Mind" (1990), discusses different mental constructions of the revolt, identifying four "meanings of Mau Mau" all held by Europeans in Kenya during the Emergency (the conservative, liberal, revivalist, and military), which he considers mutually incompatible, thus breaking down the impression of a European consensus on what it all meant and what to do about it.[47] In his 1991 article, A. S. Cleary downgrades Rosberg and Nottingham's myth to a propaganda instrument, discussing the British efforts to disseminate the myth internationally in order to convince governments and public opinion that Mau Mau was no crest of a wave of violence threatening all of Africa but a Kenyan phenomenon that the British had well in hand.[48]

In "Constructing the Colonial Myth of Mau Mau" (1992), Dane Kennedy faults Cleary for dealing with official statements exclusively and argues for the importance of the parts played by private members of the Kenyan European community in shaping the British myth. Kennedy divides European opinion during the revolt into "two rather distinct camps of explanation," which he labels the "conservative extremist" and the "liberal paternalist."[49] The explanation the liberals favored, which Kennedy argues enabled them to admit that Mau Mau was "rooted in real problems" while denying that the rebels had "genuine grievances," was the psychological explanation, and theirs was the myth of Mau Mau disseminated to the outside world, primarily through the effective public relations work of Michael Blundell.[50] The liberals used the myth to steer Kenya away from violence toward the peaceful political change then described by the catchword "multiracialism." As Kennedy concludes: "What it allowed was a reassessment of the racial foundations of the colonial order . . . providing the ideological basis for a cautious and expedient advance to that looming eventuality, decolonization."[51]

Kennedy's essay shows how far the interpretation of the myth of Mau Mau has progressed since Rosberg and Nottingham. But in his article on the private European view, which relies heavily on the writings of L. S. B. Leakey and J. C. Carothers (both of whom had close ties to the government), he does not clearly differentiate between the attitude of the liberals toward constitutional African politics and politicians and their attitude toward Mau Mau violence and forest fighters. Certainly he is right that a distinction needs to be made between conservative writings on Mau Mau that point toward the conclusion that Kenyan Africans as a whole could not be trusted with self-rule, and liberal writings that suggest loyalists might eventually work with whites in ruling the country. Conservatives questioned the capability of Africans to advance, while the writings of liberals, to quote Fred Cooper, were characterized both by "insistence on the inevitability of western modernity and fear of the power of backwardness."[52] But liberal paternalists such as Leakey, Carothers, or

Blundell did not differ from conservatives in their view of the Mau Mau movement or its fighters, men Leakey called "fanatical, murdering maniacs."[53] The myth of Mau Mau as shaped primarily by the liberals left room for the re-emergence of African politics within a multiracial context, but the liberals permanently consigned *Mau Mau itself* to the outer darkness as surely as the conservatives would have done.

The British myth of Mau Mau was a complex phenomenon formed of many strands and expressed in diverse media, including official press releases, government reports, newspaper articles, nonfiction studies, personal narratives, and novels. The materials for the myth could be found in ethnocentric attitudes of superiority, dominance, and control that emerged in the early twentieth century and developed in the environment of white colonial society in the 1920s and 1930s (which Kennedy has described so vividly in his book *Islands of White*), and in postwar assumptions about the imperatives of modernity and European-directed progressive change in Africa.[54] The myth of Mau Mau was essentially forged in the clash between these European attitudes and the anger of African rebels.

In their anti–Mau Mau discourse, in some cases guided by Gikuyu loyalists, European authors created a world of inclusion and exclusion, going so far as to appoint themselves arbiters of what was "civilized" in universal terms (meaning European) and of what was truly Gikuyu. In this discourse Mau Mau was characterized by radical otherness, as an assault against the European values of the present and as a barrier to any African civilization that might be built in Kenya in the future.

To anathematize Mau Mau, European authors relied on common key words, metaphors, catch phrases, images, and themes intended to emphasize Mau Mau's distance from both European and "traditional" Gikuyu psychological, cultural, social, and political norms. Adjectives like "atavistic," "primitive," and "superstitious" conveyed the backwardness of the African rebels, their reversion to the past.[55] References to "barbarism," "savagery," "brutality," and "bestiality" evoked images of semihuman people capable of atrocities "civilized" Europeans could not envision. Similarly, the use of "terrorists," "gangsters," and "thugs" conveyed the impression that Mau Mau was a criminal movement beyond the pale of normal politics.[56] European writers also stigmatized the movement with moral and religious epithets, attacking Mau Mau as "evil," "wicked," and "pagan" or "heathen." Leakey, Lipscomb, Corfield, and Majdalany described it as a "pseudo-religion" of "black magic" and "perverted spirituality" to convey the reactionary nature of Mau Mau and the essential superficiality of its beliefs.[57] The anti-Christian theme led some to focus on the malign transformation experienced by Mau Mau adherents through their participation in oath-taking, a transformation into "fanatics" afflicted with a spiritual sickness that could only be reversed by "confession."[58]

Sanitary and medical terms conveyed a more modern and at least quasi-scientific distaste. Writers described Mau Mau as "filthy," a "poison," a "disease," a "pestilence," a "contagion" of such infectious potential it could "spread like wildfire," even to Kamba in Nairobi who were in a situation "exposing them to the Kikuyu virus."[59] Lipscomb went further, writing in fastidious horror as if the disease of Mau Mau had actually infected the natural world itself. "The Kenya forests are among the loveliest forests in the world. Nature did a perfect job on them. They are cleaner than an English wood and free of anything noxious. . . . But now they have been sullied by Mau Mau."[60] Carothers, as a practicing psychiatrist, introduced the metaphor of psychological disease later used by Lipscomb, Corfield, Majdalany, and others; the Gikuyu affected by Mau Mau were subject to "insecurity" and "anxiety," suffering from "imbalance," prone to unnatural "suspiciousness."[61]

In contrast to the evils of the Mau Mau was the theme of loyalist virtues. Leakey, Mitchell, and others praised the Christians' steadfastness, and E. M. Wiseman commemorated them in *Kikuyu Martyrs* (1958), a collection of brief accounts of men and women beaten or killed for refusing the oath or for opposing the movement.[62] Officials and settlers saw the loyalist Gikuyu as the foundation of the future; in Lipscomb's words, "those who have stood out . . . are the skeleton of a building that must contain the future. . . ."[63] The capture and execution of Kimathi led Ian Henderson to imagine young Gikuyu in the coming years looking toward Nyandarua and saying, "'That is where an evil past is buried.'"[64] Leakey saw the loyalists as the true Gikuyu, and government officials insisted that they be called a "resistance movement," obscuring the fact that loyalists were in a minority from 1952 to 1956 and glossing over the Kikuyu Guard's brutalities and their sometimes questionable motives.[65]

The authors of the anti–Mau Mau discourse, whether racist conservatives or liberals sympathetic to African aspirations, shared certain common assumptions about the revolt and the rebels that reveal more about the European authors than about the Africans who were the objects of the discourse. Critics of the government and the settlers in Britain (whose arguments will be discussed in the next section) had to take the myth into account even as they attacked certain policies and practices during the Emergency. This interpretation of the upheavals of the 1950s retained ideological force even after 1963, as the next section will show.

Mau Mau in Independent Kenya

The Corfield report was the last major salvo of the British propaganda war against Mau Mau, and the continued promulgation of the myth lost some of its purpose in the years after 1960. After the first Lancaster House Conference, the watershed elections of 1961, and the release of Kenyatta later in 1961, any official who expressed publicly the full "myth" risked embarrassing the British government and offending Africans. Yet it hardly disappeared altogether. Rather it was pushed to the rear in official discourse by a new emphasis on constitutional advance toward majority rule, to be brought forward when European administrators wished to warn African politicians about the disturbing rhetoric of their left wing or the destabilizing effects of land agitation. Among the European settler community, where fear of Mau Mau lingered long after 1960, belief in the myth remained strong, and found expression in Robert Ruark's second novel about Kenya, *Uhuru* (1962). In other parts of Africa, the "shadow of Mau Mau, which so haunts [the] Western imagination" fell over the copy of journalists, who found material in uprisings in the Congo and elsewhere that suggested parallels with Kenya.[66]

For some still believed in the myth's predictive power. Mau Mau had been so closely associated with Jomo Kenyatta that many Europeans and some Africans assumed that after he was released from detention and won the election of May 1963, he would favor ex–Mau Mau for leadership positions and implement "Mau Mau" policies, to the detriment of settlers and loyalists. Writing in November 1963, just before independence, Michael Blundell commented that to some Europeans Kenyatta was "the personification of evil, and every bestial and murderous act of the Mau Mau is firmly placed on his doorstep."[67] As it turned out, the alarmists need not have worried. The government of President Kenyatta soon took on the character of a pro-capitalist, pro-Western regime, which placed distance between itself and the former freedom fighters while settling thousands of landless peasants (mostly Gikuyu, but not necessarily ex–Mau Mau) on subdivided farms purchased from outgoing European settlers. While it celebrated independence and Black majority rule, the regime also preached the reconciliation of Mau Mau and loyalists, Africans and Europeans, and practiced economic continuity with the colonial regime. Kenyatta appointed Waruhiu Itote, Bildad Kaggia, and J. M. Kariuki to official positions, but reserved the most important posts for old comrades like Mbiyu Koinange, younger politicians like Njoroge Mungai, or able non-Gikuyu like Tom Mboya.

The moderate-conservative political ideology and practice of the Kenyatta government influenced and in turn was influenced by independent Kenya's official view of the recent past. In the discourse of government spokesmen, the story of the 1950s was revised and the struggle for African independence extolled, but the version that emerged was hardly a reversal of the British myth. Rather, as an effort by the emerging African establishment to advance national unity, control political unrest, and maintain economic continuity by managing the public memory of Mau Mau, the official Kenyan version drew on both the British discourse and the reformist critique of British and Kenyan dissenters during the Emergency.

The Dissenting View of the Kenya Emergency

Left-wing critics had questioned the direction of government policy in Kenya for years before 1952, and their attacks intensified after the declaration of Emergency. The most prominent British critics, Labour politicians Fenner Brockway and Leslie Hale, visited Kenya in 1950 and again in October 1952, to investigate the situation on the spot. Brockway, Hale, and other sympathizers in Britain helped to form the defense team for Kenyatta and his fellow defendants at the trial in Kapenguria in northern Kenya. Throughout the Emergency Brockway, Hale, Barbara Castle, Anthony Wedgwood Benn, and other Labour politicians questioned the colonial secretary about Kenya, while outside Parliament radical lawyers like Peter Evans publicized abuses of the security services, and left-wing critics hosted dissenters like Tom Mboya during visits to Britain. The Fabian Colonial Bureau published critiques of British policy, including Mboya's *The Kenya Question* in 1956. As Stephen Howe has pointed out in *Anticolonialism in British Politics,* organizations like the Movement for Colonial Freedom, the Congress of Peoples Against Imperialism, and the Kenya Committee (dominated by the Communist Party) questioned the need for the Emergency and attacked the methods of the counterinsurgency. Although the stories published by most newspapers generally reflected the government's point of view, the *Herald* and other Labour-oriented papers were more often critical.[68]

To many British liberal and radical critics, the weakest element in the official version of the Emergency was the connection between constitutional politics and Mau Mau, a convenient association if the secret motive were to suppress African nationalism in Kenya altogether. In 1955 journalist and novelist Montagu Slater published *The Trial of Jomo Kenyatta,* which challenged the coupling of Kenyatta and KAU with Mau Mau. "To identify Kenya African Union with its educational, religious, and progressive policies with the dark, barbarous and terrorist Mau Mau was a charge of a gravity that can hardly be overstated."[69] Slater suggested that KAU's dilemma was not unusual among anti-imperial movements, comparing Kenyatta's plight to that of the Irish constitutional politician Charles Stewart Parnell in the 1880s, and to that of Mohandas Gandhi in the 1920s and 1940s, both caught between the British on the one hand and violent revolutionaries on the other. Was it reasonable or just to hold the constitutional leader responsible for the actions of the gunmen?[70]

African voices, repressed at home, were heard making similar arguments in the 1950s in Britain and in the United States. This could be risky, as Mugo Gatheru discovered when the long arm of the Kenya government reached out to Chicago and attempted to get him deported as an undesirable alien with Communist sympathies.[71] Mbiyu Koinange, sent to Britain by KAU just before the Emergency, knew that he faced detention if he returned home and was forced to spend the 1950s in exile, sometimes in difficult circumstances. During a sojourn in the United States, with help from African-American sympathizers, he published a partially autobiographical pamphlet, *The People of Kenya Speak for Themselves* (1955), which downplayed the violence of Mau Mau, highlighted British repression, and ridiculed the myth for "sowing nothing but confusion and nonsense. Let the Kenya African people establish the institutions that they are trying to build. . . . That is the cure for Mau Mau and not a lot of investigations and new theories about "back to the bush.""[72] Perhaps the most eloquent expression of the dissenting African point of view was an autobiography with the bitterly ironic title *Land of Sunshine: Scenes of Life in Kenya Before Mau Mau* (1958), written by Muga Gicaru, a Gikuyu living in Britain, with a preface by missionary Trevor Huddleston, known for his attacks on both apartheid in South Africa and Mau Mau in Kenya. Through his autobiography Gicaru depicted a Kenya blighted by injustice and racial oppression. Perhaps following the lead of Kenyatta, who had spoken in 1938 of "British fascism in the colonies" and compared the treatment of Africans in Kenya to the treatment of Jews in Germany, Gicaru wrote that the Europeans had provoked Mau Mau themselves with their "settler fascist methods."[73] Gicaru portrayed the Emergency as polarizing Kenya as never before. "When all African newspapers were banned, leaders arrested without trial, their property confiscated and destroyed, and all political meetings proscribed, the government gave the Mau Mau, both black and white, fertile ground to flourish."[74] Gicaru's Kenya was clearly on a South African path.[75]

Dissenters attacked British policy, especially the conduct of the Kenya Emergency, but, with the exception of British Communists, they usually took care to distance themselves from Mau Mau itself. In his 1955 book *African Journeys*, Brockway characterized Mau Mau in terms much like those used by L. S. B. Leakey and J. F. Lipscomb. "It cannot be denied that many of the practices of Mau Mau represent a reversion to a primitive, barbaric mentality; this has shocked, perhaps most deeply, those of us who have co-operated in the political advance of Kenya Africans."[76] Liberal journalist Colin Legum, in an article in *The New Statesman*, described Kenya as facing two challenges, the revolt of "the illegal and fanatical Mau Mau" and the tendency of settlers to use Mau Mau "to denigrate responsible African leadership."[77] Hoping to separate constitutional nationalism and Mau Mau, most critics who expressed sympathy for the victims of the counterinsurgency—the detainees, the disappeared, the women and children of the Emergency villages—did not extend that sympathy to the guerrilla movement itself. Gicaru's comment about "the Mau Mau, both black and white" suggests a reluctance to identify with either of the sides locked in the bloody struggle for Central Kenya.

Memory and Politics in Independent Kenya

In the early 1960s Mau Mau shared in the vindication of African nationalism in Kenya. The triumphalist public statements of some African politicians, especially Oginga Odinga, so inspiring to African voters and so disturbing to conservative settlers, included positive references to freedom fighters as well as praise for those like themselves who had struggled peacefully for *uhuru*. Even Tom Mboya (already suspect in the eyes of African radicals because of his American connections) devoted a section of his autobiography, *Freedom and After* (1963), to defending the patriotism of Mau Mau fighters and extolling their sacrifices.[78] The contributions of Mau Mau to Kenya's independence were also recognized internationally, at least within Africa. Milton Obote, prime minister of Uganda, speaking at Kenya's independence celebrations on December 12, 1963, proclaimed, "Today is the day when Kenya joins Algeria at the high rank of being the hero of colonial Africa," explicitly honoring the role of Mau Mau fighters in bringing freedom to Kenya.[79]

Yet in his own *uhuru* speech that night Jomo Kenyatta did not mention Mau Mau fighters at all, while acknowledging specifically the contribution of officials, missionaries, settlers, and traders to the development of Kenya, and no Mau Mau leaders had any role in the celebrations in the stadium.[80] Kenyatta was not ignoring Mau Mau altogether, however; he had met with ex-generals at his home at Gatundu in August, and on December 16—four days after independence—he, J. G. Kiano, F. L. M. Waiyaki, and Elsie Mukami (Mrs. Kimathi) welcomed a number of fighters in from the forest of Kirinyaga in a mass meeting attended by Mau Mau veterans and civilian supporters.[81] These apparently contradictory actions suggest the ambivalence of Kenyatta toward Mau Mau, and also point to the political delicacy of the situation in Kenya at the time.

In some ways Kenyatta and his government seemed to view Mau Mau as both an embarrassment and a threat. At the Maralal news conference in 1961, the conference that had begun the process of changing his image from Mau Mau leader to moderate statesman, Kenyatta had responded to a question about his responsibility for Mau Mau oathing by observing that just as the queen was not responsible for "gangsters" in Britain, he was not responsible for the acts of Mau Mau.[82] This could be considered a politic comment for international consumption, but his remarks at a public meeting in Githunguri in September 1962, after his release, went much further. "I am requesting you strongly not to hold any secret meetings or support subversive organisations. We are determined to have independence in peace, and we shall not allow hooligans to rule Kenya. We must have no hatred toward one another. Mau Mau was a disease which had been eradicated, and must never be remembered again."[83] Kenyatta's use of criminal analogies and disease metaphors recalled the British myth, suggested a strong personal distaste for Mau Mau, and expressed a fear that the Mau Mau of the past might re-emerge to destroy the peace, stability, and general political health of independent Kenya. The implication was that in order to prevent the reinfection of the country, the new government would have to innoculate public memory against the Mau Mau virus.

In *Mau Mau Twenty Years After* (1973), his study of historical memory in independent Kenya, Rob Buijtenhuijs describes the new regime's discourse on Mau Mau as the "Euro-African myth."[84] According to Buijtenhuijs, there were compelling political reasons for Kenyatta's government to condemn or downplay Mau Mau. First, it was important for the new regime to build interethnic unity, and a heavy stress on the role of Mau Mau in winning independence could alarm non-Gikuyu. Second, the independent government had to be concerned not to offend the British or the settlers. Third, Kenyatta had to be careful to avoid alienating the ex-loyalists in Central Province. Fourth, the new regime wished to place stress on the personal role of Kenyatta in winning *uhuru* for the country, and official attention to the Mau Mau contribution would weaken this emphasis. Fifth, Mau Mau veterans, including some who returned to the forests in 1964, posed a threat of physical violence against public order and even the government itself. Sixth, Mau Mau demands for rewards (such as free land), if recognized by the government, would undermine the credibility of the official slogans of "Harambee" and "Uhuru na Kazi" by providing special privileges for a particular group. Finally, Buijtenhuijs observes that Mau Mau was a kind of "skeleton in the cupboard" for independent Kenya, a kind of guilty secret.[85]

Buijtenhuijs's points can be expanded further. The ethnic issue was particularly delicate in 1963 because of the potential for clashes and even serious violence between landless Gikuyu in the Rift Valley (possibly led by the ex–Mau Mau founders of the Kenya Land and Freedom Army) and members of other groups like the Maasai and Nandi with even stronger historical claims to the area.[86] The controversy over "free land," moreover, was not only a clash of claims but a conflict of values, for many Kenyans believed that the right to land needed to be earned by traditional roads of personal achievement, not by fighting or by government largesse.[87] The Mau Mau–loyalist division after independence was for many a religious issue as well as a political one, for Mau Mau had set independent Christians (the *aregi*), many of whom supported the secret movement, against those following traditional Christianity (the *irore*) and against Gikuyu members of the Revival movement, groups whose members tended to side with the British; the independent government had to be careful, therefore, not to offend religious sensibilities in its core area of support.[88] Finally, as Greet Kershaw points out, some traditional Gikuyu felt culturally impelled to leave Mau Mau behind. "Events which had brought disaster and evil had to be exorcised. . . . The independent government's attempt to wipe it out of history was a proper Kikuyu response to a painful event."[89]

While Buijtenhuijs deals with the immediate political concerns of the Kenyatta government in the mid-1960s, other more radical writers place greater weight on long-term issues. In *Underdevelopment in Kenya,* Colin Leys presents the decisionmaking of the regime in 1963–1966 as laying the foundations for Kenya's neocolonial political economy. According to Leys, neither Kenyatta himself nor the other members of the inner circle of power had any real interest in Mau Mau demands for free land and costly social programs, for they believed such policies would weaken the economy and the state by alienating settlers, the British government, and potential investors—the very groups Kenyatta tried with considerable success to reassure in his famous "forgive and forget" speech to the settlers at Nakuru in 1963.[90] David Maughan-Brown argues that Kenyatta's calls for unity not only covered up the refusal of the new government to meet the demands of Mau Mau veterans for free land but also obscured the growing class divisions within independent Kenya.[91] In *Detained,* Ngugi wa Thiong'o observes that there were four Kenyattas—the KCA Kenyatta, the Kenyatta of KAU, the ex-detainee of 1961–1963, and the "Kenyatta of KANU in power"—and that "people tended to see what they wanted to see rather than what there was: petty-bourgeois vacillations and opportunism."[92]

Yet an argument can be made for Kenyatta's consistency and, by his own lights, integrity and loyalty to his roots. Kenyatta was not only personally disinclined by temperament and ideology to favor Mau Mau but also represented a generation, a social stratum, and a district hostile to radicalism. Ever since his entry into politics, Kenyatta's personal inclinations and political style had always been those of a conciliator and consensus-builder.[93] As the editor of the KCA's *Muiguithania* (The Unifier) in the late 1920s, his editorials had frequently argued for cooperation and concerted action, even of chiefs and people together.[94] It would have gone against the grain for Kenyatta to have strongly favored ex-detainee politicians or Mau Mau veterans, because such actions and policies would have tended to undermine Gikuyu consensus. Nor was it likely that he would have been ideologically inclined to favor the radical position after independence, for in the 1950s, as an older leader of the KCA, Kenyatta had viewed with suspicion the actions of young militants like Bildad Kaggia in using the secret movement to seize control of Gikuyu politics. Moreover, by 1952 Kenyatta was a large Kiambu landholder who had married daughters of ex-Chief Koinange wa Mbiyu and Chief Muhoho wa Gathecha; like other members of the Kiambu establishment he was likely to disapprove of the violence and social radicalism of Mau Mau (and later to react negatively to any calls in the 1960s for the distribution of free land to Mau Mau veterans). His attack on Mau Mau "criminality" (*umaramari*) at the Nyeri meeting in 1952, which Ian Henderson discounted but Bildad Kaggia took very seriously, distinguished "disciplined effort" from the irresponsible seizing of "free things."[95] When Kaggia and the rest of the Mau Mau Central Committee later forced him, with implicit threats, to cease his denunciations, this personal humiliation must have left him angry and aggrieved.[96] Kenyatta's education and worldly experience may have also contributed, when the revolt broke out, to distaste for Mau Mau methods and skepticism about its prospects. This man was no natural sympathizer with radical politics or populist rebellions.

In detention the men at Lokitaung camp divided socially and politically into two groups, with Kenyatta and Waruhiu Itote on the one side and the rest (including a new arrival, the young forest-fighting leader Kariuki Chotara) on the other. When Anglican churchman and leading loyalist Bishop Obadiah Kariuki (who was also Kenyatta's brother-in-law through the Koinange connection) visited Lokitaung in 1957, he prayed together with Kenyatta and Waruhiu Itote and he spoke with Kenyatta about the loyalist struggle against Mau Mau, while the others spurned him as a traitor.[97] The hostility between Kenyatta and fellow detainees led not only to arguments but to two physical attacks, one a 1958 possible assassination attempt.[98] During this estrangement in detention, Bildad Kaggia and the others formed the National Democratic Party, initially excluding Kenyatta from any leadership role.[99] After his release, ex–Mau Mau claims that their revolt had driven out the British must have grated on Kenyatta and on other older moderates, who disliked being told that they "could not win power except at the appalling price of owing its achievement to men they despised."[100]

After independence, Kenyatta tended to favor his home district of Kiambu, which had provided little fighting support for the revolt. In political appointments and in patronage Kiambu people enjoyed the best access and the most success, and Kenyatta surrounded himself with compatriots like Mbiyu wa Koinange, Charles Njonjo (son of Chief Josiah Njonjo), and Njoroge Mungai, so that by the end of the decade critics were referring to a "Kiambu clique."[101] The Gikuyu critics of this favoritism, like Kaggia and later J. M. Kariuki, represented districts that had been more deeply involved in Mau Mau.[102]

Other politicians—for personal, generational, ethnic, socioeconomic, or ideological reasons—saw Mau Mau and the radicals who claimed to speak for its ideals as an even more direct threat. Some seem to have concluded that the best defense was a strong offense. In his autobiography *Not Yet Uhuru,* Oginga Odinga recalls a parliamentary debate over the government's treatment of Mau Mau veterans in 1964 during which Maasai politician Ole Tiptip baldly stated, "I believe we obtained our freedom in a very nice way at the instigation of the British government and not through fighting in the forest."[103] While not necessarily typical, Ole Tiptip's comments did reflect a widespread political resistance, especially among Gikuyu loyalists and politicians from other ethnic groups, to recognizing Mau Mau's contributions in the past, the problems of veterans in the present, and the contemporary populist implications of Mau Mau social ideals. M. A. Amalemba with his criticisms of Mau Mau past and present, J. G. Kiano with his efforts to use government pressure to "reconcile" ex-detainees and loyalists, and Tom Mboya with his coded attacks on "Communist" proposals for land redistribution—all contributed to building an establishment discourse critical of Mau Mau demands and skeptical of the Mau Mau view of history.[104] As Odinga pointed out, however, "Most politicians have not been as foolish as to openly denounce the freedom fighters but have rather connived at letting this period sink into forgetfulness."[105] Kenyatta's example encouraged this common political stance.

The president's attitude at this point was best revealed in his speeches. On "Kenyatta Day," 1964, Kenyatta told his audience,

> Triumph in a struggle of this kind cannot be achieved without a long history of setbacks and sufferings, of failure and humiliation. But all this is worthwhile, and all can be forgotten, when its outcome is the foundation on which a future can be built. It is the future, my friends, that is living, and the past that is dead. In all that I have seen, in many countries and at many periods of my life, never has there seemed any purpose in arguments about the past, or any nobility in motives of revenge.[106]

In this pronouncement, Kenyatta seemed to be advocating a kind of politically convenient collective amnesia, and this became a significant official slogan in the early independent period, "Forgive and Forget." In other important speeches, however, he suggested another way of handling the past, by a revision that would emphasize the role of all in building the country. In his speech at independence, he said,

> As we start on this great task, it is right that . . . all the people of Kenya should remember and pay tribute to those people of all races, tribes and colours who—over the years—have made their contribution to Kenya's rich heritage: administrators, farmers, missionaries, traders and others, and above all the people of Kenya themselves. All have laboured to make this fair land of Kenya the thriving country it is today. It behoves each one of us to vow that, in the days ahead, we shall be worthy of our great inheritance.[107]

This consensual line on history was congruent with the contemporary slogan "Harambee," connoting harmonious communal work, which had supplanted "Uhuru," with its associations of militant struggle against illegitimate authority.

The Mau Mau fighters were a notable omission from the independence day speech, possibly because it was difficult to assimilate them into a consensual version of Kenya's history. Moreover, they were part of a potential opposition, and opponents of the government and dissenters against national policies threatened Kenya's "usable past" and stable present. This applied both to fighters still in the forests and to Mau Mau successor organizations like the Kenya Land Freedom Army in the Rift Valley, which was agitating for the distribution of free land to veterans of Mau Mau. In August 1964, after General Mwariama and his band had come out of the forest, Kenyatta chided those still dissatisfied.

> There are people who go about telling others to return to the forests. These people who go into the forests and feed on stolen things, are they not vagabonds? . . . We took oaths to regain our freedom. But if people ask you to take oaths now, it is against your Government, and therefore against yourselves. . . . If these people now refuse to co-operate, and go into the forests, will you pity them and help them again?[108]

The past was over and in the future there was no role for oathing and forest fighting; in Kenyatta's view apparently, memories of Mau Mau were potentially destabilizing and any revival of the movement threatened the very unity and integrity of the state.

The attitude of Kenyatta and other leaders was somewhat more complex, however. From 1964 to 1967 the government did not completely abandon ex–Mau Mau and their families. While the government did not set aside jobs for ex–Mau Mau during that period, or provide pensions to their widows or orphans, they did provide some settlement slots to Mau Mau veterans (but no "free land") and did register some societies of ex–Mau Mau (notably the Nakuru District Ex–Freedom Fighters Organization, which came together to buy land collectively), and they began tentatively to encourage monuments commemorating Mau Mau sponsored by local groups in Central Province.[109] Moreover, by 1967 the tone of official statements was changing. In his Kenyatta Day address of 1967, Kenyatta reiterated the well-known theme of "We all fought for *uhuru*" but also observed that without the revolt that came after October 1952, "we would still be chained and handcuffed by the colonialists."[110] While this sounded like trying to have it both ways, it was also a belated recognition of the contributions of Mau Mau fighters to the winning of independence. Buijtenhuijs suggests that by 1967 Kenyatta and others were beginning to adopt a more benign attitude toward the rebellion, its martyrs, and its survivors, citing the president's support for the restoration of the name "Hola" (the site of the notorious detention camp which the British had renamed "Galole") and for the use of local funds for the building of the Kimathi Library in Nyeri and for placing a marker at the spot of Kimathi's capture in 1956, and explaining the special honors for Kimathi by suggesting that Kenyatta needed to placate Nyeri people who resented his favoritism for Kiambu.[111] Buijtenhuijs maintains that the government had given the "green light" to "efforts to build up Mau Mau into a positive myth on the Central Provincial level and eventually in other Kikuyu-dominated areas" because Mau Mau no longer posed a political threat, and the regime was by then sufficiently confident and secure to recognize Mau Mau without fearing a backlash from the British, the settlers, the loyalists, or non-Gikuyu groups.[112]

Another explanation suggests itself, however. By 1966 the KANU government was in the midst of a bitter struggle with the Kenya People's Union (KPU), a political party with a populist and socialist platform that could potentially draw support both from the Gikuyu landless and poor and from the Luo population in general. In the short run, the government faced a twofold political challenge: (1) they needed to woo discontented Gikuyu (including ex–Mau Mau) away from the popular Bildad Kaggia, a leader with a reputation among ex-fighters rivalling Kenyatta himself, and (2) they needed to rally Gikuyu in general against the threat posed by their main ethnic rivals, the Luo, led by Oginga Odinga. Under the circumstances, a Machiavellian manipulation of the Mau Mau legacy had obvious value. In the "little general election" of 1966, KANU campaigners in Central Province, including Kenyatta himself, identified nation, party, and ethnic group with Kenyatta; they insisted that the Gikuyu people reaffirm their commitment to the man who had led them since the 1940s, and persuaded ex–Mau Mau leaders such as General Kimbo and General Mbaria Kaniu (once a backer of Kaggia) to express their public support for President Kenyatta and their opposition to Kaggia and the KPU.[113] A highlight of the campaign in Murang'a was Kenyatta's face-to-face attack on Kaggia for failing to enrich himself as other Kapenguria defendants had done.[114] As Peter Anyang' Nyong'o points out, the success of land reform in settling peasants on former estates, the rapid growth of the economy, and the general if temporary improvement in per capita incomes since independence also helped Kenyatta and KANU in 1966.[115]

Helped by favorable economic conditions, the demand for personal fealty and ethnic loyalty succeeded, undercutting class politics. Kaggia and other Gikuyu candidates of KPU lost their seats, and over the next several years the KANU regime effectively isolated the KPU in Central Province. To counter the Luo threat, Gikuyu politicians of KANU attacked the opposition as a force of disloyalty and disunion, while playing the ethnic card themselves. The government-coordinated oathing campaign of 1969— which brought thousands of willing and unwilling Gikuyu to Kenyatta's home at Gatundu, Kiambu—was clearly a revival of the principal Mau Mau instrument to enforce ethnic unity; the campaign even allowed certain Mau Mau supporters, such as the *aregi* (independent Christians) of Murang'a to take revenge against their loyalist rivals who opposed the campaign and suffered fines or even physical assault.[116] Ironically, the oathing was finally brought to an end by the objections of religious loyalists, the Gikuyu leadership of the Presbyterian Church of East Africa.[117]

Official concern with the influence of the past on the present in the late 1960s is best reflected in *Suffering Without Bitterness: The Founding of the Kenya Nation* (1968), published at the height of the struggle with the KPU. This third-person account, sometimes described as Kenyatta's autobiography, was written and edited by Duncan Nderitu Ndegwa, former permanent secretary in the President's Office and by 1968 governor of the Central Bank of Kenya, and Anthony Cullen, a journalist and member of the president's staff, with the assistance of "old friend and colleague" James Gichuru. In the foreword, Kenyatta writes that he published the book to have the facts of his arrest, imprisonment, and release made known in the context of a narrative of Kenya's history to 1963, but it soon becomes clear that he intends to use the story of the struggle against the colonialists to justify KANU's role in the conflict with the KPU. Recalling his speech on Kenyatta Day, 1964, when he "proclaimed . . . that the foundation of our future must lie in the theme: forgive and forget," Kenyatta remarks that some cannot accept that still. How unfair it is that "those whose minds reside in the past are called 'progressive,' while those whose minds are vital enough to challenge and to mould the future are dubbed 'reactionary.'"[118] It is probably no coincidence that the book appeared one year after Oginga Odinga's provocatively titled *Not Yet Uhuru* (1967), for it can be seen as a response to the autobiography of Kenyatta's principal rival.

Suffering Without Bitterness deals with the pre-Emergency period in short space, always focusing on the role of Kenyatta in protest politics, to move quickly to his arrest and trial in 1952–1953, making much of the popular response. "But not just a man had been taken away. Kenyatta was the living symbol, of aspiration, of self-respect. . . . He was their champion, their statesman, their undisputed leader. . . . Men in their loneliness, and in their anguished fury, robbed of their hope and their inspiration and their discipline, set out to rend and tear. If the bulwark of hope was taken from them, let there be catastrophe. . . ."[119] Though the book absolves Kenyatta from any responsibility for Mau Mau excesses, the tone of the references to fighters driven to rebel by the "frustrations set afire in virile men who are treated with contempt"—unlike the tone in some of Kenyatta's early speeches—is understanding.[120] There is a considerable difference between virile men and gangsters.

The revolt itself, however, is given little attention compared to the account of Kenyatta's detention. The few references to the situation in Gikuyuland during the Emergency deal entirely with the loyalty of both people and chiefs to their exiled leader Kenyatta, a martyr "in prison in the wilderness."[121] There is an extended discussion of the constitutional struggle for reform, but it is curiously impersonal, for the only African politicians besides Kenyatta mentioned, except in excerpts of speeches, are James Gichuru, Daniel arap Moi (by 1968 vice president of Kenya), and Tom Mboya; the narrative conspicuously avoids any reference to Oginga

Odinga, even managing to comment on his famous speech about Kenyatta in 1958 without naming the speaker.[122] The focus throughout this core of the book is on Kenyatta as the only man able to end the violence, unite the country, and lead Kenya to a stable independence. There is a section devoted to a condemnation of the Corfield Report, yet *Suffering Without Bitterness* is oddly reminscent of Corfield, for both stress the indispensability of Kenyatta to the development of African nationalism in Kenya.

Appended to the narrative is a long selection of speeches, many condemning dissidents. In a speech on April 26, 1966, for example, Kenyatta attributes the KPU challenge to personal ambition, foreign ideology, and the pernicious impulse to go back to the past. "What purpose could there be in sweeping the country backwards now into the barren past of power struggles and political intrigue? What progress could there be if men again took to the forest and every family must live in fear?"[123] On June 1, 1966, he ridicules the KPU's socialism. "Whether in Kiambu or Kakamega, in Kilifi or Kisumu, in Kapsabet or Kirinyaga—all things belong to someone. I have seen farms and *shambas* belonging to somebody, and worked by that man or that family. . . . I ask you, my friends, where are all these free things that can be given away?"[124] The speech on Kenyatta Day, 1967, contains both a recognition of those who struggled for freedom and a condemnation of the KPU. Recalling the day of his arrest in 1952, Kenyatta notes that he "was not the only one. . . . Hundreds of freedom fighters were taken off to different places, without any knowledge of what would happen to them." He asked the crowd for a moment of silence for the "thousands of our people who were shot dead, and those who died of diseases, and those who were persecuted by the colonialists."[125] The goals those many martyrs had died for were freedom, unity, and peace, but the "snakes" of the KPU were now bent on taking those away.[126] Kenyatta was now endorsing a carefully qualified public memory of Mau Mau that acknowledged its sacrifices while condemning anyone who suggested that the struggle was not over because some of Mau Mau's goals had not been accomplished.

Although the government of independent Kenya set aside the British myth in the early 1960s, it replaced that myth not with its antithesis, an historical version focused on the heroic role of Mau Mau freedom fighters, but rather with a complex discourse that included an indictment of the evils of the colonial system, a generic recognition of everyone who had struggled against colonialism, a glorification of the role of Jomo Kenyatta as the martyr whose sufferings represented the pain inflicted on all the people of Kenya, and a warning about the dangers of using the Mau Mau past to breed discontent and disunity in independent Kenya. This version of history, however, was not fixed but dynamic, changing to respond to new circumstances such as the challenge of the Kenya People's Union, which led the government to encourage Gikuyu to close ranks; by 1969 national unity no longer seemed as important as protecting the leader, the party, and the ethnic group. The use of oathing and of the Gikuyu ethnocentric slogan, "The flag of Kenya shall not leave the House of Mumbi," indicated a willingness of the government to manipulate rituals and symbols associated in the popular mind with the memory of Mau Mau to bolster its power.[127] By 1970 the government's line discouraged radicalism and condemned dissent, but recognized a Mau Mau contribution to *uhuru* in order to counter the class-based challenge of Kaggia with an appeal to Gikuyu solidarity, present a strong ethnic front to the Luo, and reinforce the central role of Kenyatta.

Kenyatta, the evil genius of the British myth of Mau Mau, had metamorphosed, after spending almost ten years in the chrysalis of detention camp, into the father of independent Kenya, the savior of the country's political and economic stability, and the forgiving leader of all Kenyans, including the settlers. In "a highly cultivated official myth," he had become the benevolent elder statesman whose role in official history was symbolized by the annual celebration of October 20 as "Kenyatta Day."[128] The elevation of Kenyatta to icon status was not engineered entirely by the president himself and did not serve Kenyatta and his family alone. The "Kiambu clique," the Gikuyu sociopolitical establishment in general, and even the Kenyan bourgeoisie as a whole benefited from a historical myth and a contemporary policy that stressed the unitary nature of anticolonial protest, condemned dissent as unpatriotic, and downplayed social divisions in independent Kenya, all by focusing on the symbol of the president. In Mordechai Tamarkin's words, "Kenya may not be the best example of nation-building, but it is certainly an outstanding example of *regime*-building in Africa."[129] This will be discussed further in later chapters.

Notes

1. L. S. B. Leakey, *Defeating Mau Mau* (London: Methuen, 1954), p. 52.
2. J. F. Lipscomb, *White Africans* (London: Faber, 1955), p. 142.
3. Jomo Kenyatta, *Suffering Without Bitterness: The Founding of the Kenyan Nation* (Nairobi: East African Publishing House, 1968), p. 189.
4. George Bennett, *Kenya, a Political History: The Colonial Period* (London: Oxford, 1963), Chs. 2–4.
5. Robert Tignor, *The Colonial Transformation of Kenya: The Kamba, Kikuyu, and Maasai from 1900 to 1939* (Princeton: Princeton University Press, 1976), Chs. II, III, V, VI.
6. Marshall S. Clough, *Fighting Two Sides: Kenyan Chiefs and Politicians, 1918–1940* (Niwot: University Press of Colorado, 1990), Chs. 3, 5–7; Presley, *Kikuyu Women*, Ch. 6.
7. Clough, *Fighting Two Sides,* Ch. 8.
8. John Spencer, *The Kenya African Union* (London: KPI, 1985), Ch. 3.
9. Itote, *"Mau Mau" General,* Chs. 4–5; Kaggia, *Roots,* Chs. 7–8; Muchai, *Hardcore,* p. 14; Wanjau, *Mau Mau Author,* pp. x–xi; Philip Murphy, *Party Politics and Decolonization: The Conservative Party and British Colonial Policy in*

Tropical Africa, 1951–1964 (Oxford: Clarendon, 1995), pp. 47–49; Furedi, *Mau Mau War*, Chs. 1–2.

10. Throup, *Economic and Social Origins*, Chs. 7–8; Maloba, *Mau Mau and Kenya*, Chs. 1–2; Wachanga, *Swords*, introduction.

11. Kaggia, *Roots*, Chs. 9–11; Spencer, *Kenya African Union*, Chs. 5–6.

12. Maloba, *Mau Mau and Kenya*, Ch. 3.

13. Anthony Clayton, *Counterinsurgency in Kenya 1952–1960*, 2nd ed. (Manhattan, Kansas: Sunflower, 1984), Ch. 2; see also Randall W. Heather, "Intelligence and Counterinsurgency in Kenya 1952–56" (Ph.D. thesis, Cambridge, 1993).

14. Muchai, *The Hardcore*, pp. 15–22; Michael Blundell, *So Rough a Wind* (London: Weidenfeld and Nicholson, 1964), p. 132.

15. Clayton, *Counterinsurgency*, pp. 23–27.

16. Clayton, *Counterinsurgency*, Chs. 3–4; Njama, *Mau Mau from Within*, Chs. 16–20; Wachanga, *Swords*, Ch. 7.

17. M. P. K. Sorrenson, *Land Reform in the Kikuyu Country: A Study in Government Policy* (Nairobi: Oxford, 1967).

18. Edgerton, *Mau Mau: An African Crucible*, Ch. 6.

19. Oginga Odinga, *Not Yet Uhuru* (New York: Hill and Wang, 1967), Chs. 9–11; Bennett, *Kenya*, Chs. 13–14.

20. Kariuki, *Detainee*, Chs. IX, X.

21. Kaggia, *Roots*, Ch. 18; Maloba, *Mau Mau and Kenya*, Ch. 8.

22. Press Handout, Oct. 29, 1952, PRO CO 822/438.

23. *Manchester Guardian*, Nov. 5, 1952, quoted in Buijtenhuijs, *Mau Mau Twenty Years After*, p. 44.

24. *The Mau Mau in Kenya*, foreword by Granville Roberts (London: Hutchinson, 1954); Anthony Lavers, *The Kikuyu Who Fight Mau Mau: Wakikuyu Wanaopigana na Mau Mau* (Nairobi: Eagle Press, 1955).

25. See the discussion of reporting on Mau Mau in Carolyn Martin Shaw, *Colonial Inscriptions: Race, Sex, and Class in Kenya* (Minneapolis: University of Minnesota Press, 1995), pp. 170–78.

26. J. C. Carothers, *The Psychology of Mau Mau* (Nairobi: Colony and Protectorate of Kenya, 1955), pp. 4–7; see also the discussion of Carothers in Jock McCulloch, *Colonial Psychiatry and "the African Mind"* (Cambridge: Cambridge University Press, 1995), pp. 64–76.

27. Bruce Berman and John Lonsdale, "Louis Leakey's Mau Mau: A Study in the Politics of Knowledge," *History and Anthropology*, vol. 5, no. 2 (1991), pp. 172–183.

28. L. S. B. Leakey, *Defeating Mau Mau* (London: Methuen, 1954), p. 52.

29. T. F. C. Bewes, *Kikuyu Conflict: Mau Mau and the Christian Witness* (London: Highway Press, 1953).

30. Clayton, *Counterinsurgency*, p. 1.

31. Elspeth Huxley, *A Thing to Love* (London: Chatto and Windus, 1953), pp. 66–71.

32. Charles Wilson, *Before the Dawn in Kenya* (Nairobi: English Press, 1953), p. 130.

33. Ione Leigh, *In the Shadow of the Mau Mau* (London: W. H. Allen, 1954), pp. 16, 17.

34. J. F. Lipscomb, *White Africans* (London: Faber and Faber, 1955), pp. 141, 151.

35. W. W. Baldwin, *Mau Mau Manhunt* (New York: Dutton, 1957); Dane

Kennedy, "Constructing the Colonial Myth of Mau Mau," *The International Journal of African Historical Studies,* vol. 25, no. 2 (1992), p. 247, fn. 20.

36. Ian Henderson, *Manhunt in Kenya* (Garden City, N.Y.: Doubleday, 1958), p. 149.

37. Frank Kitson, *Gangs and Counter-Gangs* (London: Barrie and Rockcliffe, 1960).

38. *A Handbook of Anti–Mau Mau Operations* (Nairobi, 1954), p. 15.

39. John Lonsdale, "Mau Maus of the Mind: Making Mau Mau and Remaking Kenya," *Journal of African History,* vol. 31 (1990), p. 407.

40. Robert Ruark, *Something of Value* (Garden City, N.Y.: Doubleday, 1955), pp. i, ii.

41. Ibid., pp. 324, 374.

42. *Historical Survey of the Origins and Growth of Mau Mau* [Corfield Report] (London: HMSO, 1960), p. 3.

43. Ibid., pp. 283–84.

44. Rosberg and Nottingham, *Myth of "Mau Mau,"* p. xvii.

45. Buijtenhuijs, *Mau Mau Twenty Years After,* pp. 43–46.

46. David Maughan-Brown, *Land, Freedom, and Fiction: History and Ideology in Kenya* (London: Zed, 1985), Chs. 3–4.

47. Lonsdale, "Mau Maus of the Mind," pp. 404–405.

48. A. S. Cleary, "The Myth of Mau Mau in Its International Context," *African Affairs,* vol. 89, no. 355 (April 1990), pp. 227–45.

49. Kennedy, "Constructing the Colonial Myth," pp. 245–47.

50. Ibid., p. 252.

51. Ibid., p. 260.

52. Frederick Cooper, *Decolonization and African Society: The Labor Question in British and French Africa* (Cambridge: Cambridge University Press, 1996), p. 360.

53. Leakey, *Defeating Mau Mau,* p. 25.

54. Dane Kennedy, *Islands of White: Settler Society and Culture in Kenya and Southern Rhodesia* (Durham: Duke University Press, 1987); Bruce Berman, "Nationalism, Ethnicity, and Modernity: The Paradox of Mau Mau," *Canadian Journal of African Studies,* vol. 25, no. 2 (1991), pp. 182–83, 188–92.

55. See particularly Wilson's last page, *Before the Dawn,* p. 130.

56. In the official Situation Reports issued during the Emergency, "terrorists" was the most popular epithet for Mau Mau fighters, followed by "gangsters" and "thugs." See PRO CO 822/455.

57. Leakey, *Defeating Mau Mau,* p. 43; Lipscomb, *White Africans,* p. 143; Corfield, *Survey,* pp. 52, 284–85.

58. Lonsdale, "Mau Maus of the Mind," p. 413.

59. Corfield, *Survey,* 203.

60. Lipscomb, *White Africans,* p. 149; Carothers, *Psychology of Mau Mau,* p. 20.

61. Carothers, *Psychology of Mau Mau,* pp. 5–15.

62. E. M. Wiseman, *Kikuyu Martyrs* (London: Highway Press, 1958).

63. Lipscomb, *White Africans,* p. 144.

64. Henderson, *Man Hunt in Kenya,* p. 239.

65. Philip Mitchell, *African Afterthoughts* (London: Hutchinson, 1954), p. xviii.

66. Jeremy Murray-Brown, *Kenyatta* (New York: Dutton, 1973), p. 383.

67. Blundell, *So Rough a Wind,* p. 296.

68. Brockway, *African Journeys,* Chs. 9–11; Stephen Howe, *Anticolonialism in British Politics: The Left and the End of Empire, 1918–1964* (Oxford: Clarendon, 1993), pp. 200–207.

69. Montagu Slater, *The Trial of Jomo Kenyatta* (London: Secker and Warburg, 1955), p. 14.

70. Ibid., p. 16.

71. R. Mugo Gatheru, *Child of Two Worlds: A Kikuyu's Story* (New York: Mentor, 1964), Ch. XIV.

72. Mbiyu Koinange, *The People of Kenya Speak for Themselves* (Detroit: Kenya Publication Fund, 1955), p. 75.

73. Muga Gicaru, *Land of Sunshine: Scenes of Life in Kenya Before Mau Mau,* preface by Trevor Huddleston (London: Lawrence and Wishart, 1958), p. 174; Kenyatta quoted in Brian Lapping, *End of Empire* (New York: St. Martin's, 1985), p. 406.

74. Gicaru, *Land of Sunshine,* p. 169.

75. The government of Kenya attempted to ban Gicaru's book, not only because of "inaccurate information" but "because of many passages designed purely and simply to denigrate the white man in general and the settlers in particular." W. F. Coutts to R. Granville Roberts, PRO CO 822/1310.

76. Brockway, *African Journeys,* p. 169.

77. Colin Legum, *New Statesman and Nation,* Oct. 10, 1952.

78. Tom Mboya, *Freedom and After* (Boston: Little Brown, 1963), pp. 37–49.

79. Quoted by Odinga, *Not Yet Uhuru,* p. 253.

80. Jomo Kenyatta, *Harambee! The Prime Minister of Kenya's Speeches 1963–1964* (Nairobi: Oxford University Press, 1964), p. 15.

81. Richard Cox, *Kenyatta's Country* (New York: Praeger, 1966), p. 55.

82. Kenyatta, *Suffering Without Bitterness,* p. 124.

83. Ibid., p. 189.

84. Buijtenhuijs, *Mau Mau Twenty Years After,* pp. 49–50.

85. Ibid., pp. 50–62.

86. John W. Harbeson, *Nation-Building in Kenya: The Role of Land Reform* (Evanston: Northwestern, 1973), 246; Kanogo, *Squatters,* 169.

87. Lonsdale, "Moral Economy," pp. 459–61.

88. David P. Sandgren, *Christianity and the Kikuyu: Religious Divisions and Social Conflict* (New York: 1989), pp. 157–58.

89. Greet Kershaw, "Mau Mau from Below: Fieldwork and Experience, 1955–57 and 1962," *Canadian Journal of African Studies,* vol. 25, no. 2 (1991), p. 293.

90. Colin Leys, *Underdevelopment in Kenya: The Political Economy of Neo-Colonialism* (London: Heinemann, 1975), p. 60.

91. Maughan-Brown, *Land, Freedom, and Fiction,* p. 196.

92. Ngugi, *Detained,* pp. 161–62.

93. John Spencer, *James Beauttah: Freedom Fighter* (Nairobi: Stellascope, 1983), p. 16.

94. *Muigwuithania,* no. 8, Dec. 1928–Jan. 1929, KNA/DC/MKS/10B.13.1.

95. Lonsdale, "Mau Maus of the Mind," p. 419.

96. Kaggia, *Roots,* p. 114.

97. Murray-Brown, *Kenyatta,* 348–49.

98. Ibid., p. 352.

99. Kaggia, *Roots,* p. 145.

100. Lonsdale, "Mau Maus of the Mind," p. 418.

101. Jennifer A. Widner, *The Rise of the Party-State in Kenya: From "Harambee!" to "Nyayo!"* (Berkeley: University of California Press, 1992), p. 96.

102. Cherry Gertzel, *The Politics of Independent Kenya, 1963–68* (Evanston: Northwestern University Press, 1970), p. 43.

103. Odinga, *Not Yet Uhuru*, p. 254.

104. Buijtenhuijs, *Mau Mau Twenty Years After*, p. 61; Geoff Lamb, *Peasant Politics: Conflict and Development in Murang'a* (Lewes: Julian Friedmann, 1974), pp. 29–30; Gertzel, *Politics of Kenya*, pp. 57, 65.

105. Odinga, *Not Yet Uhuru*, p. 254.

106. Kenyatta, *Harambee!*, p. 2.

107. Ibid., p. 15.

108. Ibid., p. 103.

109. Buijtenhuijs, *Mau Mau Twenty Years After*, pp. 69–72, 132–36.

110. Kenyatta, *Suffering Without Bitterness*, p. 341.

111. Buijtenhuijs, *Mau Mau Twenty Years After*, p. 64.

112. Ibid., 64–65. Tabitha Kanogo argues that much was done behind the scenes, especially to help veterans get access to farms. "Review of *Mau Mau Twenty Years After*," *Kenya Historical Review*, vol. 5, no. 2 (1977), p. 400.

113. Gertzel, *Politics of Kenya*, pp. 90–92; Lamb, *Peasant Politics*, pp. 32, 39; Buijtenhuijs, *Mau Mau Twenty Years After*, p. 141.

114. Lamb, *Peasant Politics*, p. 36.

115. P. Anyang' Nyong'o, "State and Society in Kenya: The Disintegration of the Nationalist Coalitions and the Rise of Presidential Authoritarianism 1963–78," *African Affairs*, vol. 88, no. 351 (April 1989), p. 239.

116. Sandgren, *Christianity and the Kikuyu*, p. 159.

117. Murray-Brown, *Kenyatta*, pp. 378–79.

118. Kenyatta, *Suffering Without Bitterness*, p. xv.

119. Ibid., p. 55.

120. Ibid.

121. Ibid., p. 67.

122. Ibid., p. 73.

123. Ibid., p. 305.

124. Ibid., p. 309.

125. Ibid., p. 341.

126. Ibid., p. 343.

127. Murray-Brown, *Kenyatta*, p. 378.

128. Mordechai Tamarkin, "The Roots of Political Stability in Kenya," *African Affairs*, vol. 77, no. 308 (July 1978), p. 298.

129. Ibid., p. 299–300.

The Mau Mau Version

The future historian of these times may well find it difficult to get our side of the story. Many documents vital to his task will be burnt before independence. But in my narrative of the camps and our strange life together inside them he may perhaps see some glimpses of the truth and justice of the movements of unity, and he may begin to understand why we do not regard the soldiers of the forest as "hardcore," "terrorists" or "murderers," but as the noblest of our fighters for freedom. May this book and our new state be a small part of their memorial. Their torture and their pain were the hard travail of a nation.

—*J. M. Kariuki*[1]

We hope that this book, valuable as it is in itself, will also help to pierce that veil of reticence which surrounds the Land and Freedom Army and go some way at least to secure to those who fought in the forests of the Nyandarua their due recognition as national heroes.
—*B. M. Kaggia, Fred Kubai, J. Murumbi, A. Oneko*[2]

T he British shaped the discourse about Mau Mau during the Emergency itself, while Kenyan politicians attempted a few years later to control the public memory of the 1950s in order to maintain national unity and preserve political and economic stability. Many Mau Mau veterans felt that these versions distorted the truth, and in 1963 some began to put forward a new perspective in the form of memoirs.

This perspective—of the oath takers rather than their inquisitors, of the guerrillas rather than the pursuers, from within the wire instead of without—represented Mau Mau as heroic, not criminal; nationalist more than tribal; central instead of peripheral; a political success (though militarily defeated) rather than a failure. Turning the tables on the British, the memoirists stressed the injustices of colonial rule, the brutality of the counterinsurgency, the harshness of the detention camps. Moreover, their focus on the revolt tended either to downplay or to appropriate the nationalist struggles of Gikuyu constitutionalists and Africans outside Central Kenya, and some accounts went further, to attack African collaborators and criticize latter-day politicians (though generally not Kenyatta). These personal narratives discredited the British myth and questioned the new rulers' control of the public memory of colonial times. The memoirists' efforts to justify themselves, that is, bestow on Mau Mau an honored position in Kenya's past, and win government recognition of the veterans had significance both as history writing and as contemporary political commentary.

The first three memoirs published (and still the most influential)—J. M. Kariuki's *"Mau Mau" Detainee* (1963), Karari Njama's *Mau Mau from Within* (1966), and Waruhiu Itote's *"Mau Mau" General* (1967)—established this characteristic Mau Mau discourse. Their effect was reinforced by Rosberg and Nottingham's *Myth of "Mau Mau"* (1966), which also portrayed the revolt as a rational response to colonial oppression similar to violent struggles for liberation elsewhere in the world. The assistant to Rosberg and Nottingham, David Koff, helped Waruhiu Itote prepare his manuscript, and John Nottingham served as Itote's editor at East African Publishing House. This chapter will examine the three memoirs, analyze their discourse on Mau Mau, and assess the conflict of interpretations that had emerged by the end of the 1960s.

"Travail of a Nation": J. M. Kariuki and *"Mau Mau" Detainee*

The key roles their authors had played in the secret movement gave the first Mau Mau memoirs immediate authority. Josiah Mwangi Kariuki, a leader of hardcore detainees, Karari Njama, secretary to Dedan Kimathi in the Nyandarua forests, and Waruhiu Itote, senior general on Kirinyaga, had important stories to tell, and, just as compellingly, a new interpretation of Mau Mau to advance.

Margery Perham, whose careful foreword introduced *"Mau Mau" Detainee,* clearly recognized its far-reaching potential. As a well-known academic expert who had both criticized settlers and the government during the Emergency and referred to Mau Mau itself as "that most ghastly of rebellions, with its bestial cult of torture and murder," she saw her role as particularly delicate, and her assertion "I had no hand in the writing" not only gave Kariuki his full share of credit, but also enabled Perham to place a comfortable distance between herself and his narrative.[3] With her eye to the British audience, she handled the issue of Kariuki's credibility with caution, declaring that "For myself I believe that he has given a substantially true account of his own experiences," but acknowledging that some European readers might reject the account as "untrue or greatly exaggerated."[4] Her apologetic observation, "For us British, whether in Britain or in Kenya, who were shocked by the character of the Mau Mau outbreak, to know all may not be to forgive all but it is still important to *know*," revealed a paternalistic Eurocentrism reflected later in the foreword by attacks on Mau Mau and defenses of British policy that recalled the themes and language of the anti–Mau Mau discourse.[5] Perham's ambivalent introduction angered Ngugi wa Thiong'o and other Africans at the time who disliked her "liberal hesitancy and apologies" and asked "Why did she and her kind want to detain the Mau Mau resistance movement in a liberal prison?"[6] For Perham herself, however, and for other European sympathizers with Africa who had believed for a decade that Mau Mau was the unacceptable, backward-looking face of African nationalism, the publication of *"Mau Mau" Detainee* enabled them to move from rejection to at least partial understanding.

Perham's painful doubts were left behind on *"Mau Mau" Detainee*'s first page. Kariuki straightforwardly spelled out his principal motivations for writing this memoir of the detention camps: to correct previous falsehoods, record a significant episode in Kenyan history, supply a background to contemporary politics, and provide a cautionary tale to other Africans:

> It is written not in any spirit of bitterness or spite but because no one has yet told the truth about them [the camps] and because they have become an important part of the history of my country. . . . Possibly too, some description of how we organised ourselves in difficult conditions will be of interest to those who may still be in danger of a similar fate today in other parts of colonial Africa.[7]

It was clear here and throughout that Kariuki was telling both a personal and a collective story, imposing on himself a keenly felt dual obligation.

He began his story, as others would who came after him, by situating himself in the web of clan, lineage, and family interrelationships that typified the Gikuyu social world. Mwangi wa Kariuki was born in 1929 into a Rift Valley squatter family living on an estate at Kabati-ini near Bahati Forest, to which they had moved from Chinga in Nyeri in 1928. His lineage was Mbari ya Mbogo of the Mungari clan. His father, Kariuki Kigoni, left the family to return to Chinga in 1940 and died in 1943, so the young Mwangi was raised primarily by his mother, Mary Wanjiku, and his maternal grandfather, Mugo Wabira, "a great warrior in the days before the British." In 1936, at the suggestion of the white farmer "Muturi" who "had been impressed by my lack of fear of Europeans compared with other boys of my age," Mwangi began to work in the kitchen of "the big house."[8] In 1938 his mother persuaded him to give up his job and enroll full time in the estate's primary school. By dint of family and personal sacrifice, he went on to a local Kikuyu Independent School Association (KISA) school and to Catholic primary and intermediate schools in Nyeri and Embu; he ultimately graduated from King's College, a Church Missionary Society secondary school in Budo, Uganda, in 1952.[9]

In general, the Gikuyu on Muturi's estate had little knowledge of politics, "though we used to discuss our land grievances through the smoke in the huts at night."[10] Kariuki was first exposed to nationalist rhetoric in independent Christian sermons, but nothing had prepared him for his first encounter with Kenyatta at a mass meeting in Njoro in 1947. "I myself was fundamentally changed by his statesmanlike words and his burning personality. I vowed there and then that I would struggle . . . to follow him in his crusade to remove the sufferings and humiliations of our people."[11] Kariuki's experience underscores Henry Muoria's observation on the force of Kenyatta's speeches, "His spoken words made many Africans become politically conscious for the first time in their lives."[12]

After completing his education, Kariuki joined KAU at Nakuru in November 1952 and became an active recruiter for the party in the Bahati area. He took the Mau Mau unity oath in December 1952 (the text reads 1953, but that must be in error because he was arrested and detained in October 1953), and the *batuni* oath probably either in late December or January 1953.[13] As an active though not prominent Mau Mau supporter in the Rift Valley, Kariuki hid forest fighters in his quarters, supplied them with money and clothes, provided bribes for the release of detainees, and travelled in a railway guard's uniform supplied by "sympathizers on the railway staff" between Eldoret and Kisumu as a messenger between groups.[14] Kariuki's hotel business in Nakuru provided him with a cover of sorts, but on October 28, 1953, he was arrested by Special Branch at his hotel.[15]

For the next seven years, the Kenya government held J. M. Kariuki in fourteen different camps of the Kenyan gulag, from Kowop in the arid Turkana lands to the steamy, subtropical Saiyusi Island camp in Lake Victoria. He sojourned involuntarily in most of the best-known places— Langata, Lodwar, Maralal, Manyani, Athi River—though he missed out on Hola. He was elected a compound leader or detainee representative in most of these camps, and assumed as his special responsibility the role of spokesman for the illiterate detainees. With other members of the educated minority, he ran classes for his fellow inmates. In addition, he took it upon himself not only to complain to camp authorities and to visiting committees from the International Red Cross about bad conditions inside, but also to write and smuggle out letters to members of Parliament and to others whom he hoped would take action to draw attention to the plight of the Kenyan detainees. There was much to complain about, from inadequate rations and medical care to harassment, incidental brutality, and systematic beatings intended to break the detainees' spirits and force them to "confess" their oath-taking and their actions on behalf of Mau Mau. Kariuki's objections to this treatment, particularly his letters sent outside the camps, drew down on him the special wrath of certain European officers, leading to a number of beatings (one of which left him with permanent injuries) and some spells without food and water in solitary confinement. Under pressure and fear of death, Kariuki eventually signed false "confessions," but he dismissed these in his memoir as a "tissue of lies" obtained under duress.[16]

Finally, officials sent Kariuki along "the pipeline" to works camps and eventually to restricted freedom in his family's home location in Nyeri. When he defied the terms of his restriction by traveling as he pleased (much as Steve Biko defied his banning orders in the 1970s) and working with others to form a Nyeri political party, he was briefly detained again.[17] Eventually, Kariuki joined KANU, met and impressed Jomo Kenyatta, and began the political career that would lead him to prominence as a populist member of the independent Kenya Parliament.

"Mau Mau" Detainee was a very self-conscious memoir, by a man as concerned with the historical record as he was with telling a personal story. The evidence suggests that Kariuki was writing on behalf of Mau Mau in general and detainees in particular but principally to the educated Kenyan and British audiences. Chapter 2, which contained little personal information, was essentially an essay in revision designed to challenge European versions of Kenya's history.

> It has amused me sometimes to read aloud in the books issued to our schools the inevitable distortions and misunderstandings that are circulating in this country in the name of "history." It has also saddened me because it is this general attitude that possibly was the biggest single contribution to the inevitable explosion in 1952.[18]

Kariuki's authority was the Gikuyu medium of oral history—"countless hours of talk over the flickering evening fires which had given me the story of my people's struggle since the days of their former freedom"—to his mind more reliable for the true history of colonial Kenya than the writing of the Europeans in which most of his people were mute.[19] But for Kariuki, as for Njama and Itote, falsity and truth lay in the heart of the teller and the gist of the story more than in the details.

Challenging Huxley, Corfield, and Ian Henderson, Kariuki traced the development of African politics in Kenya to justifiable anger over European land seizures and economic dominance and understandable fear of settler political ambitions.[20] He denied Corfield's claim that Mau Mau was the "offspring" of the Kikuyu Central Association or even the predictable outgrowth of KAU, attributing its rise solely to the refusal of the government to make the most minimal concessions to Kenyatta and the constitutional nationalists. Kariuki characterized Kenyatta and the KAU leaders as "moderates" forced by government intransigence into "more extreme positions in their desperate efforts to prevent a major explosion in the country."[21] The idealistic leaders of the secret movement itself "started slowly, indeed regretfully" through the oath of unity to organize their resistance, only to be saddled with the false name "Mau Mau" and an unfair reputation for savagery and brutality.[22]

Kariuki's presentation of the secret movement, drawn both from his own experiences and from information from fellow detainees, was deliberately the reverse of the standard British portrayal. The unity and *batuni* oaths he described bore little resemblance to the "bestial" and "obscene" savage rituals of the anti–Mau Mau discourse. He defended the use of violence against other Gikuyu to enforce oathing by asserting that only "absolute unity, implicit obedience and a sublime faith in our cause could bring victory against the guns, the armies, the money and the brains of the Kenya Government."[23] As for Mau Mau hostility toward Christians, he commented that "the struggle on earth was so desperate that Christianity could not be allowed to interfere"; after all, the "enemies, in their cunning, were using it as a weapon against us."[24] Kariuki questioned the truth of the Lari massacre, insisted that many "Mau Mau" slayings were either really murders by loyalists because of "land disputes" and other personal reasons or killings by robbers in the commission of crimes, and suggested that "sporadic murders of Europeans . . . were usually an incidental part of raids primarily aimed at getting weapons."[25] According to him, home guards were not really "loyal" but either men out to save their own skins or secret rebels, though he admitted that the British, using their massive resources, ultimately succeeded in dividing the Gikuyu and turning a straightforward anticolonial revolt into a civil war.[26]

In his early chapters Kariuki fashioned a fresh image of the men and women of Mau Mau as fighters in an heroic, beleaguered "resistance" to the implacable British juggernaut. However, because he could not claim firsthand knowledge of the forest war, his memoir gained greater authority when he turned to his personal experiences as a hardcore detainee. His characterization of the hardcore community contrasted strongly with European descriptions; his detainees were well organized and self-conscious, committed to the movement (but not fanatical), and effectively led and disciplined by their elected representatives. They set up and operated their own courts, organized their social life, and conducted classes in subjects ranging from basic literacy to current African politics. *"Mau Mau" Detainee* drew strong contrasts between the active heroism of hardcore leaders and the passive endurance of the rank and file on the one hand and, on the other, the moral cowardice of cooperators and screeners (whom he described as "traitors" guilty of "double-crossing their own souls"), the casual brutality of some of the African warders, and the authoritarianism and cruelty of some of the British prison officials.[27] But the British bore ultimate responsibility, and Kariuki was most disturbed by their unflagging self-righteousness. "What strange twists of thought made the security forces think they always had God and Right on their side whatever crimes against humanity they committed?"[28]

Kariuki isolated the British and argued for African unity by suggesting in numerous ways that most Africans—fighters and fence-sitters and home guardsmen in Central Kenya, Gikuyu and members of other ethnic groups, detainees and warders—really in their hearts hated British rule themselves and supported the revolt. In his description of the Emergency in the Gikuyu reserves, he insisted that most home guards helped the Mau Mau in secret. In his portrayal of life in the camps he mentioned non-Gikuyu detainees as often as possible, commenting, "It is another false impression that has been spread around that there were no tribes other than Kikuyu . . . there were also many from such different tribes as Jaluo, Abaluhya, Kitosh, Akamba and Masai, who provided some of the strongest resistance of all."[29] He also carefully noted acts of assistance and secret expressions of nationalist sympathy shown by warders to detainees, even claiming during his description of the response to the news of Kimathi's capture at Lodwar, that many of the guards "looked as sad as we were and it was obvious where their sympathies lay."[30] Finally, Kariuki's willingness to forgive Africans who had supported the British also enabled him to assimilate them into the freedom struggle after the fact.

But Kariuki did not unquestioningly accept Kenyatta's insistence that "we all fought for *uhuru*" and his prescription that Kenyans should forget the past. Clearly he idolized Kenyatta in 1963, and the old man had honored him by using him as a private envoy to Kwame Nkrumah and by offering him employment with the government.[31] Kariuki followed Kenyatta's lead by arguing that past oppressions and abuses needed to be forgotten in the interests of reconciliation and unity; however, as far as he was concerned, "forgive and forget" applied only to allowing amnesty for individual actions during the Emergency, not to suppressing the history of the secret movement and not to allowing Mau Mau ideals to go by the board, pushed aside by politicians in pursuit of their own interests. In the crucible of Manyani, a lifelong populist had been forged.

As a revisionist account, *"Mau Mau" Detainee* seemed credible in part because of the solid respectability of Kariuki himself. An intelligent, thrusting young man, whose struggle for education (supported by his self-sacrificing mother) and entrepreneurial spirit had lifted his family out of poverty, Kariuki came close to the British model of an ideal African, modern, Westernized, looking toward the future. The Corfield stereotype of primitive, ignorant, Mau Mau fanatic simply did not fit him at all. Moreover, *"Mau Mau" Detainee* carried a message understandable in Christian terms to both British and Africans, an instructive tale of tribulations bravely borne and temptations resisted, ending in release from bondage and forgiveness of one's enemies. Thus Kariuki pioneered a new version of the

1950s that presented the revolt as a justifiable response of oppressed people goaded beyond endurance, represented the guerrillas as freedom fighters, and portrayed the detainees (in role reversal) as men of clear-eyed principle and their British captors as misled, brutal fanatics of an unworthy and doomed cause. *"Mau Mau" Detainee* created new heroes of the Emergency, replacing colonial guerrilla fighters like Ian Henderson by African nationalists: the hardcore J. M. Kariuki; the father of Kenya, Jomo Kenyatta; and the leader of guerrillas, Dedan Kimathi. This revisionist discourse, presented with compelling immediacy in a personal account, began to undermine the British "myth of Mau Mau" in a way that the new African regime's equivocal representation of the past could not.

"A Weapon to Fight": Karari Njama and *Mau Mau from Within*

J. M. Kariuki's *"Mau Mau" Detainee* was a strong apologia for Mau Mau, but it suffered from its author's limited experience of the war itself. The next two memoirs, written by men in positions of command who had fought in the forests, added much more information on the guerrillas themselves while contributing to the emerging Mau Mau discourse on the revolt. Moreover, as fighting guerrillas Karari Njama and Waruhiu Itote shared in the blood responsibility for Mau Mau in a way J. M. Kariuki did not. There was an image shift as well; the frontispiece to *Mau Mau from Within,* showing Karari Njama on the day of his capture wearing dreadlocks and a military combat blouse, contrasted strongly with that of Kariuki in a suit working on his memoir in Kenyatta's office in Nairobi.

It was indicative of the altered circumstances of 1966 that *Mau Mau from Within* was not introduced by a liberal Briton but by four African politicians—Bildad Kaggia, Fred Kubai, Joseph Murumbi, and Achieng' Oneko—including two founding members of the populist Kenya People's Union, then locked in a struggle with KANU. Their short preface argued that the British myth of Mau Mau still lingered, even in Kenya itself. They felt nothing but sympathy for the many "self-effacing and diffident" veterans of Mau Mau, suffering from the guilt instilled by years of "brain washing" in the camps, who lived in obscurity, avoiding politics, but they attacked those "African politicians and young 'intellectuals'" who believed "that this is as it should be." Mau Mau was still "condemned by people of stature in the politics of the country today," even though "Kenya is today independent largely because of this revolt and the struggle of the men and women who participated in it."[32] Just as most educated Africans had rejected the revolt during the Emergency, the elite continued to do so in the 1960s, demonstrating once again "the wide gulf that has arisen in many parts of Africa between the intellectuals and the masses," yet one more "vicious heritage from colonialism."[33] The "humble men and women who felt passionately about the cause they struggled for" continued to see their ideals frustrated by the neocolonial system of present-day Kenya. Since "Not only politics and economics but minds have to be decolonized," they welcomed *Mau Mau from Within* as a weapon in words in the fight toward that end.[34]

This second Mau Mau memoir had its genesis in the research project of Donald Barnett, a doctoral candidate in anthropology at the University of California at Los Angeles, who met Karari wa Njama in 1962 during the process of interviewing Mau Mau veterans about their experiences as guerrilla fighters in the Nyandarua forests. Unlike the other informants, Karari Njama, who told Barnett "that he had wanted to record the history of the revolution ever since his release from the detention camps" in 1958, did not wish to be tape-recorded, choosing instead to write his story personally.[35] The result was a lengthy firsthand record of the war in the forest, with an extensive and valuable scholarly introduction by Barnett (who also introduced each chapter).

Like Kariuki, Karari Njama (whose family also came from Nyeri) was born in 1926 into a squatter household in Laikipia in the Rift Valley. His mother, Wanjiru Wamioro, died in 1932. In 1937, his father, Njama Karari, angered by the restrictive new regulations on squatter land and livestock, moved the family back to Nyeri. "I had been born and raised in the Rift Valley and did not like the idea of leaving. My resentment turned to the European farmer whose regulations about livestock and land cultivation caused my father to move."[36] Like Kariuki, he was influenced by his grandfather, an old warrior, who told him stories of precolonial days and showed him the family land that had been taken over by the government to form part of the forest reserve. "We found that we couldn't fight against the white man who was killing us with his magic fires and so he started ruling us and took away most of the best fertile lands."[37] Karari Njama's nationalism grew at home, rooted in family memories of conquest, land alienation, and racial injustice. His later youth, like Kariuki's, was taken up with the struggle to get an education. He began at the age of twelve, in Munyange KISA school in Nyeri, and worked particularly hard to make up for lost time. In a passage reminiscent of Abraham Lincoln, he wrote, "In the evenings I never went out to play with other boys. I always remained at home reading my first Kikuyu primer by the light of the fire."[38] In 1944 he entered Alliance High School, where he received a solid education in most respects but learned to resent the slanted teaching of history and the instruction in Christianity, which struck him as hypocritical. To counteract this cultural bias, the senior boys set up a secret organization to teach their juniors the other side of colonial rule and mission Christianity and inspire them with Gikuyu pride.[39]

When he left Alliance in 1947, Karari Njama, like many ambitious

Africans, tried to establish himself in business. The racially stacked economic system led eventually to his failure after several disastrous experiences, including being cheated by one European farmer and assaulted and sent to prison on the false charges of another, experiences that "created in me an ill-feeling toward the European settlers as a whole. . . . It was impossible for me not to hate them."[40] After several years eking out a living on a small farm, he took a job as headmaster of the Muthua-ini KISA secondary school in Nyeri in 1951, and helped to lead the district's opposition to the Beecher education report.

Karari Njama's first interest in politics as such came when he attended the great KAU rally at Nyeri Showgrounds on July 26, 1952. Like Kariuki, he was awakened by Kenyatta's oratory; unlike Kariuki, he did not try in his memoir to distinguish Kenyatta from Mau Mau. On the contrary, he read a Mau Mau meaning into Kenyatta's explanation of the KAU flag. "What he said must mean that our fertile lands (green) could only be regained by the blood (red) of the African (black). That was it! The black was separated from the green by red; the African could only get to his land through blood."[41] This seemed a reasonable interpretation because "most of the organizers of the meeting were Mau Mau leaders and most of the crowd, Mau Mau members" and the meeting began and ended with "Mau Mau propaganda songs."[42] (At the time Njama actually called the movement Gikuyu na Mumbi.) In the weeks after the great Nyeri meeting, the secret movement was growing in power, circulating its message through newspapers and songbooks, enforcing its boycott of European beer and cigarettes, and intimidating or assassinating its opponents. In September Njama was invited to a "feast" at the home of a prominent local businessman and took the unity oath with hundreds of others. In October activists in Kiambu killed Chief Waruhiu, the government declared the State of Emergency, and Nyeri was soon clamped in a vise of repression. In this fevered atmosphere, Karari Njama took the *batuni* oath, which involved the much more serious commitment to kill on order. By early 1953, he was buying supplies for the forest fighters and storing them in this home on the instructions of the local Mau Mau committee, even while he continued teaching, though teachers were being killed for working under Beecher Report rules. When he began to receive letters telling him "you cannot serve two masters," he chose to join the guerrillas.[43]

Karari Njama joined the band of Kigumo *mbuci* (camp), located in the bamboo forest of Nyandarua on the Gura River, about eight miles southwest of Nyeri town, and later moved to Kariaini headquarters, two miles further in. *Mau Mau from Within* described in detail the guerrilla life in the forest; the well-run camps, the ranks, the discipline, the daily routines, the substantive meetings all portrayed a guerrilla army very different from the British stereotype. Njama's main role—from May 1953 until his capture in June 1955—as one of the few well-educated men in Nyandarua, was to act as secretary and recorder, taking minutes of meetings and court sessions, corresponding with other leaders, and writing to the government. After he took the special "leaders' oath," he was present at most important meetings and privy to decisionmaking at the top, first with Stanley Mathenge and later when he joined the rival Nyeri leader Dedan Kimathi. His firsthand descriptions of the efforts to build unity among the bands and coordinate their military and political actions, including the establishment of the "Kenya Parliament" in 1954, were an invaluable record of decisionmaking at the high levels of the Land and Freedom Army. As an articulate, educated man of standing he also participated himself, for example, when he spoke to the *itungati* (guerrillas) at Mwathe in August 1953:

> You are the only ones that God has selected to deliver our country out of colonial exploitation and the settlers' slavery. Your weariness, starvation, persistence of cold, pains, and in some cases your blood or life would be the ransom . . . for the liberation of all the people of Kenya.[44]

Karari Njama soon became concerned, however, that the unity and ultimate success of the guerrilla army were potentially threatened from within: by the influence of religious leaders over military decisionmaking; by the inability of the separate guerrilla forces from Nyeri, Murang'a, Kiambu, and the Rift Valley to operate in concert; by the dangerous division between educated guerrillas and the illiterates; by the personality clashes and struggles for power among forest leaders; and by the gulf that was beginning to open between the *itungati* and the civilian population. An increasingly vigorous counterinsurgency from the summer of 1953 killed and captured many *itungati*. In late 1954 and in 1955 the forest bands dwindled from losses and desertions, and by the time Karari Njama was captured in June 1955, most bands had shrunk to beleaguered remnants.[45]

Mau Mau from Within, written—like *"Mau Mau" Detainee*—by a highly educated and self-conscious nationalist, was a portrayal of the guerrilla war that contrasted strongly with descriptions from the other side by Henderson, Kitson, Corfield, and Majdalany. While Kariuki's experience had been limited to a few months in the passive wing and seven years in detention, Karari Njama could write of the guerrilla war itself with the considerable authority of two years in the forest, much of the time traveling as a liaison from band to band. The bands he described were well organized, confident, and skilled at forest fighting, an impressive irregular force; moreover, his extensive descriptions of leaders' meetings gave an impression of a self-conscious organization, aware of the need for effective coordination to oppose the British (though rarely able to achieve it) and eager to contact the outside world to convey their nationalist aims directly. Karari Njama, however, seemed more willing, and obviously more able, than J. M. Kariuki to reveal the weaknesses as well as the strengths of the secret movement and the guerrilla army. I take exception to Robert Whittier's observation that, while Kahinga Wachanga admitted that the leaders made mistakes, Karari Njama did not.[46] Perhaps his willingness to expose those mistakes showed a confidence readers would understand, and accept Mau Mau as a genuine nationalist armed struggle in spite of them.

"To Lead Our People:"
Waruhiu Itote and *"Mau Mau" General*

In *"Mau Mau" Detainee*, J. M. Kariuki had predicted that someday General China would tell his story. In 1967, Waruhiu Itote, since the execution of Dedan Kimathi and the disappearance of Stanley Mathenge, the most important surviving forest leader, published his long-awaited memoirs, *"Mau Mau" General*.

Waruhiu Itote was born at Kaheti, in South Tetu Division in Nyeri, in 1922. His father Itote, a successful farmer, herder, and stock trader, felt that "education was all nonsense," and though the boy's mother, Wamuyu, and his aunt persuaded him to relent somewhat, the young Waruhiu was still only "semi-educated" when he left home to seek his fortune in Nairobi in 1939.[47] In the railway station he first encountered racial discrimination— the separate lavatories were marked "EUROPEANS, ASIANS, NATIVES" —and racism followed him into the King's African Rifles after he enlisted in January 1942, though he found in Burma that all were equal in combat.[48] Wartime service led to his political awakening in 1944 in Calcutta, where he was influenced by Stephenson, an African-American soldier (who told him about the liberation of Haiti and who urged the African soldiers "to fight for your own countries"), and by a nationalist Indian family who advised him to unite with other African veterans after the war to demand reform and eventual independence.[49] His experiences as a noncommissioned officer fighting the Japanese also taught him small-unit tactics in rugged forest conditions, where a "group of three or four people can easily achieve the same results as a full company by rapid movement and careful shooting."[50]

The combat veteran returned to Kenya impatient for change, only to be soon disillusioned. He was disgusted by the many overt signs of discrimination, above all by the *Kifagio* ("sweep") campaign in Nairobi against Africans found without their *vipande* (identity cards). "The large caged lorries, nicknamed by us *'haraka'* [quickly] and bursting with our people, were as familiar a sight on the Nairobi streets as the Municipal dust-carts."[51] He tried earning his living in business, but in 1947, seeking job security, he joined the East African Railways as a fireman. His frustration with the political situation and the racist conditions at work led him in 1946 into KAU; and in 1947 to join the 40 Group, and then, impressed by the fiery speeches of union leaders Fred Kubai and Bildad Kaggia, to enroll in the Transport and Allied Workers Union.[52] Like many young militants, he was appalled by the settlers' "Kenya Plan," passed from hand to hand among the Nairobi African community, which struck him as a blueprint for white minority independence on the South African model.[53] In late 1950 he took the unity oath in Naivasha. For the next two years, under the direction of the Nyeri Committee of the movement, he was "a fireman on the Railways by day and a revolutionary by night," assigned to organize and guard oathing ceremonies and to eliminate "traitors."[54] In January 1952, the movement formed a "War Council" in Nairobi, and Itote joined the secret committee within it composed of those "who knew that our people could never win their independence solely by peaceful means."[55] On August 16, Itote drove with some comrades to Gatundu for "my last meeting with Mzee before we entered the final struggle."[56] Kenyatta spoke with them for hours, telling them about Toussaint l'Ouverture and other Black leaders and charging them to keep up their courage for the struggle. "Some of you will be imprisoned and some of you will be killed. But when these things happen, my sons, do not be afraid. Everything in this world has to be paid for—and we must buy our freedom with our blood."[57] Two days later, the Nyeri Committee in Nairobi sent Itote and a group of young men to Karatina on the slopes of Kirinyaga to form a guerrilla band.

According to his memoir, the keys to the success of the Kirinyaga guerrillas under "General China" were readiness, resourcefulness, and close relations with local Gikuyu and Meru. After oathing a number of local people, Itote used his new supporters to help him locate and set up a base camp, establish caches of food, steal weapons and ammunition, and begin training his green men. His base camp was a strict military operation, with a daily schedule of exercises, drill, patrolling, and foraging for food. He used his own men, local civilians, and oathed members of the security forces to scout for him, obtain food and supplies (and intelligence), and steal weapons. He was also the first general to set up a gun-making armory. China's memoirs also contained information, based on notes taken at the time, on high-level discussions attended by generals from several different fronts dealing with critical moral and political issues facing the movement, which included a discussion in July 1953, shortly after Lari, about the morality and advisability of killing women and children and another in November 1953 about the *komerera* problem (see Chapter 5 for details).

In January 1954, General China was captured by the British. Though a judge condemned him to death after trial, the government spared his life in order to use him as a negotiator in a surrender offer to the guerrillas, exposing him to charges that he was cooperating with the enemy. After the negotiations collapsed, the British detained him for nine years; at Lokitaung Kenyatta took him under his paternal wing and patiently helped him with his English, winning in return China's unflagging loyalty. After obtaining

China's release in June 1963, Kenyatta used him as a personal emissary with remaining *itungati* in the forests of Kirinyaga; on December 12, 1963, the day of independence, China was in the forests talking with the Meru leader, General Baimungi, trying to persuade him to trust the new government and return peacefully to civilian life.[58] As with Kariuki, Kenyatta rewarded China with a position (in the National Youth Service), but his memoirs reveal that he remained troubled by Kenya's political factionalism and by how soon the independent country seemed to forget the sacrifices of the Mau Mau veterans.

In some respects *"Mau Mau" General* and *Mau Mau from Within* were much alike. The organization of bands and their camps, the relations between Mau Mau and local civilians, the challenges of fighting an irregular war in the forest were described in similar terms, and the guerrilla forces were portrayed in both accounts as self-conscious nationalist armies, fighting the British in the name of their imprisoned political leaders, led by dedicated and resourceful generals who took their responsibilities very seriously. However, this third memoir was also different in certain ways from the two that had come before. *"Mau Mau" General* was the most complete account. In contrast to the two other authors, Waruhiu Itote was poorly educated, but his life experiences were more diverse and his nationalist credentials stronger than those of Kariuki and Njama; he had served in the war, traveled widely, and had had long and varied experience in KAU, 40 Group, and the union movement prior to taking his first oath. After joining, he had had the best rounded set of responsibilities within the movement—as an organizer, oath administrator, executor of "traitors," and guerrilla general. Waruhiu Itote could write with more authority than his predecessors, moreover, because of his recognized prominence as the commander on Kirinyaga, a leadership position of a stature comparable to that of Dedan Kimathi and Stanley Mathenge.

On the other hand, Itote's role had also been more equivocal, and not only the British but some Mau Mau had reason to look on his account with skepticism. China had oathed and killed for the movement as well as led thousands of guerrillas as a fighting general. His account devoted more space than the others to explaining oathing as essential to building unity and executions as necessary to enforce security. He defended the killings he and other movement executioners had carried out by observing that "this was not wholesale, indiscriminate murder as the British Government tried to say. Only a real two-faced traitor, and there is nothing worse in the world, would be sentenced to death. Our courts were much fairer than those of the Government with their summary justice, their framed evidence, their perjuring, bought witnesses."[59] It was also clear from his memoirs that China remained sensitive to charges that he had betrayed Mau Mau after his surrender in 1954 and was eager to clear his name by telling his side of the story. He characterized his role in the peace negotiations as loyally representing the secret movement by arguing for their goals of independence, land, and the freeing of Kenyatta and the other detained leaders, and to further demonstrate his innocence included in his memoirs a letter from Dedan Kimathi given him by a Turkana policeman in prison in September 1954, expressing confidence that "you would not desert our cause."[60] Itote's conspicuous efforts to associate himself with Kenyatta—just before he entered the forest, during their imprisonment together, as a presidential negotiator with Mau Mau holdouts on Kirinyaga, and as an administrator of the new government—is another indication of his concern for legitimacy. For General China, the justification of Mau Mau and self-justification went hand in hand.

While all three memoirists required editorial assistance, Waruhiu Itote needed the most because of his limited formal education. The role of John Nottingham in encouraging Waruhiu Itote and in shepherding the project to completion over several years was quite important, and the part of David Koff "in preparing the final manuscript" was critical.[61] The organization of *"Mau Mau" General* was clear and systematic, rather different from Itote's interesting but disorganized and anecdotal second book, *Mau Mau in Action* (1979). How much of *"Mau Mau" General* was largely dictated in the form in which it appeared and how much was based on the documents his relatives had saved is not clear.[62] The final product—earnest and rather dry in parts and engagingly humorous in other places (as in the chapter on Paul Mahehu's exploits)—achieved a quasi-authoritative status within a few years, so that by 1973 Rob Buijtenhuijs observed that for many Gikuyu, *"Mau Mau" General* had become a kind of "official history" of the revolt.[63]

Themes of the Mau Mau Discourse

The Kariuki, Njama, and Itote memoirs were self-conscious refutations of the British myth that made the most of their authors' autobiographical authority—the weight of their firsthand experience as Gikuyu participants in Mau Mau. After discrediting the British version, they replaced it with one of their own, in the process creating a positive-print portrait of Mau Mau, to them clearer and more true than the negative image presented by earlier writers. To alter the metaphor, the psychological roles were switched, with the British and the loyalists now the "other" and Mau Mau the healthy norm.

It was as if the discourses described different countries. British writers had evoked a progressive colonial Kenya, whose journey toward a modern future, led by European administrators, missionaries, and settlers, was derailed by a clique of Gikuyu conspirators, headed by a demagogic Jomo Kenyatta, who deliberately encouraged unjustified resentments and unrealistic expectations in their ignorant followers, leading to an explosion of violence and a regression to a primitive past. The Mau Mau version by contrast portrayed a country of racial discrimination and oppression, where settler exploitation was abetted by cynical officials and self-interested collaborators and excused by sanctimonious missionaries, and where the only progress whites seemed to envision was the establishment of minority self-rule on the South African model. In such a colonial situation even the charismatic and idealistic Jomo Kenyatta could only fail, leaving younger African rebels to lead their followers, a nation striving to be born, into revolt. The first three memoirs insisted that this necessity of revolt validated the use of violence, discredited loyalism, and tended to diminish the importance of constitutional politics. As B. A. Ogot later observed, the "accounts of the radicals" were "a good example of the Whig interpretation of Kenya history."[64]

The counter-discourse began with the British name, which Kariuki and Itote conspicuously placed "in sanitary inverted commas" in their titles (to borrow Ali Mazrui's phrase).[65] They rejected "Mau Mau," either categorically, denying that it had any meaning in Gikuyu or Swahili or simply asserting that oathed members never called their movement by that name. Kariuki stated that the organization "did not have any special name."[66] Waruhiu Itote did call it "the Movement of Unity" and Karari Njama used several names, especially Muingi (Community) or Uigano na Gikuyu na Mumbi (Gikuyu and Mumbi Unity).[67] Symbolically, when these Gikuyu cultural insiders challenged the British name, they called into question the entire British discourse and affirmed the superior validity of their own. However, with one exception the names they mentioned were in Gikuyu, weakening their nationalist message; moreover, by not popularizing any other particular name they all but ensured that "Mau Mau" would continue to be used, much as they disliked it.

To British authors, the oaths had been the symbol of Gikuyu tribalism and primitivity, their "obscene" and "bestial" rituals the epitome of the evil that was Mau Mau. The Gikuyu writers were well aware that the use of oaths, and even more their arcane details, would be difficult to explain to outsiders. Kariuki and Njama included in their memoirs extensive descriptions of the oaths they took themselves, and Itote added an appendix explaining and defending oath-taking in general; clearly sensitive to the attacks of Leakey and others, they defended the origins of Mau Mau oathing in Gikuyu tradition, emphasized the verbal oaths more than the rituals, and defensively refuted European charges that Mau Mau went to such extremes as to use human blood and the embryos of unborn children in oathing ceremonies. As Itote complained, in the European cultural context "oath" had a positive connotation, suggesting an affirmation of honesty in court or a declaration of allegiance to one's country; but when the British spoke or wrote of the African Mau Mau movement they always associated the oath with "savagery" and "atavism."[68] The Mau Mau memoirists used personal experience and ethnographic explanation to cast the most controversial aspect of their secret movement in a more positive light, portraying oathing not as primitive tribal ritual but as a culturally rooted but creative means to build nationalist commitment.

Kariuki and Njama stressed the oaths' transforming effect on the individual. After taking his unity oath, Kariuki believed that he "had been born again"; following his *batuni* oath, he reflected, "My initiation was now complete and I had become a true Kikuyu with no doubts where I stood in the revolt of my tribe."[69] Similarly, after an extensive description of his own unity-oathing ceremony, Karari Njama commented that the new belief he had adopted "out-weighed" and thus supplanted his Christianity. "At sunrise I remembered that the next week would be my 26th birthday and that I had been born again in a new society with a new faith."[70] In his less personal, matter-of-fact descriptions, perhaps more fitting for an oath administrator, Waruhiu Itote emphasized the group more than the individual meaning of oath-taking, commenting that "we looked upon all oaths as a natural expression of people who already felt a common bond of anger and hope in their lives."[71] General China, who administered oaths to hundreds of civilians and guerrillas, understood especially well the roles of oath-taking in both binding men and women together across the divisions of family and locality and in inititiating them into a secret organization with its own ideology, discipline, and obedience. After the memoirists used their cultural authority and inside knowledge to scrape away the accretion of primitivity applied by British writers, the oath emerged as a personal rite of passage into political adulthood and as an organizational tool to weld group unity and commitment.

Kariuki, Njama, and Itote were also determined to cleanse Mau Mau of the imputations of atrocity. Just as the twentieth century has been the era of political and military atrocity, it has also been the age of atrocity mongering, and until Kariuki the British had largely dominated the propaganda war, conveying to the world the strong impression that Mau Mau revelled in killing, including the slaughter of innocent women and children. The memoirists challenged the portrayals of the most notorious atrocities, defended the use of selective violence against "traitors" killed by enforcers like Waruhiu Itote, and turned the charges against the British by accusing them in turn of nonjudicial executions, slaughters of civilians, and tortures of suspects. Kariuki and Njama showed particular concern with the case of the Lari massacre, clearly well aware that the British had used propaganda about Lari very effectively. Though neither had been involved, both had heard accounts from others that directly contradicted the British version; Karari Njama reported that eyewitnesses had told him that government forces had killed ten times as many as the attackers, and then blamed all the casualties on Mau Mau.[72] Turning the cultural tables on the British,

Njama morally distinguished scattered killings with African weapons from Western industrialized mass slaughter.

> It only made me think that the British believe that killing by a gun or bomb is right, while killing with a *panga* [machete] is evil. . . . But who has killed more innocent women and children, British or *Mau Mau*? I wondered whether the bombs dropped on towns and cities by the British during the First and Second World Wars . . . spared the innocent women and children for which they were blaming us?[73]

The memoirists also drew a line between violence to oppress and violence to liberate, as did Ngugi wa Thiong'o in 1963, when he characterized in Fanonist terms the British use of violence "to preserve an unjust, oppressive social order" as "criminal," and Mau Mau violence to liberate as justified and uplifting, "it purifies man."[74]

The Mau Mau guerrilla armies of the memoirs also differed from the familiar ragtag forces of the British accounts. The "gangs" terrorizing the countryside of Central Kenya, but fading away when faced with superior British strength, were replaced by self-conscious "freedom fighters," in a "glorious fight" against oppressive colonial rule, supported willingly by the civilian population, attacking strong targets like Naivasha and Othaya with expectations of tactical success and ultimate victory.[75] The "thugs" of British idiom in their forest "hideout" became the Gikuyu *itungati* in their well-ordered *mbuci*. Both versions praised guerrilla "bushcraft," but while the British compared it to the instinctive canniness of animals, the authors of the memoirs attributed it to their training by the elders and the skills they learned surviving in the forest. In the memoirs the guerrilla leaders were transformed; Dedan Kimathi, Henderson's "Hitler" of the Kikuyu, became Kariuki's "the greatest hero of us all."[76]

The memoirs showed the "loyalists" in a different light as well. Mitchell had described the loyalists as the "true resistance" and Lipscomb called them the "hope of the future," but to the Mau Mau authors (and, they claimed, to most Gikuyu), the loyalist leaders were "traitors" and the home guard *kamatimu*, "the little people who carry spears."[77] The Mau Mau were the real nationalists, fighting for the freedom of all Kenyans. They claimed that many reputed loyalists, including a number of Gikuyu home guards and detention camp warders of other ethnic groups, had been secret supporters of the unity movement, though they also admitted that the British had eventually succeeded in fomenting a civil war. Waruhiu Itote devoted a chapter to Dedan Kimathi's response to the loyalists' declaration in January 1954, in which Kimathi had predicted, "Those given medals for their good work in beating 'Mau Mau' will throw them away when we are free, and those pretending to be good now will hang themselves after Independence. Their children will be ashamed, while the children of 'Mau Mau' will walk strongly."[78] The characterization of the loyalists in the three memoirs both contradicted the British myth and undermined the consensualist discourse of the independent Kenya government, though both Kariuki and Itote accepted the policy of forgiving the opponents of Mau Mau.

One of the most striking contrasts between the British and Mau Mau versions was the characterization of Jomo Kenyatta, who was transformed from evil genius and cynical tribal boss to the self-sacrificing, inspiring father of his country. For Kariuki, Kenyatta "is greater than any Kenyan, he is the greatest African of them all."[79] Itote wrote that the memory of his last meeting with Kenyatta before entering the forest carried him through "the hard years to come," for Kenyatta's "confidence in our victory gave me strength."[80] The evidence the three memoirs presented about Kenyatta's link to Mau Mau was ambiguous; while Kariuki all but denied the connection, Njama's account of the Nyeri meeting could have met the approval of Ian Henderson, and *"Mau Mau" General* depicted Kenyatta dispatching Waruhiu Itote to Kirinyaga in 1952 with his blessing. In the mid-1960s the advantages to Mau Mau veterans of asserting a link to Kenyatta should be obvious, but this association squared neither with the critique of British policy during the Emergency nor with the official version of the past of the independent Kenya government. As Ali Mazrui observed in 1963, "many of Kenyatta's most ardent admirers have for years been at pains to dissociate Kenyatta from Mau Mau."[81]

This raises the issue of the attitude of Kariuki, Njama, and Itote to the political and social policies of the independent Kenya regime itself and to its stance toward Mau Mau veterans. While this will be discussed more thoroughly in Chapter 7, a few points should be made here. Karari Njama had little to say on the subject, but J. M. Kariuki and Waruhiu Itote, while they celebrated the coming of independence and took government positions themselves, felt that much more needed to be done after *uhuru* to provide Mau Mau veterans the rewards they deserved and to realize the other goals they believed Mau Mau had fought to achieve. As a recently released detainee who had just entered politics, Kariuki was disgusted with the activities of many of the politicians around him, describing them as "selfish power-seekers" unworthy of the rebel heritage. "Our politicians must stop fighting among themselves and cure each other of this unseemly hunger for great positions or everything will be lost."[82] Several years later, Itote attacked the "basic apathy" of those in "high places" towards veterans of Mau Mau, "those who fought and sacrificed," and urged a number of measures to alleviate the "plight" of the ex–freedom fighters and their families and to reward them for their contributions to independence, ranging from free land and free education to memorials for the dead. He even warned that, if nothing were done, frustrated ex–Mau Mau might take matters in their own hands at some time in the future.[83]

Conclusion

In looking back on the conflicting discourses about Mau Mau that had developed by 1967, it is important to bear several things in mind: (1) this was a debate about history emerging very soon indeed after the events themselves; (2) in spite of Margery Perham's plea that the evidence "be left to historians to sift . . . when passions have cooled," some of the most important spokesmen in the debate were lay representatives of contending positions; (3) the debate was just as much about the politics of the present as about the past; (4) the debate was not only about the meaning of Mau Mau but about its importance, with the British arguing that it was a significant development but was decisively defeated, the independent government arguing that it was no more than an episode (and not the most honorable) in the grand nationalist movement, and the Mau Mau arguing that it was essential to independence; (5) finally, a subtext of some of the major participants in the debate was who had won and who had lost—or who should have won and who should have lost—and the complex moralities of victory and defeat affected both the presentation of the history of the 1950s and the prescriptions for contemporary public action or inaction.[84]

Objectivity and partisanship make uncomfortable bedfellows, and Kariuki, Njama, and Itote, consciously representing other Mau Mau veterans as well as themselves, were aware of their partisan roles. In their memoirs they felt obliged to remove four stigmas Mau Mau still bore: those of being a primitive regression to the past, being a bloodthirsty movement, being a tribalist struggle, and being a failure. Perhaps inevitably, as Mau Mau adherents attempting to lift these stigmas, they tended to overstate the opposite case, and in the process even sanitize certain aspects of Mau Mau. Kariuki, for example, asserted that the sole legitimate oaths were the unity and *batuni,* only to have Itote contradict him by describing oaths administered to leaders well after they had taken the *batuni.* Itote himself explained away, perhaps too easily, his involvement and the involvement of others in the killing of people the movement labeled "traitors." Njama's effort to cleanse Mau Mau of the guilt of Lari relied heavily on hearsay. The Kariuki and Itote memoirs discussed Mau Mau as a rational outgrowth of the constitutional nationalist movement, even Western in certain respects, and claimed that many other Africans, both civilians and government servants (police, soldiers, warders), secretly supported the armed struggle of the Gikuyu, Embu, and Meru, suggesting a concern for a national imperative rather more characteristic of the 1960s than the 1950s. Njama and Itote also gave an impression of a guerrilla war that was more successful on the battlefield than other evidence would support; this effort to overcome the onus of military defeat was bolstered by the claims of Kariuki and Itote to moral superiority over the British and the African loyalists. Thus Mau Mau could win even though they had lost.

Were Kariuki, Njama, and Itote creating a new myth of Mau Mau to replace the British? In important writings on the significance of the memoirs, both Ali Mazrui and Rob Buijtenhuijs addressed this issue. In "On Heroes and *Uhuru*-Worship," Mazrui's review of Kariuki (which appeared just before independence), he speculated that, since the publication of this memoir suggested that "Kenya's history is going to be written afresh," Mau Mau might not only be renamed but recategorized, not as a "tribal uprising," "revolt," or "rebellion" (the term he tended to use himself) but as "the Kenyan Revolution," which would associate it with similar upheavals in America, France, Russia, and China, strike a claim to commanding importance in the history of Kenyan nationalism, and establish a "revolutionary tradition" against which the actions of national leaders like Kenyatta would be judged. He predicted that if such a tradition were established, its guardians would be radicals such as the Land Freedom Army of ex-detainees.[85]

A decade later Dutch scholar Rob Buijtenhuijs took a different stand for the virtues of an objective understanding of Kenya's past. In *Mau Mau Twenty Years After* (1973), Buijtenhuijs discussed the memoirs of Kariuki and Itote as part of an effort not only to discredit the British but to create a new African nationalist orthodoxy, "a new myth, the African myth of Mau Mau," a myth he believed had been "scientifically enshrined" in Rosberg and Nottingham's academic history. In his view, both the memoirists and the academic historians had seriously distorted the truth of Mau Mau, which Buijtinhuijs himself had represented in *Le Mouvement Mau Mau* as much more about Gikuyu "cultural renewal" than about Kenyan nationalism.[86] Bruce Berman, in a recent historiographical essay, suggests that Buijtenhuijs's points about *The Myth of "Mau Mau"* were well taken; Rosberg and Nottingham, concerned with correcting the image of Mau Mau, so emphasized the rebels' real grievances and true nationalist goals that they obscured Mau Mau's cultural traditionalism and ethnic Gikuyu character.[87] The first three Mau Mau memoirs and the first full-length academic study of the revolt thus tended to reinforce each other, but neither the expectations of Mazrui nor the fears of Buijtenhuijs were borne out; no orthodoxy emerged from the contentious and politically charged debate over the real meaning of Mau Mau.

When he reviewed *"Mau Mau" Detainee,* Ali Mazrui had not foreseen the ongoing struggles over the meaning of the revolt. Instead, he assumed that the new Kenyan nation would adopt a nationalist historiography with an important role for Mau Mau. Indeed, he argued for accepting the blood practices of Mau Mau as necessary for the achievement of Kenya's freedom; while India had its pacifist saint in Gandhi, Kenya could not have won independence by such nonviolent methods, so should adopt Dedan Kimathi as national martyr and welcome as his living avatars "the returning rebels from the Aberdares."[88] The exaltation of such heroes could form a vital part of the public history of a nation born as the result of an agonizing and bloody struggle.

But Mazrui did not address the incongruence between Gikuyu revolt and Kenyan nation, nor between guerrilla-martyr Kimathi, champion of the fighting Mau Mau and enemy of loyalism, and living statesman Kenyatta, representative of the Gikuyu elders and the constitutional politicians and apostle of peace, reconciliation, and forgive and forget. As it turned out, the lay and academic interpreters of the Kenyan past reached no consensus on Mau Mau; instead, within Kenya the debate tended to polarize along ideological, regional, or ethnic lines, with the contributions of outside scholars occasionally drawn in. The version of Mau Mau presented in these first three memoirs did not hold the field, and Mazrui's prediction that a nationally unifying myth would emerge with an important place for Mau Mau heroes did not come to pass. I will discuss these issues in greater detail in Chapter 8.

Notes

1. Kariuki, *Detainee,* p. 182.
2. B. M. Kaggia, Fred Kubai, J. Murumbi, Achieng' Oneko, preface to Njama and Barnett, *Mau Mau from Within,* p. 11.
3. Margery Perham, *The Colonial Reckoning* (New York: Knopf, 1962), p. 115; Margery Perham, foreword to Kariuki, *Detainee,* pp. xi, xxiii.
4. Perham, foreword, pp. xi, xii.
5. Ibid., p. xi.
6. Ngugi wa Thiong'o, "Born Again—Mau Mau Unchained," in Ngugi wa Thiong'o, *Writers in Politics* (London: Heinemann, 1981), p. 86l.
7. Kariuki, *Detainee,* p. 1.
8. Ibid., pp. 2–3.
9. Ibid., pp. 4–13.
10. Ibid., p. 7.
11. Ibid., p. 12.
12. Henry Muoria, *I, the Gikuyu and the White Fury* (Nairobi: East African Educational Publishers, 1994), p. 14.
13. Kariuki, *Detainee,* pp. 25, 28.
14. Ibid., pp. 40–41; government records from 1953 confirm the frequency of successful bribing of African officials to release suspects from custody. See Report of Deputy Director of Operations, Aug. 27, 1953, RH Hinde Papers, Mss. Afr. s. 1580 (4).
15. Ibid., p. 44.
16. Kariuki, *Detainee,* pp. 33, 130; John Stonehouse, however, reports that Kariuki told him, two months after his release from Aguthi Works Camp, that he had "admitted his guilt to the screening teams." Stonehouse, *Prohibited Immigrant* (London: Bodley Head, 1960), p. 127.
17. Kariuki, *Detainee,* pp. 149–61.
18. Ibid., p. 14.
19. Ibid.
20. Ibid., p. 15.

21. Ibid., p. 20; Kariuki's insistence on the distinctions among African organizations contrasts strongly with Ngugi wa Thiong'o's portrayal of the unchanging "Party" in his novel of Mau Mau, *A Grain of Wheat* (London: Heinemann, 1967), p. 13.

22. Kariuki, *Detainee*, p. 22.

23. Ibid., p. 32.

24. Ibid., p. 36.

25. Ibid., pp. 34, 38.

26. Ibid., p. 35. Kariuki's depiction of home-guard infiltration is partly confirmed by F. O. Campbell in his report "Survey of Kikuyu Guard Position, Githunguri Division, Kiambu . . . August, 1953," KNA ARC (MAA) 2/5/307.

27. Kariuki, *Detainee*, p. 65

28. Ibid., p. 182.

29. Ibid., p. 88.

30. Ibid., p. 121.

31. Ibid., pp. 178–79.

32. Kaggia et al., preface, p. 9.

33. Ibid., pp. 9–10.

34. Ibid., p. 11.

35. Njama and Barnett, *Mau Mau from Within*, pp. 14–15.

36. Ibid., p. 85.

37. Ibid., p. 87.

38. Ibid., p. 90.

39. Ibid., p. 100.

40. Ibid., p. 109.

41. Ibid., p. 75.

42. Ibid., p. 78.

43. Ibid., pp. 141–43.

44. Ibid., p. 263.

45. Ibid., p. 486.

46. Robert Whittier, preface to Wachanga, *Swords of Kirinyaga*, p. xi.

47. Waruhiu Itote, *"Mau Mau" General*, pp. 16–20.

48. Ibid., pp. 20, 27.

49. Ibid., pp. 13–14.

50. Ibid., pp. 25, 27.

51. Ibid., p. 35.

52. Ibid., pp. 37–39.

53. Ibid., p. 39.

54. Ibid., p. 41.

55. Ibid., p. 43.

56. Ibid., p. 44.

57. Ibid., p. 45.

58. Ibid., p. 253.

59. Ibid., p. 41.

60. Ibid., p. 211.

61. Ibid., preface, no number.

62. Ibid.

63. Buijtenhuijs, *Mau Mau Twenty Years After*, pp. 47–48.

64. Ogot, "Revolt of the Elders," p. 147.

65. Ali A. Mazrui, "On Heroes and Uhuru-Worship," in Ali A. Mazrui, *On Heroes and Uhuru-Worship: Essays on Independent Africa* (London: Longman, 1967), p. 23.

66. Kariuki, *Detainee*, p. 24.

67. Itote, *General*, p. 38; Njama, *Mau Mau from Within*, p. 79.

68. Itote, *General*, p. 273.

69. Kariuki, *Detainee*, pp. 27, 31.

70. Njama, *Mau Mau from Within*, p. 121.

71. Itote, *General*, p. 283.

72. Njama, *Mau Mau from Within*, p. 137.

73. Ibid., p. 138.

74. Ngugi wa Thiong'o, "Mau Mau: Violence, and Culture," in Ngugi wa Thiong'o, *Homecoming* (New York: Lawrence Hill, 1973), p. 28.

75. Kariuki, *Detainee*, p. 35.

76. Ibid., p. 35.

77. Ibid., p. 38.

78. Itote, *General*, p. 146.

79. Kariuki, *Detainee*, p. 179

80. Itote, *General*, p. 47.

81. Mazrui, "On Heroes," p. 22.

82. Kariuki, *Detainee*, p. 181.

83. Itote, *General*, pp. 270–72.

84. Perham, foreword to Kariuki, *Detainee*, p. xiv.

85. Mazrui, "On Heroes," pp. 23–24.

86. Buijtenhuijs, *Mau Mau Twenty Years After*, p. 46.

87. Berman, "Nationalism, Ethnicity, and Modernity," p. 193; on the memoirs see also Maughan-Brown, *Land, Freedom, and Fiction*, pp. 56–57.

88. Mazrui, "On Heroes," p. 34.

CHAPTER 4

The Movement and the Oaths

I then said that I would speak frankly. Nothing would obstruct me, because I was speaking for my people, for my mother's country, and for the dead traditional way of life. *Gutiri wa Iregi utuire* (No one of Iregi lives). I told them that from that day, the Forty Group had passed a law that no young girl would be forced to go to work on European farms. Further, I said that any chief or other authority not complying with this law would be "carried by the kite" (*Gutiri undu ungi agekwo tiga no rwigi rukamuoya*). After this, the crowd came to life, clapping their hands and shouting with enthusiasm *Ni gia kuguru kuu!* (That shoe fits that foot!)
—*H. Kahinga Wachanga*[1]

I, Gikoyo, agreed to take and adhere to the oath because I had been made to understand how we had been wronged. The first result of the oath was unity, the second was death, and the third was freedom. The oath commanded that I should obey Mau Mau, even if this led to killing or being killed. Those that had been initiated into the oath respected and loved each other.
—*Gucu G. Gikoyo*[2]

B Y 1967 a new discourse on Mau Mau had been established, based in part on three personal narratives. J. M. Kariuki, Karari Njama, and Waruhiu Itote had cleared the way for other authors, and over the next twenty-five years a number of memoirs were published, two written by important Mau Mau figures (Bildad Kaggia and H. Kahinga Wachanga) but most by people lower in the movement whose experiences could be taken as more typical of the ordinary member, fighter, or detainee.

The new memoirs built on the first three and often used the same themes and language, but they were different in certain respects. First, with exceptions (such as Bildad Kaggia's memoir), they were less self-conscious and less defensive; with the accounts of Kariuki, Njama, and Itote already published, most of the memoirists did not seem to feel the same need to discredit the British myth. Second, in part perhaps because the political ground had been cleared, some of the later memoirs centered on personal experiences, devoting less space to discussion of the background to the revolt or to more general issues. While Ali Mazrui criticized those particular memoirists for concentrating "on the details at the expense of the general picture," their accounts were concrete and generally credible because they tended to focus on the trees they saw before them rather than on the woods they might have perceived only through the eyes of others.[3] Third, some of these accounts described instances of violence, brutality, disillusionment, and even betrayal on the Mau Mau side unlike anything found in the first pathbreaking personal stories, suggesting that these later memoirists did not feel constrained to present Mau Mau as pure or wholly consistent. Fourth, the accounts of the 1970s (particularly those by Wachanga and Gikoyo) were in part responses to the memoirs already published, questioning or challenging certain aspects; this showed the maturity of the Mau Mau discourse, for the "second generation" did not seem to worry that negative evidence from their memoirs could be used to discredit the Mau Mau version altogether. Fifth, several of these later accounts—notably those of Joram Wamweya, Kiboi Muriithi, Kahinga Wachanga, and Gucu Gikoyo—had a less Western character and reflected the Gikuyu ethnic side of Mau Mau more unabashedly than the first three memoirs.

While the first three memoirists had contributed substantially to shaping the nationalist interpretation of Mau Mau, in collaboration or association with academic intellectuals, the role of the second generation of memoirists in influencing Mau Mau's evolving historiography was less straightforward. Foreign scholars and editors had assumed a leading role in bringing the first three memoirs to print, but African writers and translators were more active in helping to produce memoirs of the second generation, such as Joram Wamweya's *Freedom Fighter* (1971), translated by Ciira Cerere; Kiboi Muriithi's *War in the Forest* (1971), co-written by Peter Ndoria; Gucu Gikoyo's *We Fought for Freedom: Tulipigania Uhuru* (1979), which involved the active assistance of Bildad Kaggia, Isaac Kamande, and Ciira Cerere; and Gakaara wa Wanjau's *Mau Mau Author in Detention* (1988), translated by Paul Ngigi Njoroge and edited by Maina wa Kinyatti. In the 1970s the new memoirs came to assume a place among popular histories of Mau Mau such as Paul Maina's journalistic *Six Mau Mau Generals* (1977) and Waruhiu Itote's second book, *Mau Mau in Action* (1979). In the 1970s and continuing into the 1980s the memoirs in general became politicized by being drawn into the disputes between two Kenyan historians—the Marxist Maina wa Kinyatti and the more conservative B. A. Ogot; by their use as sources for the radical theater of Ngugi wa Thiong'o and Micere Githae Mugo, and as inspiration for the latter-day detention narratives of Ngugi and Koigi wa Wamwere; and by the active involvement of Bildad Kaggia, Maina wa Kinyatti, and Ngugi wa Thiong'o in the production of the memoirs of Gucu Gikoyo and Gakaara wa Wanjau. Partly as a consequence of this popularization and politicization and because the straightforward nationalist interpretation of Mau Mau embodied in the first memoirs and in Rosberg and Nottingham was challenged by new historical research and interpretation, beginning in the early 1970s there was something of an academic backlash against the personal narratives, marked by attacks by Rob Buijtenhuijs, B. A. Ogot, William Ochieng', and David Maughan-Brown.[4]

These developments have affected the role of the memoirs in Mau Mau historiography over the past twenty-five years. In the 1970s and 1980s, after the appearance of the first comprehensive studies by Rosberg and Nottingham and Buijtenhuijs, younger scholars began to publish more specialized work on aspects of Mau Mau, work which built up more detailed and nuanced understandings of the movement and advanced new interpretations. Some of these academic studies—such as those by Frank Furedi (1974), John Spencer (1985), and David Throup (1987)—were based almost entirely on archival data, interviews, and scholarly secondary sources, made few references to the memoirs, and did not discuss the personal narratives in their reviews of the historiography of Mau Mau.

Yet even during the 1970s and 1980s some scholars, including Anthony Clayton (1976), writing on the guerrilla war, Kathy Santilli (1978), writing on women and gender in Mau Mau, and Rob Buijtenhuijs (1982), writing on oathing, used the memoirs extensively. In recent years use of the memoirs as sources has become more common, notably in works by Luise White (1990), Robert Edgerton (1990), John Lonsdale (1992), and Wunyabari Maloba (1993). With the exception of Maina wa Kinyatti, most scholars who have drawn heavily on the memoirs since the mid-1970s have not been interested in them primarily as nationalist texts, but as sources on such matters as oathing, forest life, guerrilla divisions, gender, and political and social debates within the Gikuyu community. Like the second-generation memoirists, recent scholars seem less concerned about the risks of "exoticizing" Mau Mau than early scholarly commentators like Rosberg and Nottingham. Edgerton and Maloba mine the memoirs as a rich vein of information on Mau Mau organizing and forest fighting, but Luise White argues for the "authenticity" of the memoirs as popular literature and uses them as her principal source for examining Mau Mau efforts to reconstruct gender, and John Lonsdale uses them to explore expressions of Gikuyu political thought leading up to Mau Mau. The use of the memoirs by White and Lonsdale in their separate searches for fresh understandings of how Gikuyu viewed their situation in the late colonial period points toward the memoirs' greater significance—not only as sources for the details of Mau Mau but as expressions of the convictions and moral thought of an important segment of the Kenyan community.[5]

The next four chapters of this book will draw primarily on information and insights from the memoirs, using all the personal accounts published between 1963 and 1988—supported by evidence from other memoirs and autobiographies, personal papers, archival documents, and secondary sources—to describe and analyze the secret movement and its oaths, the guerrilla war, the detention camps, the end of the Emergency, and the early politics of independent Kenya. I will draw on the memoirs critically, looking at inconsistencies and points of disagreement between memoirs as well as areas of agreement. The overall purpose is to deepen our understanding of how Mau Mau veterans viewed their revolt, its aftermath, and the relationship between Kenya's past and present.

Economic and Social Pressures and Political Tensions, 1945–1952

The oldest of the Mau Mau memoirists, Karigo Muchai, was born in 1914 and the youngest, Charity Waciuma, was born in 1939, but most were born between 1922 and 1931. As Gikuyu of the second colonial generation who came to adulthood in the early 1940s, they faced the full force of postwar economic, social, and political pressures. Their testimonies—and those of Henry Muoria, Muga Gicaru, Mugo Gatheru, and other authors of personal narratives—evoke the economic conditions, the social atmosphere, the political flavor of Nairobi and the Gikuyu home districts during the watershed years of the late 1940s and early 1950s. Descriptions of the squalor and excitement of life in Nairobi locations like Pumwani, Shauri Moyo, and Ziwani; of the frustrating search for housing and stable jobs in the city (punctuated by clashes with the police); of the increasingly difficult conditions on the land; and of the pinch of poverty on rural Gikuyu families provide insight into the political ferment that eventually drew the memoirists into Mau Mau.

These difficult conditions were shaped by Kenya's particular colonial situation. Returning veterans of the war felt this situation particularly keenly. Among the 75,000 Kenyan Africans who had served in the British army—including Waruhiu Itote, Bildad Kaggia, Gakaara wa Wanjau, and Karigo Muchai—expectations were high in 1945.[6] As Karigo Muchai remembers, the British were directly responsible for raising such expectations. "While serving in the army we Africans were told over and over again that we were fighting for our country and for democracy and that when the war was over we would be rewarded for the sacrifices we were making."[7] The hopes of Muchai and other Africans for land, jobs, and improvement in conditions for Africans were soon dashed by the realities of postwar Kenya. The disillusionment of veterans misled by false political promises was hardly a new story—witness the postwar slump and unemployment that followed the "Land Fit for Heroes" campaign in Britain in 1918—but the situation in 1945 was rather different, because the British veterans of "Hitler's war" did benefit from the victory of the Labour Party and the creation of the Welfare State, while African veterans generally did not. The "second colonial occupation" of Kenya in the late 1940s under the postwar Labour government and the administration of Governor Philip Mitchell, which established a new and more systematic British economic exploitation of Kenya with officials and settlers working in close partnership, held the veterans and other Africans in a subordinate position, contributing to intense discontent soon channeled into political protest.[8]

Let us look first at conditions in postwar Nairobi—where memoirists Itote, Kaggia, Muchai, Wanjau, Kabiro, Muriithi, Eliud Mutonyi, Henry Muoria, Muga Gicaru, and Mugo Gatheru all lived. The British official assumption that Africans were only temporary sojourners in the city (an assumption not effectively challenged until the middle of the next decade) prevented the authorities from seeing clearly the socioeconomic implications of the rapid increase of the African population of Nairobi in the postwar period, which went up from 53,000 in 1945 to 77,000 in 1947, an increase of over 20 percent.[9] When Muga Gicaru came to Nairobi, the overcrowded location of Pumwani where he found a place to live was called "the Black Zoo."[10] While there were more jobs in the capital in the late 1940s and early 1950s, there were not enough to meet demand; while wages did rise, they did not keep up with inflation; the living standards of unskilled and semiskilled workers actually declined.[11] As Africans flocked to the city, including squatters evicted from the Highlands and *ahoi* tenants pushed off land in the reserves by African commercial farmers, many had to choose between unemployment, working at barely marginal wages, or attempting (usually unsuccessfully) to set up businesses for themselves. Waruhiu Itote, Karigo Muchai, Ngugi Kabiro, and Muga Gicaru were forced to change jobs several times during the period in a search for security, fair wages, and nondiscriminatory conditions. In spite of new government construction, housing was also in desperately short supply, causing many Africans to live on top of one another in circumstances of severe overcrowding. As Muga Gicaru remembers, "It was common to find two or three families in one room, sleeping, cooking and eating in a space about fifteen feet by twelve."[12] The basic infrastructure of the African locations was simply inadequate; Gicaru and "200 officially known householders together with hundreds of unregistered lodgers" had to queue up beginning at 5:00 in the morning at the single neighborhood water tap, which the city shut off at 9:00 a.m.[13] If Africans living in these conditions became ill, they had few options, unless they could afford an expensive doctor or clinic. The government dispensary was the only free clinic in Nairobi and queues were long and care uncertain; in 1949 an inadequately trained medical assistant misdiagnosed Ngugi Kabiro's bronchitis as malaria and gave him the wrong medicine for two weeks, leading eventually to his physical breakdown and hospitalization.[14]

The Kenya government, encouraged by settler politicians, tended to view the tense situation in the capital after the war as a control problem more than a social problem. The government tried to deal with the unemployed by influx control; police harassment of Africans for failure to carry their passes was common, as Mugo Gatheru experienced when a policeman challenged him in the street for his *kipande* and beat him for talking back when he could not produce the pass.[15] Municipal authorities cracked down on unauthorized slum housing and illegal markets like "Burma Market" (which served the needs of the exploding population outside the law and were kept orderly by local "watch committees") by razing such places to the ground.[16] Urban Africans developed strategies of subterfuge, passive resistance, and bribery to evade regulations. For example, to escape the Kifagio (sweep) campaign, Waruhiu Itote would listen for the Swahili command "*warefu mbele* [tall people] in front," knowing that when the police misprounounced the phrase by saying "*warevu mbele*" [clever people], they meant "those who had the money for a bribe." Developing these skills of evasion would have political value during the Emergency; as Itote puts it, "So Nairobi was a battlefield on which we learnt many tricks for evading capture which were to stand us in good stead later."[17]

Police actions like the Kifagio, however, failed to contain serious crime, which was on the rise in Nairobi in the late 1940s, especially in certain locations such as Pumwani and Shauri Moyo. Organized gangs of criminals, mostly Gikuyu, roamed the streets at night, armed with *pangas,* sometimes robbing passersby but also acting as guards for large-scale illegal activity such as the brewing of beer or distillation of spirits.[18] The understaffed police force in the capital could not cope, and the government felt compelled to import large drafts of new recruits from the Northern Province, most of whom were poorly trained, illiterate, and politically ignorant; conflicts between these new police and experienced city dwellers is a common theme of memoirs.[19] The reinforcement of the police made little difference, for crime was bred in the ever-worsening economic conditions of the Nairobi poor, nurtured by the lineage- and ethnic-based gang structure that developed in the 1940s, and fed by racial and political tension.[20] Criminal and political activity were often intermingled; by 1952, criminals were active in the secret movement in Nairobi the British had misnamed "Mau Mau," and helped shape its violent character in the capital.[21]

The tight job situation, extremely limited housing, and few municipal services, problems not effectively dealt with by the white city council or the African Advisory Council, increased the importance of unofficial African organizations and the influence of independent shapers of African opinion. Location associations in Nairobi, ethnic solidarity organizations like the Kikuyu General Union and the Luo Union, labor unions like the Transport and Allied Workers Union, independent religious sects, and age-based brotherhoods like the 40 Group provided the social support for the new arrivals in Nairobi that the government was unwilling to supply.[22] Independent African opinion expressed itself in an outpouring of pamphlets and newspapers, which soon outsold government publications. Henry Muoria, a strong supporter of Kenyatta, called in his *What Should We Do for Our Sake?* (1945) and *Life is War by Deeds* (1949) both for Gikuyu self-help and for political self-assertion. In his own angrier pamphlets, Gakaara wa Wanjau, whose *The Spirit of Manhood and Perseverance for Africans* was first published in Swahili in 1948 and reissued in Gikuyu in 1952, sought to "expose the white man's strategy of lies" and inspire Africans to challenge land alienation and racial domination.[23] The explosion of vernacular newspapers in the late 1940s and early 1950s, from Henry Muoria's *Mumenyereri* to Bildad Kaggia's *Inooro ria Gikuyu,* most of which were connected to political organizations or ethnic associations, also contributed to circulating information and raising political awareness and ethnic consciousness among Africans in Nairobi.[24]

The lineage and location associations in Nairobi, the city-based 40 Group, and the political organizations all had strong links to the rural areas of Central Kenya and the Rift Valley, where unrest was on the rise in the postwar period. The second colonial occupation in Central Kenya led the government to try to revive Gikuyu "communalism" on the land, discourage commercial farming by local entrepreneurs, strengthen the power of the chiefs, and enforce compulsory terracing in an effort to contain large-scale erosion. In 1947 members of KAU and 40 Group encouraged a strike of local women against continued terracing in Murang'a that brought the campaign in that district almost to a halt, a strike dramatically described by Kahinga Wachanga in his memoir.[25] Anger over terracing in Murang'a, the cattle-dipping campaign in Nyeri, and the handling of the Uplands Bacon Factory strike in Kiambu in 1947 fed into the growing opposition movement throughout Central Kenya. Henry Muoria helped turn the Uplands incident into a cause célèbre in Nairobi by reporting in *Mumenyereri* that the European officer had ordered his police to shoot the strike's ringleaders down in cold blood, a story that led to Muoria's conviction on a charge of sedition.[26] In the Rift Valley, the confrontation between the government and Kikuyu occupiers in Olenguruone (described by Kahinga Wachanga) and the widespread conflicts between squatters and settlers fueled Gikuyu discontent, and were publicized by activist writers like Gakaara wa Wanjau.[27]

The increasingly difficult economic situation and the rise in racial and political tension affected the authors of the Mau Mau memoirs personally and politically. In the late 1940s all of the memoirists had to struggle to support themselves and their families, often trying new occupations or changing jobs in the effort to make ends meet; economic insecurity is a common theme of the early chapters of almost all the accounts, and the memoirists tend to see this insecurity as directly or indirectly a product of the colonial situation itself, particularly of the stratification of opportunity that put Europeans at the top, Asians in the middle, and Africans at the bottom.[28] Experiences that fed the authors' anger against an inequitable system included Kaggia being passed over for promotion in the army in favor of a less qualified white corporal, Karari Njama cheated by a Boer settler, Itote refused a trading license easily obtained by Europeans and Asians, and Kabiro paid discriminatory wages as a salaried clerk. Kabiro describes his feelings:

> Since I left school, my feelings against the European and his Government in Kenya had grown more intense. I knew that it was the will of the European which caused African salaries to be so low, and I had now personally experienced the life made necessary by these starvation wages. Again, I was increasingly aware of the damage done to my family when several acres of my grandfather's land were alienated for European settlement.[29]

Personal frustrations, family grievances, ethnic patriotism, hatred of racism, and nationalist resentment of British control all drove the Mau Mau memoirists to political activism.

Unity and Divisions: The Rise of African Militancy

Though all Africans suffered in some way from European domination, they were hardly united in the late 1940s. The rhetoric of militancy, so vividly evoked in Kahinga Wachanga's description of a public meeting called by 40 Group in Nyeri on November 23, 1947, quoted at the opening of this chapter, shows how young nationalists used the politics of confrontation against Africans as well as against European settlers, missionaries, and officials. Wachanga's demands, on the authority of 40 Group, that the labor of young girls on European farms be stopped and that female circumcision continue challenged both chiefs who abetted female labor for settlers and those Christian elders who opposed the circumcision of their daughters. He backed up his demands with threats: any chief or other authority who defied this "law" would be "carried by the kite"—in other words, they would be killed and their corpses left for birds. For the moment, such threats were largely rhetorical, but the inflammatory character of the rhetoric (similar to but more extreme than that used by Harry Thuku in his attacks on chiefs in 1921) reveal the growing polarization within the African community.[30]

Among young men and women in particular a spirit of resentment grew, which was directed not only against overall white domination but also against the power of conservative elders, especially government chiefs and leaders in the mainline religious bodies.[31] Another division, quite important for the future, was developing between the growing educated African elite (*tie-ties* in the urban African *patois*), some of whom were assuming positions as chiefs in the reserves or as lower-level civil servants in Nairobi, and the semi-educated or illiterate majority.[32] Also, especially in Nairobi, the growing ethnic consciousness encouraged by the various associations that helped to build the internal unity of Gikuyu, Luo, or Kamba often contributed as well to a mutual suspicion and hostility among groups that was not successfully bridged by interethnic labor unions, political organizations, or government-sponsored bodies like the African Advisory Council in the capital.[33]

The Gikuyu were the angriest and the most internally divided of the major ethnic groups in Kenya. Colonial rule had affected them deeply, and for two generations they had suffered from its impositions and responded to the opportunities it had offered more than any other Africans. The British authorities and their policies tended to push the Gikuyu together, but for most the closer ties to lineage, locality, and district remained more important than loyalty to the ethnic group as a whole. Ever since the founding of the Kikuyu Association (KA) in 1919, their politicians had protested such grievances as land alienation in Kiambu and Nyeri, the treatment of squatters in the Rift Valley, the carrying of passes, and the nonrepresentation of Africans in the Legislative Council. In protest politics, however, disunity had been as typical as a common front, as witness the division between the KA and the East African Association (EAA) in 1921 and between the KA and the Kikuyu Central Association (KCA) in the late 1920s. Religious disputes, emerging originally from the cliterodectomy conflict of 1929–1931, divided them further among animists, followers of mission Christianity, Christian independents, and followers of prophetic sects (the *arathi*). Divisions between educated and uneducated, landed and landless, rich and poor had widened in the interwar period. Moreover, Gikuyu members of the colonial authority structure, especially chiefs, had often clashed with politicians and these conflicts would grow more intense in the postwar period as the second colonial generation entered politics.

Indicative of the new spirit of the late 1940s was the emergence of the "Aanake a 40," or "40 Age Group," an organization with a core of men circumcised in 1940 but, in Kahinga Wachanga's words, open to "all the young men of the 1940–1949 age group from Ngong to Meru."[34] Inspired by a speech in December 1946 in which Kenyatta called on the young to take action, Wachanga, Dominic Gatu, Ngari Kigecha, and others (mostly from Nyeri) founded 40 Group in early 1947. At its first large meeting in April at a field in Shauri Moyo, Nairobi, Wachanga and the other officers presented the group's principal political and cultural goals. These included to stop the digging of terraces, to stop the labor of young girls, to boycott the payment of taxes, to prevent policemen from entering the reserves, to burn *vipande* (passes), to continue the circumcision of girls, and to "block attendance of Sunday church services in foreign churches," demands that looked toward confrontation not only with the British authorities and missionaries but with chiefs and conservative Gikuyu Christians.[35] The group's slogan, "Say and Act," points to its leaders' impatience with empty rhetoric.[36]

The 40 Group (whose leaders eventually included Stanley Mathenge, Mwangi Macharia, Fred Kubai, Eliud Mutonyi, and Isaac Gathanju) was composed of wage earners, unemployed men like Wachanga, petty traders, and criminals.[37] Veterans like Waruhiu Itote were an important element as well. Defiance of white authority was a common characteristic. Muga Gicaru tells of a self-employed 40 Group member he calls only "Kamau" who refused to carry a pass, would not work for settlers, and banded together with others for mutual defense against the police.[38] The group led demonstrations against the government, called for boycotts of European products, held illegal dances, and committed crimes to raise funds and obtain weapons.[39] As its principal goals indicate, 40 Group was as much concerned with the situation in the reserves as in the capital (both Wachanga and Itote have more to say about its activities in Nyeri and Murang'a than in Nairobi) and the organization had branches in the Gikuyu districts, sometimes working in cooperation with the Kenya African Union. Wachanga tells of the violent 40 Group demonstration against terracing in Chief Ignatio's location in Murang'a, which ended in the death of one of its members, and of confrontations in locations in Nyeri over female labor (reminiscent of Harry Thuku's campaign in the districts in 1921) and cattle dipping.[40] Wachanga's vivid account, however, tends to stress the role of male militants like himself from Nairobi rather than the key part that local women played in opposing terracing in 1947.

Though 40 Group did not last long, fading away in 1948, it raised popular consciousness, trained its leaders in organizing skills, and pioneered the politics of confrontation in the late 1940s. Later, 40 Group leaders would assume important positions in the labor movement, in the Kenya African Union, and in Muhimu, the central committee of Mau Mau, an illustration of how the outlets for Gikuyu protest tended to influence and interpenetrate each other.

In the confrontations over terracing and cattle dipping in the reserves, 40 Group tended to pressure the more established Kenya African Union. KAU was founded in 1946 to bring Africans together across ethnic boundaries in concerted action for political reform. Of the Mau Mau authors, Bildad Kaggia, Waruhiu Itote, J. M. Kariuki, Karari Njama, Karigo Muchai, Kahinga Wachanga, and Gakaara wa Wanjau all belonged to KAU. Unfortunately, although KAU did score some successes in the late 1940s, its influence was uneven across the country, its position toward serious protests equivocal, its paid-up membership stagnant, and its central office poorly run.[41] When Jomo Kenyatta was elected president in 1947, many Africans, especially Gikuyu, hoped that new vigor would be injected into KAU, but, in Bildad Kaggia's words, "Little change came about in KAU's activities. Kenyatta's meetings always aroused people, but KAU, as an organization, had little success. It was lifeless."[42] KAU's leadership was multiethnic in the late 1940s, but, although Kenyatta had some success in recruiting in North Nyanza and the Rift Valley, most of the Luo of Central Nyanza remained aloof, as did the coastal peoples, and the strength of KAU remained in Nairobi and Central Kenya, principally among the Gikuyu.[43] Discontent over the moderation and impotence of KAU led Bildad Kaggia, Fred Kubai, and J. M. Mungai to plan the revival of the organization by taking over the key Nairobi branch office; the election of these militants in June 1951 galvanized KAU in the capital, but also split the KAU leadership along ethnic and political lines, even leading to clashes between Kaggia and Kenyatta.[44] KAU was broadly based and capable of bringing out large audiences to mass meetings, but it was deeply divided and its influence rivaled by other organizations that could often claim the stronger or prior loyalty of their adherents.

The postwar trade unions assumed an important role in popular organizing and in raising African political consciousness. Inspired by the Mombasa General Strike of 1947, trade union organizing burgeoned in the late 1940s, even in the face of employer hostility and government repression. Though the umbrella unions like the African Workers' Federation and the East African Trades Union Congress faded after their leaders Chege Kibachia and Makhan Singh were arrested and deported, a number of occupational unions, like the Transport and Allied Workers Union and Clerks and Commercial Workers Union, flourished in their wake, threatening strikes and issuing demands that were as much political as they were focused on workers' concerns as such. Waruhiu Itote remembers that "The trade unions had the most militant leaders and were the most active groups working for Independence in the city."[45] Union leaders such as Fred Kubai and Bildad Kaggia had an important role in rallying African opposition to the granting of a royal charter to the city of Nairobi in 1950 on the grounds that it would lead to the expansion of the white-controlled municipality into suburban African areas, accompanying their protests with the radical demand for a rapid transition to African majority rule.[46] During the general strike in May 1950, which he says had "the sympathetic support of virtually all African workers in Nairobi," Ngugi Kabiro persuaded the other Africans in his office to join this strike, and was forced to resign as a consequence.[47]

By 1950 young Gikuyu leaders of some of the Nairobi-based trade unions had close links not only with KAU but with the much older Kikuyu Central Association, which had considerable influence behind the political scenes, even though it was still illegal. With the exception of Karigo Muchai, the Mau Mau authors are too young to have been supporters of the KCA before its banning in 1940. Kaggia felt that the KCA had become outdated after the war. "The main objectives of the KCA were to demand fairer treatment for the Kikuyu from the British and to negotiate the return of alienated Kikuyu lands. It had no programme for changing the *status quo* or even for attaining independence."[48] Others, especially the memoirists from Kiambu, remained loyal to the KCA precisely because they believed that the association held out the best hope of recovering lost land, especially land lost by their own families. The stories of the seizing of the land played an essential role in awakening their political awareness. As Ngugi Kabiro remembered, "In the evenings we often sat in my old grandmother's hut and listened to tales of the coming of the Europeans and how they stole our land and burned down our huts. These stories of the 'White Bwana' take on a much deeper meaning as a man passes into adulthood and responsibility."[49]

The old KCA had been a rather selective organization, limited to elders and excluding younger men and all women, but this was about to change in the late 1940s, connected to the introduction of new oaths to replace the KCA oath of the 1920s. Since the late 1930s the KCA in Kiambu District had been closely associated with the lineage organization, the Kikuyu Land Board or *Mbari,* and after the war and the return of the KCA detainees from detention, the KCA and *Mbari* together administered a new oath to KCA members in Kiambu first, then from 1947 to KCA men in Nyeri, Murang'a, and the Rift Valley. More traditional than the original KCA oath, employing goat's meat and blood instead of the Bible, this oath of loyalty to the organization and commitment to recovery of the lost lands was particularly designed to prevent the defection of members to the government (as many believed Harry Thuku had defected after his return from detention in 1931).[50] By 1948 the oathing campaign was spreading more rapidly than the KCA and *Mbari* leaders in Kiambu had intended, and getting out of their control. When the KCA/*Mbari* leaders in Kiambu—by then based at Chief Koinange wa Mbiyu's home at Banana Hill, Kiambaa—attempted to regain control of the oathing in 1948 and spread it into Nairobi, Mbiyu Koinange approached the trade union leaders Fred Kubai and J. M. Mungai, who said they would help in return for agreements to open up the oathing to reliable Gikuyu not necessarily approved in advance by the old KCA, to reduce the fee, and to make the oath more militant.[51] For the next two years, labor union activists recruited prospects in Nairobi, oathed taxi and bus drivers drove the recruits to Kiambaa, and the new members were then oathed under the auspices of the "Kiambaa Parliament."[52] Also in 1948 the oath devised by the Olenguruone settlers protesting British policy, an oath and an oathing process that stressed unity even more than loyalty (the main emphasis of KCA oaths), which was already being administered in the Rift Valley, was brought to Kiambu by squatter leader Samuel Koina, and began to influence oathing in the Gikuyu home districts.[53]

In 1951 a critical split came. In early 1950—disillusioned by the failures of KAU, frustrated by the intransigence of the government, and apprehensive over the settlers' "Kenya Plan"—members of the Kiambaa

Parliament met at Koinange's house with KAU and union leaders to discuss a rapid expansion of the oathing campaign. Though they were determined now to build Gikuyu unity as quickly as possible, there is little evidence that the parliament was planning violence. By 1951, however, some oathed members of the Central Committee of KAU, unbeknownst to the others, formed a new "central committee" (or Muhimu, meaning "important" in Swahili) of a new secret movement to further oathing in Nairobi, and this committee and the Kiambaa Parliament eventually went their separate ways. As Kaggia explains it, "We decided to work alone without the parliament's knowledge. The committee spread the oath to all outside districts and operated from Nairobi."[54] With his strong Nairobi orientation, however, Kaggia fails to mention that the city militants attempting to spread their oath faced strong opposition in some areas of Kiambu such as Githunguri from rural-based activists loyal to other leaders, as the recently published research of Greet Kershaw points out.[55] The new movement included a "group of 30" that disseminated Muhimu's orders and a network of elders' committees from the Central Province level down to the district level and below.[56] Members of the secret movement called it variously Uigano wa Muingi, or Muingi (Unity of the Community, or Community), Gikuyu na Mumbi (the first parents of the Gikuyu), Muma (Oath), Muiguithania (the Unifier), KCA, or Muhimu.[57]

Unity and Divisions:
The Secret Movement and Muma wa Uigano

At about six o'clock on an evening early in 1952, Kiboi Muriithi was taking a nap in his room in Nairobi near Burma Market when he was awakened by loud knocking. His good friend Kamau was at the door with an invitation to "take a stroll" and drink a beer together. After a walk of some distance to the middle of Bahati Location, Kamau knocked at a strange house and slipped behind Muriithi as they both entered. "Instead of following, I found myself in front, in one of the strangest rooms I had ever seen. It was pitch black, lit by only a candle in the furthest corner. The room was small, no more than twelve feet by twelve. And it was full of people, more than twenty men and women. There was no noise. Those speaking spoke quietly. I looked around for beer, but without much hope. It was dawning on me that I was now involved in something completely different from the beer I had been expecting." In fact, Kamau had led his unwitting friend Kiboi Muriithi to an oathing ceremony.[58]

The oath of the secret movement (*muma wa uigano*) became the principal instrument to build the unity that Muhimu believed was so important to challenging British control of Kenya. The new oath that radicals like Waruhiu Itote organized and administered was different in certain particulars from earlier Gikuyu oaths.[59] Let us look at its general character-istics. To begin with, the oath was strongly militant and implicitly threat-ened violence against Europeans and those who betrayed the movement.[60] Second, the oath was administered on a mass basis as well as to small groups, a departure from tradition; Karari Njama remembers dozens at his Nyeri oathing ceremony in September 1952, while Mohamed Mathu reports thousands of people at his ceremony on the outskirts of Nairobi in June 1952.[61] Third, the oath was given to men and women equally and sometimes at the same gathering, both departures from Gikuyu tradition. During Karari Njama's first oathing, large numbers of prospective oathers of both sexes were assembled in a hut waiting to be called to the ritual.[62] Fourth, the oath was compulsory; people called to oathing ceremonies were not allowed to refuse or leave and were beaten and threatened with death if they tried. Kiboi Muriithi's mother, tricked into attending an oathing, attempted to refuse to participate. "When the calabash came round my mother foolishly refused to drink. She was dragged out of the line and man-handled, taunted with being 'Black-White' and having sold her brothers and sisters. A slap across her face sent her sprawling. Kicks and blows were rained upon her."[63] She was thrown from the hut, and later threatened with death; only her son's intervention saved her. Fifth, the secrecy of the oath was enforced by cursing, physical pressure, and the threat of serious harm to anyone who revealed the ritual to outsiders.

Most of the Mau Mau authors made their oath-taking a central episode in the early chapters of their memoirs. They did not necessarily take the oath on their own initiative; half the authors were tricked into coming, gen-erally by close friends or acquaintances from their home locations. The oathing place, usually a hut (though Mathu's group was oathed in the open), was dark and guarded by well-armed and often hostile men, who welcomed candidates with shows of bullying clearly designed to intimi-date. While the ceremony administered inside varied from place to place, the memoirs indicate that certain details were generally consistent. The administrator tells the candidate to remove his clothes (all memoir descrip-tions of oathing are by men) and any European objects like watches or keys. Often, though not always, he is then tied with goat skin to other can-didates. Naked, his wrists and neck encircled with goat skin, he passes with the others seven times through a banana stalk arch, takes seven bites from the hearts and lungs of a goat, and drinks from a gourd a mixture of goat's blood and other liquids. (Seven is a powerful number in Gikuyu cosmol-ogy.) He then repeats after the administrator a series of vows, each time saying that if he proves false, may the oath kill him. These vows commit him to struggle for freedom, never to forsake or sell the land to Europeans, to help the secret movement with firearms, money, or anything else needed, to obey superiors, and never to betray the movement to its enemies. For example, J. M. Kariuki and his comrades in the Rift Valley swore:

> I speak the truth and vow before God
> And before this movement,
> The movement of Unity,
> The Unity which is put to the test
> The Unity that is mocked with the name of "Mau Mau,"
> That I shall go forward to fight for the land,
> The lands of Kirinyaga that we cultivated,
> The lands which were taken by the Europeans
>
> And if I fail to do this
> May this oath kill me,
> May this seven kill me,
> May this meat kill me.[64]

After the initiate repeats all the pledges, the oath administrator anoints his forehead with blood, and the initiate pays his fee (which in some cases can be substantial). Sometimes the administrator then gives a talk, instructing the initiates in colonial history and in the political purposes of the movement.[65]

The unity oath had a profound impact on most oath takers. With the exception of Mohamed Mathu, all the authors who describe their oath-taking left the ceremony with a feeling of satisfaction and strong commitment. J. M. Kariuki reacted as if he had experienced a religious conversion.

> Afterwards in the maize I felt exalted with a new spirit of power and strength. All my previous life seemed empty and meaningless. Even my education of which I was so proud, appeared trivial and meaningless beside this splendid and terrible force which had been given me. I had been born again.[66]

This theme of rebirth or fundamental change recurs again and again in the memoirs, and links the oath of the secret movement, taken as an adult, to the traditional second-birth ceremony of childhood and the initiation of adolescence.[67] Thus for its initiates the oath became a third experience of personal renewal. In the case of educated Gikuyu like Kariuki, *muma wa uigano* wiped out the deracinating, detribalizing effects of Westernization (transforming them back by re-Gikuyuizing them); in the case of uneducated men like Gikoyo, who had never left their communities, the oath, the ritual, and the instructions were the first phase in their political awakening. In addition, *muma wa uigano* bound the group together, as traditional oaths had done; as Kariuki explains, "The purpose of all these oaths was to give those participating a feeling of mutual respect. . . . Envy, hate and enmity would be unknown between them."[68]

Muma wa uigano involved a culturally syncretistic ceremony containing elements of precolonial oath-taking, elements reminiscent of the Gikuyu second-birth and circumcision ceremonies, elements of the political oath of the KCA dating from the 1920s, and elements that were essentially new. Rob Buijtenhuijs, supporting his points with details from the memoirs, has argued persuasively that *muma wa uigano* was above all an "initiation into a new and purified Kikuyu tribe, proud of its past and its personality, and freed from European domination and foreign influences."[69] This theme of individual and group purification and rededication comes through clearly in Gucu Gikoyo's *We Fought for Freedom,* when the administrator tells his group after oathing "that now we were good people as we had been cleansed and had become Gikuyu Karing'a (true Gikuyu) and warriors who would fight for the independence of our country."[70] The title of "Gikuyu Karing'a," which set Mau Mau initiates apart from the unoathed, is also historically significant, because it was the name chosen for themselves by the opponents of the missions' anti-cliterodectomy campaign of 1929, distinguishing them from others who accepted the missions' direction, the *irore* (thumbprinters). Moreover, as Bildad Kaggia points out, those who had taken the oath called themselves "circumcised," not just true Gikuyu but true adults, separate from the uninitiated, who remained children in Mau Mau eyes.[71] Carrying this further, they had become genuine warriors of a true warrior age-group like those of precolonial times, with a real social purpose to defend the community against its enemies, not false men and sham warriors who accepted British rule.

The oathing ceremonies, with their potent ethnic symbolism and strong flavor of peasant irredentism, did much in themselves to further individual commitment. So did the new sense of group solidarity and community acceptance enjoyed by initiates. Ngugi Kabiro's close friend was "very pleased to hear that I too was now a true son of *Gikuyu* and *Mumbi*," and Kaggia discovered "a solidarity and closeness of all members, a confidence they had in one another, which was not evident in KAU," which he found "new and thrilling."[72] Even before he was oathed, Gucu Gikoyo was deeply impressed by the self-sacrifice and group support shown by Mau Mau men he encountered in prison. "One thing that struck me as unusual was the unity of these people. If one of them was brought food by a relation or a friend, he served it along the line until it was finished."[73]

Oathed people would not provide traditional communal support to, socialize freely with, or talk openly around those who had not taken the unity oath. Before he took his first oath, Karari Njama was shocked to find that when he and a person he later learned had already been oathed each called on friends to help him level ground to prepare to build a house, his friends failed to show up for him while the other man received all the help he needed.[74] Joram Wamweya remembers that if a person who had not taken the oath called his friends and neighbors to his home to drink beer, "nobody would decline, but he would have to drink it alone, for nobody would turn up."[75] This affected sexual interaction as well, for if a young man had not taken the oath, "No girl would so much as say 'Hullo' to him."[76] Bildad Kaggia, Karari Njama, and Kiboi Muriithi tell how the use of special handshakes and code language both enabled oathed members of the movement to recognize each other and to exclude outsiders. "If a stranger entered a room during a secret discussion someone would utter the warning 'There are plenty of fleas in this house,' or 'This house is filthy.' The conversation would switch to a safe subject."[77] All this reinforced group solidarity, protected secrecy, and ostracized Gikuyu who had not taken the oath, brought peer pressure on some to take it, and stigmatized and isolated unreconstructed "loyalists." As more and more joined, pressure on the unoathed mounted, until some holdouts found themselves desperately applying for admission. Kaggia describes how the movement responded. "Some late-comers who had previously been against the movement were fined before they could be admitted into the family. For example, if a chief had persecuted our members, when he wanted to join us he had to pay a large sum of money."[78]

The desperation of late joiners could be fueled by fear. In his appendix on oaths, Waruhiu Itote comments that "For most people, taking the oath was the final, not the first, expression of devotion to our cause."[79] Yet General China's account of his own use of compulsion when oathing civilians on Kirinyaga undercuts that assertion, as do references to intimidation and force in the narratives of Muriithi, Njama, Kabiro, and Wamweya.[80] Joram Wamweya recounts a conversation with his mother at their home in Kiambu shortly before he took his first oath:

> "Since you have come," my mother told me after she had served the food, "there is one thing about which you must take care."
> "What is it?" I asked.
> "There are people who are killing others and burying them in the very house where they live."
> "Why are they killing them?" I asked greatly puzzled.
> "They kill those who refuse to take the oath."[81]

The stories of the sudden deaths or disappearances of refusers, the deceiving of initiates inveigled to oathing ceremonies, the gratuitous violence of oathing guards, and the threats against informers built into the oathing rituals all suggest that administrators created an atmosphere of intimidation and compulsion associated with the oath to reinforce the effects of ritual bonding and political conviction. Moreover, the oath increased the stakes of noncomformity by pitting the new Gikuyu Karing'a against the Christians and collaborators who would not take it. Thus, as John Lonsdale, drawing on Gikoyo's memoir, points out, its administrators both drew on history and distorted it by calling on violence against both Europeans and other Gikuyu to redeem the past and future.[82]

Though disturbed by some aspects of the oathing ceremonies, the highly educated Karari Njama supports the necessity of oathing. "Though the oath clung on Kikuyu traditions and superstitions, yet the unity and obedience achieved by it was so great that it could be our only weapon for fighting against the white community."[83] For the willing, the unity oath heightened their sense of Gikuyu identity and strengthened their commitment to the cause; for those initially unwilling, the oath usually ensured their passive cooperation and their silence. As Bildad Kaggia attests, it was the uneducated Gikuyu who responded most enthusiastically to the oathing campaign. "When 'Mau Mau' oath-taking started it was the uneducated who were the first to accept its radical gospel."[84] Unlike Karari Njama and Bildad Kaggia, many of the educated felt that their interests, especially their hard-won if precarious positions within the colonial structure, were threatened by the movement; most educated Gikuyu probably took the oath rather than run the risks of refusal, but their support for Mau Mau was minimal. A small percentage of Gikuyu refused the oath altogether, and an unknown number died because of their refusal. Those who died tended to be Christians, for while self-interested collaborators were not inclined to martyrdom, some Christians felt a strong ideological opposition to Mau Mau, as the cases of Mary Wangeci, Andrew Kaguru, Edmund Gikonyo, and others in Wiseman's *Kikuyu Martyrs* attest.[85] Christian refusers (especially members of Revival) formed a potential counterforce to Mau Mau infused by a similar spirit of commitment; such people were a real threat to the secret movement, and could be dealt with ruthlessly.[86]

The oath also tended to separate the Gikuyu and their relatives among the Embu and Meru from other Africans. British propaganda would use this vigorously against the secret movement, particularly, Kahinga Wachanga suggests, among the Luo.[87] Gakaara Wanjau, a strong nationalist quite conscious of the need to involve other Kenyans in the struggle, was one of the leaders who recognized a need to develop oaths for other ethnic groups in order to draw them in.[88] Official evidence confirms appreciable success for the movement in oathing Kamba, many of whom lived in Nairobi and whose home area bordered Gikuyuland to the east, and less success among Maasai and among Luo in Nairobi.[89] The oath was the critical factor in building a high level of internal unity, but the movement still needed to take the next step to bring in large numbers of Africans from outside Central Kenya.

Infiltration, Intimidation, and Violence

The publication of the settlers' "Kenya Plan" (1949), the government crackdown on unions (1950), the move to elevate Nairobi to city status (1950), the banning of "Mau Mau" (1950), and the official endorsement of the unpopular Beecher Report on African education (1951) all exacerbated the tense political situation and increased the power of African political radicals. As the secret movement grew stronger and the stakes grew higher, both its power to enforce its will on the oathed and its tendency to alienate unoathed Africans increased. At the same time, divisions emerged within KAU between constitutionalists like Kenyatta and confrontationalists like Bildad Kaggia, and within Mau Mau between leaders like Kaggia, who had not fully committed to violence through armed revolt, and younger militants impatient for a test of strength with the government.

As more and more Gikuyu in Nairobi joined the secret movement, Gikuyu organizations originally established for other purposes soon became fronts for Mau Mau, a development clearly engineered by the radicals of the Central Committee, as Bildad Kaggia boasts in *Roots of Freedom*. Kaggia made the most of his position as a member of the African Advisory Council (AAC) in 1951–1952 to gain recognition for a number of Gikuyu sports and educational organizations that were really Mau Mau fronts, giving the secret movement a special ascendancy in Nairobi. "In those days having these societies controlled by 'Mau Mau' meant we could dominate the municipal halls. We could hold as many meetings as we liked without fear of being stopped. . . . These societies actually were engaged in educational activities as well. . . . But . . . were more important in recruiting new members to the 'Unity Movement.'"[90] In retaliation, the government attempted to set up front groups of its own to spy on Mau Mau; Kaggia used his position to deny AAC recognition to one of these, the "Kenya African Pointers Union."[91]

By 1952 Muhimu was establishing close links as well with the Gikuyu-dominated criminal underground of the capital city. Kaggia not only justifies this on grounds of expediency, but also claims that much of Nairobi criminal activity was politically motivated anyway. "By that time 'Mau Mau' had enlisted the help of all sorts of people, including thieves and robbers. 'Mau Mau' had a hand in almost every theft, robbery or any other crime directed against Europeans. Most of these crimes were political."[92] From Muhimu's perspective, the most important political crimes involved obtaining guns for a possible confrontation with the government. Fred Kubai reports that Gikuyu veterans began training young recruits to shoot as early as 1949–1950.[93] Unlike Kariuki's account, Kaggia's memoir suggests that the recruits embraced the prospect of violence enthusiastically.

> As membership swelled, the Central Committee became more and more aggressive. After uniting the people it was decided that if the government did not heed KAU's demands, we would be ready to fight for our rights. Word was sent out to the members to try and secure guns through all possible means—stealing, buying, robbing—according to the circumstances. Many impatient members enjoyed this, and they plunged into the job with great enthusiasm.[94]

With money from oathing fees, from the fines assessed on late-coming initiates, and from collections from local members, the movement bought guns, either directly from government workers who were oathbound members or by using such workers as go-betweens. Guns were also collected by burglary; Waruhiu Itote tells of breaking into a shop on River Road to steal twelve guns, a major coup that left his band "so elated that we did not bother with the nearby cashbox."[95] Mau Mau activists, or criminals working for Mau Mau, also attacked single policemen at night to seize their weapons. "Also our bands of strong men, led by Stanley Mathenge (Kamurwa, Gachago, and many others) used to spy on lonely policemen with guns. They snatched the gun and if necessary, killed the policeman too."[96] The Mau Mau would dismember the bodies of policemen in order to hide the evidence and deceive the government as to the men's whereabouts; eventually, a hasty killing squad left a leg with boot and puttees still on at the scene, alerting the authorities and leading them to strengthen police patrols and increase the number of posts in the Nairobi locations.[97]

In spite of the emphasis on secrecy, informers soon became a serious problem. The memoirists cite betrayal, though the resort to mass oathing itself must have posed inherent security problems. Ngugi Kabiro blames unreliable new members (especially Christians and government employees like headmen and teachers) for the rash of raids on oathing ceremonies and suspected oathing ceremonies in Nairobi and Kiambu in 1952.[98] It was not only new members who could be lured into informing, however, for a member's betrayal compromised even the Central Committee itself. As Bildad Kaggia describes, when a special oathing ceremony for the entire Central Committee of about fourteen members was scheduled to be conducted at Kiambaa, members of the committee received a message just before they left Nairobi that soldiers had arrived at the Koinange home and were posted throughout the whole area; Kaggia and the others called the ceremony off and discovered the identity of the traitor two days later through their own informers in government offices. Their "strong men" arrested him and held him for trial.

> Owing to the seriousness of the case, judgment had to be passed at once. The court session took place in a taxi, and the judges consisted of the chairman of the committee, myself and two others. The court decided that the man already knew too much. He was condemned to death. The sentence was carried out immediately. Then the postponed oath ceremonies for all members of the two supreme bodies took place.[99]

Kaggia's account of informing within the inner ranks of Muhimu and Waruhiu Itote's strong defense of the necessary killing of informers in Nairobi both suggest that betrayal had become a major concern of Mau Mau leaders by mid-1952.

The problem of informers was offset by successful Mau Mau spying from within the government. African police, headmen, and even some chiefs took the oath of unity. China reports in his second book that

Muhoya, a powerful chief in Nyeri who had taken the oath of unity, intervened to release Dedan Kimathi when the latter was arrested in April
1952.[100] Soldiers were easy to bribe because of the British "starvation wages," and Mau Mau captives could escape "for as little as five
shillings."[101] In Nairobi and other administrative centers, government
clerks, telegraphists, typists, and others were oathed into the movement so
that Mau Mau could obtain information on official plans and weapons and
ammunition from the government's own supplies. Paul Mahehu (a deco-
rated veteran of Burma), the liaison between Nairobi and the Mau Mau
bands that formed on Kirinyaga, became the main oath administrator to
government employees, and his exploits of infiltration and subversion
boosted morale and helped the movement in various ways.[102]

As pressure mounted, the secret movement turned to attacks on loyalists. Kahinga Wachanga describes the first important attempts in Nairobi in
April 1950 to assassinate prominent pro-government Africans Tom
Mbotela, moderate leader of KAU and assistant superintendent of locations, and Muchohi Gikonyo, appointed councilor of the African Advisory
Council, both of whom were wounded in the attacks. Dominic Gatu, a
Muhimu activist and an ex-leader of 40 Group, shot Gikonyo and was
arrested, tried, and sentenced to seven years in prison, though Fred Kubai
was acquitted.[103] In the reserves, especially in Nyeri, violence against loyalists was also on the rise, from assaults on policemen to arson of the
homes of headmen and chiefs.[104]

As clandestine violence escalated, the Kenya African Union continued
to operate in the open with Jomo Kenyatta at its head. By this time, the
secret movement had thoroughly infiltrated KAU in Nairobi and Central
Province. One indication is the change in the *nyimbo,* or political songs.
The political song was hardly new to Gikuyu nationalism, for some of the
most influential were those sung in the 1920s, such as the *muthirigu* song
and dance that had been used to rally *karing'a* in support of cliterodectomy
and against the missionaries, chiefs, and *irore* in 1929.[105] In the late 1940s
political songs were composed for rallies of the Kenya African Union. By
the 1950s these KAU songs were intermingled with new ones composed by
oathed men like Kinuthia wa Mugia, songs containing coded references to
muma wa uigano and praise for the secret movement; these *nyimbo* were
published in songbooks openly sold in Nairobi and at mass meetings of
KAU, such as the Nyeri meeting of July 26, 1952, attended by Karari
Njama.[106] While the songs were ambiguous, their intent was clear to initiates of the movement of unity, and ultimately to the police; when L. S. B.
Leakey working for Special Branch obtained and translated the songbooks,
the government stepped up its repression in Nairobi.

By 1952 the relationship between Kenyatta and the radicals of the
secret movement was approaching a critical point. Although there was suspicion on both sides, men like Kaggia and Kubai needed Kenyatta as much

as he needed them, for Kenyatta could win the support of older Africans.[107] As the recognized leader of African nationalism in Kenya, Kenyatta conducted his last speaking tour in the spring and summer of 1952, addressing mass meetings at Kiambu in April, Naivasha in June, Nyeri in July, and again at Kiambu in August. In spite of the evidence Special Branch would present at Kenyatta's trial, the leadership of KAU and that of Mau Mau had "no organized link," only two common members, Kubai and Kaggia.[108] Kaggia comments on Kenyatta's equivocal position, "Although the 'Mau Mau' movement looked upon Kenyatta as the national leader, it was not under his direct control. . . . He deliberately knew little of what went on in the 'Mau Mau' Central Committee meetings. He was under constant supervision from the Special Branch and had he been more directly involved it would have been impossible for us to have preserved our essential secret anonymity."[109]

The government pressured Kenyatta to prove his constitutionalism and his commitment to nonviolence by condemning Mau Mau in his speeches. Kaggia comments that Kenyatta had to give at least the public impression that he was sincerely attacking Mau Mau, "finding it politic to throw more dust in the eyes of the authorities," and Ngugi Kabiro observes that since "the Kikuyu people as a whole . . . *believed beyond a doubt* that men such as Kenyatta, Koinange, and other important Kikuyu leaders of KAU were strong supporters, if not leaders, of the underground movement," Kenyatta's denunciations were not taken seriously.[110] But the Central Committee found Kenyatta's terms of condemnation—especially at the second Kiambu meeting (where he shared the stage with the despised Chief Waruhiu), when he claimed that "Mau Mau had spoiled the country" and should "perish forever"—too harsh and confusing to ordinary members of Mau Mau, most of whom also idolized Kenyatta. Muhimu asked Kenyatta to meet with them.

> For the first time Kenyatta met the "Mau Mau" Central Committee. He was surprised to see Kubai and myself there. And he noticed to his further surprise that other leaders, whom he did not know, were running the meetings. E. Mutonyi and I. Gathanju were the chairman and secretary. The committee asked Kenyatta not to continue with the remaining meetings. After discussion he accepted the request and undertook to get the remaining meetings cancelled.[111]

This incident has ironic overtones, for in a few months the government would arrest Kenyatta as the "manager" of Mau Mau.

The Declaration of Emergency

In the early afternoon of October 21, 1952, Mohamed Mathu was heading back to work after lunch when a group of African policemen rushed up and pushed him into a line of civilians being herded, with "abusive language and occasional jabs in the back," into the Caledonia playing field across from the Coryndon Museum. As he entered the field, he could see that "screeners" (African loyalists) supervised by Europeans were passing down the long line of men to identify Mau Mau suspects. "Luckily none of the screeners from my location in Nyeri knew or suspected anything about my political activities. As they passed along the line they studied each man and then gave their opinions to the European officers accompanying them. Though I was soon released to return to the office, hundreds of others were identified as Mau Mau activists and sent into the detention camps."[112] The Kenya Emergency had begun.

In spite of all the secret preparations and the killing of police and loyalists, it was the government and not Mau Mau that determined the start of real warfare. By the summer of 1952, some bands were already in the forests, but *"Mau Mau" General* suggests that even the well led (but poorly armed) group on Kirinyaga, which had entered in August under the orders of the Nyeri elders' committee, was not ready for revolt. Rumors circulated through the Gikuyu community in 1952 about a general uprising, the Utuku wa Hiu Ndaihu (The Night of Long Swords), during which all Europeans would be killed, but the rumors were vague and no concrete conspiracy seems to have existed.[113] Certainly, as Kaggia indicates, there was pressure from the rank and file for action. "Many young initiates were very impatient. They were always asking when we were going to take up arms and fight for our rights."[114] But were their leaders prepared to give the orders to rebel, and if so, when?

While the memoirs of Itote, Kaggia, and Wachanga indicate that Mau Mau leaders were getting ready for open conflict, they do not mention any particular plans for general revolt. Kahinga Wachanga refers to the forming of a "War Council" in early 1952 whose older members at first hoped to avoid violence but "finally agreed that without bloodshed our revolt could not succeed"; this group elected Stanley Mathenge "Chairman of the Mau Mau Movement . . . because of his experience and knowledge of modern army organization and guerrilla tactics," suggesting plans for guerrilla warfare.[115] If the leaders were preparing for revolt, however, they had not communicated this to the members, and lower-echelon memoirists tend to see the stance of the movement as essentially defensive. Kariuki writes that "Africans began to prepare for the ultimate last-ditch stand that might be necessary to prevent the light of freedom being snuffed out."[116] Mohamed Mathu observes, "While violent means had been adopted to eliminate traitors, to my knowledge we had no plan for an open clash with Government prior to the Emergency declaration. . . . The most talked-about means of putting pressure on Government was the general strike."[117]

The Central Committee, though it was aware from the evidence of well-placed sources that the government was making plans to arrest some of their members, did little to prepare to go underground or lay plans for an uprising, even after the assassination of Chief Waruhiu on October 9. When a trusted spy passed a message to Kaggia during the Muhimu meeting of October 19, which told him that "all KAU leaders" would be arrested within thirty-six hours, the Central Committee scrapped its agenda, passed a resolution that if they were detained the members of the secret movement should "take up arms and courageously fight for their rights," sent messages to the district committees, arranged to hide some documents and burn others, sent out instructions "to shift weapon arsenals to new hiding places," and "made provision for our own arrest and laid down a number of directives for after our arrest."[118]

When Kenyatta, Kaggia, Kubai, Gakaara wa Wanjau, and over 180 others were rounded up on the night of October 20, 1952, and taken into detention, those who had escaped the "Jock Scott" sweep tried to pick up the pieces. Mohamed Mathu remembers a demoralized movement, with no plans for revolt and no leaders to carry out a plan, "on the defensive" and simply responding to government's repressive measures as they came.[119] In places, the structure of the secret movement crumbled. Under the pressure of government repression, for example, the Kiambu District Committee "broke down" and for a period simply ceased operations, forcing the division committees to deal directly with the Central Province Committee.[120] In Nairobi, the escalating struggle after October 20 began to separate the sheep from the goats; Mohamed Mathu witnessed the defection from the movement of most of the educated Kikuyu, including KAU leaders who bore a share of responsibility for turning "the minds of the Kikuyu people" toward "violence and revolt."[121] Ironically, however, others responded to October 20 quite differently; information from Kiambu collected by Greet Kershaw points toward a rapid increase in the oathing of Gikuyu who assumed that Kenyatta and the others would be judged not guilty and freed.[122]

Meanwhile, the government sent police patrols and military units marching through Gikuyu communities to intimidate the countrypeople, extended night curfews, arrested more and more men and women for political activity, and confiscated hundreds of head of cattle in retaliation for Mau Mau actions.[123] Headmen's police began to extract oath confessions and names of activists by violent interrogation, endangering the Mau Mau networks. At the same time, the government began to close the independent schools and repatriated many thousands of Gikuyu from the Rift Valley, Tanganyika, and Uganda to the home districts, exacerbating overcrowding, unemployment, and poverty.[124] For Gikuyu in Nyeri, December 1952 was a terrible time. "Instead of the good Christmas songs, bullets echoed everywhere, [as well as] cries for the deceased, for blazing houses, for the robbing and raping; the cry of beatings and tortures in the chiefs' centers, in police and prison cells. Instead of feasts there were fasts enforced by sorrow."[125]

Though this was a very bad period, Mau Mau was neither destroyed nor dramatically changed in character. Some entirely new leaders emerged, but others like Eliud Mutonyi and Stanley Mathenge had not been swept up by Jock Scott, and the flexible Mau Mau structure allowed committees to re-form and surviving committees to take over from those badly damaged. While government repression detained many and intimidated others, it also impelled hundreds of young men to enter the forests to join guerrilla bands "to escape the Home Guard and the security force brutality."[126] Even some Europeans criticized the harshness of the crackdown, as when C. C. Fowkes wrote to Michael Blundell, comparing the actions of the Kenya Police Reserve in the Rift Valley to the Black and Tans in Ireland and suggesting that KPR actions were likely to alienate ordinary Gikuyu and drive them toward Mau Mau.[127] The time of intermittent violence and sporadic repression was passing, and the stage was set for guerrilla warfare and counterinsurgency.

The Coming of War:
Taking the Batuni Oath and Preparing to Fight

The young men and women preparing to join the guerrilla bands forming in Nyandarua and on Kirinyaga were expected to take a new oath of loyalty to prepare them for the responsibilities of fighting. *Muma wa uigano,* eventually taken (in British estimations) by 90 percent of the Gikuyu, was only a first step for most of the authors of the Mau Mau memoirs.[128] For those who were to fight for the movement, the first oath was followed by a second called *batuni* (platoon), "Warrior," "Action," or *muma wa ngero* (the oath for killing).[129]

The *batuni* (or *mbatuni*) oath apparently varied from place to place even more than the unity oath, but oath takers agree that it was stronger, both in its use of substances and practices Gikuyu would consider *thahu* (taboo) and in its demands on initiates. Joram Wamweya and Karigo Muchai each report that their *batuni* oaths required them to wrap a strip of goat's meat around their naked bodies, either insert their penises into the meat or place the meat alongside their penises, and bite a piece of meat with each vow they swore.[130] Mohamed Mathu describes a *batuni* oathing ceremony in Kiambu in 1954 during which women swore on goat meat which they inserted into their vaginas, followed later and separately by men swearing while inserting their penises into strips of goat meat.[131] After taking the second oath, Karari Njama discussed it with his friend David Wahome. "We resolved that it was a horrible oath, though typically Kikuyu."[132]

The second oath committed initiates to risk their lives and to kill whomever the movement would require. The vows taken by Karigo Muchai were characteristically severe:

> I speak the truth and swear before *Ngai* and before everyone present here
> And by this *Batuni* Oath of *Muingi*
> That if called upon to fight for our land,
> To shed my blood for it,
> I shall obey and never surrender,
> And if I fail to do so:
>
> May this oath kill me
> May this *thenge* kill me
> May this seven kill me
> May this meat kill me.[133]

All fighters took the second oath, either just before going or just after arriving in the forest, making them in Karigo Muchai's words "blood-brothers," who "should now help and assist one another in any way possible and never think of doing harm to our own brothers."[134] The sense of being part of a fictive family created by the *muma wa uigano* was now reinforced by the *batuni* oath but also tightened to include only the select group of warriors who had accepted the awful responsibilities of killing and dying for the cause.

In order to use Nairobi as a supply base for the forests, the secret movement tried to control the African locations by eliminating opponents, maintaining internal discipline, and punishing infractions of the rules. As Kahinga Wachanga indicates, there were still many loyalists willing to help the government against Mau Mau.[135] Mau Mau activists continued to attack policemen at night, though now that patrols had been reinforced and strong police posts built in the locations, such attacks were more risky. Enforcers continued to kill informers and collaborators (such as Tom Mbotela and Ambrose Ofafa), men marked for elimination by the decisions of the elders' councils, either by the committee of their particular district in Nairobi or by the "Martial Court" in Mathare Valley.[136] A similar court, which included men and women, operated in Nakuru to deal with "anti–Mau Mau" crimes, inflicting a range of punishments including execution.[137] Nairobi Mau Mau units also carried out armed attacks on groups in the city that the secret movement had identified as hostile. In 1953, for example, in reaction against declarations of loyalty to the government by the Asians of Nairobi, Mau Mau launched a campaign of raids against shops and homes to punish the Asian community and to obtain funds.[138] In 1954, some members of Mau Mau decided that African Muslims in Nairobi were using "evil magic to help Government destroy our Movement," and attacked the Eastleigh Mosque and the Pumwani African Mosque in May 1954 with heavy Muslim casualties.[139]

The committees also dealt with internal discipline. Even before October 1952, the movement had ordered its members to boycott European cigarettes, beer, and buses, enforcing these prohibitions with fines and punishments; it encouraged members to drink African home-brew instead and permitted them to smoke *bhangi* (marijuana), popular among younger members. (After the Declaration of Emergency, the government retaliated by using the new regulations "to close *Mau Mau* adherents' shops and take their buses off the road.")[140] When another Mau Mau member caught Ngugi Kabiro smoking a European cigarette, he was taken forcibly to face a court, all of whom "were highly intoxicated on *bhangi*," and given a punishment of twelve strokes and a fine of 200 shillings.[141] The movement was concerned with issues of sexual morality as well, strongly disapproving, for example, of male members living with women outside marriage; after taking the oath, Mathu, who was living in Ziwani location with a prostitute, was told either to marry her or find another place to stay and fined 80 shillings.[142]

The need for arms increased dramatically after October 20 and Nairobi was the main source. The movement worked closely with African criminals to obtain guns, then stored the weapons in the houses of activists like Mohamed Mathu or consigned them to the special platoon of Nairobi women who concealed the firearms and transported ammunition in the frames of bicycles.[143] Asian and European criminals also took advantage of the situation, as Ngugi Kabiro relates. In May 1953, an Asian salesman at a sporting goods store struck up a conversation with Kabiro, invited him to lunch the next day at a restaurant, and in several encounters over a period of days sold him seven pistols with ammunition, which Kabiro passed on to a Mau Mau activist after extracting a 250 shillings commission for himself; at one of the meetings, a European drove the car bringing the guns, and Kabiro concluded that he was the Asian's partner.[144] The close relationship between Mau Mau and criminal activity was true of Kiambu as well as Nairobi, as Joram Wamweya describes.[145]

Recruits, arms, and ammunition collected in Nairobi were sent by various stages to the bands in the field. In 1953 and 1954, one of the main transmission lines lay through Kiambu District, and the local committees of the secret movement played a critical role in ensuring that the men, women, and materiel arrived safely. Karigo Muchai's memoir *The Hardcore* reveals how it was done. Muchai was a member of the council of elders of his location within Kiambaa Division in Kiambu; location committees were under the direction of district committees, who in turn reported to the Central Province Committee (CPC).[146] When the repression after the Declaration of Emergency severely damaged the district committee, the division committees maintained contact with the CPC themselves, and in January 1953, Karigo Muchai was elected to the Kiambaa Location Committee and told to make the rounds of the sublocations, collecting funds, gathering information on government actions (including abuses), noting the number of potential recruits for fighting bands in "the Narok, Longonot, and southern Aberdares forests," and assisting "women who had lost their husbands and men who were arrested and taken to court on Mau Mau charges."[147]

After being arrested, brutally interrogated, and released in February 1953, Karigo Muchai took the *batuni* oath, and a short time later was appointed head of the reserve units of Kiambaa fighters, men who occasionally carried out raids but were usually engaged in providing accommodation for men on the way to the forest, scouting for the forest bands, killing people condemned by the elders, and gathering information for the district committee. Muchai spent much of his own time in early 1953 arranging secret accommodations and escorting recruits, for "Almost all of the fighters recruited from Nairobi made their way into the Aberdares through Kiambu and spent a night in Kiambaa location."[148] After resucitation of the district committee in June 1953, Muchai was elected to be the representative of the fighters, their link with the elders. By that time, Mau Mau bands were operating in many places in Central Kenya.

The Movement and the Memoirs

Better than any other sources, the Mau Mau memoirs (and those of Muga Gicaru, Henry Muoria, and Mugo Gatheru as well) recreate the atmosphere of tension, fear, and excitement of the late 1940s and early 1950s, evoke the anger of young Africans against the government and the settlers, show how the secret movement channeled and concentrated that anger, and reveal the divisions that emerged among Africans in the years 1948–1952.

In *Mau Mau and Kenya,* Wunyabari Maloba points out a danger, when scholars emphasize the socioeconomic context of Mau Mau and the complexities of the movement, that they may lose sight of both the role of white racism and government repression in provoking young Africans and the role of African nationalism and ethnic patriotism in inspiring them to resist.[149] Anger against settler power and arrogance imbues the politically self-conscious memoirs of J. M. Kariuki, Waruhiu Itote, Karari Njama, Kahinga Wachanga, Bildad Kaggia, and Gakaara wa Wanjau; they returned the hostility of the settlers in kind, and saw the efforts of militants like themselves as defensive responses to white political ambitions. They resented the government in turn for its oppressive policies, its unresponsiveness to African complaints and expectations, and its efforts to divide African communities. In his clarion call, *The Spirit of Manhood and Perseverance for Africans,* Gakaara wa Wanjau argued that government and settlers had taught Africans to despise themselves and each other the better to divide and rule, and exhorted them to open their eyes, recognize their repression, and recapture their dignity and their land. "We should be people of dignified pride in spite of the evil lies of the white man to the effect that we are fools."[150]

We can look at political resistance from another angle, however, that of gender, using both the politically aware memoirs and the less self-conscious accounts. In his pamphlet Wanjau not only appealed to patriotism and race pride but to his reader's manhood, shaming him if he did not respond. In like vein, Waruhiu Itote recalled the words of a Muganda he met while on army duty in Uganda, "If you don't fight for Kenyatta to become your Kabaka you will be a useless lot of people. Are you Kikuyu just a collection of women?"[151] Wanjau, Itote, and Wachanga became political activists in part to resist the emasculating effects of white racism and foreign control and to assert their male identity as individuals and as a select community. For the less educated Joram Wamweya, Kiboi Muriithi, and Gucu Gikoyo, the gender appeal was more positive, for the movement had considerable attractions for young men keen for excitement, eager for an outlet for their restless energies, unburdened by family responsibilities, and hopeful of winning land for themselves with their strong right hands. Men who would have been warriors in precolonial times could identify with a movement of their contemporaries infused with a strong esprit de corps, a commitment to resist the ethnic enemy, and an urge to throw off the authority of conservative and cautious elders. Moreover, as Wamweya makes clear, initiates of Mau Mau were more likely to succeed with young women. Politically self-conscious memoirists like Kariuki and Kaggia credit the less educated and uneducated with devotion to the cause, but do not note that this commitment may have owed as much to the élan of youth with little to lose as to the anger and desperate courage of the downtrodden. For both the politically aware and the politically ignorant, the unity oath promised admission into a community of true men. The observations of Norma Kriger concerning the role of youth in the guerrilla war in Zimbabwe suggest in comparative perspective the importance of nonpolitical as well as political motivations for young males who join a liberation movement.[152]

Moreover, the memoirs show that the divisions that emerged among the Gikuyu had a generational as well as a political and geographical basis. Itote, Kaggia, and Mutonyi discuss the gulf between constitutionalist and gradualist older politicians of KCA and KAU, who disapproved of "wild talk," and young men confident that the system could be challenged and convinced that this had to happen before the settlers implemented their Kenya Plan.[153] Kaggia, an independent Christian from Murang'a, saw KCA as further limited by the conservative Christianity of some of its leaders and by its domination by men of Kiambu.[154] It must be acknowledged that Kaggia's outspoken rejection of the KCA is qualified in other memoirs by an identification of the secret movement *with* the KCA, not only by a man from Kiambu like Karigo Muchai but by Kahinga Wachanga from Nyeri.[155] The important issue, however, may not be the name one used for the movement but the political strategy one followed. The memoirs suggest that common to most of those who led the movement were comparative youth, confrontational spirit, and willingness to consider violence; this is supported by other evidence, including Mordechai Tamarkin's study of Nakuru, John Lonsdale's examination of Gikuyu political thought, and Greet Kershaw's microcosmic research on Kiambu.[156]

The memoirs raise questions about the leadership of Jomo Kenyatta in the years before the Emergency. Kaggia vividly recounts the confrontation between the Central Committee and Kenyatta over his speaking tour, though Fred Kubai has put the choice placed before Kenyatta even more bluntly. In Kubai's words, "If Kenyatta had continued to denounce Mau Mau, we would have denounced him. He would have lost his life. It was too dangerous and he knew it."[157] While it is hard to imagine what the effect of such an assassination would have been, this incident illustrates the political polarization that had developed by 1952 and how far the secret movement was willing to go. It also helps to explain the hostility of Kenyatta to Mau Mau in the 1960s.

In the immediate struggle for dominance, the younger radicals won, and the memoirists describe in some detail the role of Mau Mau in the African locations of Nairobi from 1951 until Operation Anvil all but destroyed it in the capital in April 1954. Their portrayal of a city in which Mau Mau militants carried out oathing ceremonies largely with impunity, defeated or corrupted the police, armed themselves by purchase or violence, terrorized loyalists, disciplined members, and enforced boycotts of European beer, cigarettes, and buses is powerful and supported by some academic histories based mainly on other sources.[158] The impression of Mau Mau domination of Nairobi conveyed by Kaggia, Itote, and Kabiro, however, is qualified by Wachanga, who suggests that loyalists still wielded considerable power themselves, and even more by Mathu, the most disaffected memoirist, who reports not only how he personally resented certain practices of Mau Mau and chafed under the movement's discipline but indicates in various ways that the movement did not control even its own members quite so absolutely as some suggest. Take Mathu's own case. Though he was assessed 80s. for living with a prostitute, how much of a deterrent this was is open to doubt, for he continued to live with her after paying his fine. Moreover, Mathu (a self-confessed follower of "a life of petty pleasures" before taking the first oath) continued drinking and smoking, as did other members who used his place in Ziwani to enjoy illicit bottles of European beer of an evening.[159] *The Urban Guerrilla* raises doubts about how effective Mau Mau discipline over the "passive wing" really was. Luise White also questions Mau Mau domination of Nairobi; according to oral evidence she collected among Nairobi prostitutes, the "Mau Mau gangs that terrorized the African locations were . . . unarmed, on foot, and substantially less competent than they were in their own accounts years later."[160] The prostitutes told White that they were more concerned about the police.

The issue of control is also raised by the relationship between Mau Mau and criminal gangs. The connection between a nationalist movement like Mau Mau and criminal organizations—particularly given the propensity of the colonial government to refer to Kenyan guerrillas as "gangsters"—is potentially embarrassing to the memory of the movement, which may explain why Rosberg and Nottingham and Waruhiu Itote are all but silent on the subject. The narratives of second-generation memoirists like Mathu, Kabiro, and Kaggia, however, are clear about the link between political activities and crime, as are recent historical accounts like Throup's *Economic and Social Origins of Mau Mau* (1987) and Maloba's *Mau Mau and Kenya* (1993); after all, if ineffective government policies and socioeconomic stress bred both crime and political discontent and the two linked up in opposition to British control, why not acknowledge it?

The memoirs, however, provide somewhat contradictory evidence about the Mau Mau–crime gang connection, even raising the question of who was influencing whom. Like the FLN in Algiers, Mau Mau tried to use existing criminal gangs to serve its purposes. Though Kaggia indicates that the secret movement dominated the criminals, his contention that "most crimes were political" does not really explain the relationship between underground politicians and criminal gang leaders, but does suggest (perhaps inadvertently) that the criminals' motives for "political" actions such as stealing guns might be mixed. Waruhiu Itote's claims that, though the movement offered rewards for weapons, few patriotic young men who obtained guns actually demanded payment, are directly contradicted in the accounts of Mohamed Mathu and Ngugi Kabiro.[161] Commenting on the role of the Nairobi criminals Mathu observes, "These men were employed in eliminating traitors and were very active in stealing guns, ammunition, other necessary supplies and money. They would not, however, perform these services for nothing. They always insisted on being paid for the goods they managed to acquire."[162] Moreover, the criminal ethic seems to have affected those whose motives were primarily political, for Mathu and Kabiro both made personal profits on arms, and Mathu justified his own actions not only by referring to the criminals' profit-making but also to the reputed corruption of "some of the elders of the Central Committee," who were said to be putting money from the movement's monthly dues into private bank accounts.[163]

Outside Nairobi the relationship between Mau Mau political activity and criminal activity was also problematic. Joram Wamweya calls Mau Mau the "Council of the Perpetrators of Crime," and the first action he and his two friends take after their *batuni* oath is to hold up an Asian shopkeeper in Limuru at gunpoint and steal two watches, acting entirely on their own, with no authorization from a Kiambu elders' committee.[164] Mau Mau used criminals but did not necessarily control them, and one of the appeals of joining the movement for a young hothead like Wamweya seems to have been the opportunity to be a criminal in the service of (or with the cover of) the secret movement.

The memoirs not only describe the structure of the secret movement before the Emergency but indicate through personal anecdote and observation how the structure functioned in practice. *Roots of Freedom,* unfortunately, tends to focus too exclusively on the role of Muhimu and on the development of Mau Mau in the capital, giving an impression of heavy centralization. Other memoirs balance this with descriptions of the structure below the Central Committee level. Ngugi Kabiro describes the committee structure from his Kiambu subdivision to the level of Central Province, while Karigo Muchai shows how the committees worked through his own involvement as an elected elder of his sublocation committee and then of the Kiambaa Location Committee. The memoirs portray a structure in which centripetal and centrifugal forces were balanced, in which the authority of Muhimu to give orders and exercise discipline from above was counteracted by the principle of election from below, in which the requirements of secrecy were weighed against the need for consultation, and in which decisionmaking about the use of resources was shared between Muhimu, the Group of 30, and the Central Province Committee on the one hand and the district and divisional committees on the other. When severe repression came after the Declaration of Emergency, the structure suffered damage, but its high degree of internal flexibility helped it to recover, as location and division committees began to assume some of the responsibilities of the higher bodies and new leaders emerged to replace those in custody.[165] While Kaggia's centralization model seems to correspond rather closely to Donald Barnett's elaborate hierarchical scheme in his introduction to *Mau Mau from Within,* the working of the committees in Muchai may fit better Frank Furedi's description of a structure "based on a network of informal ties than on a formal system."[166]

The memoirs also shed light on the relationship between the planning of revolt and the Declaration of Emergency. Kaggia, Itote, Wachanga, and Mutonyi all give the impression that the movement was simply not ready by October 1952: more time was needed to collect enough arms and to extend the oathing campaign. Under the circumstances, one would assume that Muhimu and the other committees would do their utmost not to provoke the government before they were fully prepared. But were the committees in effective control? Kaggia, for all his emphasis on the authority of the Central Committee, indicates in several places that the committee was under pressure by younger militants, who were "always asking when we were going to take up arms and fight for our rights."[167] The rural violence that broke out in Nyeri and in nearby European settled areas in 1952, including the assassination of Chief Waruhiu, was probably not Central Committee–directed, and may indeed have indicated a lack of central control. It is a bit surprising, however, that Kaggia (who does not even mention Waruhiu's death) and the other leaders apparently did not grasp the serious implications of the Waruhiu assassination; the government could hardly ignore the enormous symbolic importance of the brazen killing of an arch-collaborator, nor turn a blind eye to the "great applause" and the "three days of beer drinking" that followed.[168]

In the interval between Waruhiu's killing and the Declaration of Emergency, even though they were warned of the planning of Operation Jock Scott, Kaggia and others seemed more concerned with settling personal affairs and hiding weapons than with their own safety. Commenting on his thinking the day before his arrest, Kaggia writes, "I was anxious to know what the government had in mind. Never did it occur to me that the government had any thought of declaring a State of Emergency. I knew our organization had been successful in keeping our secrets, that there was nothing the government could prove which could justify such a step."[169] This explanation is unconvincing. For the leader of an underground that he himself calls "revolutionary" to rely on the authorities' concern for the letter of the law suggests either dangerous naiveté or a respect for constitutionalism surprising in an aspiring insurrectionist, pointing to the possibility that Kaggia was really more moderate than those who would follow him. The success of the government's preemptive strike would weaken the movement during the next months, as the accounts of Mathu and Muchai emphasize, and Kaggia and Kubai bear part of the responsibility.

Turning to Mau Mau oathing, the memoirs are invaluable sources of information—in fact the sources most used by historians. A passage in Kariuki describing a coded message and response between oathed members unknown to each other is particularly revealing of the bond created by the oath. In response to one's question "Where were you circumcised?" the other would reply, "I was circumcised at Karimania's with Karimania." Kariuki translates "Karimania" as "to turn the soil over and over."[170] The recognition phrase connected the personal "re-circumcision" of the new initiate to others who have gone through the same transforming experience and reasserts the commitment of all of them to regaining the land. Not all oath administrators considered this bond sufficient, however. Some accounts (including those of Itote, Njama, Muriithi, Kabiro, and Gikoyo) describe a political indoctrination that immediately followed the first oath, which could include a history of the European conquest, of land alienation to settlers, and of Gikuyu political organizations as well as an explanation of the goals of the secret movement. As their oath administrator explained to Ngugi Kabiro and his comrades, "The land stolen from our people by the Europeans must be returned; and this could only be achieved through an irresistible unity of all Kikuyu, who would act as a single man with a single purpose."[171] In addition to showing the role of tradition, the memoirists' descriptions of the full ceremonies also point toward the innovative charac-

ter of the oaths as tools of a mass movement. Moreover, the group solidarity of initiates and the ostracism of the unoathed described in the memoirs
also show how the oath was used in the drive for larger Gikuyu unity.
Finally, the later memoirs, particularly those of Wamweya, Muriithi, and
Kabiro, indicate the role of intimidation and force in the oathing campaign.

As well as it worked internally, the unity oath had the effect of separating the Gikuyu and their relatives from other African peoples who did not
share the same ethnic symbolism and whose anger against the British did
not necessarily include so strong an element of land grievance. Some Mau
Mau leaders were well aware of the problem and did work with activists
from other ethnic groups (notably the Kamba) to develop other oaths, but
their efforts had limited success. The unity oath was a powerful instrument
for incorporating people into the movement, for building Gikuyu resistance
to British colonial rule, and for isolating Gikuyu loyalists; but its administrators—through intimidation of reluctant joiners, through hostility to all
who remained outside the circle of the initiated, and through the use of
potent but ethnically restricted cultural symbolism—also created a large
and potentially ill disciplined Gikuyu movement subject to defections and
informing and imposed an important limitation on large-scale support from
outside Central Kenya. Yet could this have been helped, given the limited
time Mau Mau activists had before a widespread government crackdown?
J. M. Kariuki, who rejects the idea that the oath separated the Gikuyu from
other Kenyans, is probably right in his judgment that the unity, obedience,
and faith the oath instilled in so many men and women was essential to
make possible any kind of effective fight against the resources and power
of the British government.[172]

While the unity oath has not been heavily criticized for the details of
its ritual, either by Europeans or Africans, the other oaths have been, and
the memoirists are quite aware of this. They describe the *batuni* willingly
and defend its most controversial pledge, the promise to kill on demand, as
necessary for the military success of the movement, but most are less forthcoming about "advanced oaths." Kariuki and Mutonyi both deny the existence of such oaths and suggest that they were a European invention, but
neither spent time in the forest.[173] On the other hand, Waruhiu Itote makes
it clear that there were oaths taken after the *batuni,* though he is apparently
unwilling to reveal anything of the ritual details of the leadership oath,
describing it as "a highly secret ritual known only to commanders."[174] If
other memoirists can be viewed as apologists, Mohamed Mathu can be seen
as a disillusioned initiate with second thoughts about using oathing at all.
Unlike Kariuki, Njama, Muriithi, and Wamweya, he did not find oath-taking itself an uplifting experience; instead, he resented "having been
tricked" to take the unity oath and found "certain aspects of the oathing
ceremony ugly."[175] Later he was very upset by being tricked into taking an
advanced oath by members of his fighting unit, who first tested him by

accusing him of betrayal and attacking him with a knife, only relenting and allowing him to take the oath after he repeatedly asserted his innocence.[176] More serious is Mathu's secondhand description of another ritual, which involves the killing of a Kipsigis watchman by a small group of *itungati,* the taking of his heart and liver and a gourd of his blood, and oath-taking with these materials.[177] His account undermines Kariuki's assertion that oaths with human blood and flesh were practiced only by "perverted individuals driven crazy by their isolation in the forest."[178]

But if they were not necessarily rare, were such oaths typical? While General China's unwillingness to fully describe the leadership oath ritual is understandable, it makes his defensive remarks about European distortions of the details of oath rituals less credible than they might be otherwise. On the other hand, neither Mathu's *The Urban Guerrilla* nor any other memoir indicates that oaths using blood or body parts were frequent or involved large numbers of fighters. Itote quotes a speech by Dedan Kimathi in January 1954, countering a loyalist attack on Mau Mau, in which Kimathi specifically denies the use of human blood and flesh. "Not even a child can agree to drink human blood or eat human meat; you know that the blood used in our ceremonies comes from animals. We have our order that blood-stained clothes cannot be worn; if we cannot even dare to wear clothes touched by blood, how can human blood be swallowed?"[179] The elaborate cleansing ceremonies *itungati* went through after killing an enemy, reported by Waruhiu Itote and others, also suggest a fear of *thahu* inconsistent with a regular use of human blood in ritual.[180] Rebutting the Corfield Report, Kariuki objects that the "evidence" the report draws on about the excesses of advanced oaths was based on confessions extracted under duress or torture and is therefore not reliable and would not be accepted by "any court of law."[181]

Is advanced oathing important or even relevant to the better understanding of Mau Mau? Frank Furedi has dismissed the issue as a red herring, suggesting that, as far as he is concerned, Rosberg and Nottingham's failure to consider the advanced oaths was completely appropriate. "The peasants and workers who fought and died did so not for the sake of culture but to cement a unity of purpose."[182] For other scholars, oathing remains a significant issue, though discussing the "advanced oaths" is still a delicate matter because of the heavy use of oathing confessions by the colonial government in constructing the "myth of Mau Mau." In a lengthy discussion in *Essays on Mau Mau,* Rob Buijtenhuijs considers the possibility that the advanced oaths were European propaganda inventions, dismisses it by arguing that only very well informed Europeans (of whom there were few) would be able to invent oath stories so imbued with a knowledge of "Kikuyu psychology and culture," and concludes that such oaths were real but exceptional and connected not to the oath takers' commitment to Mau Mau but "to their commitment to their way of life in the forest."[183]

Wunyabari Maloba concurs that advanced oaths were probably taken by only a small minority of forest fighters after "the tide started to turn against Mau Mau in 1954" and the survivors became "desperate beings operating in a particularly hostile and trying environment."[184] Greet Kershaw does not look at forest oathing, but her evidence from Kiambu both indicates the existence of advanced oathing with taboo substances by a few people and strong community disapproval of such oaths in most cases.[185] The consensus of both memoirists and scholars seems to be that such advanced oaths involving human blood and flesh, shocking to both European and Gikuyu sensibilities and values, were taken by some Mau Mau but were not a common practice in the forest or anywhere else. We are left with the *muma wa uigano* and the *muma wa batuni* as the quintessential Mau Mau oaths for those who took up arms, and the memoirists make it clear that the details of the rituals were less important than the intense commitment the oaths instilled, a commitment that would sustain them through years of forest fighting and detention.

Notes

1. Wachanga, *Swords,* pp. xxxi–xxxii.
2. Gikoyo, *We Fought for Freedom,* p. 39.
3. Ali A. Mazrui, "Mau Mau: The Men, the Myth and the Moment," preface to Buijtenhuijs, *Mau Mau Twenty Years After,* p. 9.
4. Buijtenhuijs, *Mau Mau Twenty Years After,* pp. 45–49; Ogot, "Revolt of the Elders," p. 147; Ochieng', "Autobiography," p. 91; Maughan-Brown, *Land, Freedom, and Fiction,* p. 56.
5. Frank Furedi, "The African Crowd in Nairobi: Popular Movements and Elite Politics," *Journal of African History,* vol. 14, no. 2 (1973), pp. 275–90; Spencer, *The Kenya African Union;* (1985); Throup, *Economic and Social Origins;* Clayton, *Counterinsurgency;* Santilli, "Kikuyu Women;" Buijtenhuijs, *Essays;* White, "Separating the Men from the Boys"; Edgerton, *Mau Mau;* Lonsdale, "Wealth, Poverty, and Civic Virtue"; Maloba, *Mau Mau and Kenya.*
6. Spencer, *James Beauttah,* p. 56.
7. Muchai, *Hardcore,* p. 14.
8. John Lonsdale, "East Africa: Towards the New Order 1945–1963," in *Eclipse of Empire* (Cambridge: Cambridge University Press, 1991), ed. D. A. Low, pp. 173–76.
9. Throup, *Economic and Social Origins,* p. 183.
10. Gicaru, *Land of Sunshine,* p. 133.
11. Maloba, *Mau Mau and Kenya,* pp. 37–39; Luise White, *The Comforts of Home: Prostitution in Colonial Nairobi* (Chicago: University of Chicago Press, 1990), 187–88.
12. Gicaru, *Land of Sunshine,* p. 145.
13. Ibid., p. 144.
14. Kabiro, *Man in the Middle,* pp. 21–22.
15. Gatheru, *Child of Two Worlds,* pp. 102–103.
16. Gicaru, *Land of Sunshine,* pp. 145–46.

17. Itote, *General*, p. 35.

18. Throup, *Economic and Social Origins*, p. 172.

19. Kaggia, *Roots*, 112; Gatheru, *Child of Two Worlds*, p. 103.

20. Maloba, *Mau Mau and Kenya*, pp. 41–43.

21. Mathu, *Urban Guerrilla*, p. 18; Kaggia, *Roots*, pp. 96–97.

22. See Gicaru, *Land of Sunshine*, Chs. 19–20; Mathu, *Urban Guerrilla*, pp. 10–17; Gatheru, *Child of Two Worlds*, Chs. 5–7; *Maloba, Mau Mau and Kenya*, Ch. 1.

23. Muoria, *I, the Gikuyu*, pp. 85–123, 177–86; Wanjau, *Mau Mau Author*, Appendix 4, p. 228.

24. Muoria, *I, the Gikuyu*, Chs. 13–14; Kaggia, *Roots*, p. 83; Wanjau, *Mau Mau Author*, p. xi; Gatheru, *Child of Two Worlds*, pp. 94–98; Fay Gadsden, "The African Press in Kenya, 1945–1952," *Journal of African History*, vol. 21 (1980), pp. 515–35.

25. Itote, *General*, p. 38; Fiona Mackenzie, "Political Economy of the Environment, Gender, and Resistance under Colonialism: Murang'a District, Kenya, 1910–1950," *Canadian Journal of African Studies*, vol. 25, no. 2 (1991), pp. 233–51.

26. Muoria, *I, the Gikuyu*, pp. 53–55.

27. Wachanga, *Swords*, pp. 1–10; Furedi, *Mau Mau War*, pp. 22–37.

28. Itote, *General*, p. 34.

29. Kabiro, *Man in the Middle*, p. 19; see also Njama, *Mau Mau from Within*, p. 80; Muriithi, *War in the Forest*, p. 9.

30. Wachanga, *Swords*, pp. xxxi–xxxiii.

31. Mathu, *Urban Guerrilla*, p. 15; Kaggia, *Roots*, p. 71.

32. Wachanga, *Swords*, p. 54.

33. See Kaggia's firsthand account of ethnic tension on the AAC, *Roots*, pp. 104–106.

34. Wachanga, *Swords*, p. xxiv.

35. Ibid., p. xxv.

36. Ibid., p. xxiii.

37. Ibid., p. xxvii; Furedi, "African Crowd," p. 282.

38. Gicaru, *Land of Sunshine*, p. 131.

39. Wachanga, *Swords*, pp. xxiii–xxviii.

40. Ibid., pp. xxvii.

41. Spencer, *Kenya African Union*, Ch. 5.

42. Kaggia, *Roots*, p. 78; see also Itote, *General*, p. 38.

43. Spencer, *Kenya African Union*, pp. 179–81.

44. Kaggia, *Roots*, pp. 79–82.

45. Rosberg and Nottingham, *Myth of "Mau Mau,"* pp. 265–66; Itote, *General*, p. 38; Spencer, *Beauttah*, pp. 98–100.

46. Itote, *General*, p. 39.

47. Kabiro, *Man in the Middle*, pp. 30–31.

48. Kaggia, *Roots*, p. 63.

49. Kabiro, *Man in the Middle*, p. 20; Muchai, *Hardcore*, p. 15; see also Kariuki, *Detainee*, pp. 1–3, 14; Njama, *Mau Mau from Within*, p. 87.

50. Spencer, *Kenya African Union*, pp. 203–205; Clough, *Fighting Two Sides*, p. 170.

51. Kaggia, *Roots*, p. 108; Spencer, *Kenya African Union*, p. 208.

52. Kaggia, *Roots*, p. 108.

53. Wachanga, *Swords*, pp. 4–6; Spencer, *Kenya African Union*, p. 209; Buijtenhuijs, *Essays on Mau Mau*, pp. 8–11; Furedi has a different view of timing,

Mau Mau War, pp. 80–83; Kaggia makes no mention of Olenguruone in discussion of oathing, *Roots,* pp. 108–115.

54. Kaggia, *Roots,* pp. 109, 194.

55. Greet Kershaw, *Mau Mau from Below* (London: James Currey, 1997), p. 231.

56. Donald L. Barnett, "Introduction," to Barnett and Njama, *Mau Mau from Within,* pp. 63–65; Kabiro, *Man in the Middle,* p. 29; Kaggia, *Roots,* p. 109.

57. Barnett, "Introduction," *Mau Mau from Within,* p. 54.

58. Muriithi, *War in the Forest,* pp. 3–4.

59. Kariuki, *Detainee,* p. 25; Itote, *General,* p. 41.

60. Muriithi, *War in the Forest,* p. 5; Gikoyo, *We Fought for Freedom,* p. 36.

61. Njama, *Mau Mau from Within,* p. 117; Mathu, *Urban Guerrilla,* p. 10.

62. Njama, *Mau Mau from Within,* p. 117.

63. Muriithi, *War in the Forest,* p. 6; see also the attempted refusals of men during Karari Njama's oathing, *Mau Mau from Within,* p. 119, and during Ngugi Kabiro's, *Man in the Middle,* p. 25.

64. Kariuki, *Detainee,* p. 26.

65. Njama, *Mau Mau from Within,* pp. 119–20; Gikoyo, *We Fought for Freedom,* p. 34; Kabiro, *Man in the Middle,* p. 26.

66. Kariuki, *Detainee,* p. 27.

67. In addition to Kariuki, see Njama, *Mau Mau from Within,* p. 121; Muriithi, *War in the Forest,* p. 5.

68. Kariuki, *Detainee,* p. 31.

69. Buijtenhuijs, *Essays on Mau Mau,* p. 84.

70. Gikoyo, *We Fought for Freedom,* p. 34.

71. Kaggia, *Roots,* p. 91; Muriithi, *War in the Forest,* p. 2.

72. Kabiro, *Man in the Middle,* p. 27; Kaggia, *Roots,* pp. 107–108.

73. Gikoyo, *We Fought for Freedom,* p. 25.

74. Njama, *Mau Mau from Within,* pp. 115–16.

75. Wamweya, *Freedom Fighter,* p. 45; see description of such a specific incident in Kabiro, *Man in the Middle,* p. 34.

76. Wamweya, *Freedom Fighter,* p. 45.

77. Muriithi, *War in the Forest,* p. 6; Njama, *Mau Mau from Within,* p. 116; Kaggia, *Roots,* p. 111.

78. Kaggia, *Roots,* p. 112.

79. Itote, *General,* p. 283.

80. Ibid., p. 64. See also accounts of Wamutira and Watoro in Davison, *Voices from Mutira,* pp. 79, 103.

81. Wamweya, *Freedom Fighter,* p. 44.

82. John Lonsdale, "The Prayers of Waiyaki: Political Uses of the Kikuyu Past," in *Revealing Prophets: Prophecy in Eastern African History,* ed. David Anderson and Douglas Johnson (London: James Currey, 1995), p. 276.

83. Njama, *Mau Mau from Within,* p. 121.

84. Kaggia, *Roots,* p. 65.

85. Wiseman, *Kikuyu Martyrs,* pp. 12–14, 24–25, 29–30.

86. Buijtenhuijs, *Essays on Mau Mau,* pp. 126–27.

87. Wachanga, *Swords,* p. 12.

88. Wanjau, *Mau Mau Author,* p. 99.

89. Office of Attorney General, "Infiltration of Mau Mau into Tribes Other than the Agikuyu," PRO CO 822/780.

90. Kaggia, *Roots,* p. 96.

91. Ibid.

92. Ibid., pp. 96–97; see also evidence of Fred Kubai in which he refers to "a team of thieves," in Brian Lapping, *End of Empire* (New York: St. Martin's, 1985), p. 410.
93. Lapping, *End of Empire*, p. 410.
94. Kaggia, *Roots*, p. 109.
95. Itote, *General*, p. 44.
96. Kaggia, *Roots*, p. 112.
97. Ibid., p. 112.
98. Kabiro, *Man in the Middle*, pp. 35–36.
99. Kaggia, *Roots*, p. 110.
100. Itote, *Mau Mau in Action*, p. 9.
101. Itote, *General*, p. 86.
102. Ibid., Ch. 16.
103. Wachanga, *Swords*, pp. xxxvii–xxxviii.
104. Njama, *Mau Mau from Within*, p. 127.
105. Clough, *Fighting Two Sides*, p. 145.
106. Wachanga, *Swords*, p. 13; Njama, *Mau Mau from Within*, p. 78.
107. Lapping, *End of Empire*, p. 409.
108. Kaggia, *Roots*, p. 113.
109. Ibid.
110. Ibid., pp. 113–14; Kabiro, *Man in the Middle*, p. 37.
111. Kaggia, *Roots*, p. 114.
112. Mathu, *Urban Guerrilla*, p. 16.
113. Karari Njama, *Mau Mau from Within*, pp. 133–34.
114. Kaggia, *Roots*, p. 83.
115. Wachanga, *Swords*, pp. 24–25.; Mutonyi, *Chairman*, p. 143.
116. Kariuki, *Detainee*, p. 16.
117. Mathu, *Urban Guerrilla*, p. 17; Muchai, *Hardcore*, p. 16.
118. Kaggia, *Roots*, p. 116.
119. Mathu, *Urban Guerrilla*, p. 17.
120. Muchai, *Hardcore*, p. 17.
121. Kabiro, *Man in the Middle*, p. 40; Mathu, *Urban Guerrilla*, p. 17.
122. Kershaw, *Mau Mau from Below*, p. 248.
123. Wamweya, *Freedom Fighter*, p. 47; Wachanga, *Swords*, p. 17.
124. Njama, *Mau Mau from Within*, pp. 129–30.
125. Ibid., p. 136.
126. Njama, *Mau Mau from Within*, p. 130.
127. Fowkes to Blundell, Oct. 1, 1952, RH Blundell Papers, Mss. Afr. s. 746, Box 12/1.
128. General Erskine, "The Kenya Emergency," April 25, 1955, PRO WO 236/18.
129. Wachanga, *Swords*, p. 34; Itote, *General*, p. 274.
130. Wamweya, *Freedom Fighter*, pp. 52–53; Muchai, *Hardcore*, p. 19.
131. Mathu, *Urban Guerrilla*, p. 42.
132. Njama, *Mau Mau from Within*, p. 133.
133. Muchai, *Hardcore*, p. 19. See also descriptions in Njama, *Mau Mau from Within*, pp. 130–32; Itote, *General*, pp. 274–79; Wamweya, *Freedom Fighter*, pp. 51–53; Wachanga, *Swords*, pp. 35–36.
134. Muchai, *Hardcore*, p. 21.
135. Wachanga, *Swords*, p. 48.
136. Ibid., p. 49; Itote, *General*, p. 41.
137. Kanogo, *Squatters*, p. 148.

138. Wachanga, *Swords*, pp. 49–50.

139. Mathu, *Urban Guerrilla*, pp. 28–29.

140. Njama, *Mau Mau from Within*, p. 115; African Affairs Department, *Annual Report*, 1952 (Nairobi: Government Printer, 1954), p. 23; on smoking *bhangi* or *kibaki*, Kabiro, *Man in the Middle*, p. 61; Wamweya, *Freedom Fighter*, p. 131.

141. Kabiro, *Man in the Middle*, pp. 60–61.

142. Mathu, *Urban Guerrilla*, pp. 13–14.

143. Ibid., p. 15; Waruhiu Itote, *Mau Mau in Action* (Nairobi: Transafrica, 1979), p. 83.

144. Kabiro, *Man in the Middle*, pp. 41–42.

145. Wamweya, *Freedom Fighter*, pp. 54, 59–61.

146. Muchai, *Hardcore*, pp. 15–17.

147. Ibid., pp. 17–18.

148. Ibid., pp. 21–27.

149. Maloba, *Mau Mau and Kenya*, p. 14.

150. Wanjau, *Mau Mau Author*, p. 228.

151. Itote, *General*, p. 29.

152. Norma Kriger, *Zimbabwe's Guerrilla War: Peasant Voices* (Cambridge: Cambridge University Press, 1992), p. 168.

153. Itote, *General*, p. 39.

154. Kaggia, *Roots*, p. 194.

155. Muchai, *Hardcore*, p. 15; Wachanga, *Swords*, p. 19.

156. Mordechai Tamarkin, "Mau Mau in Nakuru, " *Journal of African History*, vol. xvii, no. 1 (1976), pp. 119–34; Lonsdale, "Wealth, Poverty, and Civic Virtue"; Kershaw, *Mau Mau from Below*.

157. Quoted in Lapping, *End of Empire*, p. 411.

158. Frank Furedi, "The African Crowd in Nairobi: Popular Movements and Elite Politics," *Journal of African History*, vol. xiv, no. 2 (1973), pp. 275–89; Maloba, *Mau Mau and Kenya*, Chs. 1–3.

159. Mathu, *Urban Guerrilla*, pp. 15, 11.

160. White, *Comforts of Home*, p. 208.

161. Itote, *General*, pp. 43–44.

162. Mathu, *Urban Guerrilla*, p. 18.

163. Ibid., p. 18; on Kabiro's profits, *Man in the Middle*, pp. 41–42.

164. Wamweya, *Freedom Fighter*, pp. 54, 59–61.

165. Muchai, *Hardcore*, p. 17.

166. Barnett, "Introduction," to Njama and Barnett, *Mau Mau from Within*, pp. 61–66; Furedi, *Mau Mau War*, p. 140.

167. Kaggia, *Roots*, p. 83.

168. Njama, *Mau Mau from Within*, p. 127; Mathu, *Urban Guerrilla*, p. 15.

169. Kaggia, *Roots*, p. 117.

170. Kariuki, *Detainee*, p. 28.

171. Kabiro, *Man in the Middle*, pp. 26–27.

172. Kariuki, *Detainee*, p. 32.

173. Kariuki, *Detainee*, p. 33; Mutonyi, *Mau Mau Chairman*, 94.

174. Itote, *General*, p. 280; Wachanga, *Swords*, p. 39; Njama, *Mau Mau from Within*, p. 191.

175. Mathu, *Urban Guerrilla*, p. 12.

176. Ibid., pp. 43–45.

177. Ibid., p. 43.

178. Kariuki, *Detainee*, p. 33.

179. Itote, *General*, pp. 143–44.

180. Ibid., p. 284.
181. Kariuki, *Detainee*, p. 33.
182. Furedi, *Mau Mau War*, p. 141.
183. Buijtenhuijs, *Essays*, pp. 110, 108.
184. Maloba, *Mau Mau and Kenya*, p. 107.
185. Kershaw, *Mau Mau from Within*, pp. 316–19.

CHAPTER 5

The War

The Whiteman has converted us into his private property, uncircumcised as he is. He is a clever man and we must prove to him that we were circumcised to get rid of all fear.

We will fight the Whiteman until the last man. There will be no rest until we expel all Europeans to their countries of origin. All this will come about through God's help and the oath of unity that we took.

—*Dedan Kimathi wa Waciuri*[1]

Mutigetigire, mworagia niri (Do not fear—it is now or never).

—*Stanley Mathenge wa Mirugi*[2]

W hen Gucu Gikoyo arrived with other recruits at Mbuci ya Njogu (Elephant's Camp) in the Murang'a forests in May 1953, they were met by General Matenjagwo, who told them:

> The war we are fighting . . . is a tough war. . . . I say it to you that in this war we have neither aircraft nor tanks nor motor cars. . . . We are the aircraft and armoured cars; we are also food carriers and ambulances. But where unity exists and where nobody considers himself better than the others, victory must surely come.[3]

A guerrilla war like Mau Mau is a military conflict of the weak and the strong; the guerrillas are usually outnumbered and always outgunned by the police and professional army of the established government, and lack equipment, training, and reliable sources of supply. They try to make up for these deficiencies by relying on the support of the civilian population; by capturing arms from the enemy; by operating out of bases in remote mountains and forests; by attacking without warning in highly mobile small bands and swiftly breaking off contact. As the writings of Mao Zedong, Che Guevara, Amilcar Cabral, and others over the past sixty years or so have shown however, modern guerrilla warfare is as much about politics as about fighting.[4]

The Mau Mau memoirs are the main source for information on the war the guerrillas fought. They also show the important role politics played in the struggle, both in the frequent meetings of forest bands during which fighters discussed the meaning of the war and the new Kenya they hoped to build and in periodic contacts between guerrilla leaders and their civilian supporters. Scholarly treatments of the Mau Mau war by Buijtenhuijs, Edgerton, and Maloba have used the memoirs, but no previous study has systematically examined the guerrilla struggle through the perspective of the Mau Mau writers.[5]

The accounts of the forest war in the memoirs are hardly identical, however. This can be explained in part by diversity; General China's experiences as the leader on Kirinyaga were not the same as those of a rank-and-file guerrilla under his command like Kiboi Muriithi, and Karari Njama's war in the Nyandarua forests naturally differed from Joram Wamweya's fighting life in Kiambu and the Rift Valley. At the level of ordinary *itungati* as well, separate memoirs can portray the guerrilla experience differently. Some personal narratives can also contradict each other. Karari Njama's *Mau Mau from Within* (1966) was the first narrative of the war from the Mau Mau side, and its author's claims of inside knowledge and his detailed descriptions of forest life, bolstered by Donald Barnett's masterful scholarly introduction and comments, won the memoir immediate credibility. Njama strengthened the reputation of Dedan Kimathi, head of the "Kenya Parliament," while damaging that of Kimathi's main rival, Stanley Mathenge, and that of Mathenge's followers in the "Kenya Riigi," especially Kahinga Wachanga. When Wachanga published *The Swords of Kirinyaga* a decade later, he questioned Njama's general credibility by casting doubt on the latter's descriptions of smooth, parliamentary-style forest meetings ("Our meetings were not very organized"); charged that Njama "was not the important man he claims to be"; defended himself against Njama's attacks; questioned Kimathi's leadership while praising Mathenge; and took the side of the illiterates of the Kenya Riigi against the Kenya Parliament.[6] Wachanga's revisionist account also somewhat damaged the credibility of Waruhiu Itote's *"Mau Mau" General* by undermining the impression both Njama and Itote conveyed of Mau Mau as a straightforward nationalist movement and the guerrilla struggle as well organized and well planned. Wachanga's interpretation was strengthened by Gucu Gikoyo's *We Fought for Freedom* (1979), the narrative of an illiterate rank-and-file guerrilla who fought in the Murang'a forest and reserve under General Kago wa Mboko; like Wachanga, Gikoyo criticized Kimathi for dictatorial tendencies and contributed to the impression of a guerrilla struggle riven by disagreements and personality conflicts among its leaders.[7]

Instead of weakening the overall credibility of the memoirs, however, the differences and the contradictions actually make them more valuable to the historian of Mau Mau. More than the accounts of the period before the Declaration of Emergency, the narrative sections dealing with the war itself provide a broad geographical picture of the struggle—with scenes from the Nyeri reserve, the northern Nyandarua forests, the Meru reserve, the slopes of Kirinyaga, the Murang'a reserve, the central Nyandarua forests, the Kiambu reserve, the periurban area around Nairobi, Nairobi itself, and the Rift Valley around Naivasha and around Longonot. There are views of the war from different angles as well, for memoirists served as generals, lower officers, *itungati,* couriers, spies, weapons suppliers, and passive-wing supporters of the movement; some guerrillas fought with large units strongly commanded and others with smaller bands under shifting leadership. Moreover, the disputes between factions and between leaders provide important information on different military, political, and social strategies (such as the debate on the role of women), show the characteristic geographical decentralization of the movement, reveal the cultural split between educated and illiterate fighters, indicate the role of leadership, and show how the fortunes of war affected the internal coherence of the Mau Mau fighting forces.

Generals, Officers, and *Itungati*

In the beginning the forest-fighting leaders saw themselves as subordinate to the elders' committees and responsible ultimately to the political leaders in the camps and in exile. Waruhiu Itote makes it clear that he entered the Kirinyaga forests with his first forty men in August 1952 under the direct orders of the Nyeri Committee in Nairobi.[8] In late 1953, in a speech to the newly formed Kenya Parliament, Kahinga Wachanga "told those present that the Parliament we had just formed was only for the duration of our armed struggle. I said that a civil Kenya Parliament would be formed after *uhuru.* Mzee Kenyatta and other political leaders then in detention would lead it."[9] The guerrillas led by Itote, Wachanga, and others called themselves *itungati,* or soldiers of the rearguard under the order of elders. The "Kenya Land Freedom Army" was not an autonomous military force but a body acting on behalf of political leaders, and ready to give way to them when victory was won.

In spite of the prestige of Dedan Kimathi (enhanced by British attention during the Emergency and since independence by the writings of Maina wa Kinyatti and Ngugi wa Thiong'o), there was no single commander recognized by all other leaders. Kahinga Wachanga remarks tellingly, "We had no one leader or commander except the oath. The oath was our leader."[10] However, a number of generals did rise to prominence during the guerrilla war, and the memoirs characterize some of the most important. Dedan Kimathi wa Waciuri, born in 1920 in North Tetu, Nyeri, founder of the Kenya Defence Council and the Kenya Parliament, became one of the two most important Nyeri leaders operating in the northern Nyandarua forests. His principal rival, Stanley Mathenge wa Mirugi, was born about 1919 in Mahiga, Nyeri, fought in Burma, became a leading member of 40 Group, an enforcer for KAU, and a leader of the strong men of the secret movement in Nairobi; from his bases in northern Nyandarua, he both planned strategy and led attacks, and was a founder of Kenya Riigi, an organization of illiterate fighters, which opposed Kimathi's Kenya Parliament. The career of Waruhiu wa Itote, or General China, who led the guerrilla forces on Kirinyaga, has already been described. Mbaria wa Kaniu, born in 1920 in Njumbi, Murang'a, led the successful Naivasha raid in March 1953, and later led bands in Murang'a and in the Kinangop area of the Rift Valley. Kago wa Mboko, born in Ruathia in Murang'a about 1920, was the leading guerrilla general in Murang'a until his death in battle in 1954; his offensive strategy in the reserve itself, in defiance of Kimathi, won the devoted loyalty of followers like Gucu Gikoyo and the respect of the British.[11]

The relationship between the leaders and the rank and file varied from area to area and band to band. The Land and Freedom Army was an irregular force, which drew on both half-remembered traditions of Gikuyu precolonial warfare and on British conventions that some fighters had learned during service in World War II. Gikuyu traditions encouraged individualism in combat and making one's mark by personal achievement, while the British regular army emphasized the importance of impersonal hierarchy and discipline; what emerged in the forests, by trial and error, was a creative blend of both.

Traditional Gikuyu warriors fought alongside their age-mates and neighbors under the command of one of their own, and Mau Mau leaders tended also to recruit their *itungati* from their own locations or divisions. As Kahinga Wachanga explains, "About three months after the Declaration of Emergency, many people entered the forest. At that time, Mathenge, Kimathi, I and others had done our best to call all the young people to the forest to join us. We made special appeals to Uthaya, Tetu and Mukurweini Divisions, for these were our home divisions. Our people heard us and began coming into the forest."[12] In the beginning there were only leaders and *itungati,* for ranks had not yet been developed. Some leaders assumed *noms de guerre,* ranging from Gikuyu nicknames like "Matenjagwo" (matted hair) to names with international revolutionary cachet like "China." Wachanga reports that top leaders began to assume ranks in June 1953, and then, presumably, distributed them among subordinates within their own bands; however, Mathenge refused rank, saying that only Kenyatta and the other detained leaders had the right to confer them.[13] Based on British army conventions, ranks ranged from field marshal and general down to lieutenant and the noncommissioned ranks of sergeant and corporal.

A camp, or *mbuci,* was commanded by an officer, usually a general. The camp leader maintained his position by a combination of kin and locality ties to his followers, personal authority (based on such qualities as skill in public speaking, bravery, and military bearing), swift discipline, and responsiveness to *itungati* needs and demands, much as a warrior *muthamaki* (big man) might have done in precolonial days. Kimathi, no field general, was a fine speaker with a good sense of humor and an ability to use his speeches to educate his audiences of leaders and *itungati,* especially by explaining "about the other nations' politics and revolutions."[14] By contrast, Mathenge was respected for his bravery, his skill with the .303 rifle, and his willingness to share the lot of the common soldier.[15] Kiboi Muriithi and other *itungati* admired Waruhiu Itote for his military efficiency. "Bushi Number Thirteen was a military camp—and General China saw to it that it was run like one."[16] *Itungati* respected generals like Tanganyika for their firmness in enforcing discipline; Muriithi describes how Tanganyika had two traitors who had revealed the location of the *mbuci* tracked down, condemned them himself, and executed them personally with shots to the head.[17] Mbaria wa Kaniu, on the other hand, was admired for refusing to place himself above the ordinary *gitungati,* for his commitment to justice, and for his skill as a mediator of disputes.[18] Kago was the epitome of the warrior leader, whose delight in trickery enabled his men to get close to the enemy, and whose reckless but contagious bravery inspired his *itungati* to risk their lives when battles were joined.[19]

The leaders of the fighting bands differentiated themselves from the *itungati* in various ways. Looking around at the hundreds of Mau Mau fighters assembled for prayers in Kariaini Camp on an evening in 1953, Karari Njama observed, "The leaders could quickly be recognized. They all tied turbans around their heads, looked more clean and healthy than the rest, wore shoes or boots, possessed either a wrist or pocket watch and carried a hidden pistol and a walking stick."[20] Most leaders wore parts of British uniforms—military overcoats, battle-dress blouses, officers' caps, or berets. In the field officers carried firearms, pistols, or sometimes automatic weapons such as sten guns. In camp officers lived in their own quarters, generally a more strongly built bamboo hut with a tight roof, and messed together, sometimes on better food than the rations of the ordinary guerrillas, though Mathenge ate with his *itungati.* Officers presided at the frequent meetings, made the speeches, and dominated most debates and most decisionmaking. As Wachanga puts it, "Decisions were made by our big leaders and set before the *itungati.* The *itungati* did not question decisions made by the accepted leaders even though they were not consulted. They followed our orders."[21] As Njama points out, however, a military leader often shared some of his decision-making power regarding military actions with the camp religious leader, its *mundu mugo,* or in some cases with a seer or prophet, a *murathi.*[22]

Most generals strongly emphasized discipline, to maintain control and promote combat readiness and for spiritual reasons. As Kahinga Wachanga points out, "There were bad men as well as good men among us. In order to avoid offending the evil spirits the conduct of these bad men had to be controlled."[23] While Wachanga includes in his memoir the "Freedom Fighter's regulations," a list of offenses and punishments that he maintains were adopted by all leaders in 1953, and Kiboi Muriithi mentions General Tanganyika consulting "our law-book," other memoirs suggest a considerable variation in the practice of discipline at the local level.[24] General Matenjagwo in the Murang'a forests established a list of offenses ranging from making excessive noise at night to desertion, the less serious punishable by the offender holding an iron bar in the air for twenty minutes at a time and the most serious (treasonable desertion) punishable by death.[25] Though some generals maintained personal discipline, camp rules could be enforced through courts; *Mau Mau from Within* contains cases of the *mbuci* court, transcribed by Karari Njama in his capacity as recorder, suggesting a real concern for procedure and fair dealing.[26] The memoirs suggest that the authority of most leaders was generally accepted and discipline well maintained, at least in 1953 and 1954.

On the other hand, the memoirs also include incidents during which *itungati* asserted themselves in defiance of their leaders. In *We Fought for Freedom,* Gucu Gikoyo describes a dramatic example, probably dating from late 1953, at General Matenjagwo's *mbuci* in Murang'a. When a captain and two sergeants questioned the food which Macaria wa Kimemia, later a top leader under Kimathi but then quartermaster of the camp, was supplying the patients in the clinic, Macaria wa Kimemia brought his accusers themselves up on insubordination charges before the general and a panel of officers. During the long hearing, officers and noncommissioned officers collected all firearms in the camp. When the accused were found guilty, some of the lower-ranking officers, NCOs, and common soldiers (including Gikoyo) responded by rising in mutiny, because "we the fighters felt that justice had not been done." Rebels took back their weapons by force, tied up some of the loyal officers, then attempted to assassinate Macaria Kimemia. At a parley called by Matenjagwo and Mbaria Kaniu, the rebels explained themselves; since they had all come voluntarily into the forest motivated by the desire for unity and could not allow anyone to break that unity by violating Mau Mau law for his own purposes, they would not only refuse to take orders from Macaria Kimemia but insist that he be executed or driven out of camp. Finally, Macaria Kimemia broke the deadlock by taking twenty followers away to form his own *mbuci*. This incident seems to contradict Wachanga, suggesting that *itungati* were willing under certain circumstances to defy even popular leaders like Matenjagwo and Mbaria Kaniu to obtain justice, challenging the discipline

they had sworn under oath to accept in their defense of principles of frater-
nity and equality.[27]

Other memoirs indicate that *itungati* not only expected to be consulted
but exercised a certain degree of choice over their military assignments or
even over which leader they would follow. Kiboi Muriithi, who fought in
the Kirinyaga forests under General Tanganyika, when describing the division of the fighters in camp one day for routine noncombat tasks outside
the *mbuci,* comments that "Groups were usually formed by choice; nobody
was forced into any group against his will, unless everyone favored a certain group. The General's decision was then final."[28] Joram Wamweya, who
fought with generals Waruingi, Nubi, and Makimei in the Rift Valley next
to Kiambu, describes how in late 1954 the leaders responded to rising discontent in the ranks over harsh discipline and limited promotions by holding a general meeting during which they allowed all *itungati* to speak their
grievances, followed by a second meeting during which they distributed
new ranks and honors. After the second meeting, the leaders announced
that the group would have to break up due to enemy pressure and the
demands of foraging for food, and "We each chose our leader and lined up
behind him accordingly."[29]

The Gikuyu men and women who joined the guerrilla bands tended to
come from Nyeri, Murang'a, or the Rift Valley (approximately in that
order); on Kirinyaga a number of Embu and Meru fighters also joined
General China's forces, making up perhaps one-third of the total of more
than 5,000.[30] Thus the geography of militant politics in Central Kenya
shifted north and west, away from Kiambu. For the most part the recruits
were young, illiterate, poor, and either owners of small farms or landless.
Their motivations were diverse. As Sam Thebere points out, young men
often joined Mau Mau to fight for land and thus earn the adulthood they
could only achieve with access to land, strong motivations for the poor.[31]
The commitment instilled by taking the oath was also an important motivating factor. As Joram Wamweya commented after taking his *batuni,*
"From the day I was initiated into the oath, I decided to give myself up to
the service of the oath."[32] Gucu Gikoyo, an enforcer for Mau Mau in
Ithanga, Murang'a, was motivated by a combination of youthful male
enthusiasm and group solidarity.[33] Others like Kiboi Muriithi, an oath
administrator and local movement secretary in Marua, Nyeri, joined the
guerrillas when they faced certain arrest and detention; in June 1953,
betrayed after an oathing ceremony and with a home guard detachment hot
on his heels, Muriithi escaped into the Kirinyaga forests.[34] Sometimes,
whole groups of Gikuyu faced the same desperate alternatives; in 1953 a
number of relocated squatters from the Rift Valley—often unemployed,
landless, and without prospects—entered the forests out of desperation and
to escape the oppressions of the chiefs and the security forces. Other Mau

Mau found themselves drawn into active combat after service with the passive wing. Karigo Muchai, after months acting as a go-between connecting the Kiambu District Committee and Mau Mau bands, was ambushed while with a supply force between Limuru and Narok in August 1953, took command and became an active fighter.[35] Characteristically, Karari Njama's motivations were the most complex of all (and he is one of the few memoirists who self-consciously recalls his reflections before entering the forest): desire to recover his family's lands, anger against settler racism and injustice, nationalist commitment, the hope of fame, male self-assertion, fear of Mau Mau retaliation if he continued to "serve two masters" by teaching under the Beecher Report, and a desire "to witness events rather than to hear them."[36]

Like most guerrilla armies in the early stages, the men and women who gathered in the large camps in Nyandarua and Kirinyaga in the spring and summer of 1953 did not seem a formidable military force. In *Mau Mau from Within,* Karari Njama describes the *itungati* at Kariaini headquarters camp in June 1953:

> Many of them dressed in the ordinary clothing while about 800 of them wore different Government uniforms which must have been acquired mainly from the dead security forces. Some had woven [or braided] their hair like women while others had wool braided in with the hair to imitate the Masai. . . . I could guess their ages; most of them were between 25 and 30 years old. There were a few old ones, well over 60 years.[37]

Kariaini at that time had a population of 2,476 men and 124 women, armed with 450 European weapons and 650 homemade guns, leaving the rest of the fighters armed only with *simis* (traditional swords) or *pangas* (machetes).[38] Few of these *itungati* had any military experience, and those who did were quickly promoted to noncommissioned or officer rank. Their enemies the British enjoyed an enormous technological advantage over this poorly armed, inexperienced, untrained guerrilla force. On their side the Mau Mau had little more than commitment, youthful enthusiasm, and faith; as Njama comments, "the ignorance of the illiterate peasants of the enemy's power was our warriors' strength and courage."[39] Yet in 1953 even he, for all his Western education, could believe that victory was certain because Gikuyu prophecies had said so.

> Moved by emotion and will, I quickly believed that the time had come for all prophesies to be fulfilled. . . . The prophesy of the Kikuyu's honored witchdoctor, Chege Kabiro, who foretold the coming of the whitemen, the building of the railways and the going of the whitemen out of this country. I remembered the star that brilliantly shown [sic] in 1946 . . . which was claimed by witchdoctors that it indicated their departure and showed the whitemen the way home.[40]

Life in the Forest, 1953–1954

By the spring of 1953, several dozen Mau Mau camps dotted the forest fringes and the deep forest of Kirinyaga and Nyandarua, with a special concentration in the northern reaches of Nyandarua next to Nyeri District. Campsites were chosen with an eye to practicality, comfort, access to fresh water (sometimes delivered to camp by pipe systems of split bamboo), and safety from attack. In both the Kirinyaga and Nyandarua forests, camps were usually situated in the bamboo belt, far enough from the Kikuyu farms or the settler estates to be reasonably secure from easy attack but close enough so that foraging parties could obtain and bring back food without having to travel too far. On Kirinyaga, General China favored sites in natural clearings, providing plenty of room "for drill and exercise," with large trees overhanging for shelter from storms and groves of bamboos nearby with which to build huts and water systems.[41] The site for Kariaini Headquarters in the northern Nyandarua forests was chosen with attention to the natural defenses of cliffs and groves of bamboo.[42] Of course, no site was entirely safe, and *itungati* had to be ready to abandon a *mbuci* at a moment's notice, as Muriithi's *War in the Forest,* full of accounts of sudden evacuations under attack, graphically portrays.

Scholarly descriptions of life in the camps have drawn heavily from the long and highly detailed early memoirs of Karari Njama and Waruhiu Itote. However, Robert Whittier's challenge to *Mau Mau from Within* has raised questions about the general picture Njama conveys. "Indeed, it seems as if Njama relates events as he thinks they should have happened, rather than as they did happen. Things are just too tidy to have occurred in the chaotic forest setting."[43] David Maughan-Brown's charge that Njama's account "would seem to be informed by a leadership ideology which is distinctly elitist and owes a good deal to the examples of British practice, military and civil" is somewhat different but raises similar questions about the credibility of the memoir.[44] In addition, Rob Buijtenhuijs has questioned the factuality of General China's account of the forest war.[45] The charges need to be considered. There is no question that both Njama and Itote portray camps run in British-style military fashion and describe leaders' meetings that resemble orderly political debates, and this may distort reality to a certain extent. However, leaders like China, Mathenge, and Kimathi did wish to assert military order and discipline at the beginning of the war, and the British example was the readiest to hand. Moreover, descriptions of Kimathi in particular suggest a personality for whom control and order were very important, and his personal ambitions and hopes for the movement depended on building a well-coordinated and organized military and political structure. Njama's and Itote's accounts of meetings are probably lacking in messy detail because they focus more on the differences of opinion and the results of discussions rather than on the circumstances in which the discussions took place; Wachanga himself comments on the frequency and importance of "meetings, debates, and lectures" in the forest, though he does not describe them in detail.[46] The picture of forest life in 1953–1954 in Njama and Itote is broadly similar to the portrayals of Gikoyo, Muriithi, and Wachanga himself. It is important to mention, however, that the large camps and orderly procedures of the early months of fighting were disrupted by the fierce attacks of the counterinsurgency beginning in the summer of 1953 (well described by Njama for Nyandarua and Muriithi for Kirinyaga); organization began to break down, and the early optimism so well evoked by Njama and Itote began to dissipate.

By early 1953 the guerrilla camps in the northern Nyandarua forests had burgeoned into substantial settlements of 300 to 400 people, in the case or an ordinary *mbuci* like Kigumo, or several thousand, in the case of headquarters camps like Kariaini. Here is Karari Njama's description of Kigumo, a *mbuci* of thirty rain shelters, each measuring twelve feet across by nine feet deep.

> Each shelter had four poles; the first pair six feet high while the hind pair was five feet high. . . . The roof, built of bamboo splits and made to overlap a pair of joints, looked like a tiled roof from the inside. The outer side of the roof was covered by bamboo bulks which provided a satisfactory rain proof. The walls were uncovered. The ground had been slightly leveled and bamboo leaves spread on the ground made a mattress. In the middle of the camp were two big kitchens measuring about twice the side of a hut. Two girls, a woman and three men were busy boiling some meat in two tins and a big saucepan; all the time taking much care that no smoke could be seen by an airplane. Thin dry bamboo splits were used to keep the fire burning without smoke. There were two leaders' houses seven by seven feet; the only ones which had walls to protect [against] wind and cold. . . .[47]

The larger camps had leaders' huts, soldiers' huts, a kitchen hut, a meeting hall, a clinic hut for the wounded and sick, and sometimes an armory. The camps were kept clean by the collection of rubbish and animal matter and by the requirement that all inhabitants leaving the camp proper for "short calls" carry *pangas* to dig holes to bury their waste.[48]

The guerrilla diet depended on what was available, and on one's rank. Some bands tried to raise crops, but the shifting geography of combat made this difficult, so most food was supplied by local African communities, raided from nearby settlers' farms and ranches, or gathered from the forest. Maize, potatoes, beans, yams, sugar cane, oranges, and bananas from African *shambas,* settler beef and mutton, and honey, wild vegetables, and wild herbs gathered in the forest were typical foods in the guerrilla diet.[49] Ordinary *itungati* did not eat as well as generals and officers, and some guerrillas complained that "the leaders had three meals a day while the *itungati* who risked their lives in order to get that food had only one insufficient meal."[50] On the other hand, some bands ate a lot of meat because the generals considered it appropriate warriors' food. Muriithi describes a typical safari ration on Kirinyaga called *wenye,* made from mutton, lamb's blood, and honey, ideal to sustain the stamina of *itungati* on long marches.[51] The guerrillas on Kirinyaga trapped game but northern Nyandarua bands did not, believing that wild animals (with the exceptions of the aggressive rhino and buffalo, nicknamed "home guards") were allies, warning them of the approach of enemies.[52] Providing a steady supply of food for the *mbuci* was a constant challenge. As Kiboi Muriithi remembers, "Provisions were an unending problem, with so many to feed. When the stores were half-empty parties were sent out to bring back what they could."[53] Many bands faced an alternation of plenty and dearth, feasting when foragers or suppliers arrived at the *mbuci* with sacks full of cobs of maize or beef on the hoof, and facing hunger when the supplies ran low. Foraging was necessary but dangerous. Karari Njama remarks that in "most cases our warriors met death while looking for food rather than in battlefields," and Muriithi's memoir describes various occasions when security forces attacked the foragers on the way home or even tracked them back to the *mbuci* itself.[54] The actions that kept the guerrilla band alive also placed their continued existence in peril.

In addition to foraging and food transport, men and women performed various forest tasks. Well-armed guerrillas were posted along the approaches to the *mbuci,* under orders to give the alarm and fight a delaying action if necessary to slow down a determined attack; newcomers passed the guards only if they knew the password, which was changed regularly.[55] Male and female scouts patrolled the forests away from the camp and went into the reserve, sometimes in disguise, to sound out the local community and spy on the security forces. Other guerrillas acted as bodyguards for the leaders and "military police" to enforce discipline and to eliminate traitors. Others took care of the food supply and its preparation; since food was often short, the choosing of a quartermaster and his helpers could be contentious. Larger bands tried to maintain a clinic of some kind to treat the sick and wounded, stocked if possible with dressings and medicines taken by supporters from European hospitals and under the supervision of a man or woman with some nursing experience. When Kiboi Muriithi was wounded in the hip during a skirmish on Kirinyaga in 1953, a movement "doctor" with a Grade Two nurse's qualification operated without anesthetic, removed the bullet, stitched Muriithi up, and nursed him back to active duty.[56] The guerrillas also used Gikuyu medicine and traditional healers to treat wounds, fractures, and sickness, with mixed results.[57] In some camps, teams of specially trained *itungati* worked in the armory, manufacturing homemade weapons. Educated people like Njama, Muriithi, and Wamaitha (China's female secretary) were assigned the tasks of writing letters, taking minutes of meetings and court sessions, and keeping a record of the band. Njama even tells of instructing "sixty-three clerks" (obviously from various camps) at the Mwathe meeting in August 1953, in the best ways to keep unit records, an indication of Kimathi's rather pedantic concern with detail.[58]

In the early days, the large camps had an established routine—a routine in which mass religious services and camp assemblies with political speeches and group singing had a role alongside military activities. At sunrise the whole *mbuci* would assemble to pray to Ngai on Kirinyaga. After a simple breakfast of gruel or soup came roll call and the assignment of *itungati* to their duties for the day. In General China's *mbuci* on Kirinyaga, the ex–sergeant major made sure that the rest of the morning was spent in martial training, "marching, laying ambushes, rifle drill, shooting, taking evasive action from a straffing [sic] aircraft, making the best use of cover when under fire."[59] Meanwhile the noncombatants policed the camp, prepared food, and tended the sick and wounded. In General Matenjagwo's *mbuci* in the Murang'a forests in 1953, the early afternoon was devoted to weapons training, cleaning weapons, and gathering firewood for the evening meal, and the late afternoon to a two-hour meeting during which the general spoke of the political meaning of the war and gave specific instructions on strategy and tactics.[60] Then all camps observed evening prayers, which were often more elaborate than the brief morning services. After dinner, the big meal of the day, the rest of the evening would be devoted to meetings, sometimes accompanied or followed by group singing. Kahinga Wachanga remembers these mass meetings as being critically important:

> We were struggling under very difficult conditions. Life in the forest was not easy. Often we were cold and hungry. . . . At these meetings we sang songs and held prayers. It was one of the ways we had of keeping the morale of our *itungati* high. The leaders, including myself, continually talked to our *itungati,* encouraging them to continue the fight as we were of one mind and all of us were fighting for the same reason.[61]

Karari Njama's memories of Kariaini suggests how effective the group singing could be in raising morale. "After dinner, the whole camp rejoiced in songs of praise to the country and warriors' leaders, songs of prayers, propagating the Movement, degrading and warning the Africans who helped the Government. The whole forest echoed in the dead night's silence. It was a great entertainment which cast away all worries and increased courage."[62]

> Even though our hearts are troubled
> Jomo will never desert us.
> Just as we were never abandoned,
> Our God, at Kapenguria by Thee.

You must display his perseverance
In the face of trouble or death;
Knowing that you belong to
The Kingdom of Gikuyu and Mumbi.[63]

While the majority of guerrillas in these camps were male, women
have received some attention in the memoirs and in studies by scholars like
Kathy Santilli, Luise White, Cora Presley, Jean Davison, and Jean
O'Barr.[64] As Cora Presley's research has made clear, Gikuyu women had
always served in the nationalist movement, though within groups like the
Kikuyu Central Association they had been limited by traditional restrictions
on women to secondary and auxiliary roles.[65] As for Mau Mau itself,
women had been deeply involved from the beginning. There is no real
debate about the critical roles women played in "the passive wing," but the
nature of the female role in the forest itself remains somewhat ambiguous.
The ambiguity is affected by the complex and shifting attitudes of male
Mau Mau leaders toward traditionalism and modernity in their construction
of the movement, by the propensity of some leaders and other male guerrillas to use women in the forest sexually, and by the tendency, probably common to many guerrilla armies under the stress of combat, to adopt forest
rules and then to evade or break them. Using the memoirs, Luise White has
argued for a clear division concerning gender relations between Kenya
Riigi leaders like Mathenge and Kenya Parliament leaders like Kimathi—
stating that the Riigi rejected binding relationships while the Parliament
favored monogamous marriages in the forest—yet Mathenge chaired the
meeting of the Kigumo and Kariaini leaders in July 1953, which decided
that women in the Nyandarua forest should all be married, each woman
should live with her husband, and the camp leader should announce the
marriages to the whole *mbuci*.[66] My reading is that male attitudes toward
the presence of women in the forest and toward female roles varied and
changed, but not necessarily as determined by the split between the educated and the illiterate.

The memoirs indicate that both uneducated generals like Stanley
Mathenge and educated leaders like Karari Njama saw the presence of
women in the forest as a problem in the beginning, a problem that men had
to solve. Although leaders discussed this problem at various meetings, there
is only one recorded case when a woman herself was able to express her
own opinion. Gucu Gikoyo's memoir (which White suggests is Riigi in
sympathy) indicates that his commanders, Generals Matenjagwo and Kago,
initially adopted the traditional Gikuyu position that sexual relations during
wartime, whether consensual or forced, not only weakened warriors physically but "was taboo and invited disaster" for the entire group.[67] Kahinga
Wachanga reports that regulations adopted in 1953 called for whipping any
guerrilla who had sexual intercourse with a woman; even a man returning

from a visit to his wife in the reserves had to be "cleansed" by a *mundu mugo* before he returned to his *mbuci*.[68] Less traditionalist male leaders like General China were doubtful about the presence of women in the camps for practical, though sexist, reasons. As Waruhiu Itote put it, "girls were forbidden to associate intimately with our own soldiers, especially with the rank-and-file. A woman who became emotionally involved with a forest fighter and then quarrelled with him might neglect her duty, either deliberately or unwittingly."[69] In the northern Nyandarua forests, some leaders attempted to deal with the presence of women by segregation, creating separate female camps, but Donald Barnett indicates that this proved impractical, both because men sought out the women anyway and because separate camps were too difficult to defend or evacuate.[70]

Sexual exploitation tainted male-female relations in the forest, although our information on this may be somewhat slanted, because it comes mostly from the rather prudish Karari Njama, who wanted to get all women out of the forest because they had always been "a source of conflict between men."[71] When Njama arrived at Mwathe for the big meeting of August 1953, a Captain Ngiriri assigned him a young woman named Wangui to be his *kabatuni* (small platoon) or personal servant, suggesting that in addition to warming his water or fetching his firewood, she would also let him have sexual relations with her. Disapproving on principle, he did not sleep with Wangui, but found out in conversation that she had been kept by force in the forest after delivering food supplies to a foraging party of *itungati*. She told him, "I have since been living with one of the warriors until we came to the meeting. We were then selected to serve the leaders."[72] When the Mwathe meeting opened, Njama spoke out on the issue of women in the forest, arguing that abduction (which he claimed was very common) sullied the movement's honor and that the contributions women made to the guerrilla effort in gathering firewood, preparing food, cleaning the camp, looking after the men's clothes, and sleeping with *itungati* did not compare to "the conflicts and difficulties arising in feeding and defending them and the possible conflicts between our warriors." Other leaders, however, praised the women who had killed police and soldiers, supplied the bands with guns, acted as spies, and served as sexual bait for members of the security forces, and argued that their contributions warranted that they "be placed in the same category as any other warriors and proved that girls had a right to come to the forest"; at the end of the debate at Mwathe, the leaders endorsed the Mumwe rules mentioned above and added new ones against abduction and for women receiving ranks according to their achievements.[73]

It is interesting that most comments on gender relations in accounts by Gikoyo, Wachanga, Itote, and Njama are concerned with protecting the male Mau Mau warrior community in the forest from the negative influence of the female presence, which in a practical sense generally meant attempting in the interests of the fighting cause to contain the tendency of young men to use women sexually. The memoirs have little to say about the women's own sexual choices, however. Given the small percentage of women in the total number of forest fighters—estimated at 5 percent in the northern Nyandarua forests and 20 percent in the forests on the edge of the Rift Valley—it is reasonable to assume that unless leaders laid effective claims on all women in a *mbuci* (and evidence indicates that they did not), a woman would be able to choose her lovers if she wished.[74] Some tough female forest veterans—whose qualities were acknowledged by Karari Njama in his speech for Wanjiru Waicanguru at her wedding to Dedan Kimathi in 1955, and later by their opponent, an admiring David Drummond—surely did just that.[75]

Moreover, Kathy Santilli has appropriately questioned the tendency of memoirists and historians to "focus on the sexual exploitation of women," arguing that this detracts from a better understanding of the women activists' real contributions to Mau Mau.[76] As Santilli points out, few women are mentioned by name in the memoirs, but two named by Gikoyo and by Itote suggest the influence strong women could wield. Gikoyo describes the role of Nyagiko, who organized the supply of food to General Matenjagwo's *mbuci* in the forest fringes of Murang'a. In November 1953, Matenjagwo met in Kikuyuni in the Murang'a reserve with local leader Mwaura wa Kagiika, his elders' committee, and Nyagiko about the forest leaders' new plan for the supply of food. As "women's leader," Nyagiko would contact other female supporters, tell them how much food each would be responsible for, and have them bring it to a central place when she gave the signal. She would then inform Wanjiru wa Ndegwa, the "female guard commander," who would recruit young women to transport the food, and Mburi wa Wainaina, the "male guard commander," who would post sentries along the route.[77] One of the most dramatic examples of the role of women recounted in the memoirs is the decisive intervention of Wamaitha, General China's Meru secretary, in the generals' discussion after Lari of the critical issue whether to kill women in the struggle against traitors and collaborators. Since she was not a leader, China at first tried to prevent Wamaitha from speaking, but she countered by arguing,

> I hope General China understands that we no longer live in the days when a woman could not eat meat before men. Although I am not a leader, I am responsible for writing down your speeches and your secrets, and I have never revealed anything. . . . Besides, this is a war of men and women. . . . when you are discussing women, you've got to listen to their representative; even fighters such as yourselves can make mistakes about the war.

After Wamaitha's speech, the group of male generals adopted her position: to kill "our enemies, the white settlers" and not to kill female collaborators but capture them and bring them into the movement.[78]

The memoirs and a number of other sources suggest that the role of women expanded and women won more respect from men as the revolt wore on. Luise White's "gendered chronology" of the forest fighting, which draws heavily on the memoirs, points to a steady development in the influence of women in the bands from 1953 to 1955.[79] In *"Mau Mau" General,* Waruhiu Itote suggests that the reliability of women under pressure may have contributed to their growing importance. "Over and over again, during the Emergency, I noticed that a woman could keep a secret much better than a man; even under interrogation, relatively few women than men would break down and reveal information."[80] Itote discusses in detail the special oath for women scouts administered on Kirinyaga; one of those scouts may have been Wanoi of Mutira Location, who also brought food from her Emergency village to Mau Mau bands.[81] On Kirinyaga, women stole weapons (as when a number of Mau Mau women took the guns of the African police they had invited to a feast at Nanyuki), sabotaged British vehicles, and joined some bands as active fighters.[82] Eventually Nyandarua leaders enlisted women as warriors and recognized outstanding female guerrillas with ranks up to colonel.[83] Cora Presley's informants described to her the active roles women took in the camps of the Kiambu forests, ranging from food supply to military operations, fighting alongside the men.[84] In the Rift Valley, according to Tabitha Kanogo's informants, Wanjiru Nyamarutu and Ruth Gathoni Gitahi, women provided food and other supplies, obtained intelligence, served on a male-female council, and fought with the men.[85] In influence, however, none of the female activists exceeded the influence of the women prophets; as Santilli points out, "in traditional Kikuyu society the position of seer was one of the few prestigious and potentially powerful positions women could occupy."[86] Female seers and prophets serving Mau Mau played an important role in the memoirs of Mohamed Mathu, Kahinga Wachanga, and Kiboi Muriithi, as the following section will show.

Religion in the Forest Camps

Following L. S. B. Leakey, British commentators had often attributed Mau Mau's popular support, the "fanaticism" of its followers, its use of violence, and its hostility to Christianity to the "fact" that it was really a religion.[87] The memoirs make it clear that religion played an important role in the camps, intensifying the commitment of individuals and strengthening group solidarity, but Mau Mau was a movement of ethnic and national resistance and not a religion in itself. Mau Mau's religious practices tended to be syncretistic, drawing on traditional Gikuyu belief and practice and on Christianity as well, especially the Christianity of the independent churches (use of the Bible was common). This was certainly a righteous army. Like

Puritan soldiers in the English Civil War or Afghan *mujahideen* fighting the Russians, the *itungati,* encouraged by prophecies and heartened by hymns, believed that they were soldiers with a religious destiny to fulfill. Moreover, they believed that spiritual power was the principal way to overcome the enemy's advantage in weapons and technology; as Kahinga Wachanga observed, "We prayed to God at all times in the forest because we knew that unless He gave us strength we had no chance against the colonial government."[88] However, although religion served to bind Mau Mau together in 1953–1954, toward the end, as the guerrilla army's fortunes declined, it could become divisive, contributing to the split between the educated and the illiterate.

Daily prayers were an essential group activity. As Joram Wamweya remembers his *mbuci* in the Rift Valley near Longonot in 1954, "Early next morning someone called out that we should rise and pray. Everybody jumped to their feet, each drawing his *simi* from its scabbard and holding its tip skywards. . . . 'Great Allocator,' the leader said, interceding with *Ngai,* 'if we ever lose the fight, it will not be our defeat but Yours. Our victory will be Your victory.'"[89] In the larger camps the morning prayers could be more elaborate and accompanied by ritual libations, as in a service led by Dedan Kimathi at Mwathe in August 1953, described by Karari Njama. After pouring home-brewed beer over his personal fire and over the door frames "so as to cleanse the house," Kimathi came out into the open with the beer-gourd in one hand and a mixture of millets in the other, faced Kirinyaga, poured beer and millet on the ground, calling first on Ngai, then on "our father Gikuyu," and next on "my father Waciuri." After pouring more beer and millet he began the public prayer, which went in part as follows:

> God, we beg you to defeat our enemies and to defend us from them; close their eyes so that they may not see us.
>
> Our Father, Gikuyu used to pray to you with these things I have in my hands. On all occasions you heard him and fulfilled his request. We are his sons and daughters. We claim that the highland grazing plateau you gave us and all the fertile land you gave our Father Gikuyu has become foreigners' plunder. We beseech Thee our Heavenly Father to restore our stolen land and drive away these strangers who have turned out to be our enemies. They have taken their strong firearms against an unarmed nation. Oh God! Be our arms. We are certain that even if they pour fire on us from their airplanes you will still protect us from their wrath. God, we request Thy peaceful and merciful eyes to look upon the blood flowing in our country, and hear the cries of the perishing lives demanding Thy help.

After calling for the protection of the Gikuyu communities and the leaders in detention camps and for the blessing of the dead, Kimathi closed by pouring the remaining beer and grain on the fire, saying, "As this fire goes, so be it with all our evils. As the wood and charcoal run cold, so may the war run cold and peace prevail. As we bury the fire, so may all the evils be buried and never rise up." As he concluded, the *itungati* came forward. "Then all the people followed with a bit of food in the right hand and a handful of wet soil in the left hand, threw these on the fire, then raised their hands high facing Mt. Kenya. By the time the last man threw what he had, there was no fire but a big heap of soil. We all together said the Christian's Lord's Prayer and ended our prayers by saying *'Thaai, Thathaiya Ngai, Thai'* three times."[90]

In Njama's rendering, this ritual and prayer is a creative blending of traditional Gikuyu rituals of invocation, libation, calling for blessings, and cursing evil, Gikuyu nationalist soil ritual, and Christian prayer. The language is evocative of both the Gikuyu ("close their eyes so they will not see us") and Christian traditions ("We beseech Thee, our Heavenly Father"). Closing with the Lord's Prayer and "Thaai, Thathaiya Ngai, Thai" ("God's Peace be with Us") links the most powerful Christian prayer with the Gikuyu words used to end all prayers, bringing as much spiritual power to bear as possible for the cause.

The political songs, some of them reworked Christian hymns and others simply using the hymn tunes with a completely different text, followed the Mau Mau activists into the forest, and became an important element in evening observances. The martial hymns had particular relevance to the struggle; Wachanga remembers one the *itungati* sang at a meeting late in 1954:

> Onward Mau Mau soldiers
> Marching as to war,
> Looking unto Jomo,
> Who has gone before.
> Jomo the Royal Master,
> Leads against the foe,
> Forward into battle,
> See his banners go.

After the hymn, Wachanga read from his Bible as Mau Mau leaders often did, choosing a text from Zephaniah 3:18–20:

> The Lord thy God in the midst of thee is mighty, he will save, he will rejoice over thee with joy; he will rest in his love, he will joy over thee with singing. . . . Behold, at that time I will do all that afflicts thee and I will save her that halteth, and gather her that was driven out and I will get them praise and fame in every land where they have been put to shame. At that time I will bring you again, even in the time that I gather you; for I will make a name and a praise among all people of the earth, when I turn back your captivity before your eyes, saith the Lord.[91]

The Old Testament—with its allusions to captivity under foreign masters, to wanderings in the wilderness, to sufferings bravely borne, to delivery by

God's hand—spoke to the Mau Mau condition and to their ultimate redemption. But they would be redeemed not by the Christian God, but by the Ngai of their ancestors.

Generals often led prayers, but Mau Mau medicine men and women and prophets carried out sacrifices, cleansed and purified soldiers, experienced and interpreted dreams and visions, and played an important role in deciding the most auspicious times or circumstances in which to launch an attack. The *mundu mugo* who accompanied a precolonial Gikuyu war party had usually been a male elder, but Mau Mau spiritual practitioners could be women or even young men. Many *itungati* took the directions and prohibitions of spiritual practitioners very seriously. General China, even though skeptical himself, obeyed the local elders' injunction against angering the spirits by firing in the direction of Kirinyaga until several battles proved to his men that the direction they faced when fighting had no effect on the outcome.[92] Unlike China, Mathenge was as strong a believer in traditional Gikuyu religion as the *itung*ati who fought under him. In June 1953, when Karari Njama was treating a wounded warrior in the hospital hut at Kariaini, the man explained to him that they had just aborted a raid because

> they were taught by the witchdoctors that if a deer or gazelle passed across the path of a group that was going to raid, it indicated bad luck and the warriors should abandon their plan. Twice a deer and a gazelle had crossed. . . . This [belief, he said] was supported by many warriors who said that when they disobeyed the same rule when they were going to raid Othaya and the result was very bad, as the seers had forecast.[93]

When seers correctly predicted success, their stock would also rise. The most famous case was that of Mungai Thiga, the sixteen-year-old seer with Mbaria Kaniu's band in the attack on Naivasha, who predicted the appearance of a star that would guide the group on their journey and then give them victory in the attack.[94]

Some Mau Mau leaders took important actions to respond to a *mundu mugo*'s directions or to fulfill the prophecies of a *murathi*. Both Kahinga Wachanga and Waruhiu Itote (in his second book) tell of the killing of Gray Leakey by men of General Tanganyika's command in the hopes of fulfilling prophecies that the British would not leave Kenya until one of their elders had been buried alive upside down, as some Gikuyu believed the British had buried Waiyaki wa Hinga in 1892 at Kibwezi. "The *arathi* told us that if we did those things, the battle could be won and *wiyathi* or *uhuru* could be achieved at long last."[95] For many of their military actions on Kirinyaga, General Tanganyika and his men depended heavily on the prophet Roda, as Muriithi describes: "She would warn the forest fighters not to approach a certain spot as the enemy would be patrolling. Her predictions were always right. . . . She was an important asset to Mau Mau. We always went to her for advice."[96] Under military pressure in 1954, Tanganyika insisted that the group travel fifteen miles to consult Roda before making any other move. She told them, "Things are getting worse. We must not forget to pray to Ngai. We must have committed a bad sin and Ngai is angry with us. You must all go to Nyamindi River, in Embu, to give a sacrifice to appease Ngai so that he will forgive us. If this isn't done within three days our losses will be even greater."[97] Educated men like Karari Njama and Mohamed Mathu, though they might participate enthusiastically in group worship, tended to be skeptical of the influence of medicine men and seers with the Mau Mau bands. Ultimately, the dependence of leaders on seers would divide the bands and contribute to their decline when conditions deteriorated in late 1954 and 1955.

Relations with Civilians

When Waruhiu Itote came to Kirinyaga in August 1952, one of his primary concerns was to establish good relations with the local civilian population. After meeting the committee at Karatina and choosing a campsite, he asked local elders to instruct him and his band in forest life and forest warfare, gaining essential information and showing respect to the traditional leaders of the community at the same time. He then began administering oaths to civilians, both in order to gain recruits and to win support, by surrounding whole communities and oathing the inhabitants *en masse*. "If they were afraid or reluctant . . . we used force to enter the houses and bring them out. Although administering an oath by force might at first sight appear meaningless, it did not prove so in practice. The explanations which we gave, as well as the effect of the oath itself, bound the people to us. . . ."[98] As he had in Nairobi, Itote followed oath administration with political instruction. "Afterwards we explained what was expected of them: the British had taken our land, we said, and we had dedicated ourselves to the fight for our liberty—those who had taken the oath must now help us in every possible way."[99] Their commitment to the oath, the pressure of intimidation, and their loyalty to kith and kin (since most of the fighters in the Kirinyaga forests came from neighboring communities), led local civilians to help the *itungati,* at least in the beginning. Recruits flocked to join (5,000 by the end of 1953); supporters gathered and transported food to the bands; scouts, both boys and young women, spied on the security forces and stole weapons; oathed sympathizers among the local home guards, police, and KAR supplied intelligence and arms; and the oath's code of silence enabled guerrillas to pass easily by or even through civilian communities without risk of exposure.

Although General China may have been particularly successful, this pattern of civilian support seems to have held true for much of Central Kenya in 1953 and 1954. The descriptions of Njama, Wachanga, and

Gikoyo point toward strong civilian backing for the guerrilla bands in the Nyandarua forests in the first year and a half of fighting. Most camps were sited within a long walking distance of the Gikuyu communities from which their *itungati* came; in the early months of the war, guerrillas visited their homes fairly often and received much of their food from their families' fields. As the forest population burgeoned and camp size grew, generals arranged with leaders of the passive wing in the neighboring communities for regular deliveries of food and supplies, organized by female leaders and carried to the camps by women guarded by *itungati,* as Gucu Gikoyo describes. Guerrilla generals tried to keep track of contributions by their supporters in order to compensate them after victory, and tried to take only loyalists' cattle so as to spare the herds of their supporters.[100] Members of the passive wing observed the movements of home guard, police, and army and got word to the camps when attacks were imminent; guerrilla leaders defended their supporters by intimidating or attacking loyalists who threatened or harassed civilian activists. ·

It was inevitable that the security forces would try to cut the links between the fighters and the passive wing, and the strong measures they took would affect guerrilla-civilian relations. In June and July 1953, General Erskine moved forcefully against the Nyeri passive wing: evicting Gikuyu families from a one- to two-mile strip at the edge of the forest, destroying *shambas* of maize, sugar cane, and bananas to deny food to the guerrillas, proclaiming strict curfews, imposing communal labor on new roads and bridges that took people away from the growing of food.[101] Guerrilla leaders now found themselves forced to calculate the effects of their actions on their supporters. When they drew supplies from the increasingly strapped communities in the reserves, the maize and potatoes they collected were food taken from the mouths of their relatives and neighbors. When they turned to seizing cattle from settlers and loyalists, their foraging parties were often attacked on the return journey and their communities faced stock confiscations and other collective punishments. In their attacks in the reserves, guerrillas tried to differentiate between the property of loyalists and supporters, but did not always succeed, and members of the passive wing were alienated by the depredations they suffered during raids, as when *itungati* under General Nyama's command robbed Joram Muchanji's shop at Ndunyu Market, Nyeri, in mid-1953, even though Muchanji was a "great comrade."[102]

But the most serious problem of this kind that guerrilla leaders had to face in 1953–1954 was the risk of deadly retaliation against the passive wing for successful Mau Mau actions against chiefs, home guards, police, and other loyalists. Fear that their relatives and neighbors would be beaten, robbed, detained, or killed persuaded some Mau Mau leaders to stay their hands. Kahinga Wachanga tells how a plan to kill all home guards in church on Christmas Eve 1952 was rescinded at the last minute by "Mau Mau headquarters" because of the fear "that the government would retaliate and cause much hardship among our people."[103] Karigo Muchai explains that the well-known controls on violence of the Kiambu elders committee were originally imposed in 1953 in response to retaliatory killings by chiefs and headmen in the district. "Killings were always followed by harsh repressive measures by the security forces. We felt they were only justified in cases where the person was found by the committee of elders to have committed grave crimes against the people."[104] In Murang'a, even Matenjagwo and Kago could be deterred by the appeals of civilians, as when they called off an attack in Kandara Division after an elderly woman begged them not to risk retaliation against prisoners in the hands of the security forces.[105] In late summer 1953, at a meeting at Kariaini headquarters in northern Nyandarua, Karari Njama and other leaders debated the wisdom of continuing to fight in the locations because "whenever we kill or burn a Home Guard's house, their revenge is between ten and twenty times." Njama argued that "We should fight our enemies in the forests, in the Special Areas, in their camps and at any other place of contact, avoiding fights in the villages and assassinations in the villages in order to safeguard the civilians."[106] Civilian supporters made the Mau Mau guerrilla effort possible, but also constituted the bands' greatest vulnerability.

Mau Mau at War

Mau Mau guerrilla warfare was shaped by material poverty. Though the movement did obtain some weapons in Nairobi before the Emergency, there were nowhere near enough to go around; when General Matenjagwo entered the forest with 250 men, his force had 6 sten guns, 20 rifles, and 6 pistols.[107] Large guerrilla bands like the group assembled at Kariaini Headquarters camp in mid-1953 had a wider assortment of European weapons, including occasionally bren guns, usually sten guns, .303 rifles, .44 rifles, shotguns, and various caliber pistols, but most of the men were armed with *simis, pangas,* and homemade guns.[108] Inevitably, leaders sent *itungati* into battle inadequately armed. The force of seventy-five who assaulted the Naivasha Police Station in March 1953, had only five precision weapons among them.[109] Many a *gitungati* marched to attack carrying only a *simi* or a *panga,* told to arm himself by killing an enemy, and instructed to always recover the gun of a dead comrade, for the loss of a weapon was more serious than the death of a *gitungati.* As General China comments, "At times our shortage of weapons made our activities seem like a series of battles to get weapons to fight more battles."[110] Ammunition was always a problem, so leaders told their men to use only the minimum necessary; during the Naivasha raid the five men with guns "only used one bullet each because they followed the Mau Mau regulations of using only one bullet unless ordered to use more."[111] The assortment of all different kinds of weapons created another ammunition headache.

Guerrilla leaders used their supply networks and their ingenuity to try to overcome the problem. Elders' committees continued to send weapons and bullets stolen or bought in the towns through the supply pipeline to the bands in the forests, but their efforts were not enough. Young women working for General China persuaded or tricked police and soldiers to part with their weapons. Oathed members of the Kings African Rifles (including Embu, Meru, Luo, and Kamba), organized into secret committees within the military camps, and arranged for arms, ammunition, and uniforms to be sneaked out of camp under the Muslim robes of women pretending to be wives of soldiers in the unit. China and other Mau Mau leaders also sent groups of men into the Northern Frontier District to buy arms, ammunition, and hand grenades.[112] Supplying Mau Mau became very risky, however, after the British made possession of even a single bullet punishable by death. The demand for arms was so high that Mau Mau bands even fought each other over them, as when a group of Kago's men (acting without his orders) disarmed some Kiambu fighters in the border area and took their guns.[113]

To compensate, the Mau Mau turned to weapons manufacturing. Waruhiu Itote describes the process:

> The stock itself was fashioned from the wood of the *Muthiti* or *Thirikwa* tree, which never cracks under any weather conditions. The barrel, generally made from water pipes, was fastened to this, and a smaller pipe or piece of iron, one which would fit smoothly within the barrel, was used as a hammer. The hammer was released by a mechanism built out of a barbed wire spring and a piece of car or bicycle tube.[114]

China's gun factory at the Kirinyaga headquarters in early 1953, with a staff of twenty, was the first, but eventually factories in every combat area turned out hundreds of homemade guns; at Kariaini in mid-1953 there were over 600 such weapons, enough to arm approximately one-quarter of the guerrillas in camp.[115] Dedan Kimathi commanded his forces to steal all the irrigation pipe they could find in order to keep the arms factories working at full capacity.[116] No forest technicians were able to master the production of ammunition, though they did succeed in filing bullets to fit different caliber weapons and in replacing part of the powder in shotgun shells with crushed glass to double the number of shells that could be fired with the same powder.[117] And no amount of ingenuity could make these guns precision weapons; they were only accurate at close range and often misfired or jammed.

For their other military supplies, the Mau Mau drew on their enemies or did without. Tents from KAR lines were used to protect leaders from the rain in Nyandarua; Very pistols from the police were used to signal during battles; military bugles called reveille and encouraged *itungati* in attacks on home-guard posts. The ill-clothed guerrillas coveted police and military uniforms, especially the wool police overcoats; even a partial uniform not only warmed a man but gave him a feeling of pride he could not derive from the often ragged garb of a peasant. Security force uniforms could also serve as disguises to enable *itungati* to approach government police or soldiers without arousing suspicion; in March 1954, General Kago led a unit of guerrillas dressed as police and home guards right into the Kiria-ini post in southern Murang'a and captured it.[118] However, stolen uniforms could unintentionally fool other guerrillas; Karigo Muchai tells of incidents in Kiambu in 1953 when bands of *itungati* fired on each other, each mistaking the others for security forces.[119]

Though the Mau Mau narrowed the gap by ingenuity and lifting from their opponents, they still fought under considerable handicaps. They tried to make up for these disadvantages, as guerrilla armies always have, by the kind of war they chose to fight. Because they were outnumbered and outgunned overall, they tried to turn the tables by attacking smaller units of security forces under conditions they could control. During the daytime they were vulnerable to spotter planes and concentrated enemy fire, so they usually attacked at night, when they could use surprise to their advantage and retreat under the cover of darkness. They usually had fewer precision weapons and less ammunition, so they often remained in hiding and attacked only when the enemy had closed to within a few yards so that their shotguns, pistols, and homemade guns could be effective and they could defeat or drive off the enemy with comparatively few shots. They often chose to attack tribal police and home guards in preference to KAR, Kenya Regiment, or British regulars like the Devons because the soldiers tended to be better armed, trained, and led. Whether attacking themselves or under attack, they usually chose to break off contact quickly to avoid being trapped by the arrival of reinforcements called in by radio, and in general preferred a rapid escape to running the risk of capture or annihilation. They used stratagems to lure the enemy into ambushes in which Mau Mau could fight on their own terms.

Because the ability to move easily through the forest and escape quickly were keys to the long-term survival of a guerrilla band, leaders put a heavy emphasis on bushcraft. During Karari Njama's first day in the forest of Nyandarua, Githae Mugweru, an officer of Kigumo *mbuci,* began the initiation of the new recruit by explaining how to approach the camp: "If you meet a green branch planted in the middle of the path, that means do not pass there, there is danger ahead. If you meet two green branches dropped on either side of a path or bent, that means that the camp is near and you are approaching the guards and that you should give a signal. We whistle like a night-bird which says '*Kuri heho-i ndirara ku?*'"[120] Communication between camps or between a camp and its patrols was either by such subtly altered natural markers or by "letterboxes," certain hollow trees or other secure places where notes could be hidden. A new *gitungati* literally needed to learn to be in tune with the wilderness. In his camps on Kirinyaga, General China required that the first half-hour after rising be a period for listening. "We would sit in absolute silence, straining to catch every sound in the forest: the varying sound of winds in different trees, the calls of birds, the noise of animals moving, the approach of rain. Above all, we trained ourselves to recognize the sounds of danger, such as a man coming near, or a frightened animal, or a low-flying aircraft."[121] When on the move between camps or between the forest and the reserve, China's men learned to travel silently through the forest while leaving no signs: no matches, no bent or broken twigs, and no footprints—even if this required a *gitungati* to walk backward and brush the footprints away behind him.[122] Smell could help conceal the *itungati* and reveal the approach of security forces. As Kahinga Wachanga remembers, "our smell aided us in our ambush, for we smelled of the forest, whereas our enemy smelled of soap, cigarettes, and hair-tonic."[123]

Experienced *itungati* were superb forest fighters, able to travel considerable distances through the forest (usually on animal trails) in short periods of time, able to double back on their paths to confuse pursuit, able to lie absolutely still in ambush until the enemy had come close enough to kill with a homemade gun. The forest ambush became the classic Mau Mau battle. Karari Njama describes the tactic most often used:

> When we saw them coming, and knowing the path they would have to follow—for we used to stay at the forest fringes, observe and count the enemies before they approached the forest—we would then deploy ourselves along the path, out of sight, and when their last man passed our ambush we would open fire, killing some and forcing the rest into the depths of the forest.[124]

A variant involved the use of a decoy force which would ambush its own back-trail. "Another way in which our fighters trapped the security forces was to go out of the forest and then march single file singing back into the forest, leaving a very clear track for Government to follow. They would then circle back and lay in wait for their trackers and forces to come along the path which they had prepared for ambush."[125] In *A Handbook on Anti–Mau Mau Operations,* General Erskine described the Mau Mau guerrilla in the forest as "a master in fieldcraft and concealment."[126]

But bolder leaders yearned to go on the offensive. In his afternoon talks, Matenjagwo was fond of telling his *itungati,* "This was not sport but serious business. We should therefore not wait to be searched for by the enemy. We should ourselves look for the enemy."[127] Outside the forest, however, the guerrillas lost some of their natural advantages, exposing themselves to possible destruction by an enemy that could call on far greater resources, so leaders relied even more than usual on secrecy, surprise, stealth, and physical stamina. In operations in Nairobi, the reserves, and the Rift Valley, the guerrillas maintained secrecy by counting on the willingness of civilians to help them while denying any knowledge of their whereabouts to the security forces who came in pursuit.[128] Surprise enabled ill-armed bands to overcome potentially devastating opposition, as in the case of the attack on the Naivasha Police Station in March 1953, which succeeded because its timing and boldness caught the police unaware. Naivasha forced the government to recognize that the Mau Mau were capable of serious military action; as Kahinga Wachanga puts it, "The Naivasha raid became well known throughout the country and forced the colonial government to admit that the Gikuyu were not *tuhii tutu* (small boys) to be cowed by the threat of hanging, shooting or even castration."[129] The stealth used at Naivasha and in other actions enabled bands of guerrillas to approach objectives without detection and escape back into the darkness and the forest before the security forces could mount an effective pursuit. Stamina enabled Mau Mau to travel for great distances at high speed; policeman David Drummond reports chasing a band in the Rift Valley which covered forty-five miles a day for five days.[130]

A notable Mau Mau success was the attack on Lukenya Prison south of Athi River Detention Camp in September 1954, led by Kariuki "Maitho Mana" and Mohamed Mathu. According to Wachanga, Mathu made a point of consulting both the Central Committee in Nairobi and the Kenya Parliament in Nyandarua for permission to attack Lukenya, while according to Mathu himself he and Kariuki only asked Parliament when their planning was well along.[131] Knowing that the prison was lightly guarded and counting on the element of surprise, Kariuki, Mathu, and twenty *itungati* arrived at Lukenya from Ndiritu, twenty miles away, on September 15. After scouting the prison during the night, they launched their assault shortly after 8:00 p.m. on the night of September 16.

> Coming to within 15 yards of the entrance we lay down and pointed our guns toward the gate. Kariuki gave the signal. He whispered "fire" to alert the men then shouted "fire!" Githongo blew the bugle and another man sent up a red and blue flare as we opened fire on the guards. They returned our fire but we ran toward the gate, shooting and shouting "kill and capture."
>
> In seconds we reached the entrance and finding one of the guards dead and the other wounded we started hacking down the wooden gate with *pangas* and with long wooden poles. Once inside we met surprisingly little resistance. . . .
>
> Hearing the shouts of the prisoners we broke down the doors of the corrugated iron barracks and told them to grab their blankets and take off their prison uniforms. When the 200 prisoners were freed we decided it was time for us to leave.[132]

Though the attackers only captured a few weapons, the Lukenya attack shocked the government, heartened the Mau Mau fighters in the Nairobi area, and provided a number of escapee recruits to the forest bands.

Naivasha and Lukenya were notable successes, part of a string of Mau Mau victories in 1953–1954, including a number of nighttime attacks on lightly defended home guard posts. Large operations were sometimes defeated, however. The Othaya (or Uthaya) raid on the night of May 27, 1953, the main attack of a coordinated assault on three home guard posts in Nyeri planned by Stanley Mathenge, Kihara Kagumu, Kabira Gatu, and Kahinga Wachanga did not fare so well. Four hundred *itungati* were assigned to attack Othaya itself in the hopes of capturing arms and releasing prisoners. While one of the subsidiary assaults on Kairuthi succeeded (the raiders assigned to Ihururu turned back), the Othaya attack itself, mounted in the middle of the night in heavy rain, went badly from the beginning. As Kahinga Wachanga tells it,

> Uthaya was very bad. Our fighters reached there at about 3:00 a.m. instead of the expected 10:00 p.m. I was among those raiders. We surrounded the camp after arriving. When the bugles were blown we opened fire into the camp. The man with our machine gun [a bren gun] was wounded immediately in his right hand and was unable to use our most important weapon. The military soldiers were very fierce and killed ten of our men. During our retreat from the camp we lost another ten men who drowned in the Thuti river.[133]

Kihara Kagumu, a survivor of Othaya, told Karari Njama that there was no surprise at all; the police within the post fired flares when the guerrillas were still 300 yards from the wire, "making every one of our warriors visible," pinned down most of the *itungati* with gunfire, and beat back those who reached the wire with grenades dropped on their heads from the guard towers. The *itungati* fell back in disorder, leaving the dead and most of the wounded behind.[134] Othaya illustrates the risk guerrillas ran in assaulting well-defended positions without the element of surprise.

Mau Mau war-making did not make much use of the sabotage that has played such an important role in irregular warfare in the twentieth century, from the French *maquis* blowing up railway lines to the Viet Cong mining the highway from Saigon to Hue. Several memoirs do mention blowing up bridges, and Kahinga Wachanga describes mining a loyalist market center, but these seem to have been atypical acts. Kenya in the 1950s offered a tempting range of targets, and by cutting telegraph and telephone lines, trenching roads, blowing up power installations, and sabotaging the railroad between Nairobi and Mombasa, the guerrillas could have disrupted the counterinsurgency and possibly extended the war, for the British would have had to spread their forces very thin to effectively guard sabotage targets. As Brigadier J. W. Tweedie remarked to General Hinde, "If Mau Mau were not such a 3rd class enemy they could make our life hell on these roads. Hope they don't think of it."[135]

Why did the guerrillas fail to use extensive sabotage? Kahinga Wachanga mentions a plan to blow up electric power installations, but indicates that the leadership vetoed the idea for fear of British retaliation against the common people, an explanation in line with other indications of Mau Mau reluctance to push the British too hard.[136] Another explanation could be the limited number of guerrillas capable of handling explosives, for making bombs is not the same as making guns. However, cutting telephone and telegraph wires and lifting fishplates from railroad tracks requires only daring (which the Mau Mau had plenty of) rather than special technical skills, and the memoirs do not provide any clear clues as to why such simple sabotage was not attempted more often, though Wunyabari Maloba has argued that the guerrillas were deterred by the religious specialists.[137]

A Brutal War

By late summer 1953, General Erskine's forces were on the offensive in the forests and the reserves. The new energy of the counterinsurgency is reflected in Karari Njama's descriptions of that summer and in Kiboi Muriithi's account of his first months in the forests of Kirinyaga. Within a few days after he joined the guerrillas in June 1953, Muriithi was caught up in a series of running battles with home guards, police, and units of the KAR. While some of this fighting can be attributed to the offensive spirit of generals China and Tanganyika, most of the skirmishes were initiated by the security forces, who were aggressively seeking out camps, pursuing foragers, and sweeping through the forest. Spotting planes, hated by all *itungati,* kept bands on the move, and war planes harassed them with strafing and bombing. Muriithi's memoir suggests that the ability of the *itungati* to escape quickly kept casualties low in the beginning, but attrition gradually took its toll and the survivors began to suffer from exhaustion and eventually from hunger.[138] When *itungati* fell in the forest, they were mourned only by their comrades. "The worst thing in those battles was that whenever people died in the forest their parents were not informed and even if they had been their real names were often not known because their original names were changed to new names when they went into the forest."[139]

As the fighting escalated, tales of enemy atrocities began to spread. The story of the slaughter of a group of recruits going to join General Kago who were captured after a battle on the Kayahwe River in Murang'a in early April 1954 and then shot out of hand circulated widely through the Nyandarua bands.[140] The killing of individual prisoners by patrols of the Kenya Police Reserve and General Service Unit (confirmed by W. W.

Baldwin's memoir) became well known. In close contact with their home communities, the *itungati* also learned of killings and brutalities by the police and home guards; the terror raids on Gikuyu communities after the Lari "massacre," when the security forces took men from their homes at night and shot them, became especially notorious among forest fighters.[141] Stories of the killings at Kayahwe and the repression after Lari, preserved in Mau Mau songs, contributed to a growing bitterness in the guerrilla bands against the British and against Africans fighting on the other side.

Mau Mau generals responded in kind. Waruhiu Itote's killing of a loyalist schoolteacher captured spying on his band in late 1952 was a cold-blooded elimination for practical reasons, but other leaders killed as vengeance and as a warning to collaborators.[142] In March 1954, General Kago took the government post at Kiria-ini. Gucu Gikoyo tells what happened to the captured garrison:

> We relieved them of the ammunition pouches they were wearing and then herded them into a house. They were thirty in number, including the one that had been on sentry duty. We locked them up in the house and set it on fire. We maintained guard until the house had burned down completely. . . . General Kago told us that anybody who did not sympathize with the Mau Mau cause could not expect any pity from us.[143]

Kahinga Wachanga makes it clear that such a slaughter of captives was by no means an isolated incident, and not only because it was difficult for Mau Mau to care for prisoners. "The forest fight was brutal, even inhuman. The colonialists used many forms of torture on us, and we in turn killed them in many different ways."[144] Wachanga claims that the British tortured men by castrating them and women by pouring hot water in their uteruses, and killed *itungati* and their civilian supporters by shooting, bombing, beating, and dragging them to death behind Land Rovers. In turn, *itungati* castrated captives and sent them back to their units, chopped up captives with *pangas,* used prisoners for target practice, broke the arms and legs of prisoners and left them to die, and strangled, drowned, and burned prisoners alive.[145] To quote *The Swords of Kirinyaga,* "The British government used all their strength to annihilate us. We, on our part, used what few strengths we had. One of our strongest points was the fear we were able to instill in them."[146]

Though these were unquestionably atrocities against helpless prisoners, British propaganda focused more often on the killing of women and children (white settlers and Gikuyu loyalists), especially on those dispatched by *panga* slashes. The British made much of the killings at Lari, presenting to the world the picture of a dead baby, its small body cut almost in half, as the symbol of Mau Mau cruelty and atavism. But Mau Mau accounts—especially those of Waruhiu Itote, Kahinga Wachanga, Karari Njama, and Gucu Gikoyo—make it clear that generals either strongly discouraged or tried to prohibit the killing of women and children. When

Gikoyo and his comrades broke into a government camp and found the wife of a home guard with her wounded husband, he finished off the man and left the woman alone, for "Mau Mau had orders never to kill women and children unless by accident."[147] Gikoyo almost certainly killed the man with his *panga*, but the *panga* was only the weapon of necessity for most *itungati*, not the weapon of choice. A British government study confirmed that no more than 10 percent of the total Mau Mau victims were women, and confirmed that the mutilation of the bodies of victims with *pangas* was rare.[148] Moreover, Mau Mau rarely committed rape because of concern with *thahu;* when Gikoyo and a comrade came across a fellow *gitungati* raping a local woman during a raid, they chopped him to death with their *pangas* "to prevent him from contaminating us with taboo."[149] Security forces on the other hand were notorious for raping women, among them Karari Njama's wife, who was attacked in 1955 and bore a child.[150] Brutalities against women and children, British claims notwithstanding, were atypical of Mau Mau.

The War in the Reserves

Drawing on the example of Malaya, the European directors of the counterinsurgency believed that success in defeating Mau Mau would depend on detaching the people from the guerrillas, and fashioned their policies—from communal punishments, to villagization, to digging the great ditch between the forests and the reserves—toward that end. Most of those who carried the policies out at the local level were African loyalists. Though Gikuyu were divided in many ways before October 1952 and the Mau Mau had already begun to kill oath refusers and loyalists, the memoirists believe that the Gikuyu civil war was a creation of the Emergency. As Kariuki writes, of all wars "no kind of conflict creates deeper hatreds"; these intense feelings would divide Gikuyu communities during the 1950s and in some cases for long afterwards.[151]

Lari is a good place to start a discussion of internecine conflict in the reserves. The attack on Chief Luka Wanganga's band of loyalists can be traced back to their acceptance in 1940 of a consolation award of inferior land in return for the confiscation of their ancestral property, when the government implemented the Kenya Land Commission's recommendation establishing the boundaries of the White Highlands in the Limuru area of Kiambu. A number of other right-holders, backed first by KCA and later by KAU, had refused the inferior land as a matter of principle, and many of these had become *ahoi* tenants in Kiambu or squatters in the Rift Valley. In 1952 a number of the Rift Valley squatters were forced out, returned to the area, took the *batuni* oath, and prepared for revenge against Luka, his family, and supporters. After coordinating with those planning the Naivasha Raid, they attacked on the night of March 26, 1953, killing Luka, his family, and almost 100 others. In the aftermath, security forces moved in quickly.[152]

Karigo Muchai, who had a special brief from his elders' committee in Kiambaa to investigate security force atrocities against civilians, may have been the first Mau Mau to visit Lari on the morning after. When he heard African soldiers talking about a "massacre," Muchai took a bus to Limuru, and spent the day concealed on a hill above Lari, observing the scene of destruction—watching huts burn, hundreds of people being rounded up by the police, and suspects being shot. After the security forces left, he walked among the bodies, noting their injuries. In the days to come Muchai talked to many people who had been at Lari during the fighting, and concluded that the initial Mau Mau killings had been followed by a counterattack on the community by security forces, who killed men, women, and children out of hand. Karigo Muchai concludes that, "In Lari there was a massacre on 26 March 1953, but most of the blood was on Government hands."[153] Ngugi Kabiro describes the climate of fear in Kiambu after Lari. "Every able-bodied Kikuyu male ran the risk of being called out of his hut at night and shot by revenge-seeking settlers or their *askari*. For myself and my family, nights were a time of fear and restless sleep."[154] At least Ngugi Kabiro's family had the good fortune to be together, for so many men were either with the forest fighters or in detention that some villages were stripped of males of fighting age, leaving boys, old men, women, and girls.

The most extended description of life in an Emergency village is in *Daughter of Mumbi,* by Charity Waciuma. A secondary student at the beginning of the Emergency, Wanjiku (the name she used at the time) returns to her community in Murang'a in 1953. Her father, though a Christian and a health inspector at the local clinic, is a supporter of the secret movement, though not an activist. While glad to leave her school, with its intensely anti–Mau Mau atmosphere, Wanjiku is shocked by her first sight of the Emergency village where her family has been forced to live. She and other villagers are forced to perform communal labor six days a week, which mostly consists of work improving the farms of chiefs and loyalists. At other times they are confined by strict curfew; with so little time for farming, there is insufficient food to eat, and many old people are suffering from malnutrition.[155] As new arrivals uncowed by the security system (they even teach new freedom songs to the villagers during communal labor), the returned students are objects of suspicion, and the chief and district officers tell them to stop talking and singing about Kenyatta or they will be sent off to "rehabilitation."[156] Wanjiku is forced with the other villagers to attend "anti–Mau Mau meetings" during which the chief and headmen harangue the villagers, condemning Mau Mau and threatening them if they support the secret movement. Her younger brother, Wanjohi, tells her, "Nearly all of us in the village have taken the Mau Mau oath, the 'loyalists' as well as the rest, except for a few Christians. Just think that the Home Guards were the oath administrators and now they are 'loyalists.' Do they think people will take any notice of what they say in their silly meetings?"[157]

Yet both Wanjohi and Wanjiku know that the relationship between their family and most of the neighbors on the one hand and the chief, headmen, home guards, and *their* families on the other is determined by power and not by political credibility. The village rules are very strict and all of them reinforce the power of the loyalists. Their mother insists that they repeat the curfew orders until they learn them by heart. "No walking about at night, go to the lavatory at six, then in your house until next morning at seven. If you break this order you will be shot. Wait for the Headman's whistle to blow. After that women will be taken down to the well to fetch water. Walk down and up together. If you leave others behind you will either be shot or severely beaten."[158] As an adolescent male, her brother Wanjohi is always under the threat of detention camp; as an attractive young woman, Wanjiku herself lives in peril of assault or rape. Eventually a home guard does attack her sexually, but she is able to use the judo she learned at school to defend herself. Thompson, the European district officer, transfers the home guard, an unusual intervention, for normally "he lets the chiefs do as they please," as it serves the government's purposes to polarize the community.[159]

The war is never far away, and when *itungati* attack nearby, severe retaliation against the civilians often follows. "Rather than face the trigger-happy security forces, the young men and women from the villages which were attacked often went back with the attackers to the bush and forests for fear of being killed. After a raid many of the old people, unable to run and hide, were beaten by the *askaris* until they could no longer stand."[160] Finally the war comes twice to their own community: the first attack results in the Mau Mau burning the village school where Wanjiku now teaches and killing Headman Wangombe, and the second leads to the death of a number of alleged "terrorists." On the morning after the second attack, Wanjiku witnesses a scene reminiscent of Sophocles' *Antigone:* "we pass by nineteen dead naked bodies half burned lying on the ground. The chickens were having a real feast. . . . Some of them are just school boys. My father is very silent tonight because one of the dead men is his cousin, and he has been refused permission by the Chief to bury the body. 'Let them lie there and teach the other villagers a lesson.'"[161] Though Wanjiku remains a strong nationalist, the violence of these two attacks shocks her; she deeply resents the guerrillas for burning down the school and distrusts her pupils, who probably knew the first assault was coming, for not warning her. She feels that she, her family, and her community are trapped. "All of us were in prison. All Central Province was a prison in one way or the other."[162] Terror, of course, works both ways, affecting collaborators and committed Christians under threat of death at the hands of Mau Mau as well as Mau Mau supporters, as the autobiography of Harry Thuku and the biography of Pastor Wanyoike wa Kamawe describe.[163] By 1955, however, the loyalists had turned the tables, and the government's plan to make civilian support for the guerrillas ever more difficult was beginning to work.

The years 1955 and 1956 broke the back of the passive wing. After his return from detention in 1959, J. M. Kariuki's Aunt Wangui told him the story of the hunger and privations that had caused the death of so many members of their community in Nyeri.

> The bell used to ring in the village and some, but not all, were allowed out under guard for one hour to gather food. Planting and cultivation were well-nigh impossible in those circumstances and much maize was, anyway, destroyed as it was thought terrorists might hide in it. . . . Because of movement restrictions no one could escape to other parts of the country or bring in food from more fortunate relatives. Famine and death trampled through the land, claiming many of our women and children.[164]

The harrowing description of work on the great ditch in Wanjiku's testimony to Jean Davison further reinforces the impression of terrible conditions in the Emergency villages in Nyeri, though General China asserts that militarily the ditch was completely ineffective.[165] Driven from their family homes, penned behind barbed wire at night, forced to work at terracing or digging the ditch, kept from their own fields, Gikuyu civilians faced a harsh and increasingly desperate existence, afflicted by hunger Red Cross relief could not alleviate and fearful of the future.

Guerrilla leaders like Kahinga Wachanga were well aware of what was happening but were helpless to do anything effective to prevent it. "During mid-1955 many Gikuyu in the Reserves turned against Mau Mau. They were working from 6:00 a.m. until 6:00 p.m. digging terraces, roads, etc. They had little food, and they were raided by Mau Mau and robbed by the homeguards."[166] The poverty of the civilians even struck the young Kiambu *gitungati* Joram Wamweya. On a raid in December 1954, he and his comrades broke into the home of a civilian family who were worse off than they were. "Far from possessing anything we could confiscate from them, these poor devils would have been happy to receive our assistance. It was nauseating to look at the dirty rags that passed for blankets. We were far better off in the forest."[167] As the civilians turned away from Mau Mau—convinced the rebellion was a lost cause, sick of the violence from both sides, and exhausted by their own suffering—the government began to receive more intelligence against the guerrillas, and in some places was able to mobilize groups of civilians to sweep the bush on the forest fringe to flush out *itungati*.

Defeat

The loss of civilian support was a prime cause of the ultimate Mau Mau defeat, but internal divisions were also important. The problems began at the upper level of the fighting forces. In spite of a succession of high-level meetings in Nyandarua in 1953 and 1954, the leaders had not been able to settle on a mutually acceptable chain of command. Although Dedan Kimathi—with the backing of the North Tetu leaders and *itungati* and some other generals—had assumed the rank of field marshall and began to give out orders as if he were in charge, he was unable to assert his power fully. Stanley Mathenge, whose authority in Nyeri predated Kimathi's, never accepted Kimathi's right to higher command, and his opposition contributed to the disaffection of others, including Generals Mbaria Kaniu and Kahiu-Itina. There is little evidence that the Central Committee or the War Council in Nairobi intervened on the side of either Mathenge or Kimathi, even though Muhimu had originally appointed Mathenge to lead the fight in the Nyandarua forests. Kago also quarreled with Kimathi, returned to the Murang'a reserve, and operated essentially on his own until his death in battle. Neither the Kenya Defence Council nor the Kenya Parliament, both set up at meetings chaired by Kimathi, were able to make decisions binding on all the leaders and all the bands.

Nor were the leaders able to agree on a coordinated strategy. The high-level meeting at Mwathe in August 1953, described by Karari Njama and Kahinga Wachanga, which was attended by many of the important leaders operating in Nyandarua, the reserves, and the Rift Valley (though not Mathenge), named and assigned general responsibilities to eight guerrilla armies and discussed such issues as ranks, the role of women, and the positions and rewards that would be distributed after victory.[168] However, the leaders were unable to agree on a key issue—whether to continue to fight primarily in the reserves or to move most active military operations into the settled areas. As Kahinga Wachanga puts it, "It had become more and more difficult to raid in the Reserves, as security measures were stepped up. Also . . . the government soldiers and the security forces killed and tortured our people in revenge and sometimes we caused their death accidentally during our raid."[169] Kimathi therefore proposed that most raiding be redirected from the reserves to the settled areas and Kahinga Wachanga pointed out that this new strategy would also damage the settlers' interests and possibly win the war by driving them from the country.[170] While Wachanga does not mention a dissenting view raised at Mwathe, he makes it clear that the subsequent actions of the generals showed that they were very divided on this issue. Some of the important leaders did follow "Kimathi's directive," including Mathenge, Macharia, Kahiu-Itina, Kibira, Kimbo, and Wachanga himself, but China, Kariba, Matenjagwo, Kago, and others continued to raid the reserves.[171] "There were several reasons for this. One, food was available, especially at this time. Two, there was less chance of being bombed. And finally, many enjoyed the company of women and preferred the easier life of the Reserves to the great hardships of the forest." Though Wachanga hastens to assert that these generals were "brave men," he states clearly, "I think it would have been better had they followed orders and raided in the settled areas."[172]

The Mwathe outcome also illustrated the characteristic decentralization of the Mau Mau military effort. This decentralization contributed to the serious distrust that developed between Nyeri and Kiambu. Kiambu, as the home district of Harry Thuku and Jomo Kenyatta, had taken the lead in the nonviolent nationalist struggle, and had acted as one of the centers of oathing during the ascendancy of the "Kiambaa Parliament" in the early 1950s. When the war came, however, far more fighters from Nyeri than the other districts joined the guerrilla bands, and there were more battles in the Nyeri and Murang'a reserves than in Kiambu. Njama even disparages Waruingi, the best-known Kiambu general, as the leader of "some small *komerera* gangs."[173] In October 1953, after General Kahiu-Itina had toured the Murang'a-Kiambu border area on Kimathi's orders, he reported that the elders had prevented the development of bands based in the southern Nyandarua forests because they did not want fighting in their reserve. Kimathi then wrote to the Kiambu elders, expressing his dismay at their lack of fighting spirit and his concern that supplies for the northern forces were actually coming through Murang'a rather than through Kiambu, even though Kiambu was "nearer the forest." Kimathi offered to send "leaders and instructors until their army was strong enough to lead itself," and complained to the Kiambu elders that "instead of their leadership, as we expected, they were helping to delay our independence."[174] Njama suspects that the better-educated, more prosperous population of Kiambu wanted to wait on the sidelines and see who won.

Kiambu memoirs reinforce the impression of comparative passivity Njama conveys. While Karigo Muchai contradicts Kimathi's opinion that Kiambu was not active in the supply effort, he confirms that after Lari, the Kiambu elders' committees forbade any military actions in the reserves without their specific authorization, for fear of retaliation against civilians. In September 1953, a guerrilla leader named Gitau Kali, who "was acting in violation of district committee rules, attacking home guard and police posts indiscriminately and giving Government an excuse to punish all nearby villagers" was called before the Kiambu District Committee, reprimanded for his actions, severely punished, and told to lead his band away to Narok.[175] Joram Wamweya's memoir confirms the intense frustration some of the *itungati* felt under the elders' restrictions. "Young men would prepare to go out and fight, but the elders would stop them, telling them to wait, sometimes even locking them up in a house for three, four or five days. At times then, young men lost patience and rebelled, sometimes even manhandling the elders."[176] Wamweya's personal experience, when he did get to fight, also underscores some of the limitations described by Muchai, for he joined the bands of Generals Waruingi and Nubi, who operated not from bases in Kiambu proper but from the area of the Kikuyu Escarpment and from the vicinity of Mt. Longonot in the Rift Valley. The military intelligence officer Frank Kitson also reports information from Kiambu informants that Waruingi was pressured to take his band to the Escarpment forest rather than endanger the supply lines going through Kiambu.[177] The memoirs point to but do not fully explain the comparative quiescence of Kiambu during Mau Mau, except to suggest that the people of the district were sitting it out for their own advantage. Rob Buijtenhuijs has advanced several reasons, including the nonviolent, constitutional tradition within the district as a whole and the involvement of the people of some divisions in internal conflicts, for there were many murders resulting from land disputes in Kiambu during the Emergency.[178] Greet Kershaw points instead to the belief of some Kiambu people that "their Mau Mau" should have been "the standard," their denial that the forest fighters ever wanted them to join in, and their conviction that the Mau Mau war was really an affair of the Rift Valley squatters.[179]

In addition to the well-known hostility between Nyeri and Kiambu, there were miscommunications and even serious disagreements between the main guerrilla leadership in the Nyandarua forests and fighting groups elsewhere. It was difficult to coordinate policy and strategy between the Nyandarua and Kirinyaga fighting bands, and Kahinga Wachanga indicates that this necessitated that a separate branch of the Kenya Parliament be set up on Kirinyaga.[180] The close working relationship between Nyandarua and Kirinyaga that General China had tried to maintain weakened after his capture. More serious was the intense resentment felt by some leaders from the Rift Valley against the leadership in Central Province. Karari Njama reports that Kimbo Mutuku, one of the most important Rift Valley generals fighting in Nyandarua, who regarded himself as the main representative of all those who had lived in the Rift Valley before forcible repatriation, referred in speeches to "WE" (the Rift Valley fighters) and "YOU" (the Central Province fighters), and claimed that the people of the Rift Valley had "contributed more for land and freedom than the Central Province" people.[181] Although Njama believes that Kimbo's main motive was personal, to build himself up as a rival to Kimathi, his attitude does reflect the suspicion felt by one group against another. The imbalance in the commitment and contribution of certain areas and the mutual suspicion led to the weakening of the Mau Mau military effort.

While some of the military difficulties the guerrilla army encountered were internal, others were caused by British action. In addition to counterinsurgency in the forests and reserves, the government moved to disrupt the flow of recruits and supplies, stop the spread of Mau Mau to other groups, and halt the rise of crime in Nairobi through Operation Anvil in April 1954, which was directed primarily against the 45,000 Gikuyu, Embu, and Meru men in the capital (75 percent of the African male population).[182] The security forces rounded up the majority of men from those groups in Nairobi, screened them, and sent most of them either to detention camp or back to their home communities. Ngugi Kabiro escaped Anvil himself due to a visit to Kiambu, but his roommates and many others were swept up. Those Gikuyu, Embu, and Meru who remained were segregated in Bahati location, and those caught outside, like Kabiro, found it almost impossible to return to Nairobi.[183] Anvil, and similar operations in smaller towns afterwards, pinched off supplies to the forest bands and made it much more difficult for the passive wing to help the guerrillas.

The two failed negotiations also contributed to internal divisions within the guerrilla army. The first, at Nyeri in March 1954, was arranged by the captured General China. The two sides, led by Kirinyaga-based General Kariba on the one hand and Ian Henderson on the other, sat down on March 30 to discuss their respective preconditions: the Mau Mau that their leaders be released first to participate and the government that the guerrillas surrender before talks began. These preliminary talks were interrupted so that the Mau Mau representatives could report back to the forest under the protection of a cease-fire; however, the cease-fire only applied to the forests, and a British unit fired on a group of *itungati* under General Gatumuki who had assembled at Itiati in Mathira Division in preparation for surrender. The first negotiations thus broke down, and some leaders came to believe that General China had cooperated with the British to save himself from execution.[184]

The next negotiations had an even more serious effect on Mau Mau unity. The background to this split was the widening gulf between the educated and illiterate fighters (connected to the growing power of Kimathi), which is well reflected in both the Njama and Wachanga memoirs. In a conversation with Karari Njama in October 1954, General Kahiu-Itina, a leader of the illiterates, charged that the educated had been too influenced by missionaries, were not strongly committed to the revolution, were "more Europeanized," and "no matter whether they were leaders in the forests, they rejected many of the old customs and tribal tradition which . . . many others believed we were fighting for as part of our freedom." Kahiu-Itina, a strong supporter of Mathenge, asserted that only illiterate leaders should hold high positions in the forests, the reserves, and the future African government.[185]

Significantly, it was the illiterate leaders (and their educated ally, Kahinga Wachanga) who took the active role in the next peace negotiations. In January 1955, the government declared a two-week cease-fire and sent planes over the forest to sky-shout and drop leaflets offering an amnesty if the Mau Mau surrendered. Initially, according to Kahinga

Wachanga, Kimathi and the other leaders rejected the amnesty offer, but events then took a fateful turn. A group of four Mau Mau turncoats contacted Wachanga on February 10 with a letter for Kimathi from General Erskine, which convinced Wachanga that the British were serious. Wachanga persuaded the government to use sky-shouting to call Kimathi, Stanley Mathenge, and Mbaria Kaniu to a meeting on February 18 at Wachanga's *mbuci*. Mathenge, Mbaria Kaniu, and others came, but Kimathi did not, instead sending Karari Njama as his representative. Over the next several weeks Kimathi "met with some Murang'a leaders and refused to join us," but Wachanga, unaware "how angry Kimathi was" decided to proceed with negotiations himself, with Mathenge's backing.[186] In Nairobi both sides appeared to assume that the other was negotiating from weakness and would be willing under pressure to give up the fight; Wachanga demanded land, freedom, and the release of the interned leaders while the British called for Mau Mau surrender in return for the promise of multiracial government. Meanwhile, as Karari Njama reports, the Kenya Parliament, angered that Mathenge, Mbaria Kaniu, Kahiu-Itina, and others were organizing a new body called the Kenya Riigi "to oppose the Parliament and express the voice of the majority of the fighters who are illiterate," voted on March 26 to assert itself and punish the negotiators for opposing Parliament and negotiating with the British without explicit approval.[187] When Wachanga returned to his *mbuci* to report to Mathenge, Mbaria Kaniu, and other senior leaders, Kimathi's *itungati* arrested all of them. "Kimathi interrogated us upon our arrival in his *mbuci*. He asked us why we had met with the government without him. Kimathi was a very jealous man. He did not want anyone to be above him. He did not like it when we negotiated without him. He had wanted to lead the negotiations himself."[188] Though the captives escaped and Kahinga Wachanga returned to Nairobi, when the talks later broke down, any trust between Kimathi and his followers and Mathenge and his was gone. General China is convinced that the breakdown was caused by spies and agents provocateurs, who "passed on Mau Mau secrets" and tried to set leaders against each other, but this conspiracy theory is not really a sufficient explanation.[189]

It is important to stress, however, that unity did not just fracture vertically between different leaders but also horizontally between *itungati* and leaders and between the guerrilla bands and their erstwhile civilian supporters. The *komerera* problem illustrates this horizontal fracturing. Small bandit groups had always been around on the fringes of guerrilla operational areas. Mohamed Mathu tells of the case of "General" Ndiritu Kirigu, who arrived in Nairobi with thirty *itungati* in January 1954, telling the Nyeri committee "many tales about Dedan Kimathi, Stanley Mathenge . . . and about the fight in the forest," and asking for money and supplies so he could return. After the Nyeri people in Nairobi supplied arms, clothing, medicine, and money, they found that Ndiritu and his band were actually hiding in the reserves as *komerera*.[190] In a high-level meeting on Nyandarua in November 1953, General China and his officers decided to "wage war" against *komerera* because their loyalty to the movement was suspect and they were preying on civilians.[191]

Njama reports that there was an increase in *komerera* groups in the second half of 1954, as five or ten *itungati* at a time left the large bands to escape their leaders' control, get away from the bombing, and be closer to the supplies of food in the reserves.[192] For some this desertion was a form of protest against their leaders. Kariuki tells of the agitation of Joseph Mbaya, who told other *itungati* that the generals

> never went to war, but only sent *itungati* to die; that they never went to fetch their own food [but] were fed with the best food available at the cost of *itungati* lives. Their tents and belongings were always carried by *itungati;* they never collected firewood or made their own fires, yet they were the most famous fighters. He had told the *itungati* that they were fighting for leaders' slavery and not for freedom. He told them that the true liberty of all persons was equality of all persons in which one was free from anyone's rule.[193]

Although Njama suspected that Mbaya was an agent provocateur, his new militantly egalitarian message did reflect radical discontent among the *itungati* that could not be mollified by promotions or promises of land and jobs after victory. Kimathi and the Kenya Parliament attempted to re-establish control by arresting radical leaders; in 1955 the court at Chieni in northern Nyandarua convicted and executed one leader for administering a "strange oath" to *itungati* in which they pledged no longer to follow leaders who would not fetch firewood and food for themselves, build their own huts, and carry their own luggage, and Kimathi judged and shot another leader out of hand.[194]

As conditions worsened in the forest, it was sometimes difficult to tell the difference between renegades and guerrillas. During a tour of northern Nyandarua in late 1954 Karari Njama was shocked by the deterioration in the state of the ordinary *itungati*.

> Most of the camps I had visited had no huts and only a few tents for shelters and many slept under trees in the open. Most of the *itungati* were dressed in oily stinky rags. A few had started making animal skin coats, jumpers, caps and pants. Their hair, which had not been shaved nor combed for more than two years and which was generally smeared with animal oil, had grown long, curling and falling over their forefaces and ears. Many of the fighters had lost their weight and their bright faces had turned to be thin and black.[195]

Joram Wamweya was one of those ordinary *itungati* on the run in the Rift Valley in late 1954. Like the men described by Karari Njama, he and his comrades had to move so frequently due to enemy pressure that they never built shelters anymore but simply slept out in the rain. Often hungry, they raided civilians for food, stealing from Mau Mau supporters and loyalists alike. By now "freedom fighters were treated like wild animals by everybody."[196]

The best example of this treatment comes from the memoir of Kiboi Muriithi, who describes firsthand his experience as the hunted prey of a sweep of soldiers and Meru civilians on the slopes of Kirinyaga in the spring of 1956:

> We lay still, watching and waiting. After half an hour a faint noise stirred the forest, gradually growing louder and louder as it drew nearer. Then through the trees we saw hundreds of people approaching in line—first soldiers, then police and men of the Kenya Regiment, then the civilian men and women of Meru in their hundreds, armed with long sharpened sticks, shouting and rattling their weapons like beaters on a lion hunt. Barring retreat was another line coming in the opposite direction. Desperately we tried another direction, only to hear the shouting again as another line moved slowly forward towards us. The trap had been sprung and was closing in on us.[197]

The terror and humiliation of this experience—described from a perspective that is the exact opposite of Frank Kitson's when he flushed Waruingi and his band from the Kiambu bush—is unmistakable. Although Muriithi escaped with a remnant of his band of Meru *itungati,* he and the other survivors were destroyed as an effective fighting force, reduced to the state of fugitives on the run, and finally wiped out several weeks later.

The end was at hand. In Nairobi loyalists and turncoats now dominated, for "so many of the fighters had been arrested through betrayal by surrenderers that all activity had come to a halt."[198] "Pseudo-gangs" of turncoats preyed on the remaining forest bands, killing and capturing many, including Muriithi's small remnant on Kirinyaga.[199] Government planes crisscrossed the forest skies, sky-shouting for the guerrillas to surrender and dropping leaflets threatening to confiscate their land and property. Cut off from most civilian aid, the bands that remained together after 1956 no longer made up a guerrilla army. In Wachanga's words, "Everyone knows that no army can defend itself against its enemies without food or weapons. The colonial government finally became successful in the long struggle by depriving us of our support."[200]

Conclusion

Mau Mau was a war of peasant rebels to win land and adulthood for themselves, land and political rights for their ethnic groups, and national independence for all Kenyan Africans. As I have suggested above and in Chapter 3, Mau Mau guerrilla life and warfare represented ingenious adaptations to unprecedented and difficult circumstances. Drawing on indigenous traditions, the heritage of African protest politics, lessons learned in building the secret movement, and experiences in the British army, leaders and the men and women under their command set up and organized camps in the forests, established links to civilian supporters in their home communities, and developed supply networks and forest weapons factories. In the forest camps—through political meetings and debates, patriotic songs, and syncretistic religious observances—the Mau Mau developed a strong culture of resistance and tested a way of living that could serve as a model for a new society and belief system after the war. From their camps the guerrillas launched military operations intended in the short term to seize arms (Naivasha), win recruits (Lukenya), damage the counterinsurgency (Othaya), and defend the home bases against attack; in the long term, overall Mau Mau goals were more political than military: to build the movement, to isolate its African enemies, to drive out settlers, and to use military pressure to force the government to release the detained leaders and negotiate for Kenyan independence and the return of the lands.[201]

The importance of politics is shown by the attention paid in the memoirs to meetings in the forest camps and to relations with civilians. The descriptions of leaders' meetings in Njama and Itote show the effort generals expended in trying to work out what their relationship should be with the detained leaders, how they should structure the movement, how they should relate to civilians, and how they should deal with the British. In the general camp meetings, and the songs and religious observances that accompanied them, leaders like Kimathi, Matenjagwo, and Wachanga strove to educate their followers on the history of government and settler oppression, convince them of their proud past and glorious future, and inspire them with enthusiasm to fight for land and freedom. As Wunyabari Maloba points out, however, the guerrilla leaders were not as successful in politicizing the Gikuyu civilian population, relying too much on the oath and not enough on real political education.[202] While General China did some politicizing of civilians on Kirinyaga in the early stages, there is less evidence of this later on and little on the other fighting fronts such as Nyandarua. This meant that the guerrilla forces had to depend too much on the civilians' loyalty to kin and neighbors in the bands, their ethnic patriotism, their resentment of the British, and their fear of the guerrillas. When the guerrilla forces suffered defeats and the counterinsurgency tightened its grip, the guerrillas lost their hold on the civilians as their prestige declined and the cost of supporting them rose dramatically. As Basil Davidson points out in *The People's Cause,* later African guerrilla movements like that of Guinea-Bissau put much more emphasis on civilian politicization, concluding that they received in return more sustained civilian support.[203]

On the other hand, in her controversial *Zimbabwe's Guerrilla War,* Norma Kriger emphasizes the role of coercion in guerrilla-civilian relations, suggesting that it can play a more important part than most scholars realize.[204] General China's description of his own use of intimidation, combined with the oath and political instruction, shows that Mau Mau leaders were aware of the power of coercion and willing to use it, though none of the memoirs discuss coercion of civilians in detail.

In the memoirs the tension between unity and division within the movement, a common problem in guerrilla forces, is a constant thread. The reader is struck by the unstable balance between the requirements of control, within each *mbuci* and across the guerrilla movement, and the need for consultation and representation. The civilian elders of Muhimu and the War Council began by giving orders to forest leaders, but their influence soon faded as the leaders gained autonomy. Ambitious generals asserted authority in the name of discipline while *itungati* demanded in return effective leadership, responsiveness to their needs, and recognition of the special nature of their volunteer service. Kimathi assumed the mantle of field marshal, set up the Kenya Defence Council and Kenya Parliament, and attempted to give orders and coordinate political and military strategy, only to face the opposition of first Mathenge and then Mbaria Kaniu, Kahiu-Itina, Kahinga Wachanga, and others. Nyeri fighters assumed a leadership role by force of numbers, then had to deal not only with the suspicions of Murang'a and Rift Valley fighters but also with the noncooperation of the Kiambu elders' committees. Generals attempted to control the *komerera* on the forest fringes, but some renegade leaders eventually attracted discontented *itungati* with a new antiauthority, egalitarian message. Educated men like Kimathi and Njama first moved to the fore, often encouraged by the illiterate (as Mathenge encouraged Njama), but eventually many uneducated fighters became disaffected and formed the Kenya Riigi in opposition to the Kenya Parliament. As Luise White stresses, this last division may have been the most significant of all, because it represented a cultural split that mirrored both the break between educated constitutional moderates and followers of the secret movement in the early 1950s and divisions within colonial Gikuyu society as constructed by the British. White also suggests that Riigi leaders were more egalitarian, which clearly applies to Mathenge himself and to Mbaria Kaniu, whose favorite proverb was *"Nyumba nene ndiri muriri"* ("a large family does not need a guardian"), but not to the rather elitist Kahinga Wachanga.[205] Barnett points out that some members of the "pseudo-gangs" Ian Henderson used against Kimathi in northern Nyandarua in 1956 were Kenya Riigi supporters.[206] But the Parliament, the rival of the Riigi, was not united behind Kimathi; Njama's account reveals his increasing dislike of Kimathi's ambitions and his effort in April 1955, with other Othaya representatives, to try to heal the split.[207]

Many anticolonial wars are civil conflicts as well, and Mau Mau both adopted internecine violence early and reconsidered it soon. As in other similar situations—from Ireland in 1919–1921, to Algeria during its war with the French, to the West Bank of Palestine during the *intifada,* to the South African townships in the late 1980s—much of the rebel violence was used against collaborating police, civil officials, and other loyalists in the effort to destroy the buffer force the government had used to divide and rule and to unite the community in support of the uprising. Though Mau Mau leaders pursued a similar strategy in the beginning, they soon developed second thoughts. In a real sense Mau Mau leaders were trying to undo the effects of their own actions, for the secret movement began the deadly cycle of internecine violence against loyalists and oath resisters. Mau Mau killings of collaborators and informers in 1952 were followed by Lari and the other guerrilla attacks in the spring of 1953, but when these attacks led to severe retaliation against the passive wing by home guards, police, and military, the civilian supporters appealed to the generals to reconsider. Facing the dilemma all guerrilla leaders must face, some Mau Mau commanders backed off, choosing to sacrifice their military effectiveness to the protection of the civilian community. Moreover, though the Kikuyu Guard acted as the first line of defense for the colonial system, many had taken the oath, and a dispute arose within Mau Mau between some who wanted to eliminate them as the main enemies, and others who argued that the principal target should be the British, who were deliberately pitting Gikuyu against each other.[208] This debate, the discussions about fighting in the reserves, and the prohibitions imposed on the killing of women and children, show that in spite of the civil slaughter, Mau Mau warfare, the propaganda of its enemies notwithstanding, was not fought "with no holds barred." Concerned about the long-term damage to their communities and to Gikuyu ethical life, the elders and the guerrillas struggled against the odds to fight a war with rules.

Turning to strategy, the debate at the Mwathe meeting in September 1953, over whether the guerrilla forces would continue to fight in the reserves or move to the Rift Valley can be seen as an important test to determine whether the leaders could accept the orders of a high command and agree on a coordinated strategy, and whether their bands would fight away from their original home areas. Njama, a Kimathi sympathizer, and Wachanga, a Mathenge man, agreed on the change in strategy and both deplored the inability of the leaders to fall in with a high-level decision. The aftermath of Mwathe also demonstrates how Mau Mau war-making was undermined by the decentralization of the guerrilla forces, a strength in the beginning but fatal to concerted efforts in the end. As General China admits, "Our fight was not a single, organised campaign carried out by a trained, disciplined and well-equipped army. It was often disorganised and fragmented."[209] A guerrilla army whose units are linked to local elders' committees and which depends on specific communities for food and recruits is certain to face difficulties in stepping up to the next level of coordinated strategy and in sending bands to fight far from their home grounds.

Guerrilla armies are usually militarily weak, but the Land and Freedom Army in Kenya fought under greater disadvantages than most irregular forces in the twentieth century. Unlike the Soviet and Yugoslav partisans of World War II, the Mau Mau forces had only a few leaders with military training, a rank and file almost completely unfamiliar with modern warfare, and no outside sources of supply. While the FLN in Algeria could set up bases across international borders and establish a government in exile, the Mau Mau were essentially isolated within Central Kenya. While ZANLA in Zimbabwe could count on the backing of both frontline African states and other members of the international community, the Land and Freedom Army enjoyed no such support.[210] Like the similarly isolated rebels in Madagascar, the Mau Mau were very short of modern arms, more so than either the resistance forces during World War II or the liberation armies that would follow them in Africa.[211]

It is common wisdom that a guerrilla movement does not have to win, it just has to avoid losing—but to do so it must remain an effective fighting force for a long period of time in order to wear down its opponent, if not militarily at least politically. While this happened in the 1950s in Algeria (and later in the 1970s in Zimbabwe), it did not happen in Kenya. By 1960 the Algerian forces were losing most of their battles with the French army, but six years of bloody, costly war and a change of government had sapped the political will to win in Paris, and negotiations began that led to an independent Algeria under FLN control.[212] In the case of Kenya, in spite of the expectations of Kahinga Wachanga, the Mau Mau–British negotiations were not going to lead to an African government with an important role for Mau Mau leaders, for the guerrillas had not damaged the British enough for a sufficiently long period of time.[213] Instead, by 1955 the guerrillas themselves were losing their civilian base and unraveling militarily.

Notes

1. Wachanga, *Swords,* p. 168.
2. Ibid., p. 170.
3. Gikoyo, *We Fought for Freedom,* p. 56.
4. Mao Tse-tung, *On Guerrilla Warfare* (New York: Praeger, 1961); Ernesto (Che) Guevara, *Guerrilla Warfare* (New York: Vintage, 1969); Amilcar Cabral, *Revolution in Guinea* (London: Stage One Publishers, 1969).
5. Buijtenhuijs, *Le mouvement "Mau Mau,"* Chs. 8, 9; Edgerton, *Mau Mau: An African Crucible,* Ch. 4; Maloba, *Mau Mau and Kenya,* Ch. 6. Rosberg and Nottingham devote only seven pages to the fighting; *Myth of "Mau Mau,"* pp. 296–303.

6. Wachanga, *Swords*, pp. x–xi, and Chap. 7.

7. Gikoyo, *We Fought for Freedom*, p. 110.

8. Itote, *General*, p. 47.

9. Wachanga, *Swords*, pp. 41–42.

10. Ibid., p. 32.

11. Ibid., Ch. 3; Njama, *Mau Mau from Within*, p. 129; Gikoyo, *We Fought for Freedom*, pp. 140–44; see also Paul Maina, *Six Mau Mau Generals* (Nairobi: Gazelle Books, 1977), pp. 33–74, 125–49.

12. Wachanga, *Swords*, p. 32.

13. Ibid., p. 29.

14. Ibid., p. 26.

15. Ibid., pp. 28–29.

16. Muriithi, *War in the Forest*, p. 32.

17. Ibid., pp. 29–30.

18. Wachanga, *Swords*, p. 30.

19. Gikoyo, *We Fought for Freedom*, Ch. 11; see also descriptions in Maina, *Generals*, pp. 33–74, 125–49, and in PRO WO 276/459.

20. Njama, *Mau Mau from Within*, p. 174.

21. Quoted by Whittier in preface to Wachanga, *Swords*, p. x.

22. Njama, *Mau Mau from Within*, pp. 205–206.

23. Wachanga, *Swords*, p. 36.

24. Ibid., pp. 36–38; Muriithi, *War in the Forest*, p. 29.

25. Gikoyo, *We Fought for Freedom*, pp. 61–63.

26. Njama, *Mau Mau from Within*, pp. 191–94.

27. Gikoyo, *We Fought for Freedom*, pp. 99–103.

28. Muriithi, *War in the Forest*, p. 31.

29. Wamweya, *Freedom Fighter*, pp. 149–50.

30. Buijtenhuijs, *Essays*, p. 57.

31. Lonsdale, "Moral Economy," p. 326; "No Easy Walk, Kenya," a film for Channel Four Television, 1987.

32. Wamweya, *Freedom Fighter*, p. 54.

33. Gikoyo, *We Fought for Freedom*, p. 43; Njama, *Mau Mau from Within*, p. 143.

34. Muriithi, *War in the Forest*, pp. 15–16.

35. Muchai, *Hardcore*, pp. 28–30.

36. Njama, *Mau Mau from Within*, pp. 141–43.

37. Ibid., p. 174.

38. Ibid., p. 176.

39. Ibid., p. 299.

40. Ibid., p. 175.

41. Itote, *General*, p. 61.

42. Njama, *Mau Mau from Within*, p. 173.

43. Whittier, in Wachanga, *Swords*, p. xi.

44. Maughan-Brown, *Land, Freedom, and Fiction*, p. 56.

45. Buijtenhuijs, *Mau Mau Twenty Years After*, p. 47.

46. Wachanga, *Swords*, p. 42.

47. Ibid., p. 161.

48. Ibid.; Itote, *General*, p. 77; Gikoyo, *We Fought for Freedom*, p. 59.

49. Muriithi, *War in the Forest*, p. 64.

50. Njama, *Mau Mau from Within*, p. 250.

51. Muriithi, *War in the Forest*, p. 29.

52. Ibid., p. 53; Itote, *General*, p. 76; Njama, *Mau Mau from Within*, p. 167.

53. Muriithi, *War in the Forest,* pp. 32–33.
54. Njama, *Mau Mau from Within,* p. 291; Muriithi, *War in the Forest,* p. 17.
55. Njama, *Mau Mau from Within,* p. 160.
56. Muriithi, *War in the Forest,* pp. 37–41; cf. Kanogo, *Squatters,* p. 147.
57. Itote, *Mau Mau in Action,* p. 142.
58. Njama, *Mau Mau from Within,* p. 257.
59. Muriithi, *War in the Forest,* p. 32; Gen. Hinde was impressed with Mau Mau training and discipline, "Brief for Commander-in-Chief," June 6, 1953, Hinde Papers, RH Mss. Afr. s. 1580 (12).
60. Gikoyo, *We Fought for Freedom,* pp. 61, 65–66.
61. Wachanga, *Swords,* p. 87.
62. Njama, *Mau Mau from Within,* p. 178.
63. Ibid., p. 181.
64. Santilli, "Kikuyu Women in Mau Mau," pp. 143–59; White, "Separating the Men from the Boys"; Presley, *Kikuyu Women;* Davison, *Voices from Mutira;* Jean O'Barr, introduction to Likimani, *Passbook Number F. 47927.*
65. Presley, *Kikuyu Women,* Ch. 6.
66. White, "Separating the Men from the Boys," p. 12; Njama, *Mau Mau from Within,* pp. 221–22.
67. Gikoyo, *We Fought for Freedom,* p. 64.
68. Wachanga, *Swords,* p. 37.
69. Itote, *General,* p. 78.
70. Barnett, in Njama, *Mau Mau from Within,* p. 226.
71. Ibid., p. 242.
72. Ibid., pp. 242–43.
73. Ibid., pp. 247–49.
74. Ibid., p. 226; Dennis Holman, *Bwana Drum* (London: W. H. Allen, 1964), p. 94.
75. Njama, *Mau Mau from Within,* p. 450; Holman, *Bwana Drum,* p. 94.
76. Santilli, "Kikuyu Women in Mau Mau," p. 152.
77. Gikoyo, *We Fought for Freedom,* pp. 91–94; see also Njama, *Mau Mau from Within,* p. 195.
78. Itote, *General,* pp. 136–38.
79. White, "Separating the Men from the Boys," p. 11.
80. Itote, *General,* p. 105.
81. Ibid., pp. 278–79; Davison, *Voices from Mutira,* pp. 160–61. Wanoi later became an informant for Jean Davison.
82. Itote, *General,* p. 101; Davison, *Voices from Mutira,* p. 160.
83. Njama, *Mau Mau from Within,* pp. 226–27.
84. Presley, *Kikuyu Women,* pp. 130–36.
85. Kanogo, *Squatters,* pp. 144–49; for an official comment on women in Mau Mau, see Police Commissioner O'Rorke, "Situation Appreciation," Feb. 18, 1953, PRO CO 822/447.
86. Santilli, "Kikuyu Women in Mau Mau," p. 149.
87. Leakey, *Defeating Mau Mau,* pp. 41–52.
88. Wachanga, *Swords,* p. 89.
89. Wamweya, *Freedom Fighter,* pp. 144–45.
90. Njama, *Mau Mau from Within,* pp. 260–61.
91. Wachanga, *Swords,* pp. 87–89.
92. Itote, *General,* pp. 61–62.
93. Njama, *Mau Mau from Within,* p. 205.
94. Itote, *General,* pp. 82–83; Wachanga, *Swords,* pp. 57–58.

95. Wachanga, *Swords*, p. 43; Itote, *Mau Mau in Action*, p. 27.
96. Muriithi, *War in the Forest*, p. 40.
97. Ibid., p. 65.
98. Itote, *General*, p. 64; compare the coercion of peasants by guerrillas in Zimbabwe, Kriger, *Zimbabwe's Guerrilla War*, p. 19, Ch. 4.
99. Itote, *General*, p. 50.
100. Njama, *Mau Mau from Within*, p. 177.
101. Ibid., pp. 189, 209.
102. Ibid., p. 188.
103. Wachanga, *Swords*, p. 18.
104. Muchai, *Hardcore*, p. 22.
105. Gikoyo, *We Fought for Freedom*, p. 70.
106. Njama, *Mau Mau from Within*, pp. 222–23.
107. Gikoyo, *We Fought for Freedom*, p. 55.
108. Njama, *Mau Mau from Within*, p. 174.
109. Wachanga, *Swords*, p. 57.
110. Itote, *General*, p. 97.
111. Wachanga, *Swords*, p. 57.
112. Itote, *General*, pp. 105–106; Holman, *Bwana Drum*, p. 162.
113. Muchai, *Hardcore*, p. 28.
114. Itote, *General*, p. 103.
115. Ibid., p. 104; Njama, *Mau Mau from Within*, p. 174.
116. Njama, *Mau Mau from Within*, p. 196.
117. Itote, *General*, p. 105.
118. Gikoyo, *We Fought for Freedom*, pp. 135–36. Security force disguises worn by Mau Mau really troubled the government, see Daily Report, April 29, 1953, PRO CO 822/454.
119. Muchai, *Hardcore*, p. 29.
120. Njama, *Mau Mau from Within*, p. 164.
121. Itote, *General*, pp. 70–71.
122. Ibid., p. 73. Army patrolling by contrast tended to be noisy and ineffectual; see report by Venn Fey of KPR in Hinde Papers, RH Mss. Afr. s. 1580 (2).
123. Wachanga, *Swords*, pp. 73–74.
124. Njama, *Mau Mau from Within*, p. 207.
125. Ibid., pp. 207–208.
126. Erskine, foreword to *Handbook of Mau Mau*, p. 1.
127. Gikoyo, *We Fought for Freedom*, p. 66.
128. Wachanga, *Swords*, p. 33.
129. Ibid., pp. 57–59; Itote, *General*, pp. 81–85.
130. Holman, *Bwana Drum*, p. 134.
131. Wachanga, *Swords*, pp. 52–53; Mathu, *Urban Guerrilla*, pp. 45–46.
132. Mathu, *Urban Guerrilla*, pp. 49–51. The Lukenya attack led the government to strengthen detention camp security. Kenya Colony, *Report on the General Administration of Prisons and Detention Camps in Kenya* (Nairobi: Government Printer, 1956), p. 2.
133. Wachanga, *Swords*, p. 61.
134. Njama, *Mau Mau from Within*, pp. 177–78; see Othaya "Incident Report" in PRO CO 822/454.
135. Tweedie to Hinde, May 25, 1953, RH Hinde Papers, Mss. Afr. s. 1580 (1).
136. Wachanga, *Swords*, p. 62.
137. Maloba, *Mau Mau and Kenya*, p. 127.

138. Muriithi, *War in the Forest,* Chs. 4–6; cf. Itote, *Mau Mau in Action,* p. 19.

139. Itote, *Mau Mau in Action,* p. 118; Wachanga, *Swords,* p. 39.

140. Wachanga, *Swords,* p. 86.

141. Muchai, *Hardcore,* p. 25; also Itote, *General,* p. 132.

142. Itote, *General,* p. 57.

143. Gikoyo, *We Fought for Freedom,* pp. 136–37.

144. Wachanga, *Swords,* p. 44.

145. Ibid., p. 44; see also on castration, Kariuki, *Detainee,* p. 41; on abuse of women, Presley, *Kikuyu Women,* p. 133; on dragging behind Land Rovers, Edgerton, *Mau Mau: An African Crucible,* pp. 152–53; on killing and dismemberment of a British soldier by Gen. Mwariama's band, see David Njagi, *The Last Mau Mau Field Marshals . . . Their Own Story* (Meru: Ngwataniro Self-Help Group, 1993), p. 52.

146. Wachanga, *Swords,* p. 44.

147. Gikoyo, *We Fought for Freedom,* p. 118.

148. J. Wilkinson, "The Mau Mau Movement: Some General and Medical Aspects," *East African Medical Journal,* vol. 31, no. 7 (1954), p. 310.

149. Gikoyo, *We Fought for Freedom,* p. 114.

150. Njama, *Mau Mau from Within,* p. 128.

151. Karuki, *Detainee,* p. 37.

152. Rosberg and Nottingham, *Myth of "Mau Mau,"* pp. 287–91.

153. Muchai, *Hardcore,* pp. 23–24.

154. Kabiro, *Man in the Middle,* p. 64; Wachanga, *Swords,* p. 92.

155. Waciuma, *Daughter of Mumbi,* pp. 112–18.

156. Ibid., p. 115.

157. Ibid., p. 121.

158. Ibid., p. 132.

159. Ibid., pp. 133, 138.

160. Ibid., p. 116.

161. Ibid., p. 138. Kandara Division had the largest Kikuyu Guard complement in Murang'a District, with more than 800 guards in fifteen posts, one of which was Waciuma's village. J. A. Rutherford et al., "History of the Fort Hall Kikuyu Guard 1952–55," p. 15.

162. Ibid., p. 129.

163. Harry Thuku, *An Autobiography* (Nairobi: Oxford University Press, 1970), pp. 69–71.

164. Kariuki, *Detainee,* pp. 147–48.

165. Davison, *Mutira,* p. 51; Itote, *Mau Mau in Action,* p. 178.

166. Wachanga, *Swords,* pp. 93–94; see similar description in Wataro's story in Davison, *Mutira,* p. 103.

167. Wamweya, *Freedom Fighter,* p. 155.

168. Njama, *Mau Mau from Within,* pp. 245–49.

169. Wachanga, *Swords,* p. 82.

170. Ibid., pp. 81–82.

171. Ibid., p. 82; but see China's comments, Itote, *General,* p. 148.

172. Ibid., p. 82. The British in fact were very concerned that Mau Mau might redirect its actions against the settled area and force the army to spread themselves thin guarding isolated farms, "Intelligence Appreciation," RH Hinde Papers, Mss. Afr. s. 1580 (12).

173. Njama, *Mau Mau from Within,* p. 297; but see Wachanga, *Swords,* p. 179.

174. Ibid., p. 297.

175. Muchai, *Hardcore,* pp. 31–32.

176. Wamweya, *Freedom Fighter,* p. 63.

177. Kitson, *Gangs and Counter-Gangs,* p. 57.

178. Buijtenhuijs, *Essays,* pp. 191, 203.

179. Kershaw, *Mau Mau from Below,* p. 330. The African Affairs Department considered the limited Mau Mau activity in Kiambu "the great enigma of the Emergency," Kenya Colony, African Affairs Department, *Annual Report, 1953* (Nairobi, 1955), p. 23.

180. Wachanga, *Swords,* p. 41.

181. Njama, *Mau Mau from Within,* p. 374.

182. Operation Anvil, Outline Plan by Joint Commanders, March 8, 1954, PRO WO 276/189, p. 5.

183. Kabiro, *Man in the Middle,* p. 63; the government was pleased, see Acting Gov. to Colonial Sec., May 9, 1954, PRO CO 822/796.

184. Itote, *General,* Chs. 22, 26.

185. Njama, *Mau Mau from Within,* pp. 397–98.

186. Wachanga, *Swords,* pp. 106–107.

187. Njama, *Mau Mau from Within,* p. 471.

188. Wachanga, *Swords,* p. 123.

189. Itote, *Mau Mau in Action,* pp. 10–13.

190. Mathu, *Urban Guerrilla,* pp. 25–26.

191. Itote, *General,* pp. 139–41.

192. Njama, *Mau Mau from Within,* p. 397.

193. Ibid., p. 406.

194. Ibid., pp. 479–80.

195. Ibid., p. 397.

196. Wamweya, *Freedom Fighter,* p. 151.

197. Muriithi, *War in the Forest,* p. 82.

198. Gikoyo, *We Fought for Freedom,* p. 199.

199. Muriithi, *War in the Forest,* p. 86.

200. Wachanga, *Swords,* p. 95.

201. See Wachanga, *Swords,* Ch. 7, on negotiation goals. The heroic ambitions of Mau Mau leaders are well evoked by Ngugi wa Thiong'o in Abdullah's description of his Mau Mau war in *Petals of Blood* (London: Heinemann, 1977), which seems to be based on the memoirs, pp. 140–42.

202. Maloba, *Mau Mau and Kenya,* p. 120.

203. Basil Davidson, *The People's Cause: A History of Guerrillas in Africa* (Burnt Hill: Longman, 1981), Chs. 11, 14.

204. Kriger, *Zimbabwe's Guerrilla War,* pp. 152–57.

205. White, "Separating the Men from the Boys," pp. 11–12; Wachanga, *Swords,* p. 30.

206. Barnett, in Njama and Barnett, *Mau Mau from Within,* p. 488.

207. Njama, *Mau Mau from Within,* p. 481.

208. Ibid., p. 214.

209. Itote, *Mau Mau in Action,* p. 5.

210. Laqueur, *Guerrilla,* pp. 202–20; Anthony Clayton, *The Wars of French Decolonization* (London: Longman, 1994), Chs. 7–9; David Martin and Phyllis Johnson, *The Struggle for Zimbabwe: The Chimurenga War* (New York: Monthly Review, 1981), Chs. 11–14.

211. Clayton, *Wars of French Decolonization,* pp. 82–87.

212. Ibid., p. 158.

213. *Handbook of Anti Mau Mau,* p. 3. Gen. Lathbury believed that exhausting the British was a Mau Mau strategy. "The Kenya Emergency May 1955–Nov. 1956," PRO WO 236/20.

CHAPTER 6

The Ordeal of Detention

The following morning the train pulled into Mackinnon Road station. The camp was a quarter of a mile away and getting down I noticed two long rows of *askari*. Each man held a rifle or a baton and they formed a pathway to the camp through which we had to pass. We were ordered to hold our belongings on our heads and run through, being hit by rifle butts and night sticks over the entire distance. Holding tightly my few possessions, I ran along trying to avoid or ward off the blows of the *askari*.

—*Karigo Muchai*[1]

To be detained on an island is an unforgettable experience An unforgettable three-days journey from Kajiado to Lamu.

Wherever they try to isolate us
Whatever tribulations they put us through
We will never give up our bid to regain our land
God is our guardian, we shall regain our freedom.

—*Gakaara wa Wanjau*[2]

With defeat, most of the surviving Mau Mau spent two to eight years detained in one or more government camps, facing privation, brutality, and pressure to confess their oaths and their actions for the secret movement. The detention camps saw a struggle between two kinds of control. The British dominated space, physical power, and time, using barbed wire and compounds, armed warders, the camp schedule, sudden interrogations, and frequent, unexpected transfers from one camp to another. In defense the Mau Mau "hardcore" turned to the less tangible but also powerful control mechanisms of movement and community, using the compound leader, the rules, the "clubs," religion, songs, group discussions. To undermine the Mau Mau collective defenses, the British then combined their basic strategy with a more subtle strategy of appeals, enticements, and threats known as "rehabilitation" in order to break hardcore cohesion by detaching the individual from the community and the persuadable from the strongly resistant. In the end, neither side won. The memoirs are the main sources reflecting the Mau Mau side of this extended struggle.

With some exceptions—notably Cora Presley, Luise White, and Marina Santoru—historians of Mau Mau have rather neglected the experience of detention, in comparison to the attention they have given to the origins of the secret movement, the oaths, the organization of Mau Mau, and the guerrilla war.[3] Though the comprehensive studies of Rosberg and Nottingham, Edgerton, and Maloba have each discussed the government's system of camps and program of rehabilitation, their analyses have not dealt at any length on what detention was like from the point of view of the detainees.[4] By contrast, most of the Mau Mau memoirists devote a substantial portion of their narratives to the camp experience, and two of the most important memoirs, those of Josiah Mwangi Kariuki and Gakaara wa Wanjau, deal almost exclusively with their lives in the camps. This chapter will use the memoirs, supported by government sources and other materials, to describe and analyze the camp experience from the hardcore detainees' point of view.

Ngugi Kabiro and Charity Waciuma were never detained, and Karari Njama's account contains no description of his detention. All the other Mau Mau authors were held in one or more camps, and describe the experience in their memoirs, usually at length. Bildad Kaggia and Waruhiu Itote were separated out as leaders for special treatment; the others lived in mass camps with other detainees, though usually in compounds specifically reserved for hardcore. Most lived in at least several and in a few cases many camps; through their memoirs, we have detailed accounts of Manyani, Manda/Takwa, Athi River, Saiyusi, Lodwar, Mackinnon Road, and Hola. Moreover, with the exception of Karigo Muchai, who ended up in the hardcore camp at Hola and was badly beaten during the "Hola massacre," most of the memoirists must have shown, deceptively or otherwise, some potential for change, for the authorities both attempted to "rehabilitate" them and eventually moved them through "the pipeline" toward home. The memoirs as a whole, then, can be taken as broadly representative of the experience of the more than 80,000 Kenyans—over 73,000 men and 8,000 women—interned in detention, works, and district camps during the Kenya Emergency.[5]

Into Detention

It is striking that in accounts not notable for chronological precision, all the Mau Mau authors remember the day and circumstances of their arrests, for the beginning of captivity marked a sharp dividing line in their lives. It was not easy to accept defeat. Gucu Gikoyo, run down and surrounded by heavily armed police and General Service Unit men in Pangani location,

Nairobi, in April 1955, thought of the proverb *"Ikurundwo ndiregaga ruoro"* (once on the ground there is no refusing the brand) and reluctantly resigned himself to his fate.[6] The others who surrendered—Karari Njama, Waruhiu Itote, Kiboi Muriithi, and Joram Wamweya—were either wounded or facing complete isolation or even starvation. Almost all evaded capture or put off surrender as long as possible, fearing that they would be either shot out of hand or soon executed.

Though they were not killed, they entered a world of constantly threatening violence. On the afternoon of Karigo Muchai's arrest, two African CID men took him out of his cell, threw him into a pit at the back of the station, and flogged him with a hippo-hide whip for five minutes at a time while they demanded that he confess his membership in Mau Mau, only stopping altogether after two hours when he fainted from the pain. Mohamed Mathu, captured after a battle outside Nairobi in October 1954, began his imprisonment with a beating by three Europeans wielding a whip, a chain, and a club. "Each time I refused to alter my story or answer their questions a flurry of blows rained upon me." When Gucu Gikoyo was brought to his first interrogation an officer beat him with a club for some time, presumably to "soften him up," before he even began to question him. The memoirs indicate that the interrogators used violence to break a captive quickly and get fresh information before his comrades learned that he had been taken into custody.[7]

British captors also used the longer-term tools of deprivation, humiliation, and psychological pressure to wear down their prisoners. The KPR officer in charge of interrogating Kahinga Wachanga degraded him by pulling out his beard, spitting into his mouth, and giving him only one meal of *posho* (maize meal) a day.[8] Karigo Muchai was deprived of water for twenty-four hours after his arrest, and later while confined at CID headquarters became convinced that the authorities were providing as little food as possible in a deliberate effort to break the prisoners by starvation. Three women prisoners held in the same building gave birth right there, in terrible conditions, with only other female prisoners to help them. In some cases cells were so overcrowded that people had to stand up all night; excrement and other filth was allowed to accumulate; inmates had to spend cold nights naked or with only a thin blanket to cover them. To demoralize or terrorize the prisoners, the officers in charge forced them to observe the beatings of others, share cells with wounded or dying men, and carry, fingerprint, and disrobe the bodies of the dead, actions that violated Gikuyu taboos.[9] Through frequent interrogations at unpredictable times, their captors took advantage of the prisoners' vulnerability to extract information.

J. M. Kariuki's first experiences of the violence, deprivation, and depersonalization characteristic of the detainee experience came at Langata reception camp near Nairobi where detainees were usually sent after the first round of interrogations at a police station or CID headquarters. His initiation began at the gate when a KPR officer reached into the open vehicle with a long stick and began beating men indiscriminately, and continued in the compound when another officer told his group to squat in lines for counting and struck the man at the end of each row as he passed by. After arrival Kariuki and his comrades were forced to go two days without food and water, and then were beaten away from their first meal at Langata to be counted once again. Racism was a part of the dehumanization of detainees; if a detainee at Langata did not call every European he met "Effendi" (a Turkish title used by KAR soldiers from Uganda), he would be savagely beaten until he did. "Since forgetting to say it involved painful reminders, it became such an instinctive reaction to a white face that whether it belonged to a clergyman or a Member of Parliament, a doctor or a lady, we greeted them all as 'Effendi.'"[10]

Langata's main purpose was the screening and classification of Mau Mau suspects. Joram Wamweya endured a number of lineups at Langata, and learned to dread the arrival of the screeners' vehicle.

> A closed truck would be brought into the compound and everyone would be rounded up and made to stand in line. The rear of the truck would then be opened and there would emerge a being encased in sacking from head to foot with only two holes for seeing through. We christened this creature *gakonia*. We would be conducted one by one before *gakonia*. A white officer sat close to the sacking and when *gakonia* said "yes" hell descended on earth. The unfortunate was kicked about and whipped and conducted to a compound reserved for "hardcores."[11]

Though the disguises were intended mainly to prevent identification of the screeners, the arrival of these sinister hooded men, with the associations of sorcery they brought, was also "another scare . . . added to the miseries of detention life."[12] Kariuki, who was also subjected to the *gakonia* (little sacks) at Langata, comments,

> The agents were a mixed lot. Some were ordinary "spivs" who became professional betrayers because this gave them a steadier income than they had known before. . . . But there were also those whom we called *Tai Tai* because they came from the class of the educated young men who wore ties. Many of these were unemployed and became agents to earn money, while others were simply cowards and did it to escape arrest.[13]

Captured men were first threatened with exposure through the *gakonia* at Langata; if they continued to resist the pressures to confess and cooperate, detainees faced the regular threat of betrayal by loyalists, informers, and "softcore" in the detention camps themselves. The hooded screeners of Langata thus came to symbolize the insidious forces constantly working to break captives down and turn committed Mau Mau into collaborators.

Most detainees were numbered and classified at Langata before being sent on to another camp. As J. M. Kariuki describes, the government had established three main categories for detainees: "'Black' was the category for the unrepentant hardcore 'Mau Mau'; 'Grey' for heavily infected but not unreclaimable 'Mau Mau'; 'White' for clear or rehabilitated people."[14] On Manda Island in 1954, where Gakaara wa Wanjau was detained, these color differentiations were reflected in the clothes issued to detainees: black shorts for those who had not confessed, yellow for the waverers, and white for those committed to collaboration.[15] Somewhat later, when, as Kariuki puts it, "the implications of these titles penetrated even the Government," officials reclassified everyone with letters instead of color designations: thus Z or Z1 for "hardcore Black," Z2 for "just ordinary Black," Y1 for "Grey," and Y2 for "White."[16] As Kahinga Wachanga explains, certain camps—such as Manyani, Mackinnon Road, Lodwar, Saiyusi, Hola—were particularly designed for Z1 and Z2 detainees, and the regime was especially harsh in such places. Y1 detainees were usually sent to work camps in the districts, closer to their homes, while those classified Y2 were sent to their villages to live under the supervision of their local chiefs. If a man first classified Z1 began to soften, he could be reclassified to a paler designation and sent along the pipeline to eventually reach home. Most of the detainees in the camps were Gikuyu, Embu, or Meru, but there were enough Kamba from Machakos District that the government created Mara River detention camp and Makueni works camp especially for them, and there were detainees of other groups held in the main camps.[17]

After screening and classification at Langata, Gikuyu, Embu, and Meru men were sent on to detention camps in Coast Province, in the far north, or in or around Lake Victoria. Guards loaded the captives on a special detainee train (*gari ya waya*), identifiable by its wire mesh windows. Potential escapees were chained with leg irons, which chafed the ankles and left open sores.[18] If the train was heading for Manyani or Mackinnon Road along the line to Mombasa—common destinations for "Blacks"—it left Nairobi in the late afternoon and arrived at the station outside the camp in the early morning. Kariuki describes his arrival at Manyani.

> When we left the train again it was to see a broad road lined on each side with an avenue of prison warders standing a few feet apart. There were thousands of them armed with long batons. As it was three miles to the camp from the station these thousands were still not sufficient, so they were leapfrogged ahead of us as we went. The warders seized anything that was not tied in a bundle or packed in a box. If anyone stopped to argue he was hit until he moved on.[19]

When Joram Wamweya arrived at Manyani and Karigo Muchai at Mackinnon Road, they also ran through a gauntlet of warders, blows raining down or whips cracking over their shoulders.[20]

After running the gauntlet, arrivals at Manyani were driven like cattle through the dip, a concrete-lined trough "twenty feet long, six feet deep and four feet wide," filled with a mixture of water and a medicine called Jeyes Fluid. J. M. Kariuki describes the experience:

> The officers told us that we would have to be dipped in this as those coming into the camp from outside were thought to be bringing infectious diseases with them. So we were sent down the ramp in single file, dressed but carrying all our spare clothes and other belongings. . . . The officers and warders standing on the top hit our heads as we came through, forcing us to submerge ourselves completely. Tears were streaming out of my stinging eyes when I came out of the dip.[21]

Kariuki, Muchai, and others who went through the dip at Manyani believed it was "aimed more at degrading our humanity than removing any possible infections."[22]

The random violence of the gauntlet and the dehumanization of the dip were apt introductions to camp life. Ironically, the belongings new detainees had suffered to protect were usually taken from them just after arrival in their compounds; any material signs of individuality—money, watches, cameras, books, food, utensils, and even clothing—were confiscated and usually never seen again.[23] Detainees whose clothes had been taken could be forced to live in their underclothing until issued prison garb, sometimes days later. New arrivals were shown and told in no uncertain terms that if they did not submit they would serve very hard time. At Mackinnon Road, the camp commandant told each new in-take, "This camp . . . is called *Kufa na Kupona* . . . 'Life and Death.' It is well named. Those who cooperate with the screening team and the rehab officers leave here alive. Those who fail to cooperate usually die at Mackinnon Road."[24]

Life in the Detention Camps

Life for the hardcores in the camps was an existence of monotony and discomfort, punctuated periodically by violence. Kariuki remembers Manyani as "hundreds of uniform aluminum huts gleaming on the plain, thousands of warders rustling to and fro in their khaki and more than fifteen thousand human beings seething inside an electric fence, black skins dressed in white prison clothes, waiting for freedom."[25] Conditions were spartan, to say the least: dusty compounds, crude barracks (the "huts"), cement floors to sleep on, a diet made mostly of gruel, posho, and beans. The detention environment softened men up by inducing intense boredom, apprehension about the future, and a sense of hopelessness.

The day began in Manyani around 6:00 when the guards unbolted the doors and lined everyone up in rows in front of the huts for the morning head count. Breakfast followed, usually a thin gruel, prepared by detainee cooks in the compound's kitchen hut. After breakfast the detainees straightened up their huts and then swept the compound and carried the latrine buckets to the disposal trenches some distance away. After cleanup the inmates of some compounds had their time largely to themselves, and spent it playing *bau*, discussing the news of the camp, or participating in classes organized by educated detainees. Others were put to work on the Manyani airfield or other labor projects, often working long hours in the hot sun and the dust, tormented by biting insects. Groups of detainees, whole compounds or selected bands of the particularly hardcore, might be subjected to special punishment details, such as being made to run and perform exercises for hours, or made to do senseless tasks like digging and filling in holes, work designed to break a person's spirit. And at any time, an individual detainee might find himself singled out for a screening or interrogation by being suddenly seized and hauled to the offices or the punishment cells. Activities were accompanied by the blaring of the camp loudspeakers, which delivered hard-sell loyalist and anti–Mau Mau propaganda at any time during the day. In the evenings the detainees would reassemble in the compounds, eat dinner (usually a more substantial meal of soup, *posho*, beans, and occasionally vegetables and meat), and socialize together until lights out.[26]

At night the Manyani detainees were confined to their huts. Most compounds had no beds or cots, and only the luckier men had pads or blankets, so most tried to protect themselves from the cold by sleeping with a partner or in a group of three huddled together on the cement floors for warmth, in hollows they created in the sand that had blown in from outside during the day. The cement was hard, but at least it retained some of the daytime heat. The men were constantly harassed by mosquitoes, and sometimes by scorpions. The nights were long and uncomfortable, and few detainees got much rest.[27] The close quarters and inadequate food, housing, and medical care led to outbreaks of disease, including typhoid at Manyani.[28]

The tone for a camp as a whole and for a compound in particular was set by the European officer in charge. At Manyani, a camp officer Kariuki identifies pseudonymously as "Marlow," generally called "Mapiga" ("the Hitter") by the detainees, created an atmosphere of violence and fear by ordering the beating of any detainee who showed signs of spirit. At Hola, an officer who had been nicknamed "Kiriamburi" or "Goat-eater" for his habit of confiscating Gikuyu goats when a district officer in Murang'a, caused a reign of terror by getting drunk on liquor or *bhangi* at night and going into the camp to beat and abuse inmates. Other officers, such as Karigo Muchai's commandant at Lodwar in June 1950, who promised prisoners they would not be beaten as long as they obeyed the rules, were humane men who refused to use routine violence.[29]

Of course, the African warders and guards were in much closer daily contact with the detainees. The attitude of the warders was affected by the attitude of the European in charge, by general warder-detainee relations, and by the personal interactions of individuals on both sides. Most of the warders were non-Gikuyu—Kamba, Luhya, Luo, Nandi, Kipsigis, Turkana, and other groups—and mutual understanding was made more difficult by barriers of language and customs. There was a great deal of suspicion and hostility on both sides, for the warders were usually apolitical colonial functionaries doing an unpleasant job for pay, sometimes indulging their greed with stealing and their resentment with beatings, while the detainees were African rebels against the colonial system. Collectively, warders and detainees were natural antagonists, and certain groups of guards, like the "Riot Squad" at Manyani, were used only for beatings and were hated by almost all detainees. But many could be influenced by money and others traded fairly with the detainees. Kariuki recalls that "Our relationship with the warders in the camp depended on how much money and goods we had."[30] Wamweya describes the use of cigarettes as a kind of currency between warders and detainees; carpenters among the detainees in Manyani would make tables and chairs in exchange for cigarettes, which they would share throughout the compound.[31] Some detainees attempted to establish good relations with friendly warders. At Kajiado camp in November 1952, Gakaara wa Wanjau and other detainees met with friendly African warders, arranged for them to deliver parcels and messages between the camp and the detainees' families for pay; the Kajiado detainees resolved not to hate the warders but to seize every opportunity to politicize them.[32] Though Kariuki was often badly treated by African warders, he maintained that they were "often reasonable people," and that warders and detainees were like "dogs and jackals together"; when the news of Dedan Kimathi's death came to Lodwar, the camp commandant (the "hunter") gloated, but it seemed to Kariuki that the warders (the "dogs") mourned along with the detainees (the "jackals").[33]

In every camp the detainees set up their own organizations, sometimes on their own initiative and sometimes with the encouragement of the camp authorities. The first such detainee committee was formed in Kajiado in early December 1952, without the knowledge of the camp commandant, by Gakaara wa Wanjau and his fellow detainees "to solve problems which arose among ourselves."[34] At Manyani the commandant asked each compound to elect a leader to act as their spokesman. When Compound 13 was set up in October 1954, its sixty detainees elected Josiah Mwangi Kariuki as their leader; Kariuki had the detainees elect a committee of six to advise him, and he and the committee set about dealing with such matters as sharing resources and dividing up labor; with leaders from the other compounds, he also presented grievances from the rank-and-file detainees to the commandant.[35] Mohamed Mathu observes that at Athi River the hardcores chose leaders based on "their loyalty to the Movement and ability to speak English."[36] Some, however, like Gad Kamau Gathumbi at Kowop, whom Kariuki calls a *muthamaki,* were not educated but rose to position through their traditional rhetorical abilities and skill in settling disputes.[37]

This internal detainee structure also dealt with matters of discipline. At Athi River in July 1954, Karigo Muchai found that each of the four hardcore compounds had elected location, division, and district committees as well as a central committee that joined all the compounds together, an organization mirroring the Mau Mau structure in Nairobi and Central Province.[38] Mathu indicates that, at Athi River at least, the elected leader was "public" and dealt directly with the camp commander, and the committees were a "secret organization" created "to keep unity among the hardcores and prevent conflicts from arising"; in order to reach an agreement of the cross-compound central committee, members would throw notes wrapped around rocks from compound to compound "until a unamimous decision was reached."[39] While hardcore activists believed that maintaining this kind of higher-level cohesion and discipline in the camps was important, for most detainees the leadership and organization that counted most, on a day-to-day basis, was that of the hut or "club," the smallest and most intimate of detainee social groups.[40]

New arrivals at a camp, like recruits at a forest *mbuci,* were introduced to the group, questioned by the leadership, and told the rules as soon as possible. On his first evening in Compound 3 at Athi River, Karigo Muchai and his fellow newcomers went through an extensive and careful interrogation by the leaders of his club, "designed to determine whether or not we were stooges placed in the club to gather information for Government."[41] After questioning each of them in turn, the head of the club carefully went over the rules and the penalties. Club members were enjoined not to fight or threaten other detainees, not to steal, not to dirty the barracks or compound, not to have sexual intercourse with any woman in the camp, not to drink alcohol or smoke *bhangi,* not to cut into the food line, not to avoid necessary work, not to appear to be attempting to escape. If a detainee broke a rule, he was made to cross the cement barracks floor one or more times on his knees.[42] The club also provided a forum for the discussion of issues, ranging from possible work stoppages to the political and land tenure systems to be established after Mau Mau had won the war.

While camp authorities usually chose to deal with detainees through their elected compound representatives, they tended to be hostile toward the committees in the hardcore compounds, suspecting correctly that these committees often reproduced Mau Mau hierarchies outside and served to maintain the cohesion of political resistance within the camps.[43] It was in the interests of the British to undermine such resistance, turning hardcores first into softcores and then into collaborators. In addition to working on individuals on a regular basis, the camp authorities attempted to use times of crisis—such as disputes about food or work—to drive wedges between them, breaking waverers away from the group and segregating them in separate compounds. In response, the committees and clubs worked to hold detainee solidarity together.

For the clubs of hardcore detainees, information was a means of self-defense in the constant struggle with the camp authorities. To Kariuki and other detainees news was "nourishment," and they took it upon themselves to discover and circulate whatever they could. There were two "news services" at Manyani; the first, called the *Manyani Times,* "was the news that was known to be true and which had been picked up from newspapers by those cleaning in the warders' lines or had been heard on a wireless by someone working near an officer's house," and the second, known as the *Waya Times* "was largely speculation, rumour or light relief." After dinner, each club would send a representative to the wire partitions to exchange tobacco with other compounds and to gather information. An individual with news would call out "Giteo" (Gikuyu for "respect") to attract attention, announce "I now begin my words of *Manyani Times* (or *Waya Times*), which are that," and then convey his piece of news, which could range from late-breaking scoops about the Emergency to local rumors about warders (who often tried to break up this exchange of news). The news services helped strengthen cohesion among the detainees, boosted morale, and provided a humorous release from the tensions of life in the camps.[44]

Resistance in the Camps

For committed men, the struggle against the British did not end with their arrest and detention, for noncooperation in the camps was resistance by other means. Gakaara wa Wanjau makes this point in his diary entry for August 15, 1953, during a conflict with the authorities over food at Manda camp, writing that the detainees had an obligation to the guerrillas in the forests and the civilians in the villages to fight back in their own way.[45] Kariuki saw resistance in the camps as "a symbol" of nationalist commitment. "If some of us had not held out, it would have been so much easier to have explained away 'Mau Mau' as a primitive and atavistic throw-back movement of a people misled by a foolish leader."[46] Effective resistance, however, did not mean striking back at the authorities on every occasion, nor did it usually mean a detainee resisting on his own; Kariuki told the men of his compound that "we would not get across the river to Freedom without Unity, even as ants clamber on each other and baboons link tails to make a living bridge over a stream."[47]

Detainees in the camps used prayer, ritual, and song to reassert commitment and strengthen morale in much the same way as *itungati* used them in the forests. Religion provided a reassuring everyday continuity with the outside world as well as lifting spirits in times of crisis. At

Lodwar, Kariuki led the morning prayers of his hutmates in the direction of Mt. Kenya; after spitting on their hands and raising them palm upwards in the attitude of respect, the detainees sang a long prayer much like the forest prayer Kimathi used at Kariaini, but including also the lines "Hasten Freedom for all Africans/Save us from our present bondage." Gikuyu prayers ending with the traditional invocation "Thaai Thathaiya Ngai Thaai" brought the day to a close within the huts at Manyani.[48] In the middle of the food dispute at Manda in 1953, when the detainees were reduced to four loaves of bread and six bottles of water, they solemnly created a ritual to help them through, using traditional Gikuyu, Mau Mau, and Christian elements. Taking as their guide the Olenguruone community's creed—"We shall all have a share, however small the portion is, even if it be a bean seed"—the detainees broke the loaves of bread into tiny pieces, and Reverend Stefano Waciira offered prayers over the food and water. "He asked God to bless the pieces of bread so that they would become like the two fish and five loaves which Jesus blessed so that five thousand people ate and were satisfied. May the pieces of bread have the strength to sustain our lives and may the drops of water cool and soothe our parched throats. May Ngai help us to overcome our enemies."[49]

Mau Mau songs from the forest raised the spirits of the new arrivals at Manyani and elsewhere, and composers within the camps wrote new ones to commemorate benchmarks in the detainee experience and in the history of African nationalism. When he and his comrades arrived at Lamu in July 1953, Gakaara wa Wanjau composed a song, set it to an Italian tune he had learned as a soldier in Addis Ababa in 1942, and within two days the whole group was singing it.

To be detained on an island is an unforgettable experience
An unforgettable three-days journey from Kajiado to Lamu.

Wherever they try to isolate us
Whatever tribulations they put us through
We will never give up our bid to regain our land.
God is our guardian, we shall regain our freedom.[50]

On a happier occasion, June 3, 1957, the day of Ghana's independence, J. M. Kariuki and Joseph Kirira composed a commemorative song, "Rwimbo rwa Africa" (the "Song of Africa"), for the celebrations at Lodwar Camp. The last verse was a panegyric to Pan-Africanism:

We shall greatly rejoice
In the unity of all the black people
Let us create in our unity
A United States of All Africa.[51]

Religion and song were thus used to bind the community of hardcores together and strengthen them for the continuing struggle.

At most camps educated detainees set up classes in the compounds to teach basic literacy and other subjects ranging from geography to politics. While some camp commandants supported these classes, the initiative almost always came from the detainees and, in Kariuki's words, "created a firm feeling of unity among us and encouraged our natural resistance to the blandishments of the screeners."[52] At Manyani, Kariuki and others set up elementary classes, using fine sand for slates and pointed sticks for writing instruments; he also took it upon himself to lecture on "the ideas and techniques of politics and current affairs to larger groups of anyone interested."[53] Tugs of war over control of classes between the authorities and the detainee leadership were common. At Athi River, rehabilitation officers offered literacy classes in English and Swahili, but the hardcores refused to participate, setting up their own classes in the compounds, with teachers who included Kimani Ruo and Henry Muli, two graduates of Makerere; Karigo Muchai first learned to read and write English in the hardcore classes at Athi River, and continued his education in other camps.[54] At Manda and Takwa camps the rehabilitation officer tried to assume supervision of all classes, pronouncing he would only allow detainees to teach English and mathematics; he "wouldn't want history or geography to be taught, for such subjects could be improperly made the vehicles for teaching the politics of agitation, which was the cause of the current troubles in Kenya. He himself would introduce the proper methods of teaching to the teachers."[55] At Manyani, the screeners and the camp authorities finally became so concerned about Kariuki's educational work that they had him transferred to another compound and cancelled his classes.[56]

While disagreements over classes for detainees did not usually lead to major disputes with camp authorities, confrontations over food and work could test the will of camp authorities and strain the commitment and solidarity of detainee communities to the limit. The issue of what work (if any) was appropriate for political detainees arose again and again in the Kenya detention camps and came to a head in the confrontation that preceded the Hola massacre in January 1959. At different times hardcores at Kowop, Manyani, Manda, Saiyusi, Mageta, Hola, and elsewhere would challenge the right of the camp officers to order them to work, on the basis of various Kenyan, British, and international laws. An early example was the conflict over food and work at Manda Camp in August 1953, which Wanjau describes in *Mau Mau Author in Detention*. The day after their arrival as the first inmate group on Manda Island, the camp commandant told the detainees to collect their food from the boat landing, draw water from the wells, gather firewood, and dispose of their night soil. The detainees refused, expressing concern that if they left the campgrounds to get the food at the landing they would be shot for trying to escape (at Kajiado they would have been), and maintaining that since "we had not been convicted in a court of law, we should, therefore, not be put into [sic] the kind of labour which virtually constituted punishment."[57] In response, the commandant refused to have the food delivered, and the detainees then persuaded a sympathetic warder to send telegrams to the governor and to the queen accusing the commandant of deliberately starving them. On August 17, after four days without any food, the solidarity of the 138 detainees began to crack. On August 18, the commissioner of prisons arrived to tell them collectively that they were required to do this work under Emergency regulations; hungry, faced with an intransigent administration, and reasoning that the oath did not require them to starve to death, the detainees gave in. It was clear, however, that their strike had attracted the attention of some very important people, a lesson they would not forget.[58]

For J. M. Kariuki, calling a work strike was both a matter of principle and a resistance strategy. Like other hardcore leaders, he believed that forcing political detainees like themselves to work was unlawful; moreover, refusing to work "seemed to be our most effective way of embarrassing the Government and helping our friends still fighting in the forest."[59] He was one of the leaders of the work strikes at Kowop in 1954 and Saiyusi in 1956, telling the Saiyusi commandant "that we were not going to work because we were not convicted prisoners and also that we were covered in our refusal under Section 18B of the International Convention" (though Kariuki did work at Manyani and at South Yatta).[60] The British came to see work strikes as a crucial test of will and strength between the government and Mau Mau in the camps, for such strikes, which often led to extended confrontations between the detainees and the camp authorities, were more common among the hardcore than among the detainees as a whole. As Michael Blundell, member of the War Council, put it, if the hardcore were not at work they were likely "to sit around in idleness hatching up other subversive plots."[61] Consequently commandants could deal with work strikes ruthlessly. At Saiyusi in 1956 the commandant tried to wear down the men by reducing their rations (which led to a hunger strike), singling out leaders for special punishment, locking the strikers in their huts all day and all night, selectively beating the detainees, and finally transferring thirty-five of the strongest resisters to Lodwar.[62]

Female resistance gave the authorities a great deal of trouble, as the work of Cora Presley on Kamiti women's camp has indicated (as does Wambui Otieno's account of her own experience at Lamu).[63] The published Mau Mau memoirs include a few but telling passages on women in detention. Karigo Muchai was impressed with the stoicism of the women who were imprisoned with the male suspects at CID headquarters in Kiambu.[64] While the apprehensions of some men about the fate of their mothers and wives at home could undermine their sense of commitment, women could also stiffen male resolve with their own steadfastness, as Likimani's autobiographical short story, "Vanishing Camp," indicates.[65] In 1956–1957, when some men were turning to cooperation at Athi River Camp, most of the women at Kamiti Women's Detention Camp were still holding out. Wanjau remembers some women putting their husbands "to shame" when the British sent the men from Athi River to Kamiti to talk their wives into cooperating. "Some women would refuse to talk to their husbands for the reason that these men had sold out by making a confession. . . . One woman told her husband point blank that she would have no dealings with the sellouts and traitors from Athi River."[66]

While detainees frequently acted in concert, leaders like Gad Gathumbi, Robinson Mwangi, and J. M. Kariuki emerged in every camp to call for hunger strikes, organize work stoppages, protest to camp commandants, and smuggle letters to the governor, members of Parliament, and the International Red Cross out of the camps. Kariuki became the most famous "camp lawyer," and his reputation accompanied him from camp to camp, propelling him into leadership; Joram Wamweya remembers arriving by train at Manyani in 1955 from Nairobi, after traveling with a Nyeri group he did not know, and the officer asking the new in-take who would be their spokesman: "At this point, a man in rags stood up. Immediately people started saying, 'Stand up Mwangi. You are our headman.'"[67] Stubborn persistence was a key to Kariuki's influence, for he persevered in his internal protests and in writing letters to authorities outside the wire (using sympathetic warders to help him get the letters posted), even though officers subjected him to severe punishments. When a visiting committee which included members of the Legislative Council came to Manyani in January 1955, and Kariuki told them frankly of the abuse of detainees during the construction of the airfield, officer "Marlow" had a warder give him twelve strokes with a cane the next morning.[68] After Kariuki sent a letter to the commissioner of prisons, the Manyani commandant assembled 4,000 prisoners, reviled Kariuki for writing letters, had him given twelve strokes, and then locked him in solitary for eight days without food or water. Although he almost died on this occasion, Kariuki and his friend Robinson Mwangi continued to send letters out. Letter-writing as a form of resistance did have an effect: letters sent to members of Parliament like Fenner Brockway led to the raising of questions in the House of Commons; a letter published in an English newspaper led to the improvement of conditions at Lokitaung; even letters sent to Kenyan officials could lead to temporary changes for the better.[69]

Direct resistance such as hitting back during beatings, escapes, or detainee uprisings were less common. Sometimes individuals, acting on their own, would oppose an officer or warder by force; when Kariuki knocked an abusive warder down, he spent a spell in solitary as a consequence, but took some satisfaction in his victory.[70] Joram Wamweya and nine comrades escaped from high-security Manyani in July 1954, and attempted to walk back to Nairobi along the railway line; the others eventually surrendered or were recaptured, but Wamweya himself eluded his pursuers, found his way to the city, and rejoined the forest fighters.[71] Escapes were always followed by retaliation. When Mwangi Mambo and Kariuki Chotara escaped from Manyani by placing planks on the electric fence and walking over it, the members of their Compound 16 "were hammered by the Riot Squad and thirty-five detainees were crippled, some permanently."[72] In decisions that mirrored the restraint of elders' committees and Mau Mau leaders described in the last chapter, the committees inside the wire attempted to limit escapes so that the remaining detainees would not suffer as a consequence. Inmate revolts were also infrequent, but at times detainee compounds would fight back, as when the striking detainees at Saiyusi in 1956 refused to be locked into their huts and fought the guards armed with batons to a standstill with tin plates, stones, and fenceposts; even as late as the summer of 1957 a group of hardcore detainees brought to Athi River from Mageta fought a brave losing battle with stones and camp utensils to resist being split up and sent to different compounds.[73]

Yet the most important kind of resistance in the camps and the most frustrating to the British authorities was the refusal of detainees to confess. A culture of resistance supported nonconfession, the hardcore compounds and clubs encouraging nonconfessors and ostracizing those they believed had confessed, but in the end confession (if and when) had to be an individual decision. The refusal to confess was an assertion of personal integrity, an affirmation of loyalty to the movement, the oath, and the land, a refusal to bend the knee to one's captors, and a denial of intelligence to the enemy that spared both oneself and one's comrades conviction for Mau Mau crimes. Yet refusal to confess the truth should not be confused with refusal to say anything at all. J. M. Kariuki admits in *"Mau Mau" Detainee:* "During all the time I was in detention never once did I tell the whole truth as I am setting it down now, although six times screeners laboriously wrote out my false confessions which had been forced out of me. There is a Kikuyu proverb, '*Njita murume*,' which is to say that when you knock someone about even if you ask him to call you God, he will do so; but the truth is still that you are not God."[74]

Kariuki takes the position that most "confessions" of oath-taking were lies extorted by intimidation, beatings, or torture, making them both invalid as evidence and useless as intelligence. Gakaara wa Wanjau confirms that invented confessions were common. "Quite a number of people from Manyani had made false confessions to save themselves from beatings. People would incriminate fictitious people in giving information about their oathing."[75]

In Kariuki's mind, false confessions preserved both one's body and one's personal integrity, for later in his memoir he observes that "Those of us who resisted 'rehabilitation' to the end did so because we considered that by confession we would lose something essential without which we could not live. We considered that the 'rehabilitated' ex-detainee screeners had sold their souls for easy time."[76] Gakaara wa Wanjau expresses this sense of integrity in Gikuyu terms. "People had made vows and and sworn secrecy by invoking the name of Ngai, the Almighty God, and invoking the eternal Earth. This was not a light thing. Some detainees would go for interrogation, carrying a symbolic lump of earth on their bodies for strength and courage."[77] Both nonconfession and false confession were forms of resistance that used the authorities' own principal weakness—their obsession with confession—to undermine their efforts to repress Mau Mau. Yet as more detainees broke ranks and made real confessions, and as the authorities gathered more reliable intelligence, it became increasingly difficult for detainees to get by with invented stories. With each new interrogation, the pressure built up on each hardcore to betray himself by telling the truth.

"Cooperation" and "Rehabilitation"

The other side of detainee resistance was detainee cooperation. The hardcores were an important target, because the British saw these men as the backbone of Mau Mau in the camps; if they could break the hardcores' resistance, they would not only gain valuable intelligence but also destroy detainee morale, turn the inmate population against Mau Mau, and perhaps bring the revolt to a speedier end. In addition to using deprivation, heavy work demands, and physical beatings, they employed subtler and more insidious means to wear individuals down and get them to confess. While the Moral Rearmament (MRA) experiment at Athi River was the most ambitious effort of any camp administration to win over the hardcore, most commandants understood their assignment to be to break down the detainees, obtain confessions and cooperation, and then empty the camp by moving the "rehabilitated" men along the pipeline to home. Just as detainee noncooperation was resistance by other means, the camp administrations fought Mau Mau by other means, less dramatic than the counterinsurgency but important to the effort to suppress the revolt and reshape Gikuyu society.[78]

African collaborators were given an important role in this effort. Teams of screeners, loyalist elders, soft-core detainees, and "rehabilitation" workers visited the compounds frequently, trolling for those who had begun to weaken. In the early years, most hardcore felt nothing but contempt for them. Kariuki describes their attitude at the time of his first detention in Manyani in the summer of 1954:

> We considered all screeners to be traitors. Most of those who had been
> brought from the Reserves to do it had allowed the love of money to

conquer their patriotism. Those who had been detainees had exchanged the life of suffering for one of relative liberty. There were a few, very few . . . who sincerely believed that the Society of the Oath was such a bad means of achieving our objectives that Independence itself would become compromised and tainted should it succeed . . .[79]

Initially the hardcores' commitment was stronger than the arguments and enticements of cooperators. But the British and the collaborators were persistent.

When Mohamed Mathu was transferred to Athi River in October 1954, he was exposed for the first time to the method of breaking Mau Mau by persuasion instead of beatings. Loyalist elders and chiefs would both speak to groups of hardcores and target young men from their localities for face-to-face sessions; since some of these same loyalists would have an important role in deciding when a detainee could return to his family, they had leverage with the young men from their home areas. These methods were successful in some cases, for Kariuki notes that detainees who had agreed to cooperate at Athi River began to show up at Manyani, wearing special uniforms marked with a red star emblem. "They lived with the screeners but every morning they would go into whatever compound they liked and try to persuade some detainees to confess as they had. They had a few converts here and there and it was unpleasant to see our former absolute unity being eroded in however small a way."[80]

Of course, one of the main aims of informers, screeners, and cooperators was to break down detainee solidarity. At Kajiado in February 1953, Dennis, the welfare officer, commented in Gikuyu to Willy Jemmie Wambugu Maina "that housed together in this camp were leopards and goats," a remark that Gakaara wa Wanjau interpreted as meaning that informers were locked up with the other detainees.[81] Wanjau, convinced his group was steadfast, was not worried about informers, but he was later surprised when the same detainees, now transferred to Manda, began to divide over the issue of the work stoppage in October 1953, and some responded to the threats and blandishments of the camp commandant Martin by volunteering for work, thus "betraying our vows to fight."[82] Volunteers were transferred to a softcore compound, and by February 1954, Martin was using these softcores to persuade others to volunteer.

> Cooperators from section 3 would have people from compounds 1 and 2, when these people were known to them from home or in other camps, summoned to the office. A rejector of work who was so summoned would face a united pack of persuaders, made up of Martin as the pack leader and his friends from the camp of cooperators.[83]

As a group, the men most likely to crack were the educated. Kariuki recalls that major defections to the ranks of the cooperators began in Manyani in late 1954 as "many of the educated young men were becoming

screeners in the camp."[84] Muchai comments that by the time he was sent to
Lodwar in the summer of 1956, there were so few educated hardcore left
that some of the compounds had no one to run the English classes. "Few
educated detainees remained hardcore for very long in the tough camps."[85]
Kariuki indicates that he and his friend Robinson Mwangi felt a particular
obligation to hold out because they believed that the illiterate hardcores
needed educated leadership, especially men who could write letters to the
outside world on their behalf, and there were so few left in Manyani to provide it.

Divisions between Kiambu and the other Gikuyu districts also widened
in the detention camps. Mathu, remembering his Hola time in 1958, comments that the Nyeri and Murang'a detainees considered the Kiambu men
"clever and cowardly"; while the people of the southern district were better
educated and had taken a more important role in the nationalist movement,
they had done little of the real fighting during the revolt and at Hola were
cooperating with the European camp officers to monopolize most of the
good jobs, "thinking they were better than other Kikuyu." As a clerk with
the Ministry of Works himself, Mathu tried to use his influence to talk up
Gikuyu unity among the detainees and to appoint non-Kiambu men when
positions he supervised fell vacant.[86] At Manda, Gakaara wa Wanjau
noticed that by February 1954, almost three times as many Kiambu
detainees had decided to cooperate as men from Nyeri (63 to 23), while
almost twice as many Nyeri men as men from Kiambu were holding out
against cooperation (52 to 27).[87] David Waruhiu from Kiambu, son of the
assassinated Chief Waruhiu and leader of a rehabilitation team, confirmed
Wanjau's impressions about the distinction between the two districts when
he visited Manda in March 1954. "Waruhiu would complain that the Mau
Mau conflict was becoming protracted because of the intransigence of
people from Nyeri; people from Kiambuu had accepted moderation and
their wish was to see an end to the conflict; but people from Nyeri were
extremists."[88]

By the end of 1954, cooperation was making inroads into the hardcore
at Manyani, Manda, Mackinnon Road, and elsewhere, but the key to this
government effort was Athi River, the largest camp and the center of the
"rehabilitation" campaign. As Gakaara Wanjau explains, Athi River was "a
major junction" in the pipeline; a detainee was sent to Athi River from
other camps as a candidate for "rehabilitation," and if he were judged sufficiently changed after his stay, he would be sent on to a "work" or "district"
camp closer to his home. Ultimately, the chief of his location would decide
if, when, and under what restrictions he would be allowed to rejoin his family.[89] The "rehabilitation" program assumed that by taking the oath and participating in Mau Mau, young men had corrupted themselves, and only by
truthfully confessing the oath and undergoing a process of cleansing and
renewal would they be ready to return to their communities again as

healthy members of Gikuyu society. Europeans like F. D. Corfield were convinced that detainees suffered from a spiritual sickness. "Many of them were no longer human; they were not even animal. The caged leopard has a fierce look of hatred in his eyes, but he does at least have a sparkle in them. The Mau Mau had a dull look of hatred which was quite frightening."[90] Government officials and missionaries were convinced that rehabilitation was essential.

Rehabilitation at Athi River went through three phases: an early experimental period in 1953–1954, the period dominated by the Christian revivalist movement Moral Rearmament in 1955–1956, and the tougher, post-MRA period from mid-1956 on. The memoirs of Muchai, Mathu, Wanjau, and Kariuki contain extensive descriptions of rehabilitation at Athi River.

Rehabilitation was thought reform, and at Athi River its symbol was the ubiquitous loudspeaker, found in every barrack. The loudspeakers would announce the names of those scheduled for interrogation; deliver speeches by visiting loyalist chiefs; pour out "streams of pro-Government propaganda," praising the British and the loyalists; issue sermons on "the virtue of confession, the evils of Mau Mau, and the benefits of being allowed to go home." Some barracks attempted to "smother the box with blankets until the noise became a comical gurgle," but this only won a brief period of respite until a cooperator called a warder and the blanket was removed.[91] The voice of Big Brother blaring into the barracks would drive some men to despair. Gakaara wa Wanjau remembers that "The system was a constant source of irritation and nagging torture for those people who had withheld confession, whom it would persistently revile. Some people would bury themselves in their blankets immediately the system started broadcasting, in an impotent protest against the propaganda."[92] The loudspeaker would simply wear people down.

Athi River posed a serious challenge to Mau Mau solidarity from the beginning. Because the camp officers there tried particularly hard to persuade or pressure detainees to cooperate, the movement committees had to make special efforts to ensure that the hardcore held firm, so hardcore rules at Athi River included a special prohibition against participation in "rehabilitation schemes" or other "unnecessary kinds of cooperation."[93] Individual detainees could find themselves caught in the middle. Shortly after his arrival in July 1954, Karigo Muchai happened upon his club's committee sitting in judgment on a member who had been seen speaking with a rehabilitation officer. An action like this "placed in grave danger the other hardcores of the club. Many of these men had been together for a long time and each knew a great deal about the others. Anyone showing signs of weakening was a threat. Thus a great deal of loyalty was both felt and demanded within the hardcore groups."[94] Muchai did not realize that the Mau Mau leadership at Athi River in mid-1954 considered voluntary work a form of cooperation (there was no concerted work stoppage at the time), and he was surprised after he volunteered for work as a way to break the tedium and get some exercise to find himself labeled a "softcore" by his club committee and placed with the other volunteers in a different club in the same compound. He later regretted his decision, because he soon found that the officers used work as a way to extort confessions; once a group of men began work, their hours became longer, their rations shorter, and their assignments harder until they agreed to confess. When Muchai's time came, he was heavily beaten for not giving a true confession.[95]

Mohamed Mathu (then David Mathu) arrived later during the Moral Rearmament period at Athi River (1955–1956), and was struck by the contrast with his previous camp, Embakasi, a very brutal place. He and other members of the in-take were housed in Compound 9, which had one barrack for new arrivals and one for cooperators assigned to the task of wearing down the new men's resistance. Screenings were initially different from the combination of demands, threats, and blows that Mathu had become accustomed to. "The early screenings involved only friendly types of persuasion and were combined with good treatment, easy work and attempts to convert us to Christianity. Elders and chiefs came regularly to preach about the merits of the Christian faith and cooperation with Government."[96] Those who responded positively to these initial screenings were given privileges and easy work, but Mathu, suspicious of the Christian message because of the "crimes" he believed Christian loyalists had committed against Mau Mau supporters in the reserves, tried to convince others that Christianity was a "white man's religion," which was simply being used as an ideological weapon to turn people against Mau Mau. His attitude led the soft cores to treat him coldly and the rehabilitators to turn violent, culminating in his public beating in the middle of the compound. After this the commandant transferred him to another compound. When a Moral Rearmament team on a world tour—including representatives from Ghana, South Africa, and Japan—visited Athi River, Mathu was elected by the members of this compound to be their representative to find out about MRA; impressed by the MRA message of reconciliation, he finally yielded to the persuasion of the team leader and the camp commandant to work with them.[97]

As a MRA cooperator, Mathu spoke to detainee groups, tried to persuade individuals to join, and acted in a drama about racial reconciliation in which he played a forest fighter alongside other detainees playing a European settler, an Asian trader, and a Jewish businessman. The play, which ended with the four characters joining the Moral Rearmament Movement and starting "to live according to the cardinal principles of Honesty, Purity, Love and Unselfishness," was put on for Athi River detainees, women prisoners from Kamiti, and visiting groups of chiefs and other loyalists.[98] Although Mathu worked for MRA for almost a year, he claims that his commitment was never complete, for he was disturbed by the accusations of betrayal from other hardcores and he came to think of the two MRA officials as hypocritical. Though he worked for months beside the "well-dressed Europeans who professed to believe in brotherhood," clad only in the rags he had worn since his capture, never did either of them offer him as much as one of their old shirts. Mathu's disillusionment set in well before the end of the MRA experiment.[99]

By the time Gakaara wa Wanjau arrived at Athi River in 1956, the government had resumed direct control of rehabilitation at the camp. Minister of Community Development Thomas Askwith, the official in charge of rehabilitation, had come to the conclusion in March of that year that the MRA philosophy that apportioned blame for Mau Mau to all Kenya communities was contrary to the government position and was actually undermining the rehabilitation effort, for while MRA adherents had turned against violent revolt, they had not abandoned African nationalism.[100] A new hardline commandant, Major Breckenridge, took over, stopped MRA activities, confiscated MRA literature, and isolated adherents like Mathu among the detainees.[101] Wanjau arrived from Takwa in early April during this period of transition. He found the routine at Athi River quite different from the other detention camps he had known. In the mornings detainees worked, but a number of different activities were scheduled for the afternoons, ranging from lectures on the benefits of British colonialism in Kenya to traditional dances to football competitions to films and concerts. All of this was background for the real reason for the existence of Athi River, "the extraction of confessions and the carrying out of brainwashing." Every night the camp authorities would announce over the loudspeakers the names of thirty detainees scheduled to be interrogated the following day in one of the special "screening courts." Then at regular intervals all the detainees came together for a mass "ceremony of confession."[102]

The first mass confession he witnessed on April 9, 1956, made a strong impression on Gakaara wa Wanjau. The detainees sat on the grass in a field between camp buildings, facing the rehabilitation officer and his screeners seated on chairs. The chief screener opened the meeting by introducing the new in-take of men from Manda and Takwa (singling out Wanjau, the writer of Mau Mau songs and prayers in particular), went on to chide detainees from Manyani for thinking that they could still get away with false confessions, and ended by reminding the detainees that the delegation of chiefs about to visit Athi River would take back with them to Division Camps only those who had made true confessions. The rehabilitation officer then called for all those willing to make public confessions to stand up, ordering a young man called "Toto Kariba" (General Kariba's assistant) to go first to show the new arrivals how it was done. Toto Kariba then gave an apparently complete description of his experience with the movement, telling of his oath-taking (naming those involved), his entry into the forest, the battles he had fought in, and the killings his group had carried out. Five more detainees followed Toto Kariba, and after each had made his presentation, interrogators questioned him further, in front of all, about those who had participated with him in oath-taking and violence, thus revealing and compromising even more people.[103]

The new arrivals were amazed and appalled by this spectacle of public confessions. Wanjau and his comrades came up with several explanations of why detainees were taking the "drastic step" of "competing to disclose secrets, to open up about the vows of the oath": some confessors were simply exhausted by detention; others had been undermined by ex-comrades writing to them to urge them to get it over with; others had been swayed by the unceasing camp propaganda; an increasing number were faced with crises at home, and the need to deal with these had finally outweighed movement loyalty. The most disturbing explanation, however, harkened back to why many men had taken the unity oath in the first place; while some had done so out of conviction, and others out of fear of reprisals if they did not, many had taken it "because it was part of a mass political action and they were carried away by the mass wave." Now at Athi River the wave was rapidly receding: "When the epidemic of confessions broke out these latter people were again carried off on the wave—and they confessed."[104]

For at Athi River the culture of resistance, built up so painstakingly in other camps, began to give way before a culture of cooperation, as intimidation, group pressure, confession, and brainwashing came to transform hardcore Mau Mau into compliant subjects of British colonial Kenya. The loudspeakers blared constant pro-British propaganda; the afternoon history lectures explained to illiterate detainees the many benefits British rule had brought the country; the touring chiefs told detainees from their locations that the British had won and advised them to confess soon and return home to their families. Public confessions put new cooperators on display as examples for their comrades. Former hardcores began to work with the British, wearing down holdouts with their examples and their persuasion. By 1957, impatient cooperators at Athi River, fearing that the remaining resisters were interfering with their own repatriation, began without official sanction to beat hardcore holdouts every night to get them to confess.[105] The detention system was beginning to turn the tide against the secret movement.

The End of Detention

The Mau Mau memoirs trace this development, as most of the authors turned toward various forms of cooperation. Some of them held out, and J. M. Kariuki, whose intransigent reputation preceded him to Athi River in October 1957, was one of these. At first the commandant tried gentle methods, pressuring him to accept a post, translating the camp newspaper into English. When this did not bring Kariuki any closer to real cooperation, camp officers tried to do it by force, beating him severely (splitting his face, breaking his kneecap, and puncturing his chest) and throwing him into an isolation cell with no food. After three days a group of detainees brought him some gruel and persuaded him to make some sort of confession so he would not die. "So I confessed a whole pack of lies, embroidered with pieces of truth, and afterwards I was returned to the compound."[106] The day after his return he wrote letters to the commissioner of prisons, the colonial secretary, Barbara Castle, John Stonehouse, Tom Mboya, and others, and had a friend bribe warders to post them; his letters brought an inquiry, and Kariuki survived Athi River without any further beatings.

By this time others were cooperating. Mohamed Mathu's cooperation during the MRA period at Athi River has been discussed above. Sometime after his first interrogation at Athi River in May 1956, Gakaara wa Wanjau decided to accept Major Breckenridge's offer of "parole," a status of cooperation that brought the parolee a khaki uniform, special food, a small salary, better housing, and passes to leave the camp and even visit Nairobi.[107] Although this was a fateful decision, Wanjau does not really explain the soul-searching that must have led up to it, perhaps because he has no diary entries from this later period of his detention and has problems reconstructing his thoughts or perhaps because the whole episode still makes him uncomfortable. His assignments were to edit the weekly camp newspaper, *Atiriri! Gitugi kia Mucii* ("The Pillar of the Home") and write pamphlets, songs, and plays with an anti–Mau Mau message. According to his own account, Wanjau wrote original songs and plays in draft which were carefully vetted by J. Kiereini, the rehabilitation officer (later a senior civil servant in the Kenyatta government), to determine if their anti–Mau Mau content was strong enough and direction clear enough. After subjecting his creations to this censorship, Wanjau would then direct public concerts of his songs and performances of his plays before camp officers, visitors, and detainees. While the authorities intended these productions to sway the detainees against Mau Mau, Wanjau asserts that he tried to write works that had the opposite effect. His most ambitious production, *Reke Aciirithio ni Mehia Maake* ("Let the Guilt of His Crimes Weigh Heavily on His Conscience") for example, was the story of the betrayal of a detainee by his old business partner who had joined the home guards; after a group of Special Branch officers from Nairobi saw the play, he was forced to go through a "rigorous interrogation" at Special Branch hands, and his release was set back.[108]

Wanjau notes that he worked with Kariuki (whom he obviously admires greatly) on the newspaper *Atiriri!* and claims that in *"Mau Mau" Detainee* Kariuki, who referred to Wanjau by the pseudonym "Benjamin," had said of him that "I valued solidarity among the detainees and always used my cunning to avoid putting fellow detainees in trouble."[109] Actually, Kariuki's characterization of Wanjau/"Benjamin" is a bit different from this.

> He was a co-operator, but a most subtle one. He never beat anyone and he always treated the other detainees well. He composed a skillful pamphlet on "confession" which was given to us all. He also produced sketches and plays in which the man who had confessed was always richer or surpassed in some way the man who remained hardcore. The warders and the soft-core liked these very much. We condemned them as The *Wamarebe* Plays [the "Empty Tins"].[110]

As a prominent Gikuyu intellectual, the author of antigovernment pamphlets in the years before the Emergency, Gakaara wa Wanjau must have been something of a prize for the British, and his cooperation an important symbolic victory for the rehabilitation program at Athi River.

Kahinga Wachanga may have played an important role as well. The brief chapter on detention in *The Swords of Kirinyaga* gives the impression that Wachanga suffered almost as badly later as he had during his first weeks of captivity, but Mohamed Mathu, who came from the same sublocation in Nyeri, reports that Wachanga was working with the British at Saiyusi and Mageta in July 1956, when Mathu himself arrived there from Athi River. Mathu encountered Wachanga and another acquaintance from Nyeri on the boat ride from Kisumu to Saiyusi. After he arrived on the island, a Special Branch officer asked Mathu "if I'd be willing to go to Mageta, another island detention camp in Lake Victoria, to help uncover some troublemakers who were turning the men against their rehabilitation program. Parkinson said that since my friends, Kahinga and Kihara, were assisting them he thought I might like to join them."[111] Although Mathu says that he turned this offer away by saying that he would think about it, officer Kellaway appointed him clerk in the main Saiyusi office. He and Kahinga Wachanga often crossed paths. "Kahinga and Kihara spent most of their time in the open camp but continued to operate as informers on Mageta and in the hardcore camp."[112] There is no evidence that this unflattering account was inspired by any prejudice Mathu may have felt against Kahinga Wachanga before Saiyusi, nor does the latter seem to have taken it badly, for he praises Mathu in *Swords of Kirinyaga* (published well after Mathu's memoir) for his role in the Lukenya Prison attack in 1954 and includes a sympathetic description of a beating Mathu suffered at Mweru Works Camp after the two of them were transferred there in May 1957.[113] Wachanga does not mention working with Special Branch at Saiyusi and Mageta, though he admits that at Mweru "I was co-operative as far as work went" and the camp authorities "thought me rehabilitated, ie 'white'" and recommended that he be released; ironically, his local chief, who would "make the final decision," refused to accept him and recommended that he be sent to permanent exile, so he was consigned to "Hola Restriction camp to rot" in September 1957.[114] Though in the end it does not seem to have benefited Kahinga Wachanga himself very much, his possible collaboration with the British may have weakened hardcore resistance at Saiyusi and Mageta.

This may have been important, for Kariuki's *"Mau Mau" Detainee* and Joram Wamweya's *Freedom Fighter* suggest that hardcore resistance to camp discipline at Saiyusi and Mageta was significant in 1956. When a number of hardcore detainees from Manyani arrived at Saiyusi in June 1956, they took strong stands against work, led by Kariuki himself, Robinson Mwangi, and Gad Kamau Gathumbi. The commandant's efforts to break this strike—which included reducing rations, placing the leaders in solitary confinement, and locking men in their barracks all day—culminated in a pitched battle between hardcores and warders. In the effort to break hardcore resistance at the Lake Victoria camps, the British isolated the worst "trouble-makers" like Kariuki, put them in fetters, and sent them to Lodwar.[115] The dispute about work continued to simmer, however. Joram Wamweya was part of a group of newly arrived hardcore transferred from Manyani to Camp 2 at Mageta who decided collectively to boycott work in December 1956, because they felt that they were being treated too much like prisoners. After this strike soon spread to the more settled detainee population in Camp 1, the British dealt with it by bringing in Special Branch (who took three of their informers out of the Camp 2 population), sealing off Camp 2 with riot police, removing a number of hardcores whom informers had identified as agitators, and sending these men to Lodwar. The decimation of his group disillusioned Wamweya and led him to decide to abandon resistance. "Having discovered that all along we had been living with Special Branch agents amongst us, I began wondering whether it was not time I thought of going home. There was no longer anything heroic in being a detainee."[116] The next day he and several friends broke ranks to work and soon were transferred to the rehabilitation center at Saiyusi, from which he was sent to Kiringiti, the district camp for Kiambu, in late April 1957.

The shooting war was now over and resisters in detention could no longer hope that their actions would strengthen comrades fighting in the forests. At Kiringiti camp with other Kiambu detainees and later at Ngenia divisional camp with acquaintances from Limuru, Joram Wamweya worked and waited. Relatives and friends came to see them and urged them to make a final and full confession, holding nothing back, so that they would not risk being returned to a detention camp. Some wives came with their mothers-in-law and the illegitimate children they had given birth to during their husbands' years in detention. At Ngenia, many men suffered the worst disillusionment they had ever experienced. "The visit from relatives demoralized many detainees: it left them feeling that they had been cheated; that they had wasted the best years of their lives for a lost cause."[117] When the interrogators came around to Wamweya himself he started to tell a carefully constructed false confession, as he had done on other occasions. The secretary of the screening team immediately stopped him, telling him that they already knew the real story of his initiation into Mau Mau, for his *batuni* oath committee, from chairman on down, had confessed. If he hoped to ever return home he would have to confess the complete truth. "I gave as much information as I had the heart to give."[118] Two months later he was back home with his family.

Others had a more difficult transition to freedom. The works and district camps, though closer to home than Athi River and Saiyusi, could be terrible places themselves. Gakaara wa Wanjau remembers that detainees would call these "Komesha Camps" ("Extermination Camps"), because they were run by home guards, who "maintained a reign of terror and they would beat people to maim and even kill."[119] One of the worst was Kanguburi in Nyeri, where Kiboi Muriithi was detained, which was notorious for overworking detainees and beating them mercilessly when they collapsed.[120] Aguthi Camp in Nyeri was known for the straightforward brutality with which its guards dealt with new in-takes. A board over the entrance to Aguthi was inscribed with the saying *"Mwiteithia Niateithagio,"* or "He who helps himself will also be helped," a proverb associated with the Local Native Councils, but which under the circumstances echoes disturbingly *"Arbeit Macht Frei,"* the legend over the entrance to Auschwitz. According to Kariuki, who spent some unpleasant weeks at Aguthi in mid-1958, the guards gave the men of each in-take fifteen minutes to decide if they would help themselves or not; those who agreed would be sent to work, the others to the punishment pits where they were beaten or made to carry buckets of earth or stones out of the pit until they collapsed.[121] Muriithi eventually won release from Karatina Camp in December 1957, by making an acceptable public confession; Kariuki was released from Othaya Camp in December 1958, on a district officer's initiative.

Muriithi and Kariuki were fortunate because the British sent other detainees into "permanent exile" in places like Hola, determined that they would never live in Central Kenya again. Several memoirists spent time at Hola—including Mathu, Wanjau, and Wachanga—but only Karigo Muchai found himself relegated with others of the blackest among the Black to the "Closed Camp." Ironically, Muchai had been sent down the pipeline to Githiga Works Camp, but was sent back up after his chief refused to take him because the secret organization Kiama kia Muingi (KKM) was active in that area of Kiambu and the chief believed he would be a dangerous influence in the location. Muchai's continued refusal to confess along with the chief's opposition convinced the Special Branch officer at Githiga to send him to Hola. In light of what was to happen to him, his comments at this point in the memoir are poignant. "I would have confessed if I thought there was a chance of being released. But having heard what the chief said about me I decided it would be wiser to remain silent."[122]

This fateful decision sent Karigo Muchai to the Hola massacre. Although Hola was an exile camp—a place where confessions and rehabilitations were not longer relevant—the British were determined to gain and retain effective control over the hardcore there. Defiance, especially the defiance represented by work strikes, were seen as threats to that control, and the authorities in Nairobi authorized a plan of carefully graduated violence—it was called "compelling force"—to break hardcore defiance. This is the background to the killings at Hola in January 1959 and the scandal that resulted. According to Muchai's memoir, the confrontation at the Closed Camp began not because the detainees refused to work but because of severe grievances over food and working conditions, and only escalated due to the reaction of the camp commandant. On the tenth morning of the strike, the commandant showed up outside the compound with 200 heavily armed *askaris;* the detainees hastily conferred, decided that they were facing force majeure, and agreed to abandon the strike, taking the commandant by surprise. After the *askaris* marched the men to the worksite, stopping once to beat them severely with batons and rifle butts, the commandant asked Kiburi, the spokesman, if the detainees were willing to work and Kiburi told him once more that they were. "Moments later the camp commandant blew his whistle and guards and warders set upon us like wild animals with their clubs, feet and fists. They continued to beat us for quite some time; I don't know exactly how long it was as I was too busy trying to protect myself against the club-swinging madmen to be concerned with time."[123] When it was all over, eleven detainees had been killed and many more—including Muchai, who had suffered injuries to the base of his spine, to his ribs, and to one knee—were hurt badly enough to require hospitalization. Muchai speculates that the commandant had resorted to violence because "He might have considered it a personal defeat if we were simply allowed to return peaceably to work after our nine-day strike."[124] Evidence from British documents suggests, however, that the officer was not acting on his own but under instructions from the Prisons Department to break hardcore resistance by violent means.[125]

After the Hola incident and the investigation that followed, the remaining camps were quickly closed down and the government sent detainees back to their homes willy-nilly, sometimes without confession.[126] Commenting on the excesses of the camps, Kariuki remarks that incidents like Hola were "the inevitable consequence of a system which was rotten through and through" and showed that "the Colonial Government of Kenya had lost its soul and was no longer capable of distinguishing between right and wrong."[127] Hola did lead to an official crisis of conscience (at least in

London), but the decision of Harold Macmillan and Ian Macleod to disengage from Africa had more to do with policy than with moral qualms. The British were cutting their losses.

Conclusion

The story of the detention camps is one of the most disturbing chapters in the narrative of the Kenya Emergency. In a certain sense, detention typified the Mau Mau experience. Far more Gikuyu, Embu, Meru, and others were detained than ever fought in the forest (over 85,000 compared to perhaps 25,000); more families had sons, daughters, fathers, mothers, brothers, and sisters in the camps than relatives on active Mau Mau service.[128] Reading Kariuki or Wanjau, it is impossible not to hear echoes from other personal accounts around the world—of POW camps (Laurens van der Post, Eric Lomax), German concentration camps (Elie Wiesel, Primo Levi), the camps of Siberia (Eugenia Ginzburg, Alexander Solzhenitsyn)—for there have been many twentieth-century memoirs describing lives "inside," possibly because the struggle of individuals with an impersonal system is one of the great themes of our time.[129] The brutality and dehumanization (including transport in "cattle cars"), the undermining of individual identity, the efforts of persons and groups to resist the regime, the complex relations between inmates and guards—all are elements the Mau Mau memoirs share with these better-known narratives of detention and political imprisonment.

Let us take a closer comparative look. The situation of Mau Mau detainees somewhat resembled that of prisoners of war. Political detainees (whether Mau Mau in the 1950s, IRA activists in northern Ireland in the 1970s, Kurdish PKP members in present-day Turkey) tend to see themselves as captured fighters, and often demand that they be treated just like prisoners of officially declared conflicts. Yet prisoners of war can claim rights guaranteed by international conventions (though not always successfully, as the World War II prisoners in Burma and Malaya discovered) while detainees have a harder time making these claims, though outside public opinion can mitigate the circumstances of their detention. Mau Mau detainees were thus faced with a struggle for legitimacy POWs did not have to deal with.

Like inmates of German or Soviet concentration camps, Mau Mau detainees often felt victimized as much for *who they were* as for *what they might have done,* seeing themselves as condemned to imprisonment and brutalization because of their convictions, their membership in a despised group, their ethnic background (as Jews or Gikuyu). The parallel with Nazi camps was noticed during the 1950s, for critics of the detention system referred to Manyani as "an African Belsen"; on the other hand, the situation of the Mau Mau detainees was not as stark or hopeless as that of the Jewish inmates of Nazi camps facing extermination. The resemblance of Mau Mau detainees to Soviet prisoners was rather closer. The complex of more than fifty British camps scattered throughout the country resembled a Kenyan gulag; Africans during the Emergency like Soviets during the Great Purge of 1936–1939 were often incarcerated on the basis of the flimsiest evidence; conditions of life and work were often brutal in both types of camps; and certain inmates were relegated to permanent exile in Siberia or in the Northern Frontier District even after imprisonment or detention was over. The resemblance suggests a parallel between colonial conditions and totalitarian conditions, a parallel noted by Frantz Fanon, though colonial camps were less isolated from public opinion in the metropole and in the international community than were the Soviet camps.[130] As Tsvetan Todorov describes in *Facing the Extreme: Moral Life in the Concentration Camps,* the Soviet camps depersonalized the inmates so that the guards could more easily regiment and brutalize them, and depersonalization was used in the Kenyan detention camps as well, as a strategy of physical control and a way of mentally compartmentalizing the "other."[131] For officials and visitors alike, individuals tended to disappear, and Europeans seemed to perceive only the "dark," "sullen" mass of the hardcore.[132] *"Mau Mau" Detainee* shocked many Europeans in part because Kariuki stepped out from that undifferentiated ethnic and racial mass to assert himself as an individual, insisting on telling his own story, refusing to go quietly into history as he had refused to kowtow to the system in the camps.

However, though the Soviet camps isolated people, they did not put a heavy emphasis on changing them. The "rehabilitation" program in the Kenya detention camps bears a closer similarity to "thought reform" practiced in "re-education" camps in China and in the Chinese-influenced POW camps in North Korea in the early 1950s.[133] For the British commandants were not simply holding the detainees. Like prison and camp authorities everywhere they tried to "break" each inmate's natural resistance to the regime inside, but they were expected to go further, to attempt to convert their charges through thought reform. While police intelligence officers concentrated on extracting information from detainees to use against Mau Mau activists still at large, camp "rehabilitation" workers tried to transform Mau Mau resisters into pliant collaborators by persuading them or physically compelling them to confess the oath and cooperate with the camp authorities against their former comrades. In most camps, then, the authorities attempted to create a controlling atmosphere, using psychological pressure, intimidation, enticement, and violence in order to dominate camp life and interfere with the development of strong and protective social structures within the Mau Mau detainee community.

The memoirs suggest that the hardcore in the camps resisted the British effectively in the first years by banding together, electing leaders, setting their own rules, and maintaining morale. Their camp classes in reading and writing, history, and politics resurrected the separatist education of Githunguri College and the Gikuyu independent schools (which must have been one reason why British officials wanted to control or close them). Kariuki and other leaders modelled a new kind of heroism in the camps; not the bravery of Mathenge and Kago under fire, fighting back, but the courage of noncooperation, risking injury and death for a principle. In turn, the struggle in the camps was a social education for Kariuki and other leaders; as Ngugi wa Thiong'o observes, "the universities of Manyani and other concentration camps" awakened Kariuki and others to the links that bound all Kenyans together within the colonial system.[134] While leaders like Kariuki inspired fellow detainees, decisionmaking in the camps was actually more collective than it had been in the forest, for the club and compound committees reproduced the hierarchies of the civilian movement in Nairobi and Central Province, preserving a sense of involvement and the faith that even those behind the wire could contribute to eventual victory. In spite of the privation, hard work, and brutality, detainee society sustained the hardcore and helped them survive.

But the authorities held most of the advantages in their hands, and this edge began to tell as the years passed. As Luise White has perceptively pointed out, the very routines of ordinary camp life may have gradually undermined the rebelliousness of even the resistant hardcore.[135] The defections of certain groups, such as the bulk of the educated and most of the detainees from Kiambu, could have been predicted from the previous history of the secret movement. While White has written, "The greatest division within Mau Mau was levelled in detention," Kariuki, Muchai, and Mathu indicate on the contrary that more educated detainees turned to cooperation than ran literacy classes or wrote letters of protest to Parliament.[136] The British first separated cooperators and then used them against the hardcore in order to wear the latter down, an effort reaching its culmination in the rehabilitation program, which was designed to establish a culture of cooperation that would oppose and eventually replace the culture of resistance among the hardcores. The confessors at Athi River, who publicly poured out secrets they had pledged under oath to conceal, modeled a new kind of behavior, at first shocking yet ultimately seductive to many men whose will had been weakened by years behind the wire and resistance worn away by brainwashing. Finally, as the research of White, Cora Presley, and Marina Santoru has indicated, the British hoped through a combination of rehabilitation in the men's and women's camps and social reform in the Emergency villages to create a new, progressive Gikuyu society, cleansed of Mau Mau, loyal, and looking toward the future.[137]

Did the British succeed? The passage of time, the separation from their families, their loss of hope in Mau Mau victory, and the pressures exerted on them in the camps all eventually took their toll on the hardcore detainees. Considered collectively, however, the memoirs suggest that detention and rehabilitation—with their dark underside of coercion and violence, brainwashing and terror—transformed rebels not into complacent cooperators, but rather into physically and spiritually exhausted men who chose to sham in order to escape. Ironically, while detention did eventually break most Mau Mau resistance, the camp system soon destroyed itself at Hola. And by 1959 the current was running strong toward decolonization and eventual majority independence.

The detention camps cast a long shadow over independent Kenya, however. Though detainees did band together in veterans' groups and farmers' cooperatives, and ex-detainee politicians like J. M. Kariuki spoke out for them, B. M. Kaggia, Fred Kubai, J. Murumbi, and Achieng' Oneko wrote in 1966 of the "self-effacing and diffident" behavior of many guerrilla veterans, and attributed this to their camp experience.[138] They were asked to "forgive and forget," but even those whose physical wounds had healed had to contend with the memory of the fear, violence, and humiliation the camps had imposed on them; like survivors who came back from the Burma Railway, the Siberian gulag, or the Nazi extermination camps, returned detainees found it hard to settle in to normal life among those who had no conception of their sufferings (or even harder to live beside loyalist neighbors who had not only beaten and shamed them but had emerged from the 1950s wealthier and facing better prospects). Finally, the experience of the camps was a dangerous repressed memory for the nation of Kenya as a whole, and exhortations simply to forget could not substitute for the painful work of confronting a bitter and conflicted past.

Notes

1. Muchai, *Hardcore,* p. 49.
2. Wanjau, *Mau Mau Author,* p. 31.
3. Presley, *Kikuyu Women,* pp. 136–50; White, "Separating the Men from the Boys," pp. 19–25; Marina Santoru, "The Colonial Idea of Women and Direct Intervention: The Mau Mau Case," *African Affairs,* vol. 95, no. 379 (April 1996), pp. 253–67.
4. Rosberg and Nottingham, *Myth of "Mau Mau,"* pp. 334–47; Edgerton, *Mau Mau,* pp. 173–201; Maloba, *Mau Mau and Kenya,* pp. 137–46.
5. Kenya Colony, *Report of Committee on Emergency Detention Camps* (Nairobi: Government Printer, 1959).
6. Gikoyo, *We Fought for Freedom,* p. 203.
7. Muchai, *Hardcore,* pp. 36–39; Mathu, *Urban Guerrilla,* p. 62; Gikoyo, *We Fought for Freedom,* p. 204.
8. Wachanga, *Swords,* pp. 137–38.
9. Muchai, *Hardcore,* pp. 38–41.
10. Kariuki, *Detainee,* pp. 58–63.
11. Wamweya, *Freedom Fighter,* pp. 81–82.
12. Ibid., p. 81.

13. Kariuki, *Detainee*, p. 60, and also Wachanga, *Swords*, p. 157. See for comparison the British use of hidden informers in Malaya, Richard Stubbs, *Hearts and Minds in Guerrilla Warfare: The Malayan Emergency 1948–1960* (New York: Oxford University Press, 1989), p. 166, and the Germans' and Greek collaborators' use of hooded informers in occupied Athens in 1944, Mark Mazower, *Inside Hitler's Greece: The Experience of Occupation, 1941–44* (New Haven: Yale University Press, 1993), pp. 342–44.

14. Kariuki, *Detainee*, p. 61.

15. Wanjau, *Mau Mau Author*, p. 84.

16. Kariuki, *Detainee*, p. 79. Similar classifications were developed specifically for women detainees at Kamiti; see Santoru, "Colonial Idea of Women," p. 263.

17. Wachanga, *Swords*, pp. 157–58.

18. Ibid., pp. 141–42.

19. Kariuki, *Detainee*, p. 63.

20. Wamweya, *Freedom Fighter*, p. 83; Muchai, *Hardcore*, p. 49. Frequent beatings at Manyani were asserted by ex-officer V. C. Shuter in Kenya Colony, *Administrative Enquiry into Allegations of Ill-Treatment and Irregular Practices Against Detainees at Manyani Detention Camp and Fort Hall District Works Camps* (Nairobi: Government Printer, 1959), p. 2.

21. Kariuki, *Detainee*, p. 85.

22. Ibid., p. 85; Muchai, *Hardcore*, p. 52.

23. Kariuki, *Detainee*, p. 64; Muchai, *Hardcore*, p. 50.

24. Muchai, *Hardcore*, p. 50.

25. Kariuki, *Detainee*, p. 84.

26. Kariuki, *Detainee*, pp. 65–67, 89; also on Athi River in 1954, Muchai, *Hardcore*, pp. 45–46; cf. Presley's information on situation for women at Kamiti, Presley, *Kikuyu Women*, pp. 139–43.

27. Muchai, *Hardcore*, p. 55.

28. See H. Stott, "Health in Detention Camps," Sept. 23, 1954, PRO CO 822/801, and Gov. to Colonial Sec., Oct. 13 & 16, CO 822/801.

29. On "Marlow," Kariuki, *Detainee*, p. 67; on *Kiriamburi*, Mathu, *Urban Guerrilla*, pp. 84–85 and Wachanga, *Swords*, p. 148; on Lodwar commandant, Muchai, *Hardcore*, pp. 57–58. Because of the rapid expansion of the camp system, few commandants or warders had any training in running camps or prisons. Kenya Colony, *Report on the General Administration of Detention Camps in Kenya* (Nairobi: Government Printer, 1956), p. 1.

30. Kariuki, *Detainee*, p. 70.

31. Wamweya, *Freedom Fighter*, p. 186.

32. Wanjau, *Mau Mau Author*, p. 7.

33. Kariuki, *Detainee*, pp. 118, 121. Government officials were concerned about the possibility that African warders could become disaffected. Kenya Colony, *Report on Administration of Camps*, p. 2.

34. Wanjau, *Mau Mau Author*, p. 12.

35. Kariuki, *Detainee*, pp. 66–67.

36. Mathu, *Urban Guerrilla*, p. 68.

37. Kariuki, *Detainee*, p. 52.

38. Muchai, *Hardcore*, p. 45.

39. Mathu, *Urban Guerrilla*, p. 68.

40. Muchai, *Hardcore*, pp. 43–45.

41. Ibid., p. 43.

42. Ibid., pp. 43–44; Mathu, *Urban Guerrilla*, p. 68. Cf. Lodwar rules, which are almost identical to Athi River, Kariuki, *Detainee*, pp. 111–12.

43. Gov. to Colonial Sec., Dec. 21, 1954, PRO CO 822/794.

44. Kariuki, *Detainee*, pp. 73–74.

45. Wanjau, *Mau Mau Author*, p. 41.

46. Kariuki, *Detainee*, p. 100.

47. Ibid., p. 68.

48. On Lodwar, Kariuki, *Detainee*, pp. 113–15; on Manyani, Wamweya, *Freedom Fighter*, p. 84.

49. Wanjau, *Mau Mau Author*, p. 39.

50. Ibid., p. 31.

51. Kariuki, *Detainee*, p. 124.

52. Ibid., p. 87.

53. Ibid.

54. Muchai, *Hardcore*, p. 48.

55. Wanjau, *Mau Mau Author*, p. 104.

56. Kariuki, *Detainee*, p. 87.

57. Wanjau, *Mau Mau Author*, p. 35.

58. Ibid., pp. 35–48.

59. Kariuki, *Detainee*, p. 104.

60. Ibid., pp. 51, 100.

61. R. H. Blundell Papers, Mss. Afr. s. 746, Box 1/4.

62. Kariuki, *Detainee*, pp. 100–105.

63. Presley, *Kikuyu Women*, Ch. 7. For information on women interned at Lamu, see Wambui Waiyaki Otieno, *Mau Mau's Daughter: The Life History of Wambui Waiyaki Otieno* (forthcoming, Lynne Rienner), Ch. 5; cf Gov's. Dpty. to Colonial Sec., Aug. 11, 1955, PRO CO 822/801.

64. Muchai, *Hardcore*, p. 40.

65. Muthoni Likimani, "Vanishing Camp," in her *Passbook Number F. 47927*, pp. 160–84.

66. Wanjau, *Mau Mau Author*, p. 194.

67. Wamweya, *Freedom Fighter*, p. 178.

68. Kariuki, *Detainee*, pp. 67–69.

69. Ibid., pp. 90–92; Kaggia, *Roots*, p. 159; cf. PRO CO 822/801 & CO 822/802.

70. Kariuki, *Detainee*, pp. 85–86. See also testimony of Allan Kenyari in Kenya Colony, *Allegations of Ill-Treatment . . . Manyani*, p. 34.

71. Wamweya, *Freedom Fighter*, Part 3.

72. Kariuki, *Detainee*, p. 71.

73. Ibid., p. 103; Wanjau, *Mau Mau Author*, p. 196.

74. Kariuki, *Detainee*, p. 33.

75. Wanjau, *Mau Mau Author*, p. 183; see also Muriithi, *War in the Forest*, p. 123; Wamweya, *Freedom Fighter*, p. 194. The evidence suggests that false confessions were more common than refusals to confess at all.

76. Kariuki, *Detainee*, p. 81.

77. Wanjau, *Mau Mau Author*, p. 186.

78. White, "Separating the Men from the Boys," p. 19.

79. Kariuki, *Detainee*, p. 65.

80. Ibid., p. 75; cf. Minister for Community Development, "Rehabilitation Teams from Athi River," PRO CO 822/794.

81. Wanjau, *Mau Mau Author*, p. 18.

82. Ibid., p. 55.

83. Ibid., p. 67.

84. Kariuki, *Detainee*, p. 67.

85. Muchai, *Hardcore*, p. 60.

86. Mathu, *Urban Guerrilla,* p. 83.
87. Wanjau, *Mau Mau Author,* p. 76.
88. Ibid., p. 82.
89. Ibid., p. 176.
90. F. D. Corfield to Alan Moorehead, Aug. 6, 1958, Corfield Papers, RH, Mss. Afr. s. 1675 (4).
91. Kariuki, *Detainee,* pp. 131–32.
92. Wanjau, *Mau Mau Author,* p. 185.
93. Mathu, *Urban Guerrilla,* p. 68.
94. Muchai, *Hardcore,* p. 46.
95. Ibid., p. 47.
96. Mathu, *Urban Gueriilla,* p. 65.
97. Ibid., pp. 65, 70–72.
98. Ibid., p. 72.
99. Ibid., pp. 71–73.
100. Wanjau, *Mau Mau Author,* p. 178; see also on attitude of new Commandant Breckenridge, R. Tretchard to Dpty. Dir. Operations, Feb. 29, 1956, Hinde Papers, RH Mss. Afr. s. 1580 (3).
101. Mathu, *Urban Guerrilla,* p. 73; Wanjau, *Mau Mau Author,* p. 177.
102. Wanjau, *Mau Mau Author,* pp. 185–86.
103. Ibid., pp. 186–87.
104. Ibid., p. 188; cf. Robert Jay Lifton, *Thought Reform and the Psychology of Totalism: A Study of "Brainwashing" in China* (New York: Norton, 1962), Ch. 14. For the possible influence of mass confession in the Christian Revival movement, see Kershaw, *Mau Mau from Below,* p. 136.
105. Wanjau, *Mau Mau Author,* 194–95; see official concern about release of large numbers of detainees, Gov. Baring to W. A. C. Mathiessson, Sept. 8, 1956, PRO CO 822/795.
106. Kariuki, *Detainee,* p. 130.
107. Wanjau, *Mau Mau Author,* p. 190.
108. Ibid., pp. 190–92; see Pugliese, "Author," p. 427.
109. Ibid., p. 192.
110. Kariuki, *Detainee,* p. 129.
111. Mathu, *Urban Guerrilla,* p. 74.
112. Ibid., p. 75.
113. Wachanga, *Swords,* pp. 51–53, 144–45.
114. Ibid., p. 147.
115. Kariuki, *Detainee,* pp. 100–105.
116. Wamweya, *Freedom Fighter,* p. 192; see also Dpty. Gov. to Colonial Sec., July 21, 1956, PRO CO 822/801.
117. Wamweya, *Freedom Fighter,* p. 196.
118. Ibid., p. 198.
119. Wanjau, *Mau Mau Author,* p. 202.
120. Muriithi, *War in the Forest,* p. 119.
121. Kariuki, *Detainee,* p. 140.
122. Muchai, *Hardcore,* p. 77.
123. Ibid., p. 80.
124. Ibid.
125. PRO CO 822/125. Also Colonial Office, *Record of Proceedings and Evidence in the Enquiry into the Deaths of Eleven Mau Mau Detainees at Hola Camp in Kenya* (London: HMSO, 1959).
126. Kenya Colony, *Report of the Committee on Emergency Detention Camps* (Nairobi: Government Printer, 1959).

127. Kariuki, *Detainee,* p. 141.

128. Buijtenhuijs, *Essays on Mau Mau,* p. 49.

129. Laurens van der Post, *The Prisoner and the Bomb* (New York: Morrow, 1971); Eric Lomax, *The Railway Man* (New York: Norton, 1995); Elie Wiesel, *Night* (New York: Hill and Wang, 1960); Primo Levi, *Survival in Auschwitz* (New York: Collier, 1961); Eugenia Ginzburg, *Journey into the Whirlwind* (New York: Harcourt, 1967); Aleksandr Solzhenitsyn, *The Gulag Archipelago* (New York: Harper and Row, 1975).

130. Fanon, *Wretched of the Earth,* p. 41.

131. Tsvetan Todorov, *Facing the Extreme: Moral Life in the Concentration Camps,* trans. Arthur Denner and Abigail Pollak (New York: Henry Holt, 1996), pp. 158–65.

132. Perham, foreword to Kariuki, *Detainee,* pp. xiv, xxi.

133. Lifton, *Thought Reform,* pp. 5–6.

134. Ngugi, "J. M.," p. 83.

135. White, "Separating the Men from the Boys, " pp. 22–23.

136. Ibid., p. 21.

137. Ibid., pp. 19–25; Presley, *Kikuyu Women,* pp. 137–50; Santoru, "Colonial Idea of Women," pp. 253–67.

138. Kaggia, Kubai, Murumbi, Oneko, preface to Njama and Barnett, *Mau Mau from Within,* p. 9.

———————————————————————————————

CHAPTER 7

Politics

Some of our leading politicians seemed to be less concerned with building up our "soon to be free" nation than with building up their own positions. What I had fought for was almost a reality, and yet I began to see it as only the beginning of a much longer fight for a better life for all the people of Kenya.

—*Waruhiu Itote*[1]

Uhuru for Kenya had to be joyful, not sombre; vigorous rather than brooding. National integrity and national dignity were the stuff of the future, and this was ours to create. And I have sometimes looked with wonder on the jargon of our times, wherein those whose minds reside in the past are called "progressive," while those who minds are vital enough to challenge and mould the future are dubbed "reactionary."

—*Jomo Kenyatta*[2]

And so in this great historical sacrifice and sacrificing, the Mau Mau became that proverbial farmer who is denied a meal. The Gikuyu have this saying: "It is not the farmer who eats the food he has grown."

—*Gakaara wa Wanjau*[3]

I n the forest camps and in detention, the future was often on people's minds. Bracing or consoling themselves with hopes of ultimate victory, many looked forward to the day when Africans would take power in Nairobi, and discussed how to distribute the spoils, compensate fighters for their services and sufferings, memorialize the movement, divide up offices, and deal with the loyalists. At the Mwathe meeting in August 1953, Dedan Kimathi told the leaders that their ranks represented promises of more substantial rewards to come. Mau Mau officers would take over, "as their pensions," farms once distributed to British army officers; the new African government would pay *itungati* the salaries they had earned through their forest service; "memorial halls" would be built all over Kenya with registers of the names of all freedom fighters "for future generations to see."[4] In his speech to the first meeting of the Kenya Parliament, Kahinga Wachanga said that, though the coming government would be a civil one led by Kenyatta, ex-guerillas would have considerable influence, for "we would remain soldiers in the civil government if we were still needed to ensure our hard-won and bloody *uhuru,*" thus guaranteeing that "all Freedom Fighters in the forest, prisons and detention camps would be given cash compensations and free land. We agreed that those who suffered the greatest should receive the greatest rewards."[5]

At Manda Camp the detainees—many of whom were prominent nationalists swept up at the same time as Kenyatta in the Jock Scott operation—saw a positive side to detention, for "We could now in togetherness deliberate on the formation of our future nationalist government."[6] Most agreed with Paulo Thiong'o and Samuel Kagotho that "after nationalist victory had swept away the colonialist administration, Kenyatta would lead the new government while Dedan Kimathi, assisted by Mathenge wa Mirugi, would lead the new nationalist army," and with Onesmus Gacoka that "Manda camp would be an appropriate recruiting ground for ministers of the nationalist government."[7] During the discussions at Manda consensus emerged on several matters: the new Kenyatta government would be led by people from all districts of Kenya, in the new government "there would be absolutely no room for colonial collaborators," and the first priority for the governing council would be to "determine the policy of reallocating the land we had been fighting for."[8] While the detainees at Manda included a number of important nationalists, a more concentrated array of potential power could be found among those detained at Lokitaung. In 1957 these detainees (with the significant exceptions of Waruhiu Itote and Kenyatta himself) formed the National Democratic Party, with a flag, a slogan ("Liberty, Equality, and Justice"), and a significant "National Day," October 19, the day of the last meeting of the Mau Mau Central Committee. The NDP elected officers (including Bildad Kaggia as president and Fred Kubai as secretary), divided up ministries, proposed policies, and agreed on those policies after thorough debate. From 1957 to 1959 the members of the NDP wrote letters to British MPs, members of the Legislative Council, and leaders of the district political unions. Although Kaggia does not say so, the NDP apparently conceived of itself as a government in waiting.[9]

One of the most delicate issues for speculation in the forest camps and in detention was the fate of the loyalists after a Mau Mau victory (though the discussions dealt almost exclusively with Gikuyu loyalists rather than people from other groups). Kimathi had predicted in early 1954 that after independence the loyalists would "hang themselves" while Mau Mau veterans would receive medals, honors, and respect, and their families would walk tall.[10] The bitterness many *itungati* felt is vividly expressed in this stanza from a forest song in Wachanga's *The Swords of Kirinyaga:*

All of us Mau Mau from Ngong Hills to Garba Tulla
will enjoy the time we defeat our enemies.

The sadness will be over;
But God will never forgive you homeguards![11]

Mohamed Mathu reports a long discussion among hardcores at Athi River Camp in October 1954, about what to do with the loyalists. While some felt that they would have to be punished, others thought that it would be better after the Emergency to "just live and let live."[12] In her "Emergency village" in Murang'a in 1953, the young Charity Waciuma had no doubt how to treat loyalists: "Traitors is what I think of them; TRAITORS, TRAITORS is written somewhere in my heart with red ink and in capital letters. Anyway our time will come one day. I am treasuring this in my heart."[13] With the possible exception of Kariuki, the authors of the memoirs believed that even if the loyalists were not specifically punished, they should be excluded from power after independence because they could not be trusted. When the fate of the loyalists came up during the discussion of the future at Manda, Solomon M' Mwiricia joked that after independence he wanted to lead the rehabilitation department "so that he could carry out the work of correcting the heads of the collaborators with the colonial administration."[14]

Things did not work out quite as many expected. Most detainees were released in the years 1957–1960; joy and relief at homecoming was often tinged by melancholy and anger as they learned of parents who had died, spouses who had been raped or unfaithful, land that had been taken away. Moreover, though they hoped for the vindication of their movement and the validation of their personal sacrifices at independence, when they returned from the camps the British were still in control of the country, and the loyalists dominated the locations of Central Kenya. The next decade would see not only the ending of colonial rule and the retreat of the settlers, but also the conflict between loyalists and ex–Mau Mau in Central Kenya, the emergence of serious ethnic divisions in the country, as a whole, and the struggle for control of the independent government between conservative-moderate forces around President Kenyatta and a faction of "radicals" particularly associated with Bildad Kaggia, ex-member of the Mau Mau Central Committee. Official admonitions that there would be "no free things" and advice to "forget the past" clashed with calls for land redistribution to Emergency veterans and their families and efforts to preserve the memory of Mau Mau sacrifices. By the end of the independence decade Mau Mau veterans themselves would be divided, some cooperating with the new regime and others isolated and alienated.

Return and Restriction

The homecomings of detainees were often bittersweet. In early 1958 J. M. Kariuki was transferred from Athi River to Othaya Divisional Works Camp in Nyeri, close enough to his home for his relatives to visit him. He eagerly anticipated seeing his mother, Mary Wanjiku, after four years' separation, but on that first visitation Sunday, Kariuki's aunt told him that his mother had died, news that shook him to his roots. His mother would never meet his wife nor witness the African independence they had both suffered so much to achieve. As a young Gikuyu man who believed in the proverb *"Nyina wa mundu ni ta we Ngai wa keeri"* ("The mother of a man is like a second God"), Kariuki's pain was worse "than all the beatings and torture that I had been subjected to in all the camps put together," and his pleasure returning to his community some months later was blighted by this sadness. (See for comparison Nelson Mandela's reflection on the death of his mother during his own long imprisonment.)[15] Karari Njama's return to Nyeri was also tainted, but in a different way. His wife had been raped by a home guard in 1955 and had born an illegitimate child; thus Njama's homecoming was like the return of Gikonyo in Ngugi wa Thiong'o's *A Grain of Wheat,* when Gikonyo learns that his wife, Mumbi, has borne the child of the loyalist chief Karanja.[16]

Others enjoyed unblemished homecomings. When Gakaara wa Wanjau returned in August 1959, his family and friends responded to his unexpected arrival with "ecstatic joy." An amazed neighbor told him that the British had sent sky-shouting planes over the village telling them to never expect to see him alive again.[17] When Karigo Muchai returned to Kiambaa in March 1960, after a six-year absence, his family prepared a traditional soldier's welcome:

> My wife and children were very excited and happy to see me. The traditional Kikuyu cleansing ceremony was performed and a feast was prepared to celebrate the return of a warrior from battle. A he-goat was slaughtered and cooked and we ate a meal to commemorate my "re-birth" into the family. Special types of herb were gathered and boiled in water. My wife insisted on my drinking this so to regain my lost strength and vigour.[18]

For some hardcore ex-detainees the joy of their return was heightened by a conviction that they had won; why would the British have released them (after telling them over and over that they would never be free) if the colonial masters were not conceding defeat? On the day of Gakaara wa Wanjau's return, his friend Mwaniki Mbariti, an ex-detainee himself, said to him, "Haven't you realised yet that we have achieved victory?"[19]

The government of Kenya did not see it that way, for while they were beginning to yield to African nationalism, they were still definitely holding the line against Mau Mau, a distinction they were beginning to recognize in practice while they continued to deny it rhetorically. Many officials—fearful of the strength of new oath-bound groups like Kiama Kia Muingi (KKM) and the Kenya Land Freedom Army (KLFA), of the depth of social unrest, and of the powerful land hunger of the Gikuyu poor—believed they had a duty to fight a rearguard battle against the forces of political and social chaos. In 1960–1961 the fearful example of the Congo was arousing considerable concern within the government and "widespread anxieties among the immigrant races"; officials believed that only a crackdown would enable them to prevent "another Congo in Kenya."[20] Keeping Kenyatta in detention as long as possible, restricting the freedom of action of the increasingly restless African politicians, preventing peasant occupation of white-held land in the highlands, and backing the loyalists in Central Kenya against radicals and returned detainees were policies designed to hold the line against Mau Mau–like unrest.

On the local level, therefore, chiefs and other loyalists continued to cling to power. Chiefs and headmen retained the right to turn homecoming detainees away and enforced restrictions on those back from the camps. After his first night at home, Kariuki's sleep was cut short by the blaring of a megaphone calling the people of his aunt's village to communal labor, or *gitati* (echoes of the loudspeakers at Athi River). He, his aunt, and all the other adult men and women gathered at the home guard post, were divided into groups, and then were sent off to dig bench terraces on the farms of loyalists. Kariuki also noticed the headman assigning women to cut firewood and draw water for his personal use; after asking around, he found that the same system was in operation in all the villages in the area. To his mind, neither he nor his relatives and neighbors were really free at all. "The whole country seemed to be in detention with the village as the compound and the works camps as the small cells. We were not released from anything."[21] The roles of the loyalists in the Nyeri villages reproduced the roles of the guards and warders in the detention camps.

Government restrictions limited the freedom to work of ex-detainees, giving the advantage to active loyalists and cooperators.[22] The families of ex–Mau Mau faced poverty and even hunger. When Joram Wamweya returned to southern Kiambu in the autumn of 1957, he and his family celebrated his arrival home, but he soon found that "It was a freedom steeped in misery. We were heavily restricted. No ex-detainee could leave his division. This meant that it was very difficult to get a job."[23] After his return in 1960, Karigo Muchai and his wife were forced to move to a new village where they had no plot to grow food for their family; restricted to his location for almost a year, where there was no steady work, Muchai was not permitted into Nairobi until the city was so flooded with job seekers that he was unable to find regular employment.[24] Even Ngugi Kabiro, who had never been arrested or detained himself but whose family remained under constant suspicion as Mau Mau adherents, also found himself, the sole possible breadwinner of his family, without a job and restricted to Kiambu by pass control regulations; in desperation, he concocted a faked confession with a number of his neighbors (each swearing the others were members of his oathing group), obtained a confession certificate, and by luck and fast-talking managed to cajole a travel permit from the district officer so that he could seek work in Nairobi.[25] Who had won and who had lost in the struggle of the 1950s? Veterans of the secret movement, the forest war, and the camps were uncertain; their return smelled like victory, but tasted of defeat.

Some freed detainees decided that the situation was so bad at home they might as well return to the forest. While Waruhiu Itote did not agree with them, he certainly sympathized.

> After years of detention, they returned to find their property destroyed or confiscated; they were ordered to report regularly to the administration authorities, something which cut into their dignity; and they were expected to pay taxes as well! They also found that many of the former home guards and prison warders, who had beaten them in detention, had important positions in the local administration and continued to dominate their lives. It was not surprising that some of them chose to return to the forest, to wait for Kenya's real Independence.[26]

Returnees joined forest holdouts, who were particularly numerous in Meru in the early 1960s, as J. T. S. Kamunchuluh and David Njagi have both described, and whose numbers actually swelled in the early 1960s due to rumors that land would be distributed to forest fighters.[27]

The Politics of Late Colonial Kenya

Gikuyu, Embu, and Meru loyalists were unsure of the situation themselves. For all the advantages they seemed to hold in their hands, active loyalists in Central Province in the late 1950s were anxious and insecure—aware of their isolation, fearful of the returning detainees, and uncertain of their fate should Kenyatta be released from detention. Gakaara wa Wanjau, finding that the home guards who supervised the forced communal labor in his village seemed unwilling to assert their authority, concluded that the loyalists were "on the retreat," fearing that the ex–Mau Mau might actually come to power at some time in the future.[28] Under the circumstances, loyalists naturally appealed to their elected representatives like J. G. Kiano, Jeremiah Nyagah, and Bernard Mate to protect their interests.[29] Tension in Central Kenya remained high.

J. M. Kariuki was acutely aware of the climate of suspicion and fear affecting relations between loyalists and returned Mau Mau in Nyeri in 1959. "Unless something were done quickly the bitter antagonism between the loyalists and the detainees would be magnified and we would lose once more the chance of unity, without which our independence would be delayed."[30] Kariuki's first effort to deal with this problem, consulting with

Tom Mboya and J. G. Kiano and forming a political party in Nyeri with a group of friends, landed him back in detention for violating his travel restrictions. Shortly after his final release in early 1960, Kiano and others returned from the first Lancaster House conference and began to organize the Kenya African National Union. However, in May "things became very bad in Nyeri" when a headman was killed; officials slapped curfews and travel restrictions on several locations, and the government arrested sixty people for holding secret meetings and oathing ceremonies ("Operation Milltown"). At the district commissioner's request, KANU leaders agreed to come up to Nyeri to calm things down, and in June James Gichuru, Joseph Mathenge, Mwai Kibaki, and others spoke to 15,000 people, "appealing for unity and condemning secret oath-taking and other similar activities as no longer necessary at this stage of our political development." Kariuki himself "personally appealed to the ex-detainees to forget the past and called upon the ex-loyalists to unite with us."[31]

Kariuki did not trust the British, believing that they were still playing "divide and rule." The political restrictions that had prevented the formation of countrywide African political parties until 1960, the refusal to release Kenyatta, and the desperate maneuvering of European settlers had led to important political consequences dangerous for the future of independent Kenya: the emergence of competing district political groups, the formation of the rival regional organizations KANU and KADU, and the selfish and undignified scramble of individual politicians for power and influence. The continuing struggle between Mau Mau and loyalists in Central Province was only one of the challenges the emerging nation had to face. By 1960 Kenya was clearly moving toward independence, but Kariuki was concerned that the divisions among Africans that had emerged over the previous decade would seriously weaken the new country.[32]

Bildad Kaggia was equally anxious about this danger. The formation of KANU and KADU had not only undercut the NDP party of detained leaders, but had raised the specter that the British could use the division to delay the country's independence. In response, Kaggia and the others brought Kenyatta into their deliberations, elected him the new chair replacing Kaggia, and the whole Lodwar group met with delegations from KANU and KADU on March 23, 1961. Although the conference resolved that neither party would cooperate with the British by accepting ministerial posts before independence, the KADU leaders soon broke the agreement, leading Kaggia and Paul Ngei to send a public letter to Ronald Ngala denouncing KADU in late April. Shortly afterwards Ngei and the others were sent home (Kenyatta was now at Maralal), and Kaggia received some "very odd visitors" at Lodwar. A Murang'a chief, a Kiambu chief, and the Nyeri district commissioner told him to support KADU in its decision to participate in government if he wanted to be released; he responded that he would not do so because KADU had violated their agreement and because it would help the British delay independence. This maneuvering was Kaggia's foretaste of what was to come.[33]

As the last Kapenguria defendant to be released, Kaggia returned to Kandara Division, Murang'a (also Charity Waciuma's home area), at the end of August 1961, to be welcomed by a large celebrating crowd. Responding as a natural politician, he spoke to them from the Land Rover, "even before I greeted my mother," with a message quite different from Kariuki's.[34]

> Although I had been away for so many years, my heart had always been with them here, I said. I had never forgotten them . . . although I had been in jail all these years, I thought they had suffered worse tortures and persecution at the hands of the colonialist military and police force. The Kikuyu home guards were especially notorious. "The time has come when all who have suffered for Uhuru should reap, for Independence is near."[35]

As Kaggia was winding up his speech a home guard in the crowd collapsed and was taken to the hospital. Though Kaggia commented that "his own conscience must have bothered him," the local home guards had more to worry about than twinges of conscience; if the Mau Mau who had suffered for independence should reap its benefits, this implied that those who had helped inflict those sufferings should lose what they had gained during the Emergency.[36]

The loyalists in the Gikuyu districts had gained more than just a temporary political advantage. The British had deliberately pushed land consolidation to strengthen the position of the forces of stability in Gikuyuland, and M. P. K. Sorrenson observes that the beneficiaries of this process tended to be "the rich, the powerful, and the loyal."[37] The competition for political, social, and economic power went hand in hand, and naturally there had been losers as well as winners. Like other Mau Mau families in Murang'a, where the land consolidation program had been plagued by partiality and corruption, Kaggia's family had lost most of their best land. "And I had no *shamba* because my original fertile land had been allocated to someone else during my imprisonment. The new plot which had been allocated to me was rocky, and nothing could grow there."[38] D. Mukaru Ng'ang'a confirms the advantages loyalists gained in Murang'a in the late 1950s and early 1960s by obtaining favorable decisions during land consolidation, by their participation in coffee societies, and by obtaining loans for agricultural development.[39] But many of the poor Mau Mau supporters hoped that returned leaders from detention would take up their cause. For weeks after Kaggia's return in 1961, delegations of well-wishers came from all over Murang'a to visit him in restriction at his home, bringing sustaining gifts of food and singing and dancing in his honor; delighted by the attention, Kaggia "addressed about six or eight groups every day."[40] Even without actively campaigning, he was building a political base, a base that could only threaten the power of the Murang'a loyalists.

In *Roots of Freedom,* Kaggia suggests that the local loyalists and some of the new African members of the Legislative Council became allies because the returned detainees threatened the political interests of both.[41] When the British had begun to relax the restrictions on African politics, younger politicians had taken over the positions of influence that men like Kenyatta, Kaggia, and Paul Ngei would have controlled if not for the Emergency. Their vision of a comfortable future had been disrupted by Oginga Odinga's call in 1958 for the recognition of Kenyatta and the Lokitaung detainees as the real political leaders; when Kiano and other politicians criticized Odinga, their hostile comments backfired and public opinion forced them to fall into line.[42] KANU soon defeated KADU in the competition for Kenyatta's favor, and fought the 1961 election under the slogan "Kenyatta na Uhuru."

Sitting members of the Legislative Council were still loath to yield their political advantage to returning detainees. The edge they held for the moment (because the British still required Africans to present "loyalty certificates" in order to vote) could not last.[43] When local newspapers reported that "the old guard" planned to take over KANU, some younger party leaders conspired "against the ex-detainees, to see that they did not get important positions."[44] This even affected Kenyatta himself, for in spite of the pledges every KANU candidate had made before the election that he would give up his legislative seat for Kenyatta, when the time came after his release, they balked, claiming that it would be inappropriate, even though he could only attend the second Lancaster House Conference, scheduled to be held in early 1962, if he were a member of the Legislative Council. It required a special conference of KANU, during which ex-detainees took an important role pressing that the pledge be honored, to obtain the seating of Kenyatta in place of Kariuki Njiri of Murang'a. But the efforts of Kaggia and others to enable Paul Ngei to attend the conference as the Kamba representative in place of Henry Mulli (who was willing to step down) were blocked by the KANU executive with the assent of Kenyatta himself, and during these discussions some party officials showed quite explicit hostility to the role of the ex-detainees. Kiprotich, a Rift Valley KANU leader, accused them of causing confusion and ignoring party decisions. "He reminded the ex-detainees that unless there were those who built KANU ex-detainees would not have found it easy to settle down into politics."[45] The controversies over the seating of Kenyatta and Ngei were the first tests in the struggle for the control of KANU.

The exclusion of Ngei from the conference convinced Kaggia "that a war was being waged between the two generations of politicians. The new was determined to push the old one off the political scene."[46] In his view, the new African politicians were encouraged in their actions by Europeans

and Asians in the Legislative Council, who thought of Mau Mau as a terrorist group, and by the actions of Kenyatta himself, who had agreed that Ngei
should not go to London. Though the Kapenguria men had all been invited
to the meetings of KANU National Executive ever since their release, on
the day Kenyatta took over the KANU presidency Tom Mboya raised a
motion to bar the presence of the others in the future because their attendance was unconstitutional. Their exclusion was followed by an attempt to
prevent Kaggia's election as chair of KANU's Naivasha branch (though
there was no residency requirement in the constitution), an attempt by
KANU headquarters to substitute J. N. Muigai for Kaggia as the parliamentary candidate from Kandara over the heads of the constituency organization, and a successful headquarters intervention to bar Paul Ngei from election as KANU chair in Machakos. The hostile KANU leadership targeted
not only the Kapenguria men like Kaggia, Ngei, Achieng' Oneko, and Fred
Kubai, but also less prominent ex-detainees. "Every day became more
intensified, and KANU Headquarters became the centre of the offensive
against the former prisoners."[47] Kaggia does not mention, however, the
concern of Tom Mboya and others in the KANU leadership that radicals
were taking over the KANU Youth Wing, causing major problems for headquarters.[48]

In Kaggia's view, the general election of 1963 was a crucial test of the
direction KANU was taking, especially in several key constituencies where
"older KANU and 'Mau Mau' leaders"—including James Beauttah for
Kigumo constituency, Stanley Kagika for Kiharu, and Stephen Ngobe for
Githunguri—ran against the nominees of KANU headquarters. The
Kigumo election campaign in Murang'a was particularly telling. Beauttah,
a nationalist veteran of forty years and a founder of the Kikuyu Central
Association, was pitted against Kariuki Njiri, "a young man completely
unknown to the freedom struggle," the American-educated son of the leader
of the Kikuyu Guard in Murang'a, ex-Senior Chief Njiri Karanja. In this
bruising campaign the party headquarters pulled out all the stops, accusing
Beauttah of being a sympathizer with KADU and an agent of colonialism.
Beauttah, Kagika, and Ngobe were all defeated. In Beauttah's own words,
"We had done more than they ever had, fought and gone to jail while they
were studying in UK and America. And they pushed us out, we who put
them where they were."[49]

However, though the election of 1963 was a defeat for the radicals, it
was only a temporary setback. Kaggia's memoirs, which do not extend
beyond the end of 1963, may leave the rather misleading impression that
the Kenyan left had been defeated; the reality was rather different, for political radicals—operating first from the KANU backbenches in Parliament
and from within extraparliamentary oragnizations like the trade unions and
the KLFA, and later from leadership positions in the Kenya People's Union

(KPU)—would continue to wield influence in Kenyan politics for six more years.

The Radical Challenge

The election of 1963 was only one round in the bout for the political control of Kenya. Indeed, some outside observers in Kenya at the time, like British journalist Richard Cox, believed that "the Mau Mau had, in the end, won" and were "now in a position of influence" while the loyalists were in decline, both at the national and at the local levels, as Kenya moved toward full independence.[50] In December 1963, Jomo Kenyatta shared the speakers' platform at Ruringu stadium in Nyeri with Dedan Kimathi's widow, Elsie Mukami, to welcome fighters in from the forest. While Kenyatta listened, Mrs. Kimathi, after leading the crowd of 40,000 in a cheer of *"Uhuru na Mau Mau,"* spoke strongly for official rewards for Mau Mau veterans and their families.[51] As Atieno Odhiambo puts it, in an essay evoking the atmosphere of 1963, "the Mau Mau freedom fighters" advanced "their hegemonic claim that only they had fought for Uhuru, and therefore that only they should rule," a claim that, though not accepted by the regime, could not be simply ignored.[52]

In spite of the setbacks they had suffered in 1962–1963, ex–Mau Mau and their political allies wielded some power in the first years of independence. Kenyatta appointed Kapenguria colleagues like Kaggia and Achieng' Oneko, prominent former detainees like Waruhiu Itote and J. M. Kariuki, and left-wing politicians sympathetic to Mau Mau like Oginga Odinga to positions of responsibility in the first independent government. Ex-detainees like Kaggia, Kariuki, Joseph Mathenge, and Waweru Kanja were elected to the Kenya Parliament. In 1963 prominent ex-detainees and other left-wing politicians established a formal backbench group separate from the Parliamentary Group of the party to challenge the cautious economic and social policies of the government, and Kaggia assumed the leadership of the backbenchers after he gave up his post in the Ministry of Education in June 1964.[53] The left-wing politicians tended to respond positively to demands from outside Parliament, from critics like union radical Dennis Akumu and Mau Mau veterans, for social justice and land redistribution.

A number of controversial issues pitted the backbench critics of official policy, sometimes supported by Vice President Oginga Odinga, against the KANU government. Kaggia, Waweru Kanja, T. Okelo Odongo, and others demanded more rapid Africanization of the civil service, attacked the continued influence of Western capital in Kenya, urged the adoption of limitations on land purchase, demanded strong government support for agricultural cooperatives, called for nationalization of some public utilities and some industries, and urged greater public expenditure on social services, especially on the provision of free education. In foreign affairs the radicals attacked "neocolonialism," demanded a loosening of ties with Britain and the United States, and called for closer relations with the Eastern Bloc. The power of the radicals during this early period peaked in late 1964 and early 1965, when radical politicians and students used the platform of the Russian-financed Lumumba Institute to attack KANU and the policies of the government.[54] But the most critical struggle as far as Mau Mau veterans were concerned involved the land in the former "White Highlands."

Land was the most contentious issue of racial and ethnic debate; the restoration of lands lost to Europeans had been a demand of African political groups from the East African Association to Mau Mau, while European farmers had always claimed their own rights to sell or keep their highland farms as they chose. In the early 1960s radical parliamentarians like Joseph Mathenge and members of Mau Mau veterans groups like the Kenya Land and Freedom Army called for the seizing and free distribution of land, many landless moved on to Rift Valley farms to stake claims, and European settlers threatened to abandon their farms unless they were offered a fair price.[55] Although the political and economic influence of the mixed-farming settlers had precipitously declined since 1959, neither the British government, the large agricultural companies whose holdings dominated the highlands, nor the Kenyatta administration wanted to risk the political and economic consequences that might follow the invasion of highland farms by the landless and the collapse of the land market. The government also feared the potential for serious ethnic violence if Gikuyu landless occupied highland areas farmed by settlers but also claimed by other ethnic groups such as the Maasai, Kipsigis, and Nandi.

The strongest voice for the rights of the Gikuyu landless was that of the Kenya Land and Freedom Army (KLFA). Beginning in 1957 as a new oath-bound organization, the KLFA began to spread among the Gikuyu peasantry in Central Province and the Rift Valley, winning an especially strong response from ex–Mau Mau detainees. Its goals were to win independence and take over (or "recover") the highlands. According to Tabitha Kanogo, "the KLFA was better organised, commanded stronger allegiance and had greater clarity of purpose than Mau Mau. Composed of hardcore ex–Mau Mau leaders and followers, it clearly anticipated using physical violence if events went contrary to their expectations."[56] The KLFA was a strong potential threat to a smooth process of decolonization on the land. Members called themselves *thigari cia bururi,* or guards of the land, and "they sought to ensure that the land did not get into the wrong hands, such as those of loyalist Gikuyu, other groups like the Kalenjin or Maasai who might claim land in the Rift Valley, or even settlers who might want to stay."[57] Although the KLFA did not endorse violence as such, its stand implicitly threatened violence in the Rift Valley if it did not gain its ethnocentric aims, and members stockpiled arms to use if necessary. Moreover, the KLFA was not only for land for Gikuyu, but for *free* land. A proposal to confiscate land and distribute it free challenged the property claims of the remaining settler landowners, threatened the market in land, and even undermined the capitalist Kenyan economy as a whole. Although it was infiltrated by the police, who arrested dozens of members from 1960 on, the KLFA was difficult to suppress because of its secrecy, wide popular support (especially among returned squatters in the Rift Valley), backing from left-wing members of KANU such as Bildad Kaggia, and influence within KANU branches in the Rift Valley, especially in Nakuru District.[58]

While the need to supply land to the landless was not really in dispute among Kenyan politicians at the time, there was a great difference between the government buying up land for resale to peasants and others on the one hand, and redistributing free land to the poor in general or to Mau Mau veterans in particular on the other. The land issue drew the line between Kenyan radicals and conservatives. Kaggia expressed the radical position in a speech to Parliament in February 1965:

> Our policy, Mr. Speaker, Sir, has been that the land in Kenya belonged to the African people and this land was stolen from us. This is the policy not the slogan as many people tend to make us believe. We have used this for all these years as a policy and in fact it has been the backbone of our political struggle.[59]

Kaggia and other radical politicians argued that for Africans to pay for "stolen land" was "absurd"; instead, white-controlled land in the highlands should be confiscated and redistributed to cooperatives of the landless.[60] Kenyatta and other KANU leaders strongly opposed demands for free land, partly in order to mollify the British and international lenders but also because of their personal convictions. As early as his return to Gatundu in 1962, Kenyatta had spoken to the crowds who had gathered to see him about the issue of land in the highlands, saying "It is for everybody. Whoever wants to buy—whether he is Indian, European or African, let him do so."[61] Individual rather than group rights to land, the necessity to purchase land, and the refusal to distribute land free of charge (to Mau Mau veterans or anybody else) were positions taken up by the conservative KANU leadership even before independence and held consistently throughout the 1960s.

The decolonization of the "white highlands" has received a great deal of attention from scholars, so only its main results will be summarized here. Any free land redistribution was firmly rejected; loans were provided under the auspices of the British government and the World Bank on a "willing buyer, willing seller" basis to African individuals and groups to purchase land in the highlands. Schemes like the "Million Acre" scheme ultimately bought out hundreds of settler farmers, brought to the highlands thousands of new African landowners (ex–Mau Mau received no special priority), helped to prop up the market in land, defused some of the potentially "destabilizing" land hunger (among the Gikuyu especially), and left many new African owners with a burden of long-term debt. The British government, European farmers, international investors, and African conservatives were pleased that the principle of private property had been ensured and potential violence between Gikuyu and other ethnic groups averted, while radicals in KANU and in the KLFA criticized the solution as a sellout. Most scholars agree that the resolution of the issue was a victory for the proponents of gradual change within the economic system inherited from colonial times and a defeat for those who hoped for populist land redistribution, including ex–Mau Mau.[62]

The Conservative Counterattack, 1964–1969

Even at the height of radical influence, conservatives in the party and the government were taking steps to meet the challenge. The dissolution of KADU in 1964 had swelled the ranks of conservatives in KANU, for many who had crossed the aisle were suspicious of the ex–Mau Mau, fearful of the land hunger of the Gikuyu poor, and resentful of what they saw as Gikuyu and Luo pretensions to dominance. After dismantling the federalist constitution in 1964, the regime moved to return power to the provincial administration, eventually lifting the new African district and provincial commissioners to positions of strength greater than any local politicians. New government policies on industrial disputes in 1964, worked out by Tom Mboya, largely neutralized the independent power of the unions. Mboya's Sessional Paper No. 10, *African Socialism and Its Application to Planning in Kenya* (1965)—which emphasized the need for capitalist growth, encouraged official incentives for free enterprise, called for greater foreign investment, and decried class politics—pointed toward an economic future along Western lines. These statist, capitalist, and pro-Western policies excited considerable criticism from KANU backbenchers and extra-parliamentary organizations.[63]

In 1965–1966 conservatives responded to the criticism by mounting a fateful offensive of their own. Led by Tom Mboya, they accused the radicals of favoring "communism," of accepting financial support and weapons from foreign powers, and even of planning to overthrow the government. In March 1966, Mboya called an unconstitutional KANU conference at Limuru, in spite of the opposition of radical politicians and union leaders, who voted to tighten the control of the central authorities over KANU and to replace the position of vice president, held by Oginga Odinga, with eight provincial vice presidents.[64] This conservative counteroffensive drove almost thirty MPs, led by Odinga and Kaggia, out of KANU and into an opposition party, the Kenya People's Union (KPU), founded in April 1966.

The KPU manifesto echoed Mau Mau in its attack on big estates, but now the broad acres had come into the hands of "a new class of big landlords," ministers and other officials of the new African government. The manifesto stated boldly that "A radical change in land policy is obviously necessary. The *wananchi* shed their blood to secure it." The KPU program included "distribution of free land to the neediest," reduction of the size of individual farms, an emphasis on cooperative farming ("in line with the socialist policy of the KPU"), democratic land consolidation, and free education for all.[65] Kaggia, Odinga, Achieng' Oneko and their colleagues presented the KPU as a real socialist party espousing class politics on behalf of the *wananchi,* and themselves as the true inheritors of the militant tradition of the fight for independence. KPU leaders spoke of the responsibility of independent Kenya to the ex–Mau Mau and their families and extolled the role of the revolt in winning *uhuru.* Although the strongest base for the KPU was the Luo heartland of Central Nyanza (not Mau Mau territory), Oginga Odinga had consistently praised the role of Mau Mau in liberating the country, and the KPU could also claim significant support in Kaggia's stronghold of Murang'a and in Nakuru District in the Rift Valley. There is reason to question, however, whether the KPU really represented a continuation of a Mau Mau political program, because there is little evidence in the memoirs or elsewhere that the Mau Mau struggle for land and freedom was ever articulated in socialist terms.

The KANU government wasted no time in striking back. Although Tom Mboya had fought as the point man for the conservatives in Parliament and KANU in the struggle with the radicals leading up to the KPU split, Kenyatta himself led the assault on the opposition in the "little general election" of 1966. Although Kenyans of various political leanings, including some radicals, had claimed to speak for him, Kenyatta had been moving in a more and more conservative direction, typified in the early 1960s by his rejection of "free land" and his hostility to the Kenya Land Freedom Army, which can be contrasted with his efforts to reassure the British government and the settlers, particularly in his famous Nakuru speech of August 1963. By 1966 his government was well prepared for a challenge from the left. From 1963 to 1966 the regime had been consolidating power at the top, marginalizing Parliament and local organizations, and continuing the colonial pattern of strengthening the ministries and the provincial administration. Informally, Kenyatta himself contributed to this growing centralization by relying more and more on his Kiambu inner circle. Although parliamentary backbenchers and the press exercised considerable freedom of speech, the government was quite successful in neutralizing or turning aside criticism. In 1966 the KPU faced a governmental structure experienced in containing potential opposition and unprepared to tolerate serious dissent, and for the first time government critics had to contend with a president directly involved in the effort to silence them.

During the short life of the KPU (early 1966 to late 1969), the KANU government succeeded in using its administrative powers to severely circumscribe opposition activities and its propaganda to brand the KPU as an ethnic party fostering disunity. The refusal of local authorities to register KPU branches, the intimidation of KPU supporters by KANU men, the official restrictions on party meetings, and the attacks on KPU gatherings in the Rift Valley and Kandara were accompanied by the detention of KPU officers under the Public Security Act in 1966 and later by the six-month imprisonment of Kaggia in 1968 for holding an illegal meeting.[66] In statements by government spokesmen, including Kenyatta himself, support for the KPU was equated with disloyalty to the Kenyan nation and betrayal of Kenyatta; to counter Kaggia's claims to represent Mau Mau veterans, the government won pledges of loyalty to Kenyatta from General Kimbo, General Mbaria Kaniu, and "Field-Marshal" Mwariama. In addition, the government offered access to land to landless families in Central Province to undercut the KPU's appeal.[67] Although KANU portrayed the KPU as antinational and tribal, as so jealous of Gikuyu success as to be willing to destroy Kenyan unity, the clique around Kenyatta decided themselves in 1969 to reassert ethnic unity and reinforce loyalty to the president by conducting mass Gikuyu oathing at Gatundu. The ethnic gulf widened further with the assassination of Tom Mboya in July 1969. In August Kaggia and the other Gikuyu leaders within the KPU left the opposition and applied for re-admission into KANU. Although Kenyatta ended the oathing campaign in response to the demands of African Christians, this did not ease the pressure on the KPU, and in October, after Kenyatta's provocative speech in Kisumu led to rioting and killings by the police, the government banned the KPU and put Oginga Odinga and other leaders into prison.[68]

A good example of official manipulation of ex–Mau Mau during the struggle with the KPU is the case of the Nakuru District Ex–Freedom Fighters Organization (NDEFFO), an agricultural cooperative exclusively for Mau Mau veterans and their families founded in 1968. Mau Mau veterans' organizations had often struggled to win government registration and toleration. Between 1964 and 1969, the government either denied registration to or banned a number of them, including the Kenya Freedom Fighters' Union, the Kenya War Council, the ex–Freedom Fighters' Union, and the Walioleta Uhuru Union ("Those Who Brought Freedom Union"). The government declared the Ex–Freedom Fighters' Union, headed by M. P. James Njiru, illegal in 1969 because it persistently demanded free land for Mau Mau veterans and free education for their children.[69] In 1972 the Kenya Old Mau Mau Company, set up to publish books and make films on Mau Mau, was officially banned.[70] NDEFFO was different. "Completely nonpolitical," according to its manager (a code expression for "progovernment"), NDEFFO was composed of members who pooled their resources to buy farms as cooperative ventures.[71] Frank Furedi argues that KANU encouraged NDEFFO as a way to "outflank the KPU" among Gikuyu voters in the Rift Valley. "KANU celebrated not so much Mau Mau as the ethnic ties that linked Kenyatta with the Kikuyu 'freedom fighters.' This link, which promised material rewards, was understood in ethnic terms. In much the same way the KPU was dismissed as an ethnic threat to Gikuyu interests from the Luo."[72]

The banning of the KPU did not end popular discontent in the volatile and heavily populated Rift Valley. Unrest over government land policy in the Rift Valley began to well up again in the early 1970s, led by an interethnic group of populist politicians headed by J. M. Kariuki and John Seroney, and only subsided after Kariuki's murder in March 1975 and the official repression that followed.[73] The government used the NDEFFO once more to rally Mau Mau support. A picture in *Mau Mau Twenty Years After* shows assembled members of NDEFFO, in Mau Mau dress, carrying a sign supporting Kenyatta and KANU and condemning revolution. "NDEFFO CO LTD/ MZEE JUUUU!!/MAU MAU IS STILL ALIVE/HATUTAKI MAPINDUZI KENYA/ HANG ALL CONSPIRATORS. WE ARE READY WITH/ OUR PANGAS AND OUR HOME MADE GUNS./ HESHIMU KENYATTA NA K.A.N.U." The caption explains that the photograph was taken "during a solidarity meeting for President Kenyatta in November 1971."[74] NDEFFO, an association formed by ex–Mau Mau for economic purposes but based in a strategically important district, was being used by the government for its own political ends. Official minds seemed to perceive a clear distinction between good Mau Mau and bad Mau Mau.

The Fate of the Mau Mau

Twelve years after independence the wartime expectations of the fighters and the detainees had not been realized. The African government in Nairobi had not rewarded generals with large estates and *itungati* with land and back wages, appointed freedom fighters to high positions in the army, expropriated settlers and distributed land to the landless, provided compensation to the widows of veterans and education to their orphans, punished the loyalists for their betrayal of the cause, or built memorials around the country in honor of dead heroes. Instead, the regime, serving the interests of a new African establishment well articulated with the international economic system, continued many of the policies of colonial times.[75]

Some of the authors of the Mau Mau memoirs expressed serious concern about the direction of independent Kenya, especially about the widening separation between the political elite and the *wananchi*. Kariuki, who revered Kenyatta in the early 1960s and agreed to his policy of forgiving the loyalists in the interests of unity and stability, also had an agenda for social change inspired by his experience in the camps, which made him harshly critical of the self-serving careerism of many African politicians.

> Our leaders must realize that we have put them where they are not to satisfy their ambitions so that they can strut about in fine clothes and huge Cadillacs as ambassadors and ministers, but to create a new Kenya in which everyone will have an opportunity to educate himself to his fullest capabilities, in which no one will die or suffer through lack of medical facilities and in which each person will earn enough to eat for himself and his family. This will require responsible leadership, hard work, unity, honesty and a sincere love of our country in all our hearts. Selfish power-seekers will have to go.[76]

Mohamed Mathu commented, "I have closely watched the activities of our political leaders and am not happy with much of what I see. . . . Some leaders are becoming rich Africans. . . . They rarely talk with the poor peasants and workers whose interests they say they represent."[77] Referring to 1962, Ngugi Kabiro remarked that he could not tell what the two Kenyan parties really stand for. "Mau Mau has been crushed under the heel of British might and now it seems there are no spokesmen for the great aspirations or hopes of my people."[78] It seemed to some that nothing was really changing, and that the sacrifices of the Mau Mau fighters would be ignored. In Mathu's view, this would be intolerable because "we did not make these sacrifices just to have Africans step into the shoes of our former European masters."[79] The politicians who introduced Karari Njama's *Mau Mau from Within* in 1966—including Kaggia and Achieng' Oneko, leaders in the KPU—connected the nation's neglect of its rebel heritage and its Mau Mau veterans to the system that had developed in postindependence Kenya; in their minds, the "conspiracy of silence" about the contributions of Mau Mau to *uhuru* was related to the neocolonial politics and economics of the country.[80]

Waruhiu Itote would not go nearly so far, but he was surprisingly critical in 1967 given his official position in the National Youth Service and his close links to Kenyatta; though his memoir described his efforts on Kenyatta's behalf in 1963 to bring Mau Mau in from the forests and though it supported the reconciliation of old enemies, in his last chapter he attacked the neglect of veterans and their families, and in so doing raised serious questions about the political values of the postindependence regime. He attributed the poor treatment of the veterans in part to the apprehensions of Gikuyu loyalists and members of other ethnic groups that ex–Mau Mau might challenge their positions.

> Thus, in many high places, there appears to be a basic apathy towards the plight of those who fought and sacrificed. Some of those who now enjoy

the fruits of Independence, who sit in places made available to them partly through the blood and sweat of those who fought, look down upon the fighters as fools. They prefer to give them no opportunity at all to come up, to regain what they sacrificed.[81]

Itote was contemptuous of the "many politicians" who "claim in public that 'we all fought for Uhuru,'" for as a guerrilla and a detainee he knew that "there are different degrees of fighting."[82]

The Mau Mau memoirists themselves experienced a variety of fates. Three—J. M. Kariuki, member of Parliament and landowner; Bildad Kaggia, influential politician; and Waruhiu Itote, well-placed bureaucrat—did well. Others at least held their own: Gakaara wa Wanjau resurrected his publishing business and became a moderately successful writer in the Gikuyu language; Karari Njama took a position as a primary school teacher; Mohamed Mathu recovered his job as a draftsman with the Nairobi City Council; Ngugi Kabiro found work as a typist; and Joram Wamweya landed a job as a plumber with the Bata Shoe Company. While in most cases these men had regained something like their social and economic positions, they had received no benefits for their efforts or for the time they had lost fighting or in detention. Others faced poverty and an uncertain future. At the time of the publication of his memoir, Karigo Muchai had no regular job, was "unable to provide adequate food and clothing for my family and have had to borrow money for my eldest childrens' school fees." He had just been arrested for nonpayment of poll tax, and was only saved from imprisonment by the generosity of friends.[83] After Gucu Gikoyo served out his colonial prison sentence, he emerged to find his contribution to *uhuru* unrecognized and without "land on which to make a living, a trade to follow or a job to do to maintain myself."[84] Poor before and poor again, he was forced to eke out a marginal existence herding goats, a job traditionally allocated to Gikuyu boys.

Several of the memoirists suggest that those who had risked their lives for the cause often failed to enjoy the fruits of *uhuru* while their old enemies frequently prospered. In his final chapter, Kahinga Wachanga comments that "Many of the beggars you see on the streets of Nairobi are products of the so-called rehabilitation programme. There is a village called *Mji wa Huruma* (Mercy Village). Most of the women who live there are widows. Their husbands were Freedom Fighters."[85] Gakaara wa Wanjau complains that, by contrast, many of the "very good servants in the colonial administration were readily absorbed into the Government administration of nationalist Kenya."[86] In an effort to obtain compensation "for the torture, loss of lives and property they had suffered during the struggle for Uhuru," a number of Mau Mau veterans in Murang'a sued the government in 1974, but the court decided against them in 1976.[87]

In the last pages of *"Mau Mau" General,* Waruhiu Itote called for a number of specific official actions to benefit both living veterans and the memory of the dead: free land ("this is what they fought for"), aid for their wives or widows and their children, compensation for lost land or property, housing and employment for the disabled, official identification and marking of the graves of the fallen. With the exception of the last, none of these actions were officially carried out. Though he made clear his loyalty to Kenyatta and noted that his comments "should not be misconstrued as a sign of dissatisfaction with our African government," Waruhiu Itote remarked pointedly that "they should be seen as a reminder to the Government that it has not recognized the Freedom Fighters in the same spirit with which the struggle for freedom was prosecuted."[88] He closed his memoir with a warning:

> Many former Freedom Fighters remain disappointed by the efforts of the Government to help them, and others deplore the attempts to make everyone's contribution to Independence appear of equal weight and importance. While I do not foresee any undue threat to security arising from the dissatisfaction felt by some former fighters, it would probably not be wise to assume that they will tolerate their present position indefinitely.[89]

General China's warning went unheeded, probably because the government saw no pressing need to pay attention.

Conclusion

When the British sent the detainees home, declared an end to the Emergency, and called the first Lancaster House conference, it seemed to many, British and Africans alike, that the ex–Mau Mau now held real power to shape Kenya's future. But the strength of their position was more illusory than real. First, as a militarily defeated guerrilla force, the Mau Mau, unlike the ALN in Algeria or ZANLA in Zimbabwe, lacked the prestige or the political clout of an active body still in the field (the remnants in the Kirinyaga forests were not militarily important, as Waruhiu Itote makes clear). Second, the leading generals of the guerrillas (with the exception of the compromised General China), possible popular rivals of African politicians, were dead or, in the case of Stanley Mathenge, had disappeared. Third, by 1960 the African politicians in the Legislative Council had not only gained years of political experience while Mau Mau leaders had languished in detention but had also successfully built up local power bases (which included the support of loyalists). The somewhat naive tone of outrage in the last chapter of Bildad Kaggia's *Roots of Freedom* suggests that he had not seriously considered how reluctant the new generation would be to gracefully yield power to the older men returned from detention (and after all he himself had been quite willing to push older KAU leaders, and even Kenyatta, aside in the early 1950s). Fourth, the British government, European politicians like Michael Blundell and Bruce Mackenzie, and the European companies, recognizing how much was at stake, had begun to work with constitutional politicians without Mau Mau connections to strengthen them against the returned detainees. Fifth, Mau Mau had not sufficiently considered the potential political power of the ethnic groups outside Central Kenya, people who were not necessarily hostile to their movement but could not share all their hopes and expectations. Sixth, ex–Mau Mau continued to bear the stigma of involvement in past violence and killing. Seventh, the involvement of ex–Mau Mau in conspiracy, oathing, and populist agitation, in Kiama kia Muingi and the Kenya Land and Freedom Army, allowed their enemies to condemn them as representing forces of chaos and disunity. Finally, Mau Mau relied much too heavily on Jomo Kenyatta to take their side and redeem their sacrifices, especially through the distribution of free land.

The maneuverings of the new KANU politicians in 1962–1963 are discussed briefly by Kariuki, Itote, Wachanga, and Mathu, and thoroughly analyzed by Kaggia. In Murang'a loyalists were afraid that Kaggia and his allies would undermine the social and economic positions they had built up in the 1950s, while in the Rift Valley ambitious young Gikuyu politicians and members representing other groups suspected that ex-detainees leading returned squatters would even bypass the electoral process and seize land and political power by popular action. The election of 1963 was both a KANU-KADU contest and a conflict within KANU (at least in Central Kenya) between veterans of the nationalist struggle (mostly ex-detainees like James Beauttah) and younger men backed by KANU headquarters.

But electoral politics in 1963 were probably less important than the maneuvering behind the scenes. In the early 1960s Kenyatta was beginning to assemble the combination of personalities, factions, and subethnic and ethnic elites that would make up his independence coalition. Within Kiambu he brought together (partly through his own family connections) old antagonists, the loyalists and the former Kikuyu Central Association supporters. His cabinet, which was heavily dominated by Kiambu men, included both older nationalists like Mbiyu Koinange and younger technocrats like Njoroge Mungai. Using the largesse of official positions, government loans, and access to land on favorable terms, he eventually built up a network of supporters, not only among the Gikuyu but also among the Kalenjin, especially the followers of Daniel arap Moi, eventually his vice president. However, although Kenyatta did include certain powerful non-Kiambu Gikuyu politicians in his cabinet, like the loyalist J. G. Kiano from Murang'a and the technocrat Mwai Kibaki from Nyeri, the central and northern Gikuyu districts were comparatively neglected. Not neglected as much, however, as populists who questioned the emerging system in the name of Mau Mau. As David Throup puts it, "those who challenged the morality of the system or who appealed to their role in the 'Mau Mau War of Liberation' secured little. Their demands were subversive of the new political order, which was predicated on the social engineering that had taken place in Kikuyuland under cover of the disruption caused by Mau Mau."[90]

Many Mau Mau veterans who still saw Kenyatta as the leader of the movement suffered considerable disillusionment. As Tabitha Kanogo comments, Kenyatta's position on land "came as a great shock to many landless Kikuyu" for "The peasant had come to equate Kenyatta's release with the inception of a millenium that would be epitomised by the recapturing and redistribution of the stolen lands."[91] Kenyatta's regime became a government of landowners and property holders, who condemned the demand for "free things," and whose slogans "Forgive and Forget," "Uhuru na Kazi," and "Harambee" stressed consensual politics and self-help and gave no priority to "freedom fighters" over any other interest group. The defeat of the KPU challenge in 1969 only reinforced the political and institutional direction of the country. The regime also managed to contain the political crisis that followed the murder of J. M. Kariuki in 1975. As William R. Ochieng' points out, the salient characteristic of the Kenyatta period was continuity: "due to the Western and capitalist orientation of Kenyatta and his regime, Kenya's colonial heritage—laws, parliament, civil service, police, army, economy, education and provincial administration—remained largely unchanged and unsympathetic to and remote from popular wishes."[92]

In the 1960s and 1970s Mau Mau was suppressed, co-opted, or marginalized. Leaders who spoke for the veterans and their cause were persecuted if they did not conform to the demands of the regime, brought into the fold if they did. The government permitted ex–Mau Mau associations to operate only if they concentrated on economic concerns and publicly supported Kenyatta and KANU when called upon to do so. Mau Mau veterans gained access to land and jobs, but only on the same terms as everybody else; the government established no particular benefits for Mau Mau veterans, their widows, or their children; some memorials were built in honor of Kimathi and others but only in Central Province and only with local funds. As Buijtenhuijs points out, independent Algeria did far more than Kenya to recognize the contributions of veterans of its liberation war and to alleviate their sufferings and those of their families.[93] When in the late 1960s the Kenyan regime began to recognize Mau Mau's historical contribution in certain ways, it did so only when it served the government's purposes and upheld the centrality of the president. At the stops on Kenyatta's tours of Central Province and the Rift Valley, along with the groups of traditional dancers who turned out in the president's honor there usually appeared one of the "Mau Mau freedom fighters' teams"—their hair in forest dreadlocks, wearing ragged clothes, and carrying *pangas* and homemade guns.[94] Their performances were symbolic of the government's effort to appropriate the

Mau Mau memory, domesticate it, and reduce the image of its *itungati* to folklore. As the next chapter will show, however, this populist memory was more difficult to control than politicians expected.

Notes

1. Itote, *General*, p. 233.
2. Kenyatta, *Suffering Without Bitterness*, p. xv.
3. Wanjau, *Mau Mau Author*, p. 212.
4. Njama, *Mau Mau from Within*, pp. 249, 247.
5. Wachanga, *Swords*, p. 42.
6. Wanjau, *Mau Mau Author*, quoting Waira Kamau, p. 60.
7. Ibid.
8. Ibid.
9. Kaggia, *Roots*, pp. 145–47.
10. Itote, *General*, p. 146.
11. Wachanga, *Swords*, p. 23.
12. Mathu, *Urban Guerrilla*, p. 67.
13. Waciuma, *Daughter of Mumbi*, p. 130.
14. Wanjau, *Mau Mau Author*, pp. 60–61.
15. Kariuki, *Detainee*, pp. 138–39; Nelson Mandela, *Long Walk to Freedom* (Boston: Little Brown, 1994), p. 388.
16. Njama, *Mau Mau from Within*, p. 128; Ngugi wa Thiong'o, *A Grain of Wheat* (London: Heinemann, 1967), p. 132.
17. Wanjau, *Mau Mau Author*, p. 205.
18. Muchai, *Hardcore*, p. 84.
19. Wanjau, *Mau Mau Author*, p. 205.
20. See Extract from the Minutes of the Security Council, July 26, 1960, PRO CO 822/2024, and W. F. Coutts to F. D. Webber, Feb. 9, 1961, PRO CO 822/2031.
21. Kariuki, *Detainee*, p. 145; see also experiences of Gakaara wa Wanjau doing forced communal labor in Nyeri after his release in 1959, Wanjau, *Mau Mau Author*, p. 207.
22. Loyalists were allowed to seek jobs in Nairobi. See War Council, "Movement of KEM," March 4, 1958, PRO CO 822/1241.
23. Wamweya, *Freedom Fighter*, p. 198.
24. Muchai, *Harcore*, p. 85.
25. Kabiro, *Man in the Middle*, pp. 72–75.
26. Itote, *General*, pp. 257–58.
27. J. T. Samuel Kamunchuluh, "The Meru Participation in Mau Mau," *Kenya Historical Review*, vol. 3, no. 2 (1975), pp. 208–11; Njagi, *The Last Mau Mau Field Marshals*, pp. 4–7.
28. Wanjau, *Mau Mau Author*, p. 207.
29. David Goldsworthy, *Tom Mboya: The Man Kenya Wanted to Forget* (London: Heinemann, 1982), p. 102.
30. Kariuki, *Detainee*, p. 148.
31. Ibid., pp. 167–68.
32. Ibid., pp. 165–66.
33. Kaggia, *Roots*, pp. 162–73.
34. Ibid., p. 178.
35. Ibid.

36. Ibid.
37. Sorrenson, *Land Reform*, p. 212.
38. Kaggia, *Roots*, p. 179.
39. D. Mukaru Nganga, "Mau Mau, Loyalists, and Politics in Murang'a," *Kenya Historical Review*, vol. 5, no. 2 (1977), pp. 366, 372.
40. Kaggia, *Roots*, p. 180.
41. Ibid., p. 182.
42. See W. F. Coutts to Granville Roberts, Aug. 21, 1958, PRO CO 822/1310; Goldsworthy, *Tom Mboya*, p. 104.
43. See Legislative Council (African Representation) Bill, 1956, which required evidence of loyalty of potential Gikuyu, Embu, and Meru voters by certification of district commissioner, PRO CO 822/926.
44. Kaggia, *Roots*, p. 183.
45. Ibid., p. 189.
46. Ibid., p. 187.
47. Ibid., p. 191.
48. W. F. Coutts to F. D. Webber, Feb. 9, 1961, PRO CO 822/2031.
49. Spencer, *James Beauttah*, p. 110; Kaggia, Roots, pp. 192–93; Lamb, *Peasant Politics*, p. 16 fn.
50. Cox, *Kenyatta's Country*, p. 50.
51. Ibid., p. 55.
52. E. S. Atieno Odhiambo, "Democracy and the Ideology of Order in Kenya," in Michael G. Schatzberg ed., *The Political Economy of Kenya* (New York: Praeger, 1987), p. 193.
53. Gertzel, *Politics*, pp. 40, 45.
54. For a thorough discussion of this period see Gertzel, *Politics*, Ch. 2.
55. Many settlers had been afraid of expropriation ever since the first Lancaster House conference. Gov. Renison to F. D. Webber, June 10, 1960, PRO CO 822/2025; John W. Harbeson, *Nation-Building in Kenya: The Role of Land Reform* (Evanston: Northwestern, 1973), pp. 122–23.
56. Kanogo, *Squatters*, p. 165.
57. Ibid., p. 166.
58. Furedi, *Mau Mau War*, p. 177.
59. Quoted in Gertzel, *Politics*, pp. 45–46.
60. Harbeson, *Nation-Building*, p. 122.
61. Rebmann M. Wambaa and Kenneth King, "The Political Economy of the Rift Valley: A Squatter Perspective," paper presented to the Historical Association of Kenya Annual Conference, 1972, p. 20.
62. Harbeson, *Nation-Building*, p. 332; Christopher Leo, *Land and Class in Kenya* (Toronto: University of Toronto, 1984), p. 144; see also Gary Wasserman, *The Politics of Decolonization: Kenya Europeans and the Land Issue, 1960–1965* (Cambridge: Cambridge University Press, 1976) and D. F. Gordon, *Decolonization and the State in Kenya* (Boulder: Westview, 1986).
63. Gertzel, *Politics*, Ch. 2.
64. Goldsworthy, *Tom Mboya*, pp. 241–43.
65. Odinga, *Not Yet Uhuru*, pp. 304–305.
66. Suzanne Mueller, "Government and Opposition in Kenya, 1966–69," *Journal of Modern African Studies*, vol. 22, no. 3 (1984), pp. 409–18.
67. Nicholas Nyangira, "Ethnicity, Class, and Politics in Kenya," in Schatzberg, ed., *Political Economy*, p. 30.
68. See Chapter 2 above, and Leys, *Underdevelopment in Kenya*, pp. 234–38.
69. Buijtenhuijs, *Mau Mau Twenty Years After*, pp. 131–32.

70. Ng'ang'a, "Mau Mau, Loyalists, and Politics," p. 381.

71. Buijtenhuijs, *Mau Mau Twenty Years After,* p. 133.

72. Furedi, *Mau Mau War,* p. 211.

73. Jennifer A. Widner, *The Rise of a Party-State in Kenya: From "Harambee!" to "Nyayo!"* (Berkeley: University of California Press, 1992), Ch. 3.

74. Buijtenhuijs, *Mau Mau Twenty Years After,* facing p. 57.

75. Bruce Berman, *Control and Crisis in Colonial Kenya: The Dialectic of Domination* (London: James Currey, 1990), p. 417.

76. Kariuki, *Detainee,* p. 181.

77. Mathu, *Urban Guerrilla,* p. 87.

78. Kabiro, *Man in the Middle,* p. 75.

79. Mathu, *Urban Guerrilla,* p. 87.

80. Kaggia, Kubai, Murumbi, Oneko, preface to Njama and Barnett, *Mau Mau from Within,* pp. 10–11.

81. Itote, *General,* pp. 270–71.

82. Ibid., p. 271.

83. Muchai, *Hardcore,* p. 85.

84. Gikoyo, *We Fought for Freedom,* p. 325.

85. Wachanga, *Swords,* p. 159.

86. Wanjau, *Mau Mau Author,* p. 211; for the unhappiness of some Zimbabwean liberation war veterans, see Teresa Barnes, "The Heroes' Struggle: Life after the Liberation War for Four Ex-Combatants in Zimbabwe," in Ngwabi Bhebe and Terence Ranger, eds., *Soldiers in Zimbabwe's Liberation War* (London: James Currey, 1995), pp. 118–37.

87. Ng'ang'a, "Mau Mau, Loyalists, and Politics," p. 382.

88. Itote, *General,* pp. 271–72.

89. Ibid., p. 272.

90. David Throup, "The Construction and Destruction of the Kenyatta State," in Schatzberg, *Political Economy,* p. 42.

91. Kanogo, *Squatters,* p. 171.

92. William R. Ochieng', "Structural and Political Changes," in Ogot and Ochieng', eds., *Decolonization and Independence,* p. 106.

93. Buijtenhuijs, *Mau Mau Twenty Years After,* p. 146.

94. Ibid., p. 132.

CHAPTER 8

Past and Present

The lives of Kenya's Freedom Fighters should not be forgotten by all future generations who must defend the freedom we fought for.

—*H. Kahinga Wachanga*[1]

Let this be the day on which all of us commit ourselves to erase from our minds all the hatreds and the difficulties of those years which now belong to history.

—*Jomo Kenyatta*[2]

History is subversive. . . . So they try to *rewrite* history, make up official *history;* if they can put cottonwool in their ears and in those of the population, maybe *they* and the *people* will not hear the *real* call of history, will not hear the *real* lessons of history.

—*Ngugi wa Thiong'o*[3]

Mau Mau: war/rebellion/civil war/revolution? Each choice of epithet both absolves and accuses the users irrespective of whether they claim the expertise of professional or guild historians or partake in the popular debate of the various interested parties. The point is that there are layers of spoken knowledge, but also of critical silences, that inform one's choice of each word both within the academy and in the larger society. This is because there are, in fact, various Mau Mau pasts calling for their own historians.

—*E. S. Atieno Odhiambo*[4]

At the end of his introduction to Kahinga Wachanga's Mau Mau memoir, *The Swords of Kirinyaga,* published in 1975, editor Robert Whittier called on Kenyans to take a new look at their history.

Although sufficient time has elapsed for historical perspective . . . many Kenyans are unwilling to look at their recent past in a critical, scholarly and objective way. They seem to avoid asking the basic questions of who got what, and why. They seem to avoid understanding the immediate past and its deep effect on their present. Most appear to have taken the *uhuru*

239

celebration words of President Kenyatta literally, and have, at least concerning Mau Mau, "forgotten the past." Perhaps the time for remembering
and understanding the past and its effect on post-independent Kenya is at
hand.[5]

In the year of J. M. Kariuki's murder and the clampdown on dissent which
followed, it was difficult for Kenyans to cast their view over the past in a
"critical, scholarly, and objective way." The questions "who got what, and
why" were not merely issues for debate around a graduate seminar table,
but matters of serious, even dangerous political import. For many Kenyans
the historical objectivity Whittier exalted may not have seemed possible or
even desirable. This is not to say that Kenyans did not need to deal with
their past—quite the contrary—only that this task would be necessarily difficult, painful, and complicated.

In an essay, in the 1992 collection *Unhappy Valley,* John Lonsdale
shows more awareness of the sensitivity of Kenyans toward the subject of
Mau Mau. "At the heart of Kenya's modern history broods the enigma of
Mau Mau. The rising and its suppression were the forcing house of the
country's freedom from British rule and white settler power, yet its memory
disturbs more Kenyans than it inspires; it divides them." This tendency of
history to disturb and divide does not surprise Lonsdale, as it "is often true
of the formative events in any human past, brutal as they tend to be," nor
should it surprise most modern historians, for in the contemporary world
academic history, popular history, and public memory are very difficult to
separate from the social and political tensions of the present time.[6] As
recent controversies in France about collaboration during the Occupation,
in Russia about the purges of the Stalinist period, in Germany about the
Holocaust, in the United States about the history of white and minority
relations, in Argentina about the "dirty war" of the 1970s, in South Africa
about "apartheid crimes" all indicate, the past can be a minefield for historians and politicians alike, not to mention ordinary citizens. If "forgive and
forget" is a questionable formula for the reconciliation of past and present,
zealous efforts to either publicize or suppress a version of historical truth
may not only threaten the power of a particular regime, but also upset an
uneasy sociopolitical balance and exacerbate tense ethnic relations. History
is often disputed terrain, its "real lessons" subject to intense, divisive
debate.

How do the Mau Mau memoirs help to elucidate the Mau Mau enigma? And what is their role in the ongoing debate about the Kenyan past?
This chapter will look through the prism of the memoirs at the interpretation of Mau Mau and at Mau Mau in memory and history. It will also suggest comparisons, for Mau Mau may be easier to understand by looking at
the ways in which it resembled and differed from other insurgencies and
guerrilla wars, both while it was going on and since in the academic, official, and popular memories. In making comparisons, however, it will not

lose sight of the special character of Mau Mau, which Greet Kershaw's recently published research so vividly demonstrates.[7]

The Interpretation of Mau Mau

The essential nature of Mau Mau has remained controversial ever since the 1950s. Atieno Odhiambo comments that the term any writer or speaker most relies upon to describe Mau Mau tends also to label the user in turn.[8] But should Mau Mau itself be compartmentalized? John Lonsdale has suggested that the labels usually applied, often derived from Western ideological categories, are a poor fit, while Rob Buijtenhuijs has warned that using any particular term as the descriptor for the movement tends to oversimplify "the very complex, many-sided, contradictory phenomenon Mau Mau really was."[9] Mau Mau has been described as a nationalist revolt, an anticolonial war, a resistance movement, a class struggle, a peasant uprising, a movement of cultural renewal, an ethnic revolt, and a civil war. The memoirs indicate that it was all of these.

The progenitors of the Mau Mau discourse—J. M. Kariuki, Karari Njama, and Waruhiu Itote—had a key role in refuting the British version of Mau Mau as atavistic regression. Though Kariuki, Njama, and Itote took pains to explain the Gikuyu characteristics of the movement in order to refute what they saw as British distortions, they focused on certain Western and universalist aspects—the militant opposition to racial and political oppression, the goal of national liberation, the effort to involve all ethnic groups in the struggle. The first memoirs, then, made the case for an historical memory of Mau Mau as a predictable, understandable, and legitimate revolt against oppressive and irresponsible colonial rule, a movement whose violence played an important role in establishing a Kenyan nation. Moreover, as Bruce Berman points out, the memoirists and Rosberg and Nottingham "were intent on proving that it was a modern movement" rather than a return to the past.[10]

The interpretation of Mau Mau as militant anticolonialism and nationalism can be linked to the description of it as a resistance movement, a term applied by Peter Evans in *Law and Disorder* (1955), in which he described Mau Mau as having "a mystique among Kenya Africans comparable to 'the resistance' in Europe during the war."[11] The memoirs indicate that some Africans saw Kenya in late colonial times as an occupied country (and historians have written of the "second colonial occupation" of Kenya in discussions of the late 1940s), not fundamentally different from countries controlled by the Germans or the Japanese during World War II. Consider this reflection on the German presence during the Occupation from *The Blood of Others,* Simone de Beauvoir's autobiographical novel of the French Resistance: "In our midst, they were like a nation of colonizers amongst a crowd of natives; two worlds that ran parallel with each other without ever intermingling. They lived at the level of motorcars and planes; we had only our feet and at best, our bicycles. Distances did not mean the same for us as for them, nor did the price of a glass of wine."[12] While the phrase "a crowd of natives" suggests that it was difficult for French people to see themselves in the position of conquered colonials, the parallel would not be lost on Frantz Fanon from Martinique who trained in Algeria to fight in the liberation of Provence (and would later write that the "colonial world is a world cut in two" in terms like de Beauvoir's), on Malagasy who fought with the Resistance and later rose against France in 1947, or on Waruhiu Itote and others who served in India and Burma and later fought the British in Mau Mau.[13] Though the British attempted to obfuscate the issue by stigmatizing Kimathi as a Hitler, comparing the Gikuyu to the Germans, and regularly referring to the home guards as the "Kikuyu Resistance," many Africans understood that this was propaganda designed to mask the reality that the Mau Mau were patriots fighting the foreigners. Greet Kershaw has questioned the use of "resistance" to describe Mau Mau, arguing that it represents an inappropriate foreign concept that flattens out the complexity of the situation in Kenya in the 1950s.[14] This is a danger, but the memoirs indicate that in their hatred of foreign rule (again and again memoirists stigmatize the British as "the foreigners") and in their commitment to fight for liberation, both expressed vividly in the forest songs in the memoirs, the Mau Mau *itungati* saw themselves and were seen by many others as a fighting opposition to occupation.

The most direct heir of Itote, Kariuki, and Njama, the first generation of Mau Mau memoirists, was Bildad Kaggia, whose *Roots of Freedom* (1975) carried forward the anticolonial nationalist interpretation of Mau Mau. Kaggia went beyond his predecessors, however; by expressing his impatience for the constitutionalists of KCA and KAU, including Kenyatta, he pointed more clearly than earlier writers toward violent revolt as the only solution. His actions in detention, organizing, and initially leading the National Democratic Party, also suggest that he believed that Mau Mau had superseded the previous political groupings, though after his release he found that KANU had leapt over Mau Mau in turn. Finally, as a very self-conscious memoir published after the die of neocolonial Kenya had already been cast, *Roots of Freedom* is a history of the violent struggle for independence unquestionably influenced by its author's sense of the present.

In the late 1970s and in the 1980s the nationalist interpretation was taken up and transformed in the historical writings of Maina wa Kinyatti and the novels, plays, essays, and detention memoir of Ngugi wa Thiong'o, both of whom used Kariuki's and Karari Njama's accounts to support their own class analysis of Kenya's history. Moreover, it was Ngugi wa Thiong'o, recently freed from political imprisonment himself, who approached Gakaara wa Wanjau in the early 1980s and urged him to publish his detention diaries in Gikuyu, and Maina wa Kinyatti who edited *Mau Mau Author in Detention.*[15] These Kenyan Marxists use the memoirs to support an interpretation of the late-colonial past that characterizes the Mau Mau as the vanguard of all the African common people of Kenya and strongly attacks collaboration. Thus anticolonialism and nationalism are linked to class struggle, both in the colonial period and against the neocolonial African establishment of independent Kenya. Ngugi and Kinyatti handle the ethnic nature of Mau Mau in one of two ways, either by placing it last in a line of Kenyan resistance struggles (Koitalel of the Nandi, Me Kitilili of the Giriama, Kimathi of the Gikuyu) or by downplaying its Gikuyu character altogether.[16] In Maina wa Kinyatti's introduction to *Kenya's Freedom Struggle: The Dedan Kimathi Papers,* he writes of the "Kenyan masses" and the "African masses" but does not refer to the Gikuyu once, and his discussion of Mau Mau nationalism ignores the movement's ethnic cultural roots.[17] Kinyatti and Ngugi openly push Kenyatta off the pedestal of nationalist hero and replace him with Dedan Kimathi and J. M. Kariuki, who, separately and together, embody the heroism of resistance and the heroism of suffering and martyrdom. In *Detained,* Ngugi contrasts Kimathi's role in the forests and Kariuki's role in detention with that of the "political opportunist" Kenyatta after independence, and in *The Trial of Dedan Kimathi* he uses Karari Njama's memoir as an "invaluable guide" to understanding Kimathi, "the great man of courage," who is "still the hero of the Kenyan masses."[18]

There is some irony in this exaltation of Kimathi, both because hero worship has reactionary potential and because other left-wing writers have questioned Kimathi's revolutionary credentials. The radical South African scholar David Maughan-Brown has argued that there was an "ideological split" between guerrilla groups, which he refers to as "the state-building/ parliamentarist 'Freedom' component" (Dedan Kimathi, Karari Njama, and the Kenya Parliament) and the "peasant/Land component" (Stanley Mathenge, Kahinga Wachanga, and the Kenya Riigi).[19] The memoirs do portray Kimathi as an elitist with high ambitions and Mathenge as a populist who refused rank and chose to mess with his men rather than maintain his dignity by eating separately.[20] Maughan-Brown argues that the "peasant" followers of the Kenya Riigi were truly revolutionary, while the educated followers of Kimathi just wanted to defeat the British and replace them with an African government on the same model. While this certainly goes too far, it does point to the division within the forest, described in several memoirs, between the educated nationalists and the illiterate peasant/ethnic leaders.

In fact, the later memoirs (at least prior to that of Gakaraa wa Wanjau) point away from interpretations of Mau Mau based on Western-style nationalism or on Marxist class analysis and toward an understanding of Mau Mau in ethnic terms. Among the memoir authors, a division emerged in the 1970s not only between the adherents of Kimathi and those of Mathenge but also between those who took the "high road" of anticolonialism and Kenyan nationalism (reflected in the descriptions of political meetings in Kaggia and forest conferences in Njama and Itote), and those who immersed the reader in the particular beliefs, culture, and practice of Mau Mau itself, thus emphasizing its peasant and Gikuyu nature (e.g., Wachanga, Wamweya, Muriithi, Gikoyo). The flavor and character of the second set of memoirs come through not only in the *gitungati* account of Gucu Gicoyo, *We Fought for Freedom,* but also in Wachanga's *The Swords of Kirinyaga,* written by an experienced nationalist and prominent forest general.[21] It is difficult to imagine the scene Wachanga describes during the negotiations in 1955, in which he and other guerrilla leaders surreptitiously administer a leadership oath to the British over a cooking black lamb, appearing in Waruhiu Itote's narrative.[22]

The memoirs of Wachanga, Gikoyo, and Wamweya remind us of the key importance of oathing, for Wachanga tells us that the oath was their real leader. Rob Buijtenhuijs is convinced that oathing is the best evidence for the interpretation of Mau Mau as an ethnically based movement of cultural renewal.[23] The oaths have always been considered the most characteristic Mau Mau feature. However, the use of oathing to build a secret movement among peasantry, including oaths with a strong religious component, was hardly peculiar to Kenya or Africa; in eighteenth- and nineteenth-century Ireland, the use of secret oaths among peasant organizations opposed to the English landlords, such as the "Whiteboys" and "Ribbonmen," was common, and oathing was also used to bind members of European revolutionary organizations like the Carbonari in Italy and the Irish Republican Brotherhood.[24] In Europe as in Africa, oathing was used to enforce solidarity and ensure secrecy.

Mau Mau oathing was typified by the use of *muma wa uigano* to build ethnic and regional unity in 1952 and 1953. After the radicals had snatched oathing away from the control of the Kiambaa Parliament, it became inclusive (involving women and adolescents as well as men) and compulsory, developments that reflected a change in the intentions of oath administrators and an increase in their ambitions. While the administrators drew on the traditional Gikuyu past in constructing the ritual and pledges of the unity oath, they hoped to make something new; as Buijtenhuijs puts it, citing Kariuki, "The new Kikuyu nation, created by the oath of unity, was meant to be the beginning of a new life, for each initiate individually and for the Kikuyu people as a whole."[25] The oath brought initiates into a new circumcision group while excluding and ostracizing the uninitiated others, especially *irore* Christians and political moderates, some of whom were elders who would customarily have presided at circumcisions or oathing ceremonies. As Maia Green argues, through the unity oath, "An alternative structure of eldership was instituted within the movement, itself reconstituted as the 'tribe.'"[26] Thus the new "true Gikuyu" ("Gikuyu Karing'a") were led by a new set of elders, the oath administrators and other leaders of Mau Mau. The *muma wa uigano* was the beginning of a cultural renewal of the Gikuyu while also constituting an essential precondition for ethnic revolt against colonialism.

Oathing can be also connected through the concept of cultural renewal to the role of religion during the guerrilla war itself. The descriptions of prayers, libations, songs, dreams, visions, and signs in the memoirs point to the critical role religion played in the Mau Mau efforts to build commitment, maintain morale, and overcome the government's substantial military advantage. Though this reliance on neotraditional religion sets Mau Mau apart from most modern insurgencies in Europe, Asia, and Latin America, Terence Ranger's and David Lan's work on Zimbabwe and other comparative studies show that African revolts have often contained a strong religious component drawn from the spiritual roots of the peasantry.[27] While anticolonial nationalism, ethnic feeling, and peasant grievances have provoked revolts, religion has been a strong motivating factor for guerrillas and a significant support for morale in African insurgencies, beginning with Mau Mau.

Both the oath and Mau Mau religion were creative, syncretistic developments of renewal, drawing on Gikuyu cultural roots but pointing in new directions. Luise White has argued that another effort of cultural renewal lay in Mau Mau's reconstruction of gender and of relations between the sexes.[28] In the crucible of the guerrilla war in the forest, men and women assumed new roles in their struggle with the enemy and in their relations with each other. This led ultimately, as Waruhiu Itote, Karari Njama, Gucu Gikoyo, and Wambui Otieno have indicated, to women assuming important roles, not only in support of men but alongside men, and claiming thereby a new power to influence male-female relations and to shape their own destinies. This carried from the forests into the camps, where, as the memoirs of Gakaara wa Wanjau and Wambui Otieno and the research of Cora Presley indicate women were among the strongest resisters.[29]

Mau Mau had many characteristics of a peasant uprising. The war was rooted in the Gikuyu, Embu, and Meru peasantry, who provided most of the support and most of the fighters and in whose countryside much of the war was fought. The bases of operation in the Nyandarua and Kirinyaga forests—like the guerrilla bases in the rugged mountains of the Peloponnese in Greece, the dense forests of the Malayan peninsula, the Aurès range of northern Algeria—were within easy traveling distance of the peasant communities that supported them.[30] In Kenya as elsewhere this made for strength as long as the fighting was localized, but also made it harder to coordinate operations and increased the tendency of guerrilla leaders to fight among themselves. In Kenya (as in Greece, Malaya, Algeria, and later in Vietnam, Mozambique, and Zimbabwe) the guerrillas' dependence on the peasantry led naturally to counterinsurgency campaigns based on removing that support. Anger against settlers and wealthy Gikuyu landholders coupled with land hunger were important motivators of peasant *itungati,* as references to the land in the oaths and the songs indicate. This could lead to ethnic chauvinism and expansionism, for, as Tabitha Kanogo points out, when many Rift Valley Gikuyu "took the oath for land" they assumed that when the Gikuyu had driven out the settlers, they would have stronger claims to the land than largely quiescent groups like the Maasai.[31] The peasant/ethnic particularism of oathing, songs, and land hunger has led some Kenyan scholars such as Ogot and Atieno Odhiambo to label Mau Mau non-nationalist.[32] Frank Furedi disagrees: "No nationalist movement develops evenly among all the constituent peoples of a nation. Mau Mau can no more be dismissed as non-nationalist because it was based on the Kikuyu than German nationalism can be caricatured as a Prussian affair."[33]

Guerrilla warfare and counterinsurgency, terror and counterterror often pitted Mau Mau generals and *itungati* against chiefs and home guards, leading the British to refer in a self-exculpating way to a "Kikuyu civil war." The memoirists try to undercut this British version by emphasizing how many "loyalists" had taken the oath and helped the guerrillas, but the accounts of Kariuki, Njama, Muchai, Waciuma, Otieno, and others indicate that the conflict did culminate in a war between Gikuyu and Gikuyu. In Kenya—as in France, Greece, China, and elsewhere—civil conflict was very divisive, and "collaboration" has remained a moral and political dilemma. As Ogot points out, there are few sources for the loyalist side, for no one has written a loyalist memoir of Mau Mau, though chapters on the Mau Mau period are included in the autobiographies of Harry Thuku and Bishop Obadiah Kariuki.[34] In the Mau Mau memoirs loyalists are characterized either as secret Mau Mau or cynical and brutal men out for themselves, while loyalism as a conviction is given short shrift—Kariuki suggesting that only a tiny minority really believed in it—and this appears to be a real blind spot.[35] As Ogot has observed, there is evidence that an important minority of Gikuyu, Embu, and Meru opposed the revolt from early on for traditional cultural and religious reasons, because of Christian conviction, or because of their commitment to constitutional change and opposition to violence, even if in some cases they also wished to protect familial positions of wealth and privilege within the colonial system.[36] Ogot's argument is strengthened by evidence from the memoirs that many educated Gikuyu refused to support Mau Mau and that backing for the rebellion was weaker in Kiambu than in other districts. Ogot's apparent "defense" of loyalism has led radical historians to brand him a reactionary much as the attempts of some French historians to explain the Vichy regime has led to attacks on them from the left.[37] In her recent book, however, Greet Kershaw has questioned the terms "loyalists" and "collaborators," pointing out that their use reduces the complexity of the political situation in Central Kenya to polarized opposites; Kershaw's conclusion, based on local interviews, is that Gikuyu believed that a collaborator during Mau Mau was an informer out for personal gain, not simply someone who dealt with government, and such people were "relatively rare."[38]

The civil war interpretation of Mau Mau can be extended into later times, for Kenya's postcolonial experience can be compared to similar aftermaths in other countries in which collaboration and resistance traditions were established during liberation wars. Liberation and independence can bring dramatic changes, but these changes may not be those the guerrillas believe they fought for. After the occupiers are forced out (sometimes by the guerrillas directly but more often with outside help or as the result of negotiations), the people who take power are not usually fighters but politicians, bureaucrats, and property holders, most of whom had sat on the sidelines and some of whom had directly collaborated. In a recent essay on decolonization, Atieno Odhiambo makes a shrewd comment on the guerrillas' fate: "Mau Mau played a constructive role, albeit unwittingly, in that the military defeat of the Mau Mau militants cleared the political arena and enabled the loyalists to re-emerge as nationalist politicians in a postcolonial society."[39] The guerrilla veterans in Kenya and elsewhere, especially the peasants among them, are often disappointed in the rewards they receive and in the socioeconomic policies of the new regime. In their frustration some veterans may take up the gun again, while others may turn to opposition political parties. The regime will suppress the rebel bands, persecute guerrilla veterans who turn to political dissidence, and use economic concessions to undercut support for the cause. Fighters for liberation are difficult to assimilate socially and politically when the shooting is over.

Though the pattern described above has not always held true, there are numerous twentieth-century examples besides Kenya itself. In Ireland in 1922, the treaty negotiated with the British proved unacceptable to a large portion of the IRA (particularly its left wing), who returned to guerrilla fighting to oppose the treaty in the Irish Civil War of 1922–1923, only to be defeated by the soldiers of the Irish Free State, many of whom had previously served in the British army. The Free State government of the 1920s, dominated by large farmers and businessmen, vigorously suppressed the IRA, as anxious about its social radicalism as about its political dissidence.[40] In France and Italy, in the immediate aftermath of World War II, struggles developed between forces associated with the left-wing of the Resistance, who saw the fight against the Germans and the collaborationist regimes of Vichy and the "Italian Social Republic" as the first battle in a war to change permanently the social and political makeup of their countries, and moderate and conservative political groups (in some cases tainted by collaboration themselves) who wanted no more than limited reforms in order to avoid revolution and a possible Communist takeover.[41] In Greece from 1944 to 1950 the conflict that emerged between the social radicals who had dominated the Resistance and the indigenous conservatives spilled over into a new full-scale civil war; the conservatives, many of whom had collaborated with the Germans, won that struggle, and for years persecuted not only Communists who had fought in the civil war but many guerrilla veterans whose only offense was their participation in the Resistance.[42] To cite an Asian example, after the expulsion of the Japanese, some of the Filipino guerrilla bands believed that liberation should be followed by broad social and political reforms that would go beyond the decolonization promised by the United States to effect real change in the indigenous power structure. This did not happen and the Hukbalahap revolt followed, which was finally put down by a combination of moderate land reform and counterinsurgency.[43] After the negotiated independence in Zimbabwe, many veterans, especially among the Ndebele, felt dissatisfied with the fruits of independence, and the Mugabe government dealt with what it perceived as the threat of ethnic unrest by sending military force into the Ndebele area in the mid-1980s; the government-sponsored attempt since then to memorialize "fallen heroes" has been attacked for elitism and ethnic bias.[44] In all of these countries the social and political demands of the guerrillas and their leaders clashed with the desire of politicians and government officials for stability. In all of these countries bitter feelings between resistants and "collaborators" in general, and the unsettled scores between individuals and families would affect private and public life for many years to come.[45]

History, Memory, and Politics

One of the ways people of the twentieth century have commemorated the traumatic past has been through the building of monuments. In Britain and France in the aftermath of World War I there was a construction boom of memorials "to the fallen," from grandiose battlefield structures to small commemorative memorials in many country towns, a collective effort to mourn and to purge grief.[46] Memorials of the second war are less common; in fact, as Henry Rousso points out, monuments to the dead of World War II alone are "extremely rare" in France and when they are found their inscriptions can be misleading. The memorial to the prominent leader of the Third Republic, Georges Mandel, outside Paris, for example, is simply inscribed "Here died Georges Mandel, murdered by the enemies of France on 7 July 1944." Those who shot Mandel, however, were not Germans but members of the Milice, the paramilitary force of French collaborators. Monuments of World War II are uncommon because they remind the French of internecine betrayal and civil slaughter (*la guerre franco-française*) as much as they evoke memories of heroic struggle against the foreign enemy.[47] Kenya has faced a similar but more complicated problem in its efforts to remember, or forget, the Mau Mau war.

Discussions of history cannot be extricated from contemporary political controversies or separated from efforts of national leaders to control both the memory of the past and the politics of the present. Kenyatta's situation in the early 1960s can be compared to the circumstances faced by Charles de Gaulle of France at a critical time in his career and his nation's history. When they assumed power both leaders had to deal, immediately and urgently, with the politics of remembrance and forgetting. Nation-mending and nation-forming can be similar.

When de Gaulle returned to his country from exile in 1944, he faced two major political problems: what to do about the defeated collaborators, Marshal Petain and his followers, and how to handle the Resistance. The Vichy supporters were his wartime enemies, but his own social background, conservative politics, and authoritarian inclinations aligned with theirs in many ways; the Resistance had fought alongside his Free French forces to liberate France, but many of the Resistance fighters were Communists, with a view of both the French past and the French future very different from his own. While de Gaulle permitted without encouraging a purge of collaborators (the *épuration*), in his concern for national unity he also fostered an official memory of the Occupation that focused not on "the Resistance" but on "the people in Resistance" (suggesting that those not actively collaborating must have been resisting), much as Kenyatta constructed a discourse downplaying Mau Mau and emphasizing "We all fought for *uhuru*."[48] In the late 1940s, with France facing major social and economic problems and all Europe split by the first battles of the Cold War, de Gaulle came to view his old French Communist allies as his new enemies, as partisans of the Soviet Union. Politicians and intellectuals who had supported Vichy demanded rehabilitation and sought to influence French collective memory of the painful past, while some old resistants demanded further retribution and warned of betrayal.[49] In Kenya, as we have seen, the regime led by Kenyatta stressed unity in its view of both past and present, held the veterans of Mau Mau at arm's length (though using them when politically expedient), incorporated loyalists into the governing structure, and attacked left-wing politicians who claimed to be acting in the spirit of the liberation as allies of communist forces from outside the country.

Michael Kammen, in *Mystic Chords of Memory,* his brilliant book on history and memory in the United States, shrewdly observes that "amnesia is more likely to be induced by a desire for reconciliation," while "memory is more likely to be activated by contestation."[50] In France after liberation and Kenya following the achievement of majority rule, the national leader assumed an important initial role in shaping a discourse on the terrible period the country had just passed through, a discourse of unity characterized by a certain politic forgetfulness. In both nations, however, controversy reemerged, affected by what Rousso has called "unfinished mourning," by a desire of some for justice or retribution, by the inability of the national leadership to impose historical consensus, and by the return of competition between political antagonists, rival interest groups, regions, and ethnicities.[51] In Kenya the proponents of Mau Mau memory opposed the adherents of amnesia not only to set the record straight from their point of view but to stake political claims, such as the claims of Gikuyu Mau Mau veterans to land, and these claims in turn provoked political responses, some by proponents of rival historical memories, such as the Maasai and Kalenjin of the Rift Valley. Beyond ethnicity, however, the memory of Mau Mau also became a touchstone for political leaders who wished to claim authority and legitimacy and for dissidents who wished to draw attention to poverty and social injustice.

Ernest Renan's observation about the need "to get one's history wrong," interpreted by Ali Mazrui as "being selective about what did happen," is reasonable advice on how to construct a public history for a nation, but it does not address the issue of who is to make the selection and on what grounds.[52] The personal ambitions of leaders and factional, ideological, class, ethnic, and regional conflicts within the country may frustrate the forming of any national consensus on what should be forgotten and what remembered. In France "crises of memory," often connected to contemporary political conflicts, have flared up periodically since the Liberation (e.g., in the 1950s over amnesty for Occupation crimes, in the 1970s over Marcel Ophuls' film *The Sorrow and the Pity,* in the 1980s over French complicity with Klaus Barbie).[53] In Kenya the publication of writings on the history of Mau Mau has often coincided with national political controversies that have sometimes mirrored issues originally raised by Mau Mau; as Frederick Cooper observed in 1988, "In Kenya, Mau Mau has become a politically charged topic, and discussing it has become a way—in some cases a risky way—of saying something about the present."[54]

A brief and selective chronology of political controversies and publications in Kenya can roughly illustrate this point. Let us look first at the Kenyatta period. The Kenyatta government's treatment of Mau Mau in past and present can be divided into two periods, the first (1963–1966) characterized by the careful placing of distance between the regime and Mau Mau, and the second (1966–1978) by an equally careful rapprochement with Mau Mau veterans and Mau Mau memories the regime could use for its purposes and repression of organizations and individuals who would not conform. Kariuki's *"Mau Mau" Detainee* was published in 1963 just before independence, when the struggle between ex–Mau Mau and ex-loyalists was reaching its first peak. In 1966–1967 several important books on Mau Mau, including *Mau Mau from Within, "Mau Mau" General,* and *The Myth of "Mau Mau,"* came to print in the midst of the intense struggle between KANU and the KPU. The publication of Buijtenhuijs's *Mau Mau Twenty Years After,* the first in-depth study of historical memory in Kenya, coincided with serious discontent in the Rift Valley in 1973. The year 1975 saw the publication of Wachanga's *Swords of Kirinyaga* and Kaggia's *Roots of Freedom,* the murder of J. M. Kariuki, and the official suppression of dissent over Kariuki's killing (marked by the detention of Koigi wa Wamwere and others). In 1976 and 1977 articles on Mau Mau, pro and con, appeared in the *Kenya Historical Review;* Paul Maina published his popular history, *Six Mau Mau Generals;* Ngugi wa Thiong'o published his novel *Petals of Blood* and produced his play *Ngaahika Ndeenda;* and in December 1977, the government imprisoned Ngugi.

Upon the death of Kenyatta in 1978, Daniel arap Moi, a Kalenjin politician from Western Kenya, who had no personal connection to the liberation struggle, became president after turning back an effort of some Gikuyu leaders to exclude him. After freeing political prisoners (including Ngugi wa Thiong'o) and easing up on repression, Moi pursued "populist" policies in his first several years, generally in order to gain widespread popularity irrespective of ethnicity and region and more specifically to undermine the power of the Gikuyu establishment. In the long term he intended to shift political and economic power from Central Kenya to Western Kenya. Moi's honeymoon period did not last long. In 1982 he attacked university lecturers for encouraging subversion, detained Maina wa Kinyatti for suspected membership in the shadowy underground movement Mwakenya (and possibly for his editing *The Dedan Kimathi Papers,* published in 1980), and turned back an attempted coup by dissidents in the Air Force in August.[55] In 1983, at the urging of Ngugi and Kinyatti, Gakaara wa Wanjau published his memoir of detention in Gikuyu, received the Noma award in 1984, then was arrested for suspicion of involvement in Mwakenya. In 1985–1986 the government arrested university researchers for involvement in Mwakenya, and rumors circulated that ex–Mau Mau supporters in Nyeri and Nakuru were disseminating populist Mwakenya reform proposals among local farmers.[56] In 1985, after removing the durable Gikuyu establishment figure Charles Njonjo from his post of attorney general in 1984, Moi adopted "a strategy of faction" to ally with two important ex–Mau Mau leaders, Fred Kubai and Kariuki Chotara, breaking the Kenyatta tradition of relying on Gikuyu leaders "from loyalist backgrounds" in the hopes of splitting the Gikuyu politically and neutralizing Mwai Kibaki and Charles Matiba.[57] In 1986, debate over Mau Mau in the Historical Association of Kenya meeting overflowed into the newspapers and into the community, involving in particular several groups of Mau Mau generals; one of these groups, led by Mbaria Kaniu, received a grant of two million shillings from President Moi to document the story of Mau Mau.[58] This coincided with the internal crackdown on dissent of 1986–1988, and was shortly followed by an outpouring of new academic books on Mau Mau (from David Throup's in 1987 to Wunyabari Maloba's in 1993 to Greet Kershaw's in 1997), by public debates and street demonstrations against presidential authoritarianism and one-party rule, and by the return to multiparty politics in 1992, in an election during which candidates from arap Moi to Mwai Kibaki to Oginga Odinga claimed to be heirs to the legacy of Mau Mau (Moi pointing to his devotion to Kenyan unity, Kibaki to his roots in Nyeri, Odinga to his long-term commitment to social justice).[59]

Let us look more closely at the connection between history, memory, and politics in writings about Mau Mau. The first study to examine broadly the issue of the historical memory of Mau Mau was *Mau Mau Twenty Years After* (1973), in which Rob Buijtenhuijs discussed the representation of Mau Mau history largely in terms of the "European myth," "the African myth," and the "Euro-African myth." He faulted the Kenya government for its failure to deal with the needs of the Mau Mau veterans and their families, yet discussed sympathetically the early "forgive and forget" policy of the Kenyatta government and endorsed as politic and reasonable the local approach to the public memory of Mau Mau the regime developed later.[60] In contrast, Bildad Kaggia's *Roots of Freedom* (1975) was a tract demanding the national rectification of the memory of Mau Mau. Though Kaggia prudently ended *Roots of Freedom* in 1963, his attack on the misrepresentation of Mau Mau was really a disguised assault on the handling of its public memory by the independent state. Kariuki, Njama, Itote, and others had demolished the British myth, so when Kaggia wrote in his last pages that Mau Mau "must be recognized and praised for the true liberation movement it was," he was not targeting the British themselves but those Africans he believed were perpetuating the *mzungu* version of the past for their own purposes.[61]

While moderate academics like Buijtenhuijs condemned myth-making, radicals within and without the scholarly community attacked the colonial myth in order to further one of their own. Radicals (mostly Gikuyu) exalted Mau Mau heroes, condemned loyalism, and held up Mau Mau as the exemplary popular struggle, using the memoirs selectively to support their interpretation of the past, glancing over the exaltation of Kenyatta and the calls by Kariuki and Itote for reconciliation between rebels and loyalists. Maina wa Kinyatti, in an influential article in the *Kenya Historical Review* in 1977 (which drew heavily on Mohamed Mathu, Bildad Kaggia, and Karari Njama), condemned Gikuyu chauvinists who claimed Mau Mau as theirs exclusively and launched a vigorous assault on historians who argued that Mau Mau was un-national because its oathing and symbols were Gikuyu and because it lacked support outside Central Kenya.[62] In 1981 Ngugi wrote in *Detained* on the differences between false neocolonial history and real resistance history; the one focused on national days celebrating politicians while the other condemned collaborators and restored to history those with the courage to fight—against imperial conquerors, against soldiers and settlers during Mau Mau, and against neocolonialism.[63] David Maughan-Brown, though not a myth-maker, carried on the radical analysis of distorted memory in *Land, Freedom, and Fiction: History and Ideology in Kenya* (1985).[64]

Through the years B. A. Ogot, Benjamin Kipkorir, William Ochieng', Atieno Odhiambo, and others have challenged some of the historical assumptions of nationalists and radical writers on Mau Mau and some of the political implications of those assumptions for the present. These Kenyan conservatives, moderates, and non-Gikuyu have tended to stress the constitutional politics of the 1950s and downplayed Mau Mau, explained the political and economic continuities linking the colonial and independent regimes, and questioned the historical value of the memoirs. This tradition of analysis culminated in 1991 in a probing essay by Atieno Odhiambo on history and memory. "History in Kenya: The Mau Mau Debate," published almost twenty years after Buijtenhuijs' book, shows clearly that Mau Mau remains as controversial as ever, and his question "whose history?" not only raises startlingly the issue of ownership but reminds us that Mau Mau means one thing to an ex-general from Tetu, something else to a woman from Kandara who survived detention in Kamiti, and something else again to a young, middle-class politician from Githunguri. Its meaning for a Luo historian from western Kenya may be quite different for a radical Gikuyu novelist from Limuru. Atieno Odhiambo criticizes Buijtenhuijs for suggesting that historians from Western Kenya have deliberately minimized the importance of Mau Mau but also charges that Gikuyu have wanted to appropriate Mau Mau, as if remembering and writing about the revolt were no other Kenyan's business.[65] At the same time, he observes that "the present generation of Gikuyu elders" are very conscious of "the dangers of raking up surface history for study: the worms may still be turning on the putrefying corpses of our murdered or betrayed fathers."[66] A way for Gikuyu politicians to avoid dealing with this threatening past, as Kenyatta and others with national ambitions have done, is to "cast a network of discrete belongings and emphasize the least intimate of them," that is, to represent themselves as Kenyans.[67] But their constituencies in Central Kenya will always remind them of their first and most demanding loyalties. Many people from other regions, feeling excluded from this tight circle, may think of Mau Mau as exclusive and non-national, resenting and perhaps fearing the "hegemonism" of the Gikuyu they consider implicit in the continued exaltation of the historical role of Mau Mau.[68]

John Lonsdale has long been concerned with these issues, and in *Unhappy Valley* (1992) he proposes a way to both elucidate the Mau Mau enigma and address the reservations and resentments of non-Gikuyu concerning the memory of Mau Mau. His careful analysis of "The Moral Economy of Mau Mau" attempts to bridge the gap dividing African nationalism from Gikuyu ethnic feeling by distinguishing between "political tribalism" (the amoral competition that places ethnic groups at odds) and "moral ethnicity" (an ethos all can share). In a tour de force of thick description, Lonsdale develops a detailed analysis of the Gikuyu past to reflect on Kenya's present, arguing that the Western ideologies so often applied to the contemporary Kenyan situation have less explanatory value than "reference to deep historical memory," memory that includes the Gikuyu political debates of the 1940s and the 1950s.[69] Lonsdale's essay examines the role of Gikuyu political thought in shaping both Mau Mau itself and its opposition within the Gikuyu community; according to his analysis, the young *itungati's* fight was in part a moral protest against the denial of traditional access of the poor to land, while the counterattack by elders expressed a moral rejection of the proposition that people should obtain land by violence as opposed to winning it by the long, hard road of peaceful struggle. In spite of Mau Mau's military defeat, this philosophical conflict was never resolved, but it modeled debates of the future. Western political scientists may attribute the comparative stability of Kenya to "the high-political resort to the auction room of tribalism," but Lonsdale believes that it has more to do with the political leaders' awareness of the force of "moral ethnicity," the popular critique of leadership that demands that power be linked with virtue.[70]

> Folk memories of a time when poor men and women were goaded beyond endurance . . . must make today's rulers uneasily aware of the potential of popular censure. Moral ethnicity may not be an institutionalized force; but it is the nearest Kenya has to a national memory and a watchful political culture.[71]

Lonsdale argues that "moral ethnicity" has meaning not only to the Gikuyu but to others as well. Thus the debate over "civic virtue" that developed among the Gikuyu before and during Mau Mau not only could model but *has* modeled a nationally integrating ethos of popular accountability of leadership, one not based on "forgive and forget" but on memory as a guide to action.[72]

Here are two different views of Kenya's historical memory. Atieno Odhiambo sees the Mau Mau legacy as a kind of unhealed wound deceptively covered with skin, which one lances periodically without ever completely relieving the pressure or curing the infection for good. His vivid image of the "putrefying corpses of our murdered or betrayed fathers" suggests that the blood debts of the past cannot be paid by distributing spoils, making political concessions, or rhetorically acknowledging the sacrifices of the past. For whenever the "Mau Mau debate" erupts, it is characterized by an immunity to compromise, a resistance to differing viewpoints, an intolerance of the right of certain people to speak at all. Ethnic, intraethnic, class, and ideological barriers prevent intellectuals, politicians, and citizens in general from reaching any kind of consensus on Mau Mau. There is no purge through mourning, no effective reconciliation, no closure.

Certain indications support this rather bleak picture. In *Mau Mau Twenty Years After,* Rob Buijtenhuijs remarks that when he discusses the 1950s with Gikuyu, it is the Emergency they mention and not Mau Mau, saying that "these were hard times" and not "these were heroic times." He concludes that the Mau Mau military defeat and the period of years between that defeat and independence has meant that "the collective Kikuyu memory remembers the hardships and the sufferings during the Emergency period rather than the battles in the forest."[73] This may hold true for Mau Mau veterans as much as for civilians, as the exhaustion that characterizes the end of the memoirs of Joram Wamweya, Kiboi Muriithi, and Gucu Gikoyo suggests. Moreover, individuals and families may deal with their bitter memories of Mau Mau murders or loyalist betrayals by repressing memory if they no longer nurse any serious hope of obtaining justice. Greet Kershaw reinforces Buijtenhuijs's impression of a popular mood (at least in Kiambu), and provides a specifically Gikuyu validation for the Kenyatta regime's policy of forgive and forget. "Events which brought disaster and evil had to be exorcised and discussion would resurrect it. . . . The famine around the turn of the century belonged in this category, as did Mau Mau as soon as it was finished. The independent government's attempt to wipe it out of history was a proper Kikuyu response to a painful event."[74] One may ask, however, if there were such strong personal, familial, and cultural motivations to forget, why did the memory of Mau Mau resurface so frequently just the same? Probably because the cultural unity that would enable Kenyatta and local leaders effectively to impose historical amnesia no longer existed. The effort of neotraditional elders to enforce forgetfulness was countered by the effort of younger Mau Mau veterans (like Kahinga Wachanga) and still younger admirers of the rebels (like Ngugi wa Thiong'o) to pressure the regime and the community to remember. The Gikuyu struggle about remembering Mau Mau mirrors the original internal conflict of the 1950s in Central Kenya.

As for people in other parts of the country, there is less to remember. However, while hundreds of non-Gikuyu fought in Mau Mau or helped the movement in substantive ways, thousands served the colonial government against it as policemen, soldiers, guards, and functionaries, and this memory is problematic, for it can be seen as not only anti–Mau Mau but possibly anti-national. The effective integration of such regional colonial servants into the independent system required some degree of forgetting on the national level. More studies are needed of the attitude of local communities outside Central Kenya to the involvement of members in Mau Mau or in the fight against it. For non-Gikuyu peasants of the Rift Valley, Mau Mau is also problematic, for the memory of conflict with the Gikuyu during the Emergency has bled into the competition with the Gikuyu for land in the 1960s (and again in the government-instigated struggles of the 1990s); historical amnesia is not a solution for these Kenyans, but their memories cannot be the same as the memories of Mau Mau veterans and Gikuyu Rift Valley squatters. For others the emphasis of Gikuyu on their predominant role in the freedom struggle can be a frequent irritant and a threat to national cohesion.

Turning to John Lonsdale's more optimistic discussion of historical memory, the concept of "moral ethnicity" he explains with such care may be the most important legacy of Mau Mau to the independent nation, for it can be shared by all Kenyans. Other aids to memory such as monuments carry special burdens. There is Kimathi Street in Nairobi (centrally located but shorter than Kenyatta Avenue) and Kimathi Library and Kimathi Institute of Technology in Nyeri; there is a monument to Mau Mau in Nyeri town; some graves of forest fighters have been marked; the name of the site of a notorious detention camp has been returned from Galole to Hola. Concrete reminders of Mau Mau can be divisive, however, which may partly explain why there are few. Like monuments, hero cults (Kenyatta, Kimathi, Mathenge) can create problems of their own, for they can be used to validate a factional view of the past, promote a "great man" interpretation of historical change that is potentially antipopular and sexist, exclude non-Kikuyu, oversimplify historical complexity, and promote a political or ideological agenda. On the other hand, "moral ethnicity" is a bequest of Mau Mau to the present that is indigenous, rooted in the *wananchi,* and representative of a broad national consensus about authority that may be capable of limiting the abuse of power at the highest level. Thus the pre-Emergency pamphlets of Gakaara wa Wanjau and others and the Mau Mau memoirs are forerunners in spirit to the outbursts of dissent after the killing of J. M. Kariuki in 1975 and to the political developments of the past ten years. The protest of the *matatu* drivers in 1988, the "war of the cassettes" (during which the authorities attempted to suppress cassette tapes of songs drawing on Mau Mau themes to criticize the government) in 1988–1990, the "Saba Saba Day" riots of July 7, 1990 (and since), the hunger strike of the mothers of political prisoners in March 1992—all evoked the memory of Mau Mau against political authoritarianism.[75] Thus when Moi and other politicians used Mau Mau themes and placed Mau Mau fighters on their platforms during their election speeches in 1992 they were showing recognition of this popular power inherent in the memory of the movement.

The struggle of Kaggia and Mutonyi in Nairobi, of Njama, Itote, Wachanga, Gikoyo in the forest, of Waciuma and Otieno in the Gikuyu communities, of Kariuki, Muchai, Wamweya in the detention camps was not just for victory but for the principles that power must be authentic (held by Africans) and responsible (supported by and attuned to popular will). This lesson of Mau Mau is conveyed directly to secondary and university students who read *"Mau Mau" General* and other memoirs or in a more qualified form to those who use such recent texts as *Themes in Kenyan History.*[76] It is also available to the public at large in the memoirs, in other popular writings about Mau Mau, and in the cassettes still circulating among the *wananchi*. As Lonsdale has suggested, it is part of the oral culture of politics in Kenya, an invisible, elusive, but real contribution of the past to the present.

Since Kenya's independence, armed conflicts have typified the struggle for liberation from minority control in Africa. While Zimbabwe, whose liberation war resembled Kenya's in certain ways, has thus far produced little in the way of African memoirs, such a tradition may be emerging further south. J. M. Kariuki's *"Mau Mau" Detainee,* which described not only his own courage but the heroism of ordinary people struggling against a depersonalizing system, was a culturally pathbreaking document—the model for all future Mau Mau memoirs and the inspiration for later journals of political imprisonment. It is the real progenitor of detention memoirs from southern Africa like John Ya-Otto's *Battlefront Namibia* (1982), Moses Dlamini's *Robben Island Hell-Hole* (n.d.), and Nelson Mandela's *Long Walk to Freedom* (1995).[77]

When Mandela visited Kenya in July 1990, shortly after his release from imprisonment, he recognized Mau Mau in a public speech. "In my twenty-seven years of imprisonment, I always saw the image of fighters such as Kimathi, China, and others as candles in my long and hard war against injustice. . . . It is an honor for any freedom fighter to pay respect to such heroes."[78] If the original Mau Mau was an inspiration to Mandela, he should bear in mind that the story of the Mau Mau memory is a cautionary tale. Like Kenya, South Africa not only had a long, hard fight with a minority regime but has had to come to grips with a recent history marked by civil struggle between resistants and collaborators and ethnic conflict fostered by the divide-and-rule tactics of the previous government. Like Kenyatta, Mandela was released from detention to negotiate with his former captors, and some of his actions have angered supporters. After the majority rule elections in 1994, President Mandela tried to conciliate the Zulu power structure, reached out to Western investors, and endorsed economic policies that angered many radicals. In 1996, Mandela established a Truth and Reconciliation Commission to investigate "apartheid crimes," which was attacked by the right as going too far and by the left as not going far enough.[79] If the struggle over historical memory in Kenya has anything to teach South Africa, it is these lessons: it is futile for a regime to attempt to impose historical amnesia; it is important to allow people to mourn; it is dangerous to allow political, ideological, or ethnic polarization to be exacerbated by selective use of the past; it is constructive to use the past to model popular political values for the present. For *"Mau Mau" Detainee* is also the inspiration for memoirs of prisoners of independent African regimes, of Wole Soyinka's *The Man Died* (1972), Ngugi wa Thiongo's *Detained* (1981), Koigi wa Wamwere's *Conscience on Trial* (1988), and Bola Ige's *Detainee's Diary* (1992).[80] It is the voice of private conscience, but also the voice of civic virtue, speaking from the African past to the African future.

Notes

1. Wachanga, *Swords*, p. 163.
2. Kenyatta, *Suffering Without Bitterness*, p. 241.
3. Ngugi wa Thiong'o, preface to Maina wa Kinyatti, *Kenya's Freedom Struggle: The Dedan Kimathi Papers* (London: Zed, 1987), p. xiii.
4. Odhiambo, "Production of History," p. 302.
5. Robert Whittier, introduction to Wachanga, *Swords*, p. xx.
6. Lonsdale, "The Moral Economy of Mau Mau: The Problem," in Berman and Lonsdale, *Unhappy Valley*, vol. 2, p. 265.
7. See Kershaw, *Mau Mau from Below*.
8. Odhiambo, "Production of History," p. 302.
9. Lonsdale, "The Moral Economy of Mau Mau: The problem," p. 270; Buijtenhuijs, *Essays*, p. 79.
10. Berman, "Nationalism, Ethnicity, Modernity," p. 192.
11. Peter Evans, *Law and Disorder, or Scenes of Life in Kenya* (London: Secker & Warburg, 1956), p. 4.
12. Simone de Beauvoir, *The Blood of Others*, trans. Yvonne Moyse and Roger Senhouse (Hammondsworth: Penguin, 1981), p. 187.
13. Peter Geismar, *Fanon* (New York: Grove, 1971), Chs. 1–2; Frantz Fanon, *The Wretched of the Earth* (New York: Grove, 1968), p. 38; Weigert, *Traditional Religion and Guerrilla Warfare*, p. 14.
14. Kershaw, *Mau Mau from Below*, p. 324.
15. Wanjau, acknowledgements to *Mau Mau Author*, pp. vii–viii.
16. Ngugi, *Detained*, pp. 64–65.
17. Maina wa Kinyatti, introduction to Kinyatti, *Kenya's Freedom Struggle*, pp. 1–12.
18. Ngugi, *Detained*, pp. 95, 90; Ngugi wa Thiong'o and Micere Githae Mugo, preface to *The Trial of Dedan Kimathi* (Oxford: Heinemann, 1977), n.p.
19. Maughan-Brown, *Land, Freedom, and Fiction*, p. 47.
20. Njama, *Mau Mau from Within*, p. 290.
21. Lonsdale, "The Moral Economy of Mau Mau: Wealth, Poverty, Civic Virtue," p. 458.
22. Wachanga, *Swords*, pp. 126–27.
23. Buijtenhuijs, *Essays*, p. 80.
24. Maureen Wall, "The Whiteboys," Joseph Lee, "The Ribbonmen," T. Desmond Williams, "The Irish Republican Brotherhood," all in T. Desmond Williams, ed., *Secret Societies in Ireland* (Dublin: Gill and Macmillan, 1973), pp. 15, 32, 147; Denis Mack Smith, *The Making of Italy 1786–1870* (New York: Walker, 1968), p. 45.
25. Buijtenhuijs, *Essays*, p. 84.
26. Maia Green, "Mau Mau Oathing Rituals and Political Ideology in Kenya: A Re-analysis," *Africa*, vol. 60, no. 1 (1992), p. 80.
27. Terence Ranger, *Peasant Consciousness and Guerrilla War in Zimbabwe* (London: James Currey, 1985), Ch. 5; David Lan, *Guns and Rain: Guerrillas and Spirit Mediumship in Zimbabwe* (Berkeley: University of California Press, 1985); Weigert, *Religion and Warfare*, Chs. 2, 3, 5, 6.

28. White, "Separating the Men from the Boys," pp. 10–15.

29. Presley, *Kikuyu Women,* pp. 136–50.

30. See Mazower, *Inside Hitler's Greece,* Ch. 12; Stubbs, *Hearts and Minds,* Ch. 3; Alistair Horne, *A Savage War of Peace: Algeria 1954–1962* (Harmondsworth: Penguin, 1977), Ch. 12.

31. Kanogo, *Squatters,* p. 151.

32. Ogot, "Mau Mau Songs," p. 286; Atieno Odhiambo, "Rebutting 'Theory' with Correct Theory: A Comment on *The Trial of Dedan Kimathi,*" *Kenya Historical Review,* vol. 5, no. 2 (1977), p. 387.

33. Furedi, *Mau Mau War,* p. 141.

34. Ogot, "Revolt of the Elders," p. 148.

35. Kariuki, *Detainee,* p. 65.

36. Ogot, "Revolt of the Elders," p. 142.

37. Maina wa Kinyatti, introduction to Kinyatti, *Thunder From the Mountains: Mau Mau Patriotic Songs* (London: Zed, 1980), p. 9.

38. Kershaw, *Mau Mau from Below,* p. 325.

39. E. S. Atieno Odhiambo, "The Formative Years 1945–55," in *Decolonization and Independence in Kenya 1940–93,* ed. B. A. Ogot and W. R. Ochieng' (London: James Currey, 1995), p. 42.

40. Erhard Rumpf and A. C. Hepburn, *Nationalism and Socialism in Twentieth Century Ireland* (New York: Barnes and Noble, 1977), Chs. 2, 3.

41. Hilary Footitt and John Simmonds, *France 1943–1945* (New York: Holmes and Meier, 1988), p. 40; Rousso, *Vichy Syndrome,* Chs. 1–2; Luigi Meneghello, *The Outlaws,* trans. Raleigh Trevelyan (New York: Harcourt, Brace, 1967), Chs. 9–11.

42. Mazower, *Inside Hitler's Greece,* Chs. 20–23 and epilogue.

43. Benedict Kerkvliet, *The Huk Rebellion: A Study of Peasant Revolt in the Philippines* (Berkeley: University of California Press, 1977), Chs. 3–5.

44. Norma Kriger, "The Politics of Creating National Heroes: The Search for Political Legitimacy and National Identity," in *Soldiers in Zimbabwe's Liberation War,* ed. Ngwabi Bhebe and Terence Ranger (London: James Currey, 1995), pp. 147–54.

45. See Marcel Ophuls' film, "The Sorrow and the Pity" (1970).

46. See J. M. Winter, *Sites of Memory, Sites of Mourning* (New York: Cambridge University Press, 1995).

47. Rousso, *Vichy Syndrome,* p. 22.

48. Ibid., p. 18. As Andre Malraux comments, de Gaulle knew "that for millions of men he was their alibi. In the Resistance France recognized what she should have been rather than what she had been." *Anti-Memoirs,* trans. Terence Kilmartin (New York: Holt Rinehart and Winston, 1968), p. 94.

49. Rousso, *Vichy Syndrome,* pp. 27–28; see also Philippe Burrin, *France Under the Germans: Collaboration and Compromise,* trans. Janet Lloyd (New York: New Press, 1996), p. 460.

50. Kammen, *Mystic Chords of Memory,* p. 13.

51. Rousso, *Vichy Syndrome,* p. 15; Burrin, *France Under the Germans,* p. 460.

52. Mazrui, "On Heroes, " p. 21.

53. Rousso, *Vichy Syndrome,* pp. 311–16.

54. Cooper, "Mau Mau and Discourses of Decolonization," p. 313.

55. B. A. Ogot, "The Politics of Populism," *Decolonization and Independence,* ed. Ogot and Ochieng', pp. 198–99.

56. Widner, *Party-State in Kenya,* pp. 177–78.

57. Ibid., p. 148–49.

58. Odhiambo, "Production of History," p. 304.

59. Galia Sabar-Friedman, "The Mau Mau Myth: Kenyan Political Discourse in Search of Democracy," *Cahier d'études africaines,* vol. 35 (1995), pp. 120–27.

60. Buijtenhuijs, *Mau Mau Twenty Years After,* pp. 43–72, 145–49.

61. Kaggia, *Roots,* p. 193.

62. Maina wa Kinyatti, "Mau Mau: The Peak of African Political Organization in Colonial Kenya," *Kenya Historical Review,* vol. 5, no. 2 (1977), pp. 303–305.

63. Ngugi, *Detained,* p. 64.

64. Maughan-Brown, *Land, Freedom, and Fiction,* Chs. 4–7.

65. Odhiambo, "The Production of History," p. 302, on Buijtenhuijs's comments in *Mau Mau Twenty Years After,* p. 74.

66. Ibid., pp. 301, 306.

67. Ibid., p. 307.

68. Odhiambo, "Democracy and Order," p. 193.

69. Lonsdale, "The Moral Economy of Mau Mau," pp. 317, 465.

70. Ibid., pp. 446–48.

71. Ibid., p. 467.

72. Ibid., p. 468.

73. Buijtenhuijs, *Mau Mau Twenty Years After,* p. 110.

74. Kershaw, "Mau Mau from Below," p. 293.

75. Widner, *Party-State in Kenya,* pp. 182–83; Angelique Haugerud, *The Culture of Politics in Modern Kenya* (Cambridge: Cambridge University Press, 1995), pp. 22–23, 28–30; Sabar-Friedman, "The Mau Mau Myth," p. 123.

76. William R. Ochieng', ed., *Themes in Kenyan History* (Nairobi: Heinemann, 1990).

77. John Ya-Otto, *Battlefront Namibia* (London: Heinemann, 1982); Moses Dlamini, *Robben Island Hell-Hole: Reminiscences of a Political Prisoner in South Africa* (Trenton, N.J.: Africa World Press, n.d.); Mandela, *Long Walk to Freedom.*

78. Sabar-Friedman, "Mau Mau Myth," p. 116.

79. See Alex Boraine, Janet Levy, Ronel Scheffer, eds., *Dealing with the Past: Truth and Reconciliation in South Africa* (Rondebosch: Institute for a Democratic Alternative, 1994).

80. Ngugi, *Detained;* Koigi wa Wamwere, *Conscience on Trial* (Trenton, N.J.: Africa World Press, 1988); Wole Soyinka, *The Man Died: Prison Notes* (London: Rex Collings, 1972); Bola Ige, *Detainee's Diary* (Lagos: NIALS, 1992).

Glossary

Anake a 40	the "40 Group" of Gikuyu activists
arathi	(sing. *murathi*) prophets; sometimes, followers of a prophetic religious group
aregi	independent Christians
askari	Kenyan soldier employed by colonial regime
batuni	the "platoon" or fighting oath
bau	board game played with rocks or seeds
bhangi	marijuana
gakonia	"little sacks," name given to hooded informers
Gikuyu na Mumbi	the first ancestors of the Gikuyu, and one of the names for the secret movement
gitati	communal labor
gitungati	warrior; see *itungati*
irore	(sing. *kirore*) Christian Gikuyu who agreed to abandon female circumcision; by extension, sometimes used to mean "collaborators"
itungati	(sing. *gitungati*) warriors under elders' orders, the Mau Mau guerrillas
kamatimu	"little spears," a term used for the home guard
kipande (pl. *vipande*)	identity/employment card carried by Kenyan Africans
Kirinyaga	Gikuyu name for Mt. Kenya
komerera	renegade separated from a band
matatu	the automobiles that serve as "taxis" in periurban and rural areas
mbari	a Gikuyu lineage or subclan

261

mbuci	a guerrilla camp
mundu mugo	a medicine man
Muhimu	"important," used to designate either the Central Committee of the secret movement or the movement itself
Muiguithania	"the unifier"—sometimes used for the movement
Muingi	"the community," a term used for the secret movement
muma wa ngero	"oath for killing," the same as the *batuni*
muma wa uigano	the unity oath
murathi	prophet; see *arathi*
muthamaki	(pl. *athamaki*) an outstanding man, or spokesman
mzungu	(pl. *wazungu*) European
Ngai	the Gikuyu high god, believed to dwell on Kirinyaga
Nyandarua	Gikuyu name for Aberdares mountains
nyimbo	poitical songs
panga	a long, curved knife; machete
posho	maize meal rations
Riigi	the traditional Gikuyu doors made of sticks; the guerrilla council of the illiterate warrriors
shamba	African garden or small farming plot
simi	Gikuyu traditional sword with double edge
"Thaai, thathaiya Ngai thai"	"God's peace be with us," traditional ending to Gikuyu prayers
uhuru	freedom
wananchi	the common people
wiyathi	male adulthood

Bibliography

Official Sources

A number of official sources were consulted, including Kenya National Archive (KNA) sources, especially Ministry of African Affairs and Ministry of Community Development; and Public Record Office (PRO) sources, those of the Colonial Office, particularly the CO 822 series (443–802, and 1235–1250) and War Office, especially the WO 216, WO 236, and WO 276 series. Among the printed official reports consulted, those most useful to the book were *Historical Survey of the Origins and Growth of Mau Mau* (London: HMSO, 1960); J. C. Carothers, *The Psychology of Mau Mau* (Nairobi: Colony and Protectorate of Kenya, 1955); and Kenya Colony, *Report of Committee on Emergency Detention Camps* (Nairobi: Government Printer, 1959).

Private Archival Sources

Various collections of papers at Rhodes House, Oxford (RH), were consulted, the most directly useful being the papers of Sir William R. N. Hinde (Mss. Afr. s. 1580), the papers of Michael Blundell (Mss. Afr. s. 746), the papers of F. D. Corfield (Mss. Afr. s. 1675), and the papers of Sir Arthur Young (Mss. Brit. Emp. s. 486).

Books, Book Chapters, Pamphlets, Articles, and Dissertations

Anderson, Benedict. *Imagined Communities: Reflections on the Origin and Spread of Nationalism*, rev. ed. New York: Verso, 1993.

Andrews, William L. *To Tell a Free Story: The First Century of Afro-American Autobiography, 1760–1865*. Urbana, Ill: University of Illinois Press, 1986.

Baldwin, W. W. *Mau Mau Manhunt: The Adventures of the Only American Who Fought the Terrorists in Kenya*. New York: Dutton, 1957.

Barnes, Teresa. "The Heroes' Struggle: Life after the Liberation War for Four Ex-

Combatants in Zimbabwe." In *Soldiers in Zimbabwe's Liberation War,* ed. Ngwabi Bhebe and Terence Ranger. London: James Currey, 1995, Pp. 118–37.

Barnett, Donald L. "Introduction" to Karari Njama and Donald L. Barnett, *Mau Mau from Within.* New York: Modern Reader, 1966. Pp. 23–72.

Bennett, George. *Kenya, a Political History. The Colonial Period.* London: Oxford, 1963.

Berman, Bruce. *Control and Crisis in Colonial Kenya: The Dialectic of Domination.* London: James Currey, 1990.

————. "Nationalism, Ethnicity, and Modernity: The Paradox of Mau Mau," *Canadian Journal of African Studies,* vol. 25, No. 2 (1991), pp. 181–206.

Berman, Bruce, and John Lonsdale. "Louis Leakey's Mau Mau: A Study in the Politics of Knowledge," *History and Anthropology,* vol. 5, No. 2 (1991), pp. 143–204.

Blundell, Michael. *So Rough a Wind.* London: Weidenfeld and Nicholson, 1964.

Brockway, Fenner. *African Journeys.* London: Gollancz, 1955.

Buijtenhuijs, Robert. *Essays on Mau Mau: Contributions to Mau Mau Historiography.* Leiden: African Studies Center, 1982.

————. *Le mouvement "Mau Mau": Une révolte paysanne et anti-coloniale en Afrique noire.* The Hague: Mouton, 1971.

————. *Mau Mau Twenty Years After: The Myth and the Survivors.* The Hague: Mouton, 1973.

Clayton, Anthony. *Counterinsurgency in Kenya.* Manhattan, Kans.: Sunflower University, 1984.

————. *The Wars of French Decolonization.* London: Longman, 1994.

Cleary, A. S. "The Myth of Mau Mau in Its International Context," *African Affairs,* vol. 81, No. 355 (April, 1990), pp. 227–45.

Clough, Marshall S. *Fighting Two Sides: Kenyan Chiefs and Politicians, 1918–1940.* Niwot: University Press of Colorado, 1990.

Clough, Marshall S., and Kennell A. Jackson, Jr. *A Bibliography on Mau Mau.* Stanford: Stanford University Press, 1975.

Cooper, Frederick. *Decolonization and African Society: The Labor Question in French and British Africa.* Cambridge: Cambridge University Press, 1996.

————. "Mau Mau and the Discourses of Decolonization," *Journal of African History,* vol. 29 (1988), pp. 313–20.

Cox, Richard. *Kenyatta's Country.* New York: Praeger, 1966.

Davidson, Basil. *The People's Cause: A History of Guerrillas in Africa.* Burnt Mill: Longman, 1981.

Davison, Jean, with the women of Mutira. *Voices from Mutira: Lives of Rural Gikuyu Women.* Boulder: Lynne Rienner, 1989.

Edgerton, Robert B. *Mau Mau: An African Crucible.* New York: Macmillan, 1989.

Fanon, Frantz. *The Wretched of Earth.* New York: Grove, 1968.

Furedi, Frank. "The African Crowd in Nairobi: Popular Movements and Elite Politics," *Journal of African History,* vol. 14 (1973), pp. 275–90.

————. *The Mau Mau War in Perspective.* London: James Currey, 1989.

Fussell, Paul. *The Great War and Modern Memory.* New York: Oxford, 1977.

Gatheru, R. Mugo. *Child of Two Worlds: A Kikuyu's Story.* Introduction by St. Clair Drake. New York: New American Library, 1972.

Geiger, Susan. "Women's Life Histories: Method and Content," *Signs,* vol. 11 (1986), pp. 344–51.

Gertzel, Cherry. *The Politics of Independent Kenya.* Evanston: Northwestern, 1970.

Gicaru, Muga. *Land of Sunshine: Scenes of Life in Kenya Before Mau Mau.* Foreword by Trevor Huddleston. London: Lawrence and Wishart, 1958.

Gikoyo, Gucu. *We Fought for Freedom/Tulipigania Uhuru.* Nairobi: East African Publishing House, 1979.

Goldsworthy, David. *Tom Mboya: The Man Kenya Wanted to Forget.* London: Heinemann, 1982.

Gordon, David. *Decolonization and the State in Kenya.* Boulder: Westview, 1986.

Green, Maia. "Mau Mau Oathing Rituals and Political Ideology in Kenya: A Re-Analysis," *Africa,* vol. 60, no. 1 (1990), pp. 69–87.

Harbeson, John W. *Nation-Building in Kenya: The Role of Land Reform.* Evanston: Northwestern University Press, 1973.

Haugerud, Angelique. *The Culture of Politics in Modern Kenya.* Cambridge: Cambridge University Press, 1995.

Heather, Randall W. "Intelligence and Counter-insurgency in Kenya 1952–56." Ph.D. diss., Cambridge University, 1993.

Henderson, Ian, and Philip Goodhart. *The Hunt for Kimathi.* London: Hamish Hamilton, 1958.

Itote, Waruhiu. *"Mau Mau" General.* Nairobi: East African Publishing House, 1967.

———. *Mau Mau in Action.* Nairobi: Transafrica, 1979.

Kabiro, Ngugi. *Man in the Middle: The Story of Ngugi Kabiro,* ed. Don Barnett. Richmond, B.C.: Liberation Support Movement, 1973.

Kaggia, Bildad. *Roots of Freedom, 1921–1963: The Autobiography of Bildad Kaggia.* Nairobi: East African Publishing House, 1975.

Kaggia, B. M., Fred Kubai, J. Murumbi, and Achieng' Oneko. Preface. In Karari Njama and Donald L. Barnett, *Mau Mau from Within.* New York: Modern Reader, 1966.

Kammen, Michael. *Mystic Chords of Memory: The Transformation of Tradition in American Culture.* New York: Knopf, 1991.

Kamunchula, J. T. Samuel. "The Meru Participation in Mau Mau." *Kenya Historical Review,* vol. 3, no. 2 (1975), pp. 193–216.

Kanogo, Tabitha. *Dedan Kimathi: A Biography.* Nairobi: East African Educational Publishers, 1992.

———. *Squatters and the Roots of Mau Mau 1905–1963.* London: James Currey, 1987.

Kariuki, Josiah Mwangi. *"Mau Mau" Detainee: The Account of a Kenya African of His Experiences in Detention Camps 1953–1960.* Foreword by Margery Perham. London: Oxford University Press, 1963.

Kennedy, Dane. "Constructing the Colonial Myth of Mau Mau," *The International Journal of African Historical Studies,* vol. 25, no. 2 (1992), pp. 241–60.

———. *Islands of White: Settler Society and Culture in Kenya and Southern Rhodesia, 1890–1939.* Durham: Duke University Press, 1987.

Kenyatta, Jomo. *Facing Mt. Kenya: The Tribal Life of the Gikuyu* [1938]. With an introduction by B. Malinowski. New York: Vintage, 1965.

———. *Harambee! The Prime Minister of Kenya's Speeches, 1963–1964.* Foreword by Malcolm MacDonald. Nairobi: Oxford, University Press 1964.

———. *Suffering Without Bitterness: The Founding of the Kenya Nation.* Nairobi: East African Publishing House, 1968.

Kershaw, Greet. *Mau Mau from Below.* Oxford: James Currey, 1997.

———. "Mau Mau from Below: Fieldwork and Experience, 1955–57 and 1962," *Canadian Journal of African Studies,* vol. 25, no. 2 (1991), 274–97.

Kinyatti, Maina wa. "Mau Mau: The Peak of Political Organization in Colonial Kenya." *Kenya Historical Review,* vol. 5, no. 2 (1977), 287–311.

———, ed. *Kenya's Freedom Struggle: The Dedan Kimathi Papers.* London: Zed, 1987.

———, ed. *Thunder from the Mountains: Mau Mau Patriotic Songs.* London: Zed, 1980.

Kitson, Frank. *Gangs and Counter-Gangs.* London: Barrie and Rockcliffe, 1960.

Koinange, Mbiyu. *The People of Kenya Speak for Themselves.* Detroit: Kenya Publications Fund, 1955.

Kriger, Norma J. "The Politics of Creating National Heroes: The Search for Political Legitimacy and National Identity." In *Soldiers in Zimbabwe's Liberation War,* ed. Ngwabi Bhebe and Terence Ranger. London: James Currey, 1995. Pp. 139–62.

———. *Zimbabwe's Guerrilla War: Peasant Voices.* Cambridge: Cambridge University Press, 1992.

Lamb, Geoff. *Peasant Politics: Conflict and Development in Murang'a.* Lewes: Julian Friedmann, 1974.

Lapping, Brian. *End of Empire.* New York: St. Martin's, 1985.

Laqueur, Walter. *Guerrilla: A Historical and Critical Study.* Boston: Little Brown, 1976.

Lavers, Anthony. *The Kikuyu Who Fight Mau Mau / Wakikuyu Wanopigana na Mau Mau.* Nairobi: Eagle Press, 1955.

Leakey, L. S. B. *Defeating Mau Mau.* London: Methuen, 1954.

———. *Mau Mau and the Kikuyu.* London: Methuen, 1953.

Leigh, Ione. *In the Shadow of the Mau Mau.* London: W. H. Allen, 1954.

Leo, Christopher. *Land and Class in Kenya.* Toronto: University of Toronto Press, 1984.

Likimani, Muthoni. *Passbook Number F. 47927: Women and Mau Mau in Kenya.* Introduction by Jean O'Barr. New York: Praeger, 1985.

Lipscomb, J. F. *White Africans.* Introduction by Elspeth Huxley. London: Faber and Faber, 1955.

Lonsdale, John. "Mau Maus of the Mind: Making Mau Mau and Remaking Kenya," *Journal of African History,* vol. 31 (1990), pp. 393–421.

———. "The Moral Economy of Mau Mau: Wealth, Poverty, and Civic Virtue in Kikuyu Political Thought." In *Unhappy Valley: Conflict in Kenya and Africa, Book Two: Violence and Ethnicity.* By Bruce Berman and John Lonsdale. London: James Currey, 1992. Pp. 315–467.

———. "The Prayers of Waiyaki: Political Uses of the Kikuyu Past." In *Revealing Prophets: Prophecy in Eastern African History,* ed. David M. Anderson and Douglas H. Johnson. London: James Currey, 1995. Pp. 240–91.

Mackenzie, Fiona. "Political Economy of the Enviroment, Gender, and Resistance under Colonialism, 1910–1950," *Canadian Journal of African History,* vol. 25, no. 2 (1991), pp. 226–54.

Maina, Paul. *Six Mau Mau Generals.* Nairobi: Gazelle Books, 1977.

Majdalany, Fred. *State of Emergency.* Boston: Houghton Mifflin, 1963.

Maloba, Wunyabari O. *Mau Mau and Kenya: An Analysis of a Peasant Revolt.* Bloomington: Indiana, 1993.

Mandela, Nelson. *Long Walk to Freedom: The Autobiography of Nelson Mandela.* Boston: Little Brown, 1994.

Mathu, Mohamed. *The Urban Guerrilla: The Story of Mohamed Mathu,* ed. Don Barnett. Richmond, B.C.: Liberation Support Movement, 1974.

The Mau Mau in Kenya. Foreword by Granville Roberts. London: Hutchinson, 1954.

Maughan-Brown, David. *Land, Freedom, and Fiction: History and Ideology in Kenya.* London: Zed, 1985.

Mazrui, Ali A. Foreword to Robert Buijtenhuijs, *Mau Mau Twenty Years After: The Myth and the Survivors.* The Hague: Mouton, 1973. Pp. 7–13.

———. "On Heroes and Uhuru-Worship." In Ali A. Mazrui, *On Heroes and Uhuru-Worship: Essays on Independent Africa.* London: Longman, 1967.

Mboya, Tom. *Freedom and After.* Boston: Little Brown, 1963.

Mitchell, Philip. *African Afterthoughts.* London: Hutchinson, 1954.

Muchai, Karigo. *The Hardcore: The Story of Karigo Muchai,* ed. Don Barnett. Richmond, B.C.: Liberation Support Movement, 1973.

Mueller, Susanne D. "Government and Opposition in Kenya, 1966–69," *Journal of Modern African Studies,* vol. 22, no. 3 (1984), pp. 399–427.

Muoria, Henry. *I, the Gikuyu and the White Fury.* Nairobi: East African Educational Publishers, 1994.

Muriithi, Kiboi, with Peter Ndoria. *War in the Forest.* Nairobi: East African Publishing House, 1971.

Murray-Brown, Jeremy. *Kenyatta.* New York: Dutton, 1973.

Neubauer, Carol E. "One Voice Speaking for Many: The Mau Mau Movement and Kenyan Autobiography," *Journal of Modern African Studies,* vol. 21, no. 1 (1983), pp. 113–31.

Ngugi wa Thiong'o. "Born Again: Mau Mau Unchained." In Ngugi wa Thiong'o, *Writers in Politics.* London: Heinemann, 1981. Pp. 86–93.

———. *Detained: A Writer's Prison Diary.* London: Heinemann, 1981.

———. *A Grain of Wheat.* London: Heinemann, 1967.

———. "J. M.—A Writer's Tribute. " In Ngugi wa Thiong'o, *Writers in Politics.* London: Heinemann, 1981. Pp. 82–85.

———. "Mau Mau: Violence and Culture." In *Homecoming.* New York: Lawrence Hill, 1973. Pp. 26–30.

———. *Petals of Blood.* London: Heinemann, 1977.

———. and Micere Githae Mugo. *The Trial of Dedan Kimathi.* London: Heinemann, 1976.

Njama, Karari, and Donald L. Barnett. *Mau Mau From Within: Autobiography and Analysis of Kenya's Peasant Revolt.* New York: Modern Reader, 1966.

Nyong'o, P. Anyang'. "State and Society in Kenya: The Disintegration of the Nationalist Coalitions and the Rise of Presidential Authoritarianism 1963–1978," *African Affairs,* vol. 88, no. 351 (1989), pp. 229–51.

Ochieng', William R. "Autobiography in Kenyan History," *Ufahamu,* vol. 14, no. 2 (1985), pp. 80–101.

———, ed. *Themes in Kenyan History.* Nairobi: Heinemann, 1990.

Odhiambo, E. S. Atieno "Democracy and the Ideology of Order in Kenya." In *The Political Economy of Kenya,* ed. Michael G. Schatzberg. New York: Praeger, 1987.

———. "The Formative Years 1945–55." In *Decolonization and Independence in Kenya 1940–93,* ed. B. A. Ogot and W. R. Ochieng'. London: James Currey, 1995.

———. "The Production of History in Kenya: The Mau Mau Debate," *Canadian Journal of African Studies,* vol. 25, no. 2 (1991), 300–307.

Odinga, Oginga. *Not Yet Uhuru.* New York: Hill and Wang, 1967.

Ogot, B. A. "The Decisive Years 1952–63." In *Decolonization and Independence in*

Kenya, ed. B. A. Ogot and W. R. Ochieng'. London: James Currey, 1995. Pp. 48–81.

———. "Politics, Culture, and Music in Central Kenya: A Study of Mau Mau Hymns 1951–1956," *Kenya Historical Review*, vol. 5, no. 2 (1977), pp. 273–86.

———. "Revolt of the Elders: An Anatomy of the Loyalist Crowd in the Mau Mau Uprising 1952–1956." In *Hadith 4: Politics and Nationalism in Colonial Kenya*, ed. B. A. Ogot. Nairobi: East African Publishing House, 1972. Pp. 134–48.

Olney, James. *Tell Me Africa: An Approach to African Literature*. Princeton: Princeton University Press, 1973.

Otieno, Wambui Waiyaki. *Mau Mau's Daughter: The Life History of Wambui Waiyaki Otieno*. Boulder: Lynne Rienner, forthcoming.

Perham, Margery. *The Colonial Reckoning: The End of Imperial Rule in Africa in the Light of the British Experience*. New York: Knopf, 1962.

———. Foreword to Josiah Mwangi Kariuki. *"Mau Mau" Detainee*. London: Oxford University Press, 1963. Pp. xi–xxiii.

Presley, Cora Ann. *Kikuyu Women, the Mau Mau Rebellion, and Social Change in Kenya*. Boulder: Westview, 1992.

Pugliese, Christiana. "Author, Publisher and Gikuyu Nationalist: The Life and Writings of Gakaara wa Wanjau." Ph.D. diss., University of London, 1993.

Ranger, Terence. *Peasant Consciousness and Guerrilla War in Zimbabwe*. London: James Currey, 1985.

Romero, Patricia, ed. *Life Histories of African Women*. London: Ashfield, 1988.

Rosberg, Carl. G. and John Nottingham. *The Myth of "Mau Mau": Nationalism in Kenya* [1966]. New York: Meridian, 1970.

Rousso, Henry. *The Vichy Syndrome: History and Memory in France Since 1944*, trans. Arthur Goldhammer. Cambridge, Mass.: Harvard University Press, 1991.

Ruark, Robert. *Something of Value*. Garden City: Doubleday, 1955.

Sabar-Friedman, Galia. "The Mau Mau Myth: Kenyan Political Discourse in Search of Democracy," *Cahiers d' études africaines*, vol. 35, no. 1 (1995), pp. 101–29.

Sandgren, David P. *Christianity and the Kikuyu: Religious Divisions and Social Conflict*. New York, 1989.

Santilli, Kathy. "Kikuyu Women in the Mau Mau Revolt," *Ufahamu*, vol. 8, no. 1 (1977–78), pp. 143–59.

Santoru, Marina E. "The Colonial Idea of Women and Direct Intervention: The Mau Mau Case," *African Affairs*, vol. 95, no. 379 (1996), pp. 253–67.

Schipper, Monika. *Beyond the Boundaries: Text and Context in African Literature*. Chicago: Ivan R. Dee, 1990.

Sicherman, Carol. *Ngugi wa Thiong'o: The Making of a Rebel. A Source Book in Kenyan Literature and Resistance*. London: Hans Zell, 1990.

Slater, Montagu. *The Trial of Jomo Kenyatta*. London: Secker and Warburg, 1955.

Sorrenson, M. P. K. *Land Reform in the Kikuyu Country*. Nairobi: Oxford University Press, 1967.

Spencer, John. *James Beauttah*. Nairobi: Stellascope, 1984.

———. *The Kenya African Union*. London: KPI, 1985.

Stubbs, Richard. *Hearts and Minds in Guerrilla Warfare: The Malaya Emergency 1948–1960*. New York: Oxford University Press, 1989.

Tamarkin, Mordechai. "Mau Mau in Nakuru," *Journal of African History*, vol. 17, no. 1 (1976), pp. 119–34.

———. "The Roots of Political Stability in Kenya," *African Affairs*, vol. 77, no. 308 (1978), pp. 297–320.

Throup, David W. *Economic and Social Origins of Mau Mau 1945–53.* London: James Currey, 1987.

Thuku, Harry. *An Autobiography.* Nairobi: Oxford University Press, 1970.

Tignor, Robert L. *The Colonial Transformation of Kenya: The Kamba, Kikuyu, and Maasai from 1900 to 1939.* Princeton: Princeton University Press, 1976.

Wachanga, H. Kahinga. *The Swords of Kirinyaga.* Introduction by Robert Whittier. Nairobi: East African Literature Bureau, 1975.

Waciuma, Charity. *Daughter of Mumbi.* Nairobi: East African Publishing House, 1969.

Wamweya, Joram. *Freedom Fighter,* trans. Ciira Cerere. Nairobi: East African Publishing House, 1971.

Wanjau, Gakaara wa. *Mau Mau Author in Detention,* trans. Ngigi wa Njoroge. Nairobi: Heinemann, 1988.

Wamwere, Koigi wa. *Conscience on Trial. Why I was Detained: Notes of a Political Prisoner in Kenya.* Trenton, N.J.: Africa Word Press, 1988.

White, Luise. *The Comforts of Home: Prostitution in Colonial Nairobi.* Chicago: University of Chicago Press, 1990.

———. "Separating the Men from the Boys: Constructions of Gender, Sexuality, and Terrorism in Central Kenya, 1939–1959," *International Journal of African Historical Studies,* vol. 23, no. 1 (1990), pp. 1–25.

Whittier, Robert. "Editor's Introduction." In Kahinga Wachanga, *The Swords of Kirinyaga.* Nairobi: East African Literature Bureau, 1975. Pp. xiii–xx.

Widner, Jennifer A. *The Rise of a Party-State in Kenya: From "Harambee!" to "Nyayo!"* Berkeley: University of California Press, 1992.

Wilson, Christopher. *Before the Dawn in Kenya.* Nairobi: English Press, 1953.

Winter, J. M. *Sites of Memory, Sites of Mourning.* (New York: Cambridge University Press, 1995).

Index

About the Book

The still contentious issues of the Mau Mau revolt are thrown into stark relief by the *Mau Mau Memoirs,* personal accounts by Kenyans of the events of that violent period. Marshall Clough deftly analyzes these memoirs, making a strong case for not only their historical value, but also their role in the struggle to define Mau Mau within Kenyan historiography and politics.

Systematically studying thirteen memoirs as a group, as a kind of "discourse" about the revolt, Clough demonstrates that the recollections of their authors—whose experiences ranged from organizing the secret movement, to supplying the guerrillas, to active fighting, to resistance in the British detention camps—serve to refute both the British version of the revolt and that of the leaders of the independent Kenyan state. They also point unequivocally to the importance of Mau Mau in the making of modern Kenya.

Marshall S. Clough is professor of history at the University of Northern Colorado. He is coeditor of *A Bibliography on Mau Mau* and author of *Fighting Two Sides: Kenyan Chiefs and Politicians, 1918–1940.*